GHOSTS, BUGGA

KARL ROEDER'S MA

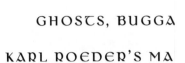

❀

Content first published in the Isle of Man Examiner, 1901–1904, and subsequently as Manx Notes & Queries by S. K. Broadbent, Douglas, 1904. Reproduced here from the original newspaper columns with added material. This edition © Culture Vannin.

First published by Culture Vannin 2019
PO Box 1986, Douglas, Isle of Man IM99 1SR
www.culturevannin.im

Edited by Stephen Miller: chiollaghbooks.com

Front cover design by Kim Gee Studio: kimgeestudio.com

Photographs on the back cover © Manx National Heritage:
Karl Roeder (PG/7692) and Edward Faragher (PG/0990)

Printed and bound by Words and Spaces

ISBN: 978-1-912668-05-2

PREFACE

꙳

Karl Roeder's Manx Notes & Queries is one of the most important books of Manx folklore ever published.

It presents one of the richest and most important collections of tales dealing with fairies, bugganes, ghosts, giants, the Phynnodderree, King Orry, Manannan and more. No other book is like it in the quantity and breadth of the folklore that it holds.

Here we also find fragments and tales which would be too baffling or messy for other collectors – two white serpents slithering about the road, a giant hare attacking two men in a boat, or a stack of fire breaking up a drunken fight. Their inclusion reflects the truthfulness of the tales as presented here by Roeder, in a way perhaps more reliable than any other Manx collection.

A large number of the tales are gathered from Edward Faragher ('Ned Beg Hom Ruy'), the poet of Cregneash, and so predominantly relate to the South of the Island. The book therefore offers an essential counterpart to Sophia Morrison's better-known Manx Fairy Tales, which focusses on the West.

As well as folklore, this collection contains fascinating pieces on history, language, literature and other things of Manx interest, as well as some more theoretical discussions of Manx matters unmatched then or since. All of it has been faithfully transcribed and introduced by Stephen Miller, whose knowledge of the material is second to none.

James Franklin, Culture Vannin, 2019

INTRODUCTION

੨₹

In the *Isle of Man Examiner* for the 21 September 1901, the following announcement appeared:

> In response to requests made by gentlemen who take a deep interest in questions concerning the Isle of Man and the Manx people, we have decided to devote space as occasion requires to "Manx Notes and Queries."

The proposed scope of this column was then outlined:

> In connection, with these notes and queries, we invite contributions and inquiries in connection with elucidation and points on Manx language, Manx history, Manx biography, Manx antiquities, Manx folk-lore, Manx place-names, the natural history of the Island, and kindred subjects.

It concluded:

> We feel sure that Manx people and others will appreciate this new departure, which commences this week, and will assist us to make "Manx Notes and Queries" interesting and instructive.[1]

What followed under were the first two notes in a column that would run in ninety issues of the *Examiner* until 24 October 1903. Whilst there was mention of "gentlemen" behind the column, it was the idea of a single individual, namely Karl Roeder (1848–1911), a German national resident in Manchester, long interested in Manx folklore.[2] The title echoes the periodical *Notes and Queries* established in 1849, and such columns, variously short or long-lived, were a feature of English provincial newspaper titles in the nineteenth century. A number of these colums were reproduced later in book form, as was the *Examiner* one in 1904.

Any such column always relied on the enthusiasm of others to submit material and in this particular case it was not forthcoming. Roeder was not shy in coming forth on this topic as the introduction to *Manx Notes & Queries* (1904) made clear. Here he stated that the idea behind the column was due to himself but "with a view to animate others to contribute to it." This did not come to pass:

> [...] this first experiment has so far been rather sterile. It was fully expected that a certain amount of interest would be evinced by the Manx people in general to further the scheme. But, as it is, the main share has actually fallen upon myself,

---

1 Karl Roeder, "Manx Notes and Queries: Nos 1–2," *Isle of Man Examiner* 21 September 1901.
2 For his folklore publications, see Stephen Miller, "Karl Roeder: An Updated Checklist of Writings on Manx Folklore," *Manx Notes* 16 (2004).

i

and I am consequently responsible for the entire work, with the exception of a few stray contributions by Mr G.W. Wood and Mr Kneen.[3]

That said, J.J. Kneen had once been given short shrift over one of his contributions by Roeder. Having contributed a note on "Manx Names of Fish and Shell Fish" [35] he was then publicly taken to task by Roeder later on: "He seems to be unaware that many years ago Mr J.C. Crellin, MA, has drawn up already a very careful and scientific List of Fish of the Isle of Mann, for the Isle of Mann [sic] Natural History and Antiquarian Society [...]." [69] This was not the best of ways to encourage others to submit material.

On one occasion he expressed his general frustration over the colum:

> I regret to see so extremely few Manxmen assisting the Manx Notes and Queries, their help would preserve many valuable and now perishing traits, and besides a little support in many other directions—biographical and domestic—descriptive of the old peasantry and their habits and life, indoors and outdoors, would increase the value of the columns considerably. I hope my appeal will fructify, and then we may gradually obtain a more faithful mirror of the old customs, habits, and life in Man during days gone by. [203]

It is a credit to Roeder at the end of the day that he persisted with the column, although that doggedness led him at times taking others to task. There were, however, two individuals who were singled out for praise:

> I have to render sincere thanks for the valuable and unswerving assistance given to me privately by the veteran Manxman, Edward Farquhar, whose knowledge of everything Manx is inexhaustible, and also to Miss Sophia Morrison, of Peel, who has valiantly stood by me, and whose support has been beyond words to express.[4]

Edward Faragher (1831–1908),[5] a fisherman living in Cregneash, was Roeder's main informant and folklore collected from him was later to be used to fill out the columns in the *Examiner*. That this relationship between the pair was known led to an extraordinary intervention by Roeder. A contribution under the heading of "Scaayn Goanlysagh (Malicious Spirits)" [83] was introduced so:

> Spirits of living people haunting those they had any spite to. There are several stories of such on record in the Island, and of psychological interest. I give them in the same form as related to me by my old Manx friend[.]

Faragher is clearly not named here but it was assumed that he was the "old Manx friend" and Roeder had to use a subsequent note in order to correct this view: "It appears that my recent note, No. 83, on 'Malicious Spirits,' and previous matter, has

---

3 Charles Roeder, "Introduction," *Manx Notes and Queries* (Douglas: S.K. Broadbent, 1904).
4 Roeder, "Introduction."
5 For a biographical note see the introduction to George Broderick, "Manx Stories and Reminiscences of Ned Beg Hom Ruy," *Zeitschrift für celtische Philologie* 38 (1981).

greatly vexed some of the good people in Cregneish whom I much esteem." [88] He went on to add:

> I am really sorry to have unwillingly given cause for raising any bad feeling, but I may assure them that I alone am responsible for the publication of these notes, which I have collected during the last six or eight years from a variety of old people in the neighbourhood.

However, "[u]nfortunately, the odium is cast on my old friend Mr Ed. Farquhar, who is absolutely free from any share; the information in question, along with many other items of folklore from that place, was given me at various times from a worthy old man now dead some years." And Faragher was suffering the consequences:

> But there really is no personal reflection intended or expressed on any one, and I trust those who feel aggravated will accept my assurance, and desist from venting their ire on Mr Farquhar, who has nothing at all to do with the matter, and who suffers greatly by the general animus against him, which I sincerely hope will cease after the explanation I have given, and that the former good relations will be established.

The *Examiner* was being read in Cregneash and on this occasion what was being published was not to their liking.

In 1903, the year after this incident, Sophia Morrison (1859–1917)[6] received a letter from William Boyd-Hawkins, who wrote that "I am fascinated by the lore of the Island, which I hope you will not allow to pass away without record. All the fragments should be collected so that nothing be lost. You can do this quietly in Peel—without publishing for the present—I fear, that, if you publish, the old people will not tell you anything!"[7] Later, when passing on part of her folk medicine collection on to Roeder, her letter has a note of caution, "I will ask you please not to publish the names of any of the givers of the prescriptions & charms, though I have put them down for the sake of remembering them."[8]

Folklorists were not just dealing with a literate populace in the Island, but also one with a strong Nonconformist religious culture. Morrison collected "Arrane Sooree" from Joseph Moore of Dalby and she commented that while he once knew twelve or thirteen verses of it, "now he remembers the first verse & the chorus which came after each verse."[9] Moore attempted to find others who could recollect more of the song than he could but to no avail. "However, he tried to console me by saying that the missing verses were no loss, 'jus' [just] boghtynid.'"

---

6   For an overview see Breesha Maddrell, "Speaking from the Shadows: Sophia Morrison and the Manx Cultural Revival," *Folklore* 113.2 (2002).

7   Letter from William Boyd-Hawkins to Sophia Morrison, 15 August 1903, MNHL, MS 09495, Box 1.

8   Copy letter of Sophia Morrison to Karl Roeder, undated [April? 1906], MNHL, MS 09495, Box 4, Letter Copybook (1904–07).

9   "Manx Fragments of Music," undated, hand of Sophia Morrison, MNHL, MS 09495, Box 7.

Cregeen glosses *boghtynid* as meaning "poverty, poorness"[10] with Kelly the same sense as "poverty, need."[11] Moore is using it here in the second notion, that the missing verses were no great loss. This was not the only time that Morrison encountered this feeling. When reporting to the Manx Language Society in 1905 about the activities of the recently purchased phonograph she mentioned a major problem she had encountered in collecting material:

> One difficulty in the way of obtaining the material which we want, has been, as I have found by experience, the unwillingness of our intensely earnest and religious peasantry to speak into the instrument such "boghtynid" as folk-stories and sayings and secular songs. They prefer that such a serious thing as a record which is to be handed down to posterity shall consist of Hymns, Scripture, or Carvals.[12]

As A.W. Moore had earlier noted in his *Manx Ballads and Music* (1896), "[t]o this day a score of Manx men will know one or more Manx sacred songs for every one that knows a Manx secular song."[13]

"The items of the Peel Sea Lore are all too valuable to be shelved & I have therefore taken the liberty to send them to the <u>Examiner</u> for Notes & Queries; leaving names out, as desired. I am most obliged to Mr Cashen."[14] So wrote Roeder to Sophia Morrison on 15 January 1903, and her material appeared in the columns for 24 January 1903, and the week following, 31 January, regardless as to whether she intended that or not. [218–19] Roeder wrote to her again a few days later on 20 January:

> I am sorry I make you acquaintance so late, but fortunately it comes very opportune & I rely upon your previous help in continuing to collect what is still to be had. Mr Cashen may know many <u>haaf words</u> & things pertaining to sea lore & customs.[15]

From the extant letters from Roeder to Morrison it is evident that she supplied notes on the herring fishery to him and amongst her own papers there is a notebook dating from 1903 containing material on that topic.[16]

---

[10] Archibald Cregeen, *A Dictionary of the Manks Language* (Douglas & London & Liverpool: J. Quiggin & Whittaker, Treacher, and Arnot & Evans, Chegwin, and Hall, 1835 [but 1837]) 27a.

[11] Rev. William Gill, ed., *The Manx Dictionary in Two Parts. First, Manx and English; and the Second, English and Manx* (Douglas: Manx Society, 1866) 26b.

[12] Sophia Morrison, "The Secretary's Report," *Annual Meeting, 1905* (n.p.: Manx Language Society, 1905) 4.

[13] A.W. Moore, "Introduction," *Manx Ballads and Music* (Douglas: G. & R. Johnson, 1896) xv.

[14] Letter from Karl Roeder to Sophia Morrison, 15 January 1903, MNHL, MS 09495, Box 6.

[15] Letter from Karl Roeder to Sophia Morrison, 20 January 1903, MNHL, MS 09495, Box 6.

[16] "Manx Folk Lore | Collected by self 1903". Notebook compiled by Sophia Morrison. MNHL, MS 09495 Box 8.

Roeder's column never covered the range of topics that were outlined at the start and it became in effect one for Manx folklore. Whilst Faragher was just one of a circle of informants that Roeder had built up in the Island, he was, nevertheless, the principal one.[17] Moreover, he was an active collector for him. In 1896, he wrote to Roeder that "I am not meeting with any fairy tales as I have not been from home for some time now but christmas is near and folks often go a visiting at christmas times and if all is well I will be trying to have a stroll myself."[18] The next year, "I have been to ballakilperic But my old aunts could not tell me about any old tales the old yarns was forgotten by them they are both over Eighty years."[19]

Roeder supplied him with blank notebooks for him to fill with whatever he could find, a fresh one often sent with queries arising from the previous one. This from 1897: "I am sending you the books and I wish I would have had a chance to take some more pains with them I should have had a room to myself and not to have been called from them every ten minutes."[20] Four of these notebooks are known, one from 1897,[21] two from the following year 1898,[22] and a final one dated 1901.[23]

The folklore that appears is not that familiar from other columns of this nature, notably the one in *Notes and Queries*, where short notices of customs and superstitions were sent in by outsiders, often puzzled or bemused individuals. Faragher's material is altogether different and also comes from someone who was an insider. One example that makes this plain is a contribution to the *Examiner* column such as this:

> A Buggane was often seen between Ballagawne and Ballacurrie, sometimes it was in the shape of a black pig, and sometimes like a man with officer's cloths. He is said to have followed a woman and her boy all the way home, and when they were in bed he was seen standing at the window, but she put the boy the floor side and he disappeared; then she put the boy the wall side again and he was at the window in a moment, and she to keep the boy the floor side all night. [16]

And as the start of another piece: "There was an old man from Foxdale telling about a changeling in Foxdale. He said it was a true story, for he knew the man and woman and the house, and he had seen the fairy child many times." [138] Here we have the recounting of both memorates and fabulates, which in the course of the column are

17 As regards one of his other informants, see Stephen Miller, "'We write you a few lines.' Karl Roeder and the Hudsons of Ballafesson," *Manx Notes* 35 (2004).
18 Letter from Edward Faragher to Karl Roeder, 21 December 1896, MNHL, MS 11064, Box 2. All transcripts from Faragher's letters are diplomatic ones.
19 Letter from Edward Faragher to Karl Roeder, 28 January 1897, MNHL, MS 11064, Box 2.
20 Letter from Edward Faragher to Karl Roeder, 28 January 1897, MNHL, MS 11064, Box 2.
21 MNHL, MS 09447, Karl Roeder Papers.
22 MNHL, MS 09447, Karl Roeder Papers; MNHL, MS 09495, Box 5.
23 MNHL, MS 09447, Karl Roeder Papers.

recounted both in number and at length.[24] There is the impression given that Roeder was using the notebooks compiled by Faragher to keep the column afloat, and by so doing a remarkable amount of essentially narrative folklore appeared.[25] This also put into print material now gone with the loss of Roeder's personal papers.

Towards the end of the column's life, Roeder himself contributed a series of lengthy notes on the Finn MacCooil cycle of legends [**229–31**] & [**233–37**] and the history of the Manx herring fishery [**249–56**] & [**260**]; this latter topic was carried on after the column finished with a further series of contributions, "The Herring and Its Habitat" in ten parts (1903–04) and "Gastronominal Notes on the Herring" in two (1904). The *Examiner* also carried a number of other pieces by Roeder later in 1905 and 1906 under the "Manx Notes and Queries" heading.

In 1904, the column was reproduced in book form and Roeder in his preface mentioned:

> I have enough material left to fill another volume, but at present it is wiser to see first if this volume will find favour and public appreciation sufficient to encourage the *Examiner* to undertake its publication.[26]

It is not clear how well *Manx Notes & Queries* sold; the *Examiner* carried sales notices between December 1904 and July 1905, but nothing further after that date. Whatever the situation was as regards sales, there never was a second column in the newspaper, and in any case Roeder lost interest as an undated letter by Morrison written to J.J. Kneen shows:

> I had a 'breezy' letter from Mr Roeder last night. He thinks we are but a poor lot not to be able to keep open the Manx N. & Queries in the Examiner. "there is nothing doing in the Isle. The indifference is great."[27]

That said, she once wrote herself to Roeder in 1903, "[i]t is fortunate that the work brings its own reward, otherwise the buckets of cold water so lavishly thrown over one would quench the most ardent lover of Manx."[28]

STEPHEN MILLER, 2019

---

[24] Memorates are personal recollections whereas fabulates are accounts retold on the basis of someone else's experience.

[25] Work is still needed to see the full extent of the overlap between the notebooks and the material that appeared in the column.

[26] Roeder, "Introduction." For a description of the contents, see pp. 275–76 here.

[27] Letter from Sophia Morrison to J.J. Kneen, 28 December [?], MNHL, MS 1046 (C) C.

[28] Letter from Sophia Morrison to Karl Roeder, 9 November 1903, MCL, Manchester Archives, M277/12/1–196.

INTRODUCTION

REFERENCES

INTRODUCTION

Broderick, George. "Manx Stories and Reminiscences of Ned Beg Hom Ruy." *Zeitschrift für celtische Philologie* 38 (1981): 113–78.

Cregeen, Archibald. *A Dictionary of the Manks Language*. Douglas & London & Liverpool: J. Quiggin & Whittaker, Treacher, and Arnot & Evans, Chegwin, and Hall, 1835 [but 1837].

Gill, Rev. William, ed. *The Manx Dictionary in Two Parts. First, Manx and English; and the Second, English and Manx*. Douglas: Manx Society, 1866.

Maddrell, Breesha. "Speaking from the Shadows: Sophia Morrison and the Manx Cultural Revival." *Folklore* 113 2 (2002): 215–36.

Miller, Stephen. "Karl Roeder: An Updated Checklist of Writings on Manx Folklore." *Manx Notes* 16 (2004): 1–2.

———. "'We write you a few lines.' Karl Roeder and the Hudsons of Ballafesson." *Manx Notes* 35 (2004): 1–2.

Moore, A.W. "Introduction." *Manx Ballads and Music*. Douglas: G. & R. Johnson, 1896. xiv–xxx.

Morrison, Sophia. "The Secretary's Report." *Annual Meeting, 1905*. n.p.: Manx Language Society, 1905. 3–7.

Roeder, Karl. "Introduction." *Manx Notes and Queries*. Douglas: S.K. Broadbent, 1904. [unpaged].

———. "Manx Notes and Queries: Nos 1–2." *Isle of Man Examiner* 21 September 1901: 3c.

*

A NOTE ON THE TEXT

The texts here are taken from the original columns in the *Isle of Man Examiner* with any obvious typos corrected. The numbering of the original newspaper column was erratic in places and here it has been renumbered; however, this does not match the similar exercise that was undertaken for the 1904 edition. The column is obviously of its time and Roeder's comments in places reflects contemporary ideas and the then state of philological knowledge and so needs to be read with a cautionary note in mind.

❀

KARL ROEDER

MANX NOTES AND QUERIES

THE ISLE OF MAN EXAMINER COLUMN
(1901–03)

❀

MANX NOTES AND QUERIES

MANX NOTES AND QUERIES

*

MANX NOTES AND QUERIES

In response to requests made by gentlemen who take a deep interest in questions concerning the Isle of Man and the Manx people, we have decided to devote space as occasion requires to "Manx Notes and Queries." In connection, with these notes and queries, we invite contributions and inquiries in connection with elucidation and points on Manx language, Manx history, Manx biography, Manx antiquities, Manx folk-lore, Manx place-names, the natural history of the Island, and kindred subjects. We feel sure that Manx people and others will appreciate this new departure, which commences this week, and will assist us to make "Manx Notes and Queries" interesting and instructive.

1. STORY OF THE BEE-STUNG PARSON

Among the old stories which I have obtained from the South of the Island, at Cregneish, the one of the bee-stung patson is of particular interest. It was given me in Manx, and runs thus:

Ta mee er chlashtyn skeeal veg mysh saggyrt ren coyrt e vreechyn gys thalear dy cherraghey ad fastyr Jesarn, as ren yn thalear cur y vac thie lhieu moghrey Jydoonee. Mry ve'h er yn raad gys thie yn taggyrt, haink eh er edd shellan, as ghow eh breechyn yu taggyrt dy yeealley ny shellanyn ersooyl. As tra ve'h er gheddyn yn vill hie eh gys thie yn taggryt lesh ny breechyn. Ren eh lhiggey shaghey spooileil ny shellanyn, as ve traa da'n saggyrt dy gholl ayns yn cheeil, chur eh ny breechyn er anys siyr, as ghow eh toshiaght dy lhaih ny padjeryn ayns y cheeyl as ghow ny shellanyn toshiaght dy chur nyn gahyn ayns e lheeayst, as ghow eh toshiaght dy lheimyragh as dy stampey, as haink eh magh lesh goan nagh row cairagh dy ve loayrit ayns keeyl: Va er ve paart dy shellanyn ayns e vreechyn.

Or Englished: I have heard a little tale about a parson that sent his pants to a tailor on Saturday evening to get mended, and the tailor sent his son with them on Sunday morning, and he came on a bees' nest and he took the parson's pants to beat the bees. When he got the honey he went on his way to the parson's house, and as he had delayed by robbing the bees' nest, it was about time for the parson to go to church. So he put on the pants in a hurry, and began to read the prayers in the church, and the bees began to sting his thighs, and he began to jump and stamp, until at last he came out with words that were unlawful to be said in church: Some of the bees had been in the pants.

Readers of Edwin Waugh's *Jannock, or the Bold Trenchman* (1873), will recognise the outlines of the above anecdote again, so racingly told in Chapter vii, 60–68. He puts it into the mouth of Adam Ritson, of Broughton, who thus says: "It happened a long time ago, at a little chapel somwheer Kes'ick way on. It was yan o' my gran'fadder's cracks." It is a delightful bit of writing, and the question is where did Waugh really pick up the material?

Waugh visited the Isle of Man in 1869, and the fruits of that trip are laid down in his *Guide to Castletown, Port Erin, and Adjacent Parts of the Isle of Man* (Manchester, 1869).

It is a striking coincidence to find the tale simultaneously in Manx, at Cregneish, which Waugh also visited and described. Did he get the story here, or did he obtain possession previously, during his rambles in the Lake Country in 1861, and merely amused the Port Erin or Cregneish fishermen with it when he cracked his jokes with them? When he went to the Island he was fifty-one years old. His fame was then already established, and his was a Lancashire household name.

2. QUERY

Can any of your readers supply information in regard to the old mound on Castleward (near the old shooting range)? Evidently this mound has been fortified, for there are yet to be seen the remains of defensive works. There is a very similar mound close to the Parish Church of Malpas (Cheshire).

B. E. P.

3. THE WORD GROOSNIÚYS, OR GROONÓAYS

Groosniúys, also *grissniuys* signifies, according to Cregeen, "beastings," or new curd, made of the milk of a cow newly done calving. I picked up the word again recently in the South of the Island. It is derived from *groo*, Manx, *gruth*, 'curds,' Gaelic and Irish. In Gaelic *beastings*, or *biestings*, is also called *bhainne*, first milk, or *nos* or *bainne nuis*. The latter is doubtlessly derived from the word *nuadh*, Gaelic and Irish, 'new,' 'fresh'; so that the Manx *groosniuys*, which, as it clearly is the more correct rendering, would correspond to *gruth nuadh* in Gaelic and Irish and thus means fresh, or new curds.

4. MANX PROVERBS

Amongst the many Manx Proverbs relating to meteorological phenomena the following has been collected by me:

    Tra ta bayrn er Baroole Yiow
    Kione Vaughold ayrn jeh shen
    Tra ta'n sniaghtey lhie er thie Bushel
    Bee eh tammylt roish nee eh tennue

Or in English:

    When Barrule will have a cap,
    Maughold Head will get share of that,
    When the snow lies on Bushel's House.
    It will be a while before it thaws.

This old weather rule runs on the same lines as the distich found in Cumberland, viz:

If Skiddaw hath a cap, Scuffel wots full well of that.

These are two neighbouring hills, the one in this country and the other in Annandale. If the former be capped with clouds and foggy mists, it will not be long ere rain falls on the other. It is spoken of such who must expect to symphathise in their sufferings by reason of the vicinity of their inhabitants. See *A Complete Collection of English Proverbs*, by John Ray, revised by John Balfour, (1813).

Turning to Lancashire we have another parallel:

If Riving-pike do wear a hood,

Be sure that day will ne'er be good.

(A mist on the top of the hill is a sign of foul weather.)

Also:

When Pendle wears its woolly cap,

The farmers all may take a nap.

And again, as present in Lancashire folklore and dialect:

"Owd Know (Knoll, a hill between Rodden and Ronesdale) has bin awsin (offering) to put hur durty cap on a time or two today, an' as soon as hur can shap to see it, ther'll be waytur among us, yo'll see."

In Leicestershire we meet with:

If Bever hath a cap,

You churles of the vale, look to that.

(When the clouds hang over Bevis Castle, it is prognostic of rain and moisture, to the much endangering of that fruitful vale lying in the three counties of Leicester, Lincoln, and Nottingham.)

We see that the Manx proverb does not stand alone, and is not specifically Manx. It points to Cumberland and North-Western Lancashire for its origination, and most probably applied at an early period by Lancashire and Cumberland settlers in the Isle of Man. To the former, particularly, as I shall be able to show on a later occasion, the Manx peasantry is very much indebted for their popular nursery rhymes, songs, ditties, and games, many of which became naturalised in the Island with the incoming of the Stanleys.

5. ADDITIONAL VERSES FROM OUR CREGNEISH POET
LINES TO —

Time will change the fairest flower,

Time will change the gayest bower,

Time will waste the giant oak,

Time will end all human hope.

Time the palace walls erases,

Time the fairest scenes defaces,

Time will change the monarch's crown,

And lay all his glory down.
Time will change the golden hair,
Time the hardest marble wear,
Time will change the brightest dye,
Steal the light from beauty's eye,
Stop the sweetest birds that sing,
Change the charms of rosy spring.
Time will change the sylvan grove,
But time cannot alter love.
Time will change all things beside,
Yet the stream of love will glide,
Till the eye is closed in death,
And the fond heart laid beneath.
When the ties of earth are riven,
Love lives on afresh in Heaven.
When the spirit hence has fled,
And the heart is cold and dead—
Then in some Arcadian grove
We shall live again in love.
Time may change and life may flee,
Yet the heart that beats for thee
Shall as fondly round thee twine,
And each throb respond to thine,
Till the sun of life has set,
Nor e'en then can we forget.
Like yon star that marks the Pole,
The re-animated soul
Lives of love again to dream:
Love shall then be all the theme.
Lovers here may droop and die,
Yet 'twill blossom in the sky,
By no jealousy distrest,
Where no rival can molest.
Let the world say what it will,
Love shall live and flourish still.

The above were composed in his younger days by my friend Edward Farquhar, and for their mellow cadence, great beauty, and originality, although not perfect in form, deserve preservation in your valuable columns.

6. HOW TO STOP BLOOD!—A CHARM

Perhaps the following Manx charm will be of interest:

KYS DY LHIETTAL ROIE FOALLEY!—PISHAG

Trooid magh yn Ellan shoh veagh persoonyn (deiney dy-cadjin) baghey lech pishagyn oc oddagh lhiettal roie foalley. Ayns Skeeyley Chreest ny Hayrey va dooinney baghey oddagh slaanaghey yn roie foalley ec deiney as beiyn myrgeddin. Dy beagh muc ny booa lhiggey fuill, roieagh yn theay faasechredjuagh dy gheddyn yn "fer-obbee." Shiartanse dy vleeantyn er dy henney haghyr roie foalley ayns Laxey my-e-chione ta mee er chee dy insh diu. Va boirey eddyr daa pherson, as va'n derrey yeh er woailley yn jeh elleyer y chione lesh cainleyr, huitt y dooinney neealloo, as va'n "fer-obbee," haink eh, as hug eh pishag er y dooinney boght. Ren yn uill sthappa!—agh roish my dug eh yn phishag er, hug eh boandey-aanrit er e lhott!

HOW TO STOP BLOOD!—A CHARM

Throughout this Island there used to be people (generally men) living with charms at them who could stop the running of blood. In Kirk Christ Lezayre there was a man living who could heal the running of blood at men and beasts also. If there would be a pig or cow letting blood the superstitious peasantry would run to get the "charmer." A few years ago there happened a running of blood in Laxey, about which I am going to tell you. There was trouble between two persons, one had struck the other on the head with a candlestick, the man fell in a swoon, and the blood poured out of his wound. They sent for the charmer, he came, and he put a charm on the poor man. The blood stopped!—but before he put the charm on him, he put a bandage on his wound.

JUAN Y CRUIN

7. MANX RIDDLE

"Myr yeeagh mee harrish boalley chashtal my ayrey honnick mee yn marroo cur lesh ny bioee ersooyl." Lhong. In English: 'As I looked over my father's castle wall I saw the dead carrying the living away.' Solution: A ship.

8. PUZZLE

"Abbyr: 'abb' as ny gleaysh dty chab." "Say 'abb' without moving your chin." It was a kind of puzzle; you cannot say "abb" without moving your chin.

9. THE SCAA BUGGANE USHAG

"The ghost of a scarecrow" is an old coat and hat set up in a field to scare the birds away. When anyone had very ragged clothes on people said he was like the ghost of a scarecrow. It is also called *buggane doa*, 'the adhering buggane,' and *dollaghan*, 'the frightful figure,' from *doal*, 'blind.' Some also put two empty bottles in the field, and the wind makes a peculiar noise in the bottles and frightens the rooks away.

10. THE PHRASE GAARDERYN SLOCK

'Squalls of wind' coming through the Slock. The Slock is the hollow between Cronk -ny-irree-Laa and Surby mountain; when the wind is N.W. there are squalls coming in through the hollow, and somtimes tumbling the stacks of corn and unroofing the houses. In Lingague there was once an old farmer living, and he was very "fearful" of these Gaarderyn Slock.

11. THE BUGGANE Y SMELT

"The Buggane of the Smelt" was held in great fear. There is a story of a very old woman who said she had seen him standing on a stile at the roadside, and she turned round and repeated the Lord's Prayer; and, lo! he was gone. Some man, that met him was in great fear to pass him, when the *Buggane* accosted him thus: "Ny cur boirey orryms, as cha derrym biorey orts" ('Don't molest me and I will not molest thee'). It used to be a common word with the people living there: "What did the *Buggane* say?" The Smelt is at the Nennagh, close to the big mill. It was thought that the *Buggane* was the spirit of some man that had been murdered there.

12. THE GOOD BROTH

Once upon a time a manservant went to see his sister who was living in another part of the Island. When he arrived at his sister's house it was dinner time, and his sister had broth for dinner. She gave some to her brother, and all the time he was supping it, she kept saying to him, "Isn't that good broth, Boree? Thou'll not get broth like that from Nancy (his wife) I'll warrant." Every time she said this, Boree replied, "It's hot, it's hot," and she could not get him to say that it was good, a fact which annoyed her greatly. As soon as he was done dinner, Boree had to start for home again. When he had gone, she discovered that she had forgotten to put the meat in the broth. "Aw well," quoth she, "no wonder for Boree to say, 'It's hot, it's hot.'"

JUAN Y CRUIN

YN BROTT MIE

Keayrt dy row hie fer mooinjerey dy chur shilley er e huyr va baghey ayns paart elley jeh'n Ellan. Tra ve'h er roshtyn thie e hayrey va traa jinnairaghayn, as va brott ec e huyr son jinnair. Hug eh paart da e vraas, as choud as v'eh gee eh, v'ee gm rish, "Nagh vel shen brott me Bovee? Cha now brott mie myr shen voish Nancy (e ven) Var-a-mish" Dagh keayrt v'ee gra shoh, va Bovee freggyrt. "T'eh çheh, t'eh çheh," as cha n'yiarragh eh dy row eh mie, as er yn oyr shoh v'ee dy-mooar seaghnit Cha leah as v'an brott eeit ec Bovee, b'eign da goll er yraad dy-valley reesht. Tra v'eh ersooyl, hooar ee magh nagh row yn eill currit 'sy vrott eck, "Ochannee," dooyrt ee, "cha nhyrrys da Bovee gra, 't'eh cheh, t'eh cheh.'"

13. **THE MOUND AT CASTLEWARD**

I was pleased to see a query on this subject, and have copied from Thwaites' and Train's Histories the items below. They cannot, however, be described as ample and sufficient, and it would be instructive to learn whether the old fort was ever used in actual warfare, and if any relies of such usage have been found upon the spot. Perhaps some member of the Antiquarian Society will aid us in the matter?

I also wish to mention that at the top of Castleward, where a clump of trees grows by the highroad, the place is locally known as "The Sod Castle." What does this name signify? Apologies for mixing up my notes and queries together.

A. Cannan.

14. **REPLY**

"Castleward, one of the most entire remains of a Norwegian station that has reached our times, is situated in a valley, on the banks of the river Glass."—Train's *History*, p. 276 (Mounds and Fortifications).

"In this parish is the ancient fortification of Castleward, one of the most perfect Norwegien encampments which have been preserved It is situated on the banks of the river Glass, but its original character has considerably suffered on account of the numerous trees which are now growing on its site."—Thwaites' *History*, p. 388 (Topography of Braddan Parish).

15. **QUERY**

Is there any Gill or Glen named Glen Gawne between Groudle and Ballameanagh in the parish of Kirk Lonan?

Mac.

16. **A BUGGANE CHANGING HIS SHAPE**

A Buggane was often seen between Ballagawne and Ballacurrie, sometimes it was in the shape of a black pig, and sometimes like a man with officer's cloths. He is said to have followed a woman and her boy all the way home, and when they were in bed he was seen standing at the window, but she put the boy the floor side and he disappeared; then she put the boy the wall side again and he was at the window in a moment, and she to keep the boy the floor side all night.

17. **SEEING THE WIND AND THE BLACK PIG**

They say that if a man would keep from getting his face washed for nine days, he would see the wind as well as the black pig.

18. **THE OLD MANX FEMININE CHRISTIAN NAME BAHEE**

There is an obsolete woman's Christian name which occurs frequently in the recital of names in the 16th and 17th centuries in Manx deeds and documents, spelt Bahee,

Bahie, or Bahy, sometimes also Baggy. The name has not entirely disappeared, and has been given to me in various forms. It is pronounced Puy, Puiy, and Poy, also Phiy, and stands for Margaret, Peg, and Peggy. But is not used much now. I heard it in Cregneish. The best name now, however is Morgaid or Morgeid in Manx. Bahee, of course, is the same as Puy, Peg, or Peggy, and no doubt the proper derivation.

19. SHEEP SHEARING

Formerly in the time of sheep shearing in the Island the sheep owners used to meet on an appointed day to gather all the sheep on the mountain into the *paail* for the purpose to impound them. All the owners in the different parishes had their own mark to identify their sheep, and this mark was called *cowrey keyrrach* or *beim er y chleaysh*. The grandfather of a friend of mine in the South had, for instance, a split of half an inch in the point of both ears (*scoltey ayns baare dagh chleaysh*), some had a small piece cut out of one place or another, some had holes in their ears (*daa howl as un towl*), just like the Westmorland farmers, who likewise ear-marked their sheep with particular notches cut in the ear. In the Shetlands each family also had its own particular mark, which was registered and went to the youngest son. When the old Manx were shearing their sheep, and just as the shorn animals bounded away from their grip they had an old rhyme which they used to sing on the occasion, an accompaniment still to be heard sometimes, as in Glen Aldyn, and in the South. It ran as follows:

Gow dy lhome as tar dy mollagh,
Cur lesh dy eayn braue bwoirrin,
As dy loamrey braue saillagh:
My aikys oo moddey croym dty chione,
As my aikys oo maarliagh, roïe er-y-hon.

Go away bare, and come back rough,
Bring a good she-lamb and a good fleece,
If you see a dog, stoop your head,
And if you see a thief run for it.

20. MANX SHIPPING

The following shipping news, referring to the Isle of Man will be of interest to readers. The list is extracted from R. Whitworth's *Manchester Magazine*, during 1741–42, it is headed:

Ships entered outwards, and imports at Liverpool to and from "Isleman," with indication of the captains.

Charming Molly, N. Cumming, Nich. Shimmin, with Manx cattle, Isleman; *Charming Nancy*, H. Woods, with Manx frize, calf skins, linnen cloth, hides, Isleman; *Ann and Mary*, R. Pennington, Castletown, Manx cattle; *Ann and Francis*, Geo. Willis, Isleman; *William & Mararet*, Wm. Thomson, Isleman; *Betty*,

Alex. Crocket; *Michael*, Jas. Kown, Isleman; *Edward*, John Kissack, from Douglas;
Thomas, Rich. Holland, Isleman; *Love's Encrease*, Henry Lowey, Isleman;
Friendship, Wm. Robinson, with linnen cloth; *Prosperity*, David Bitton, Ramsey,
Manx cattle; *Resolution*, T. Rymer, Derbyhaven, Manx cattle; *Endeavour*,
Jonathan Saul, Isleman; *Speedwell*, John Peace, Isleman; *Dispatch*, John
Woodhouse, Isleman; *Dove*, John Hough, Isleman; *Squirrel*, Thos. Wilson,
Isleman; *Lyon*, Rid. Rutter, Isleman.

21. LAA BOALDYN (MAY DAY)

The season has returned again,
When the *bwillogh* is all in bloom,
By April's sun and showers of rain,
And evening dew and midnight gloom.

I still remember days gone by,
When I was but a little lad,
We plucked the yellow flowers with joy,
And on May-eve we all were glad.

At every door we laid them down,
That fair Titania might see
The beauteous flowers scatter'd round,
And dance around with fairy glee.

The Fairy Queen—the old folk said—
Was going round on old May-night
When all mankind was gone to bed,
And in the flowers did delight.

She kindly blessed each little cot,
Where yellow flowers did appear:
If there were none—she blessed them not
But gave bad luck through all the year.

I still remember on May-day,
Those flowers scatter'd in Cregnaish,
But since the Queen is gone away
No flowers at the door we place.

No more among the *trammon* trees,
The little elves or fairies swing,
Hopping amongst the leaves like bees,
Or little birds upon the wing.

And branches of the rowan tree
Were carefully in crosses made,
And placed in holes where none could see,
To keep away each witching jade.

While bonfires blazed on every hill,
To keep the *buitching* crew at bay.
And some folks kindle fires still
To scare the witches—people say.

The little elves now dance no more,
Nor sing in Manx their midnight song
Among the flow'rets at the door,
And home to fairy-land are gone.

But these are now things of the past,
For witch alike and elf are flown,
From all the hills, save Cronk Glenchass—
'Tis said they claim that as their own.

Note: The *bwillogh* is the *Caltha palustris*, and a grand Manx fairy flower. The *trammon*, or elder tree, is dear to the Manx elves and fairies. The rowan tree, or mountain ash, plays an important part in the celebration of May Eve and its berries, when placed on cow byres, and tied in the tails of cows, or hung over the threshold of the house, or worn by the milk-maids and fastened to the pails and milk vats, *etc.*, acted as powerful agencies against witchcraft and evil spirits and their dark work. Cronk Glenchass, or the dry glen, was and still is supposed to be a favourite haunt of the Manx fairies, and I have a large collection of stories and legends referring to it.

I sent you above little composition from Edward Farquhar, descriptive of old Manx May-day, which will interest many of your Insular readers.

22. THE WITCH OF GLEN RUSHEN

"There is a story, sir, of a witch that lived in Glen Rushen. She could command the wind to blow so sudden as to dismast the vessels sailing on the coast. She also would command the *gobbags*, or dog-fish to eat and destroy the fishermen's nets. She often used to go about in the form of a hare, and a great many had tried to shoot her, and often chased her with dogs, but no gun could hurt her nor any greyhound catch her in running. But there was a young gentleman out with his gun one morning pretty early, and the game birds very scarce, but at last he started a very fine hare; he fired at him, but the gun only gave a little crack, and the hare did not run away, but turned round and looked at him: so by that he thought it was a witch. He had silver buttons in his wristbands, and he pulled them out as fast as he could and loaded the gun again, putting in the silver buttons for shot. He went towards the hare, but she

10

seemed to feel no alarm, so he took aim and fired. He saw that he had hit the hare, but she went away limping, and he gave chase expecting to catch her, but he could only keep her sight, until she got in the house. When he came to the house he went in and saw nobody. Then he went to the *cullee*, and the old witch was in bed, and seemed as if she was dying. He lifted up the bed clothes and the bed was all over blood—she was wounded in the thigh. It appears she did not live very long after that, for the people said she was not seen in the form of a hare afterwards in the bruit fields in the morning."

23. THE BUGGANE AT THE FISTARD
"My grandfather, sir, was coming home from Port St Mary at a late hour one night, and he came Fistard-way, and he got on the stile to cross a field—for that road leads through two fields. There was a black cat, just beyond the stile, sitting beside the path, and he gave the cat a kick, but did not feel his foot touching anything, but the cat grew like a big black bull in a few minutes, and he had such big long horns! The monster stood in the path before him, and he could not get past, so he made as if he would go across the field another way, but the bull was before him every way he turned, and he had to go backward until he got to the stile again, and there was a house near the stile. So he went backward to the door and kept his face toward the bull, and beat against the door with his heels until the man in the house got out of bed and let him in—he had to stop there all night."

24. MANX CHRISTIAN NAMES
I am much pleased and interested with the column devoted to Notes and Queries on Manx subjects. I differ, however, with the recent contribution numbered 18. I have found in my experience that Bahee in Welsh is a pet term, or expression of endearment, for a child; and I knew an instance in the North of the Isle of Man where the same word was equivalent to the English name Phoebe. Peggy and Puy, I understand to be Manx for Margaret, or Maggie.

J.R. L., Douglas.

25. ORIGIN OF KING WILLIAM'S BANK
In the fourth volume of the *Historic Society of Lancashire and Cheshire*, 1852, a very interesting account is given by Joseph Mayer, the antiquarian, of King William the Third's royal progress to Ireland to suppress the rebellion. According to it, he left London on the 4th June, 1690, slept at Peel Hall, near Tarvin, on the 9th. The next day we find him at Chester, from thence, the same afternoon he travelled to Gayton Hall, near Parkgate, and the next morning he proceeded to Leusowe, and the troops striking their tents, were put in motion and embarked on board the Royal Fleet (on a point since called the King's Gap) lying in the Lake, and sailed out with the tide at noon-day. Edward Tariton, master of the *James*, of Liverpool, piloted the King's

vessel from Hoylake to Carrickfergus. By a computation of the state of the tide on the 10th June, 1690, old style, it was high water at Hoylake and Liverpool at nine o'clock, a.m. The King's ship, on board of which William III was, grounded on a bank near the Point of Ayre, off the Isle of Man, at about four o'clock the next morning. This being the low water of a spring tide, his vessel did not get off for more than an hour afterwards; and the bank has ever since been called King's William's Bank. The origination of the naming of this dangerous sandbank will no doubt prove of great interest to Manxmen.

26. THE FOXGLOVE (DIGITALIS PURPUREA)

The foxglove in Irish plant lore is intimately connected with the fairies under the appellation of *lusmore;* the *shefro* wears the corolla of its flower on his head. The Welsh call it:

menygellyllon, elf's glove; *bysedd ellyllon,* fairy fingers; *bysedd y cwn,* dog's fingers.

In Gaelic we have:

meuran sith, fairy thimble; *meuran na daoine marbha,* dead men's thimble.

And in Irish:

meregan na m'na sioh, thimble of the fairywomen.

In Manx we meet various more or less corrupted forms:

slieggan sliean (Kelly); *sleggan slieau* (Quayle and Ralfe); *slegon slieau* (Laxey, Rydings); *slachan slieau* (Cregneish); *slingan slieau* (W.F. Peacock (1863) from Colby); *slian slieau* (Spaldick); *slang y slieau* (Spaldick).

And A.W. Moore derives it from:

sleggan slieau, Manx = *cleaver* or *wood cleaver.*

In the Norwegian and Danish language it is called:

raev bjaelde, the fox tinkle-bell

so named with reference to a favourite instrument of earlier times, a ring of bells hung on an arched support—*tintinnabulum*—which this plant with its hanging bell-shaped flowers so exactly represents. We also find a popular German plant name for the *digitalis purpurea:*

Wald schelle, Wald glöcklein, the little tinkle-bell of the wood

and Threlkeld in his *Sinopsis stirpiurm Hibernicarum,* Dublin 1727, cites:

Shihan sleivhe = mountain or wood bell, and

Shihan na m'na sioh = fairy women's bell

from the root *seinn* = music, chant, melody, with reference to the jingle or tinkle the little bell produces. We also have the phrase *seinn an clag, gilong an c'og* = to ring the bell. We find thus that the Manx name has nothing to do, according to analogy and comparative folk-names, with *sleggan* = a cleaver, but is in all probability derived from Gaelic: *clag* or *glag* = bell; *claggan* or *glaggan* = little bell, and German *glocke* = bell, and the Manx *slieggan* and *sleggan* is but a corrupted form of *claggan,* as *c* is often in Manx interchanged for *s.*

So far the Manx peasantry seems to be short of any fairy lore relating to the Foxglove. In Britten and Holland's *Dictionary of English Plant-Names* the following quotation occurs: "The Kirk Session of St Cuthbert (1636) examined Heleine Profeit, whether she had given her child ane drink of fox-tree (foxglove) leaves or not."

This seems to be connected with another bit of folklore of the County of Donegal, given in the *Cornhill Magazine*, vol. 35, 1877:

> Get foxy leaves (foxglove) said the old woman, an' boil them and bathe the wean three times in the water, and then weigh him in the scales. If he's your ain child he'll live, but if he is what I think he is—a changeling—he'll die.

Has the Island anything similar? The Island also appears to be destitute in the use of the foxglove for folk-medicine at least I have not come across any medical recipes. Its application for paralysis, headache, abscesses, epitheliac cancer, swelling, *etc.*, was already known in Wales in the middle of the 13th century, and prescriptions of the use of the foxglove are given by the *Physicians of Myddroi* (Caermarthensbire). The Irish peasantry, according to Threlkeld (1727), used it as remedy for epilepsy and the running ulcers of the King's evil.

I hope my note on the Manx *claggan slieau*, for such I consider the only correct form—the little mountain bell—also called by the Welsh in the 13th century *ffion ffridd*—the forest crimson—two beautiful and poetical descriptions—may induce any Manxmen who happen to remember any fairy lore about the foxglove, to record it permanently in your valuable columns.

27. CHRISTIAN LEWAIGUE'S DOG

I was told a little incident in Ramsey lately about Christian Lewaigue and Craine the Glaick, which I think ought to be recorded. Christian was in the vanguard of teetotalism while Craine was a big farmer and powerful preacher. They both went up and down through the Island advocating doctrines of reform, preaching against the pride that had come over the people, their habit of drinking *jough*, and so forth. Craine, on his way to Maughold to preach, called for "Lewaigue," and encountered a big dog chained on the street. The two reformers proceeded to the chapel together, and in the course of the sermon Craine called "Lewaigue" to account on the ground that he kept the big dog to frighten the poor and beggars from going near the door!

Mac.

28. MANX FISHING-BOAT NAMES

I have collected a number of old Manx names given by the fishermen to their boats, which are both interesting and instructive. I hope others may add to the list. The names come from the south-east of the Island: *Collagh vuck*, Boar; *Muck vooar and veg*, Big and Little Pig; *Loayr ghoal*, Blind Mare; *Molt*, Wether; *Cabbyl shuttle*, Shuttle Horse; *Thollag faiyr*, Titmouse; *Guiy minnagh*, Nippy Goose; *Shellan tarroogh*, Busy Bee; *Shellan mill*, Honey Bee; *Kishan shellar*, Beehive; *Colmane*, Dove;

Beisht y kione dhoo, The Beast of Black Head; *Glashtin mooar and beg,* Big and Little Glashtin; *Ben-rein fairish,* Fairy Queen; *Buggane y Smelt,* The Buggane of the Smelt; *Bill ny fairishyn,* Fairy Bill; *Kione mooar,* Big Head; *Jenny stoamey,* Bonny Jane; *Ben aeg stoamey,* Bonny Lass; *Kitty Balda,* Kitty of Balda; *Kerry thion mooar,* Big-Backed Katherine; *Guilley mie,* Favourite; *Breeshyrs yn Joan Doghernee;* John Doghernee's Breeches; *Baatey yn clieau,* Mountain Boat; *Baatey chirrym,* Dry Boat; *Billey feeyney,* Vine Tree; *Corlhea* (name of a farm); *Buinney cabbash,* Cabbage Stalk; *Collagh sniper,* is the snipe fish (when they made sharp bows in the boats they called them *sniper* bows); *Smugler mooar,* Big Smuggler; *Boteil,* Bottle; *Cleps,* (boat-hook); *Lhiattee yiarn,* Iron-side; *Trattley,* the name was *Australia,* but pronounced Trattley by the owner.

29. AN OLD MANX HARVEST RHYME

Ta mee shleeuit my chorran dy-geyre,
Dy ghiarrey yn choonlagh marish yn aiyr,
Dy laboragh fo chiass yn ghrian,
Gollish myr dy beign 'sy cheayn,
Dy churt ny bunneeyn fo haïee,
As paart dy lhie er yn laare-vooice.

I have whetted my sickle sharp,
To cut the straw and the grass,
To toil under the heat of the sun,
Sweating as if I was in the sea,
That I may get the sheaves under the kiln,
And some laid on the threshing floor.

30. THE MERMAN

The Manx fishermen, when out on the sea, used to call the merman *yn guilley beg,* 'the little boy.' This was his *haaf,* or sea name, by which alone he was allowed to be alluded to on the sea; his land name is *pohllinagh.* There were many other words which were tabooed by the fishermen while engaged on the sea, and the same custom was followed by the Shetlanders and the Scotch fishermen. Even the surname was changed at sea by the men, and I could quote some instances to that effect. Mermen and mermaids have been known sporting and gamboling round the creeks and coves on the south-west part of the Island, and I have heard many a tale about their doings—and as I was told by an old friend:

"Tra veagh ad fakin eh, veagh ad jannoo braghtan dy arran corkey as eeym, as ceau magh eh. Ta mee er chashtyn jeh dooinney ren cheet er unname jiu er yn traie, as ren eh coyrt eh ayns yn cheayn reesht; ny lurg shen, tra veagh sterrym ergerrey, veagh yn pohllin-agh cheet dy chur raaue da, as cha row eh goit ayns steerym, choud as ve'h goll gys yn cheayn."

When they saw him they made a cake of oaten bread and butter and threw it out. I have heard of a man that came on one of them on the shore, and put him in the sea again; after that when there was a storm near, the merman was always coming to inform him, and he was not caught in a storm as long as he went out to sea.

31. FRAGMENT OF AN OLD SONG

Ta'n ushag veg ruy ersooyl gys yn chrow,
Ny eayin gys ny moiraghyn roie,
Ta'n oie er yn aarkey lesh co-caslys grouw,
Dy gastey cheet voish y shiar-hwoaie.

Ta fainagh ny ghreiney ersooly harrish 'oyr,
Gys faarkaghyn lhean y sheear-ass,
Ta'n eayst ayns shiar er n'irree ayns gloyr,
As yn sheear ayns y coamrey glass.

The little brown bird has gone to the bush,
The lambs to their mothers now run,
The night on the ocean appears gloomy,
And quickly comes from the north-east.

The chariot of the sun is gone over the edge,
To the wide waves of the south-west,
And the moon in the east is risen in glory,
And the west in its robe of gray.

32. THE MANX MAY FLOWERS

On May Day (I quote *Mona's Herald*, May 5th, 1837) the people in the Isle of Man from time immemorial burnt all the (yellow-flowered) whin bushes in the Island, conceiving that thereby they burn all the witches and fairies which they believe take refuge there. Then also old and young gathered particular herbs and planted them at their doors and in their dwellings for the purpose of preventing the entrance of the witches. In another place we read: "On May Eve they gathered primroses and strewed them before the doors of their dwellings to keep away the fairies on that night. They congregated in the mountains on May Eve, and to scare the fairies and witches supposed to he roaming on that particular night in numbers greater than ordinary, set fire to the gorse or *conney* and blew horns."

Folkard in his *Plantlore* tells us that on May Day country people strew Marsh Marigold before their doors, and twine them into garlands, and in another passage: "To yellow flowers growing in the hedgerows the fairies have a special dislike, and will never frequent a place where they abound. Timorous folk took precautions for excluding elfin visitors from their dwellings by hanging over their doors boughs of

St. John's Wort (which also bears a yellow flower) at midnight on St. John's Eve." In some parts of Russia, according to Folkard, the country people heat their baths on the eve of St. John's and place in them the herb *kunalnitza* (a yellow crowfoot or *ranunculus*), in other parts they place herbs, on the same anniversary, upon the roofs of the houses and stables, as a safeguard against evil spirits; the French peasantry rub the udders of their cows with similar herbs to ensure plenty of milk, and place them over the doorways of cattle sheds and stables.

We see that these customs were observed both at May Eve (*Oie'l Voaldyn*) and on midsummer Eve (*Oie'l Eoin*) which mark two very important Manx festivals. The May Day in Gaelic is the *la buidhe bealtuinn* = the day of the yellow or golden *bealtain;* and in Irish plant lore the marsh marigold, or *caltha palustris*, is called, amongst other names, *lus buide bealtaine* = the flower of yellow bealtaine, and in Cregneish I have likewise heard it called *lus y voaldyn* = flower of *Bealtain.* Another Irish name is *bearnan bealtine*, or the *bealtin* chaplet, probably because it was worn as a covering for the head, as was likewise the mugwort. We notice the frequent recurrence of *buidhe* = yellow or golden, in all these words. Besides this name we find another word for it used by the Manx peasantry, variously spelt: *bellióch, bwillógh, booaliúgh* and *bluight; bluight* in Manx means milk (Gaelic *blvochd*, Irish *bleachd* = milk, kine, cows, giving milk) which seems also to be traceable in the Gaelic plant name: *bliochan* = marigold. There is another plant name in Manx: *bluightagh vheaun* a plant not botanically defined in Kelly's *Dictionary*, but which I surmise is to be equated with the Irish, *bainne bo bleacht*, or verbally, milk of the milch cow, a name given to the cowslip. *Bluigtagh* in Manx is milch cattle (Gaelic *bliochdach* = milk producing) and *vlieaun* is derived from *blieaun*, Manx = milking.

From this it would appear that both the marsh marigold and the primrose played a very interesting part in the observation and celebration of thes festivities and that it was particularly applied to the milch kine—their chief wealth—and use to protect them from the evil influence of the fairies, evil spirits, and witches. The French custom above alluded to seems to explain the meaning of the Manx *bluight* or *bwillogh*, the *bluightagh vlieaun*, and the Irish *bainne bo bleacht.* Perhaps the Manx may also, like the Gallo-Celtic peasantry, have in times gone past rubbed and stroked the udders of their cows with marsh marigold, cowslip, and other yellow May flowers, in order to "ensure plenty of milk."

The subject deserves the attention of your Insular readers. I should like them to add to this lore, and increase the store of information to throw more light on the beliefs and customs observed during these early stages of pastoral life.

[Several other contributions, which are in type, are unaoidably held over.—ED.]

33. THE MEANING OF MANX FAIRY TALES

The Manx are a very superstitious folk and one evidence of their superstitious nature is the large number of fairy tales everywhere current in the Island. That the Manx for generations past have been superstitious will be admitted. But did they always believe their fairy tales? For instance, there is one which runs something like this (the exact details do not matter):

"A man was walking home through the country on a dark and stormy night. As he was passing the side of a hill he saw a cavern brightly lighted up and filled by a company of elves, who were feasting merrily. Upon seeing the wayfarer, two or three of their number ran out to the man with a cordial invitation to join their banquet, at the same time pressing upon him a goblet of wine. The man was sorely tempted, but knowing that if he joined their company he would be committing a deadly sin he, in spite of all entreaty, refused, and finally to mark his determination threw the wine on the ground. No sooner had he done this than there was a thunder-clap, the cavern disappeared, and the man was left alone, weary and footsore. He reached home, however, and had just entered his house when he found that the goblet (which like most goblets in fairy tales was of gold and mounted with precious stones) was still in his hand."

That is the story, was it ever believed literally? We think not, for the antiquity of this and similar stories justifies us in believing that they may have been circulated by the Druids. The Druids were in the habit of conveying religious teaching by parables. And is not the above quoted story a beautiful parable? A man is treading life's journey, weary and often discouraged. Then come the temptations of the world—"eat, drink, and be merry." But they are successfully resisted, with the result that in after years the man can look back and see that although he lost the fleeting pleasures then offered to him, he had retained something which was far better. Some people may already hold this view, but there are many who, in regard these stories are in the position of Wordsworth's character:

A primrose by the river's brim,
A yellow primrose is to him,
And it is nothing more.

It is certainly a more dignified interpretation of these tales, and one more in accordance with reason, to suppose that they were originally of some real value apart from their character as "fairy" tales.

LL. JONES.

34. MANX NAMES OF FISH AND SHELL FISH

Appended below are the Manx names of the piscatorial family, which will no doubt be of interest to Manx fishermen. As it would be very desirable to make the list as complete a one as possible, criticism and corrections are invited. There are many old Manxmen with whom not a few of these names will be familiar, and there are many points which may require clearing up, so I shall esteem it a pleasure to have the list freely criticised. In some cases, two or more Manx names appear for one fish, in others it is hard to determine their English equivalent, while a great many seem to have no Manx name. Some of these are merely translations of their English equivalents, which I have taken the liberty to make. No doubt, not a few of these have Manx names, so I hope that Manx fishermen will peruse the list and send in any additions or corrections. A list of animals, birds, insects, &c., will follow in due course.

J. J. K.

Angel or Monk Fish, *Eeast-Vaynagh;* Butterfly Fish, *Eeast-Foillycan;* Carp, *Carroo;* Sea-Horse, *Cabbyl Marrey;* Cod, *Boiddagh;* Cod (rock), *Boiddagh Ruy;* Crab, *Partan;* Crab (soldier), *Partan Sidoor;* Cray Fish, *Gimmagh Awin;* Dog Fish, *Gobbag, Gobbag Ghoal?;* Eel, *Astan;* Conger Eel, *Astan Vooar;* Flounder, Flook, *Liehbage;* Flying Fish, *Eeast Etlee;* Gold Fish, *Eeast Airhey;* Grampus, *Perkyn Vooar;* Gudgeon, *KioneTramman;* Gurnard, *Crodane;* Gurnard, gray, *Crodane Ghlass;* Haddock, *Attag;* Herring, *Skeddan;* Limpet, Flitter, *Baarnagh;* Lobster, *Gimmagh;* Mackerel, *Brack-Varrey* (*Cheayin*); Minnow, *Burdoge;* Mussel, *Gobdoo;* Sea Owl, *Hullad-Varrey;* Oyster, *Ooastyn;* Plaice, *Liehbage Vreck;* Porpoise, *Perkyn;* Salmon, *Braddan;* Salmon Trout, *Brack Ghiaal;* Saw Fish, *Eeast Saaue;* Sea Wolf, *Moddey Oayldey Marrey;* Shark, *Sharkagh, Bock Glass;* Shrimp, *Strimp;* Skate, *Scarrag;* Sole, *Lichbage Chiare;* Sucking Fish, *Eeast Jiolee;* Sun Fish, *Eeast Greiney;* Sword Fish, *Eeast Cliwe;* Tench, *Bollan;* Toad Fish, *Gailley Pern;* Trout, *Brack;* Trumpet Fish, *Eeast Hellym;* Turbot, *Turbait;* Sea Unicorn, *Eeast Eairkagh;* Whiting, *Fynnag;* Whelk-Mwatlag, *Buckee;* Pollock Fish, *Blockan;* Periwinkle, *Feoghaig;* Sand Eel, *Gibbin;* Stinging Sand Eel, *Gibbin-Kialgerey;* Scollop, *Raucan; Glarechutt? Callag? Keilleig? Bulkione?*

There seems to be no Manx equivalent for the following: Admiral, Anchovey, Bream, Chama, Char, Chub, Cockle, Dace, Dolphin, John Doree, Father Lasher, Gar Fish, Grayling, Horned Silure, Kraken, Lucerna, Lump Fish, Narval, Perch, Pike, Pilchard, Pilot Fish, Prawn, Reinora, Roach, Flying Scorpion, Smelt, Snipe Shell, Sparling, Sprat, Sturgeon, Thornback, Torpedo Whale.

35. THE MANX SHEALINGS OR AIREYS

In ancient times there was no parish and sheading in the Island but had its *Airey* on the upland hills, wherever they would yield fair pasturage. It was a merry, happy time, this, and the Highlands of Scotland owe to their existence some of their finest ballads and songs. Then when the summer came at last the black cattle and milch cows and goats were driven to the *Aireys*, and booths were built from the Hebrides, Shetland, the Highlands, down to Mann and Donegal. Pennant in his Highland travels gives us some picturesque sketches of their daily life during that jolly time, and shows us some of their quaint sugar-loafed and heather and turf-built erections. The Norsemen, too, had their shealings, and called them *Setr*, and they had their *Sels*, or as we call it, shealings and booths. They soon, in their Gaelic intercourse, became acquainted with the term Airidh and used it, but they pronounced it *Erg* or *Arg*, as we know from early Icelandic records.* *Airidh*, now contracted in Manx variously into *ary, eairey, irey, harry, ari,* or *eree,* means originally a place for summer grazing in the mountains, a hill pasture for black cattle, or a shieling, or shed, or booth in the secondary sense. Indication of an early use we have in the word *Airey Steane* or *Stane* (pronounced now by the peasants *Harry Stane*). The Lewis, the islands par excellence with their hundreds of *Airidhs, Airidheen's,* and *Gearridheens,* always affix the owner's or clan's name to it, and amongst them we have also the *Airidh Stein an Totair,* or *Stein's an Totair Shealing,* so that we see how closely Norwegian surnames run in Lewis and Mann. The name Steane is found in the Ballaugh Burial Register of 1598, and of course is much older in the Island. I will not count up here the numerous *Aireys* in the Island; no parish, as Arbory, Patrick, Marown, Braddan, German, Garff, &c., is without them. They were either communal, going then simply by the name *The* Airey, *Airey glass, mooar, lhean, ny Kione, ven,* but they have also proprietory names given to them, as *Airey Cushlin, Steane, Torkell, Kelley, Wind* (Quinn), *Carrigan,* and there is also an *airey of the Strangers (jora)*—but that is long ago, the system has crumbled, and the aireys have become enclosed. The commune which held out longest was Rushen. An old Manx friend told me:

"I can remember when there were a great many of the farmers sending their heifers to Paark Staine somewhere near Airey Staine (known in Manx Folklore by the legend of the weaver's leaping beam). There used to be great wide common between Lhinguage and Airey Staine, and many cattle were sent to the pasture every summer, but the farmers of Rushen all joined, and sold the common and have done away with all."

But the interest does not end here; we also have our Aireys even in name in Lancashire, implanted by the early Norseman, as proved by Dr Colley-March,† and preserved in such names as Grimes arge, Anlasasghe, Gusharge, Skelmerserghe, Mansergke, *etc.* (Grimes, Anlafs, Goose, Skelmers, Mani, Olaf's son, arghe; in Amounderness, Furness, West and East Riding, *etc.* Did these Norsemen come from Garff to Cumberland and North Lancashire, crossing from Laxey, Maughold, and Onchan, where they had large settlements, or did they descend rather in their ships from Lewis and other Western isles? The connection between the Norsemen of Mann and the opposite west coast of England was very intimate I believe the former assumption is the more likely one.

* See Vigfusson's *Icelandic Dictionary, sub nomen.*

† *Transactions of the Lancashire and Cheshire Antiquarian Society* (1890), specially 93–96.

36. KEEPING CHRISTMAS* (A MORE SUCCINCT ACCOUNT)

They have a peculiar way of keeping Christmas. In the evening of the 24th of December, all servants are allowed to knock off business, who ramble about till the clock strikes twelve; and then the bells ring in all the churches to call them to prayers, which, being ended, they go to hunt the wren, kill the first they find; lay her with great solemnity on a bier, bring her to the parish church, bury her with whimsical ceremonies, singing dirges over her in the Manks tongue, which they call her knell. This done, Christmas begins. Every barn is occupied for the twelve days. Every parish provides fiddlers at the public charge, to accommodate the young people, who spend the nights in dancing. On the twelfth day the fiddler lays his head in one of the women's lap, which posture they look upon him as a kind of oracle. For one of the company coming up, and naming every maiden in the company, asks this fiddler, who shall this or that girl marry? And whatever he answers it is absolutely depended upon as an oracle. This is termed: The cutting off the fiddler's head, because he becomes useless till the next year.

* *An Historical and Geographical Description of the British Empire*, by the Rev. John Entick, MA, vol. iv, pp. 274–75, London, 1774.

37. LITTLE AND BIG CHRISTMAS
An old saying of the people at Christmas time was:
Ta'n Ullick veg fe'n vink,
Ta'n Ullick vooar cooil thie,
Tra yiow mayd lune dy iu,
As glout browe mooar dy fie.

The little Christmas is under the bench,
The big Christmas at the back of the house,
When we will get ale to drink,
And a good big lump of pie.

They used to, and still call the new Christmas the little Christmas, and the old Christmas, the big Christmas, and most of the houses in Cregneish had a stone bench near the front door, to set tubs and other things on to dry. It was called *bink*, in Manx, and when the Christmas was very near at hand, they used to say: it is under the bench, that is to say, at the door; and the big Christmas is at the back of the houses *(cooil)*, that was: it is near, when we'll get ale to drink and pie with merry cheer. The people of Cregneish keep old Christmas, for they think it is the right Christmas.

38. CHRISTMAS SONG
The old men at Christmas times were dancing in the public-houses and singing:
Darrey dy Graase Vorgaig,
Cha vaik mee rieau dty lheid;
Fiddler ayns Bradda, as piver s'yn Howe,
As shen Hommy gonnagh ec y thie cloïe er yn clou.

Dorothy Grace Margaret,
Never saw I the like of you;
A Fiddler in Bradda, and piper in the Howe,
And old sore Tommy at home, playing with the tongs.

39. CHRISTMAS CUSTOM
In old times the farmers and fishermen used at Christmas time, after coming from the *Oie'l Verree*, to go to a public-house and have a spree of Manx ale. They called it *jough vie*. Every house had a big candle made for the occasion, and the men would be enjoying themselves until the large Christmas candle would be burning down in the socket. And then they would be singing before they left the house: "*Ta tra gholl thie dy gholl dy lhie,*" &c.

40. HOLY EVE
On Holy Eve the girls used to go at 12 o'clock at night and carry a ball of woollen yarn in their hand, and steal to a barn without anyone knowing anything about it, and twisting the end of it round their wrist threw the ball in the darkness as far as they could; then after a little while they began to wind it up, beginning at the end twined around their wrist. If the thread was held they could cry out: "Who is holding the thread?" and they expected whoever held it to say who he was; if there was no answer they were to be old maids.*

  * Also current in Ireland, Scotland, &c., &c.

41. THE MANX UNNESUP
I alluded in the first part of my Manx Folklore (see *Yn Lioar Manninagh*) to a custom still remembered in Cregneish on Christmas. The fiddlers then used to go about after twelve o'clock playing and singing some Manx song which they called the *Unnesup*. It ran thus:

Goll er yn Unnesup, goll er yn Unnesup,
Daa oor roish yn laa,
Dooinney ta ny lhie marish ben dooinney elley,
Te bwaagh dy girree ayns traa.

Goll er yn Unnesup, goll er yn Unnesup,
Daa oor lurg y vean oie,
Dooinney ta ny lhie marish ben dooinney elley,
Te bwaagh dy girree ayns traa.

Unnesup was likewise a common word with the old people, and meant a good thrashing, when the young ones played some tricks. They gave them *unnesup* on being caught.

My attention was drawn recently to the above word by a passage in *Anderson's Cumberland Ballads*:

Thy fadder's comin' frae the croft,

A bonnie hunesup faith he mek.

Hunesup is rendered "to scold, quarrel,"* and was a word current in the central part of Cumberland. In slang it would be to give you a taste of the "tune." The *hunesup* is also the name of a lively old tune peculiar to Christmas, called "The hunt's up through the wood." John Briggs† informs us that the inhabitants of the Westmoreland cottages were aroused from their dreams on Christmas night by the elegant aid of this song. Going a step further we find‡ that "Hunesup" was a tune played on a horn under the window of sportsmen very early in the morning to awake them—hence the term was applied to any noise of an awakening or alarming nature. In Craven§ it denoted "a clamour, a turbulent outcry." But the great interest of the Manx song of the "Unnesup' (the masked "Hunt is up") consists in the early rendering of it in English, which is found in *The Merry Drollery Complete*, 1661, and in the *New Academy of Compliments*, 1694, which runs:

The hunt is up, the hunt is up,

And now it is almost day,

And he that's in bed with another mans's wife,

It's time to get away.

Our Manx song contains a second strophe, and appears to be a close verbal translation. We learn, further,¶ that it is in the same measure, and was probably sung to the same tune, as the old ballad:

The hunt is up, the hunt is up,

And it is well nigh day,

And Harry our King has gone hunting,

To bring his deer to bay.

which was one of Henry VIII favourite melodies, and has been traced back to 1537. It is certainly one of the finest tunes in the whole history of English ballad-literature, and has maintained its hold upon the people for centuries, and to find therefore a faint echo of it reverberating in the little secluded hill-village of Cregneish, in Manx garb, with its old meaning and origin, however unknown to the old people, gives its re-discovery a peculiar charm. It passed over, no doubt, with Stanley's "merrie men," who carried it from Mid-Lancashire to the South of the Island, to Castletown and Peel, from whence the catching tune was quickly taken up by the Manx morris-dancers and fiddlers who went on Christmas from village to village, playing and singing, and merry-making and *goll er yn unnesup*. And the Christmas festival used to be ushered in not so many decades ago by the young men perambulating the streets fantastically dressed up and playing the White-boys. For several nights, just preceding the festival, the fiddlers went about the streets of the town for hours together, playing a tune called the "Andisop." This is of course the same as the

"Unnesup" of Cregneish, and was played in the Northern parts, as Ramsay, &c. The blowing of horns at weddings was a very old custom, and formerly not very complimentary to the bride.|| This was also a kind of "hunesup," of an indelicate nature, in vogue in England in the 17th century, to which allusion is made in Chappell's *Ballad Literature.* A good many old so-called Manx tunes are really of English origin, introduced to the Island at different periods.

P.S. I see from the programme of the inaugural meeting of the Manchester Manx Society, November 27th, 1901, that the Manx air, "Yn Unnesup' is associated with the song "Mannin veg villish veen." Why not restore it now to the proper and original fine old tune "The Hunt is up," current in the time of Henry VIII, which is given in *Chappell's Ballad Literature of the Olden Times,* page 61?

* See also *Dialect of Cumberland,* by W. Dickenson, London, 1878.

† See *Westmoreland as it was.*

‡ See *Halliwell.*

§ See *Craven Glossary.*

¶ See *Ballad Literature and Popular Music of the Olden Times,* by W. Chappell, F.S.A., and harmonised by G.A. Macfarran, London, page 61.

|| See *Quiggin's Illustrated Guide through the Isle of Man,* page 191.

42. THE ORIGIN OF ERYSTEIN

The note referring to Erystein in a recent issue in "Manx Notes and Queries" must have been read with interest. It would appear, however, that the derivation ot the word from Steane (Stephen) is hardly correct. Tradition says that this place formerly belonged to the Austeyns from whom the name is probably derived—it being originally "Eary Austeyn." This is borne out by the Rent Roll of 1511, where we find the following entries of Lord's rent for this treen:

John Brice, senr., and Patric Brice, with Michael McAusteyn xvjs. vjd.

And Michael McAusteyn iijs. iiijd.

The McAusteyns were, of course, the descendants of the Austeyns, and the name has become corrupted into the modern Costain. Austeyn is a shortened form of Augustin and this is the diminutive of Augustus (see Moore's *Surnames and Place-Names*). The same remark applies to Park Stein and Slieu Eary Stein. From Erystein would probably come the Costains who settled at Ballachrink, and gave rise to that numerous family. Tradition also asserts that these Austyns were originally Dutch immigrants; and the Stevensons of Balladoole are said by some not to be Stephensons, but Steynsons. Indeed the whole subject is a most interesting one, and worthy of thorough investigation.

43. QUERIES

Can any reader give an account of the origins of the name of "The Horse Leap" on Douglas Head Marine Drive?

44. QUERIES

Is there any historical data of the use of the old fort at Castleward, or what is the most feasible theory of its purpose and age?

45. MANX CATTLE, ETC.

A few notes on the old native breeds will not be amiss in this place. Sacheverell* says the Manx cattle were generally small. The swine used to be in abundance, and a small mountain kind, called Purs, formed admirable meat. The old country stock of cows was already seldom in Feltham's† time, and short legged and thick bodied, and more remarkable for fattening than for milk. Of sheep they had a breed of yellow, or rather buff colour (Sacheverell). Feltham writes:

The native stock is small and hardy, and would endure the hardest weather with little loss, and the meat tasted fine. This (he adds) is still the mountain breed. There is also (he continues) a peculiar breed, called Laughton, of the colour of Spanish snuff, and these are not so hardy, and more difficult to fatten. The natives like the cloth and stockings made of this wool.

More recently‡ a writer offers the following remarks about the Manx breed of sheep:

The sheep are small on the hills, seldom exceeding 8 to 10th the quarter, and producing a fleece of short or middle wool, weighing 2½ lbs.§ They have much resemblance to the Welsh sheep, and have most of their peculiarities and bad points. They are narrow chested, and narrow-backed, long in leg, and deficient in shoulder. They are both found horned and polled, mostly of white colour, but some of them grey, and others of a peculiar snuff or brown colour, termed in the Island a laugton colour, this colour either covering the whole of the sheep, or appearing in the form of a patch on the neck, is considered as the peculiar badge of the Isle of Man. In the valleys a larger sheep, with longer wool, a proper long woolled sheep, the fleece averaging 7 lbs, and the quarter from 12 to 16 lbs is found. The flesh of both breeds is said to be good, and the wool of the hill sheep valued in the manufacture of stockings, and some of the worsted goods. Some attempts have been made to improve the vale breed by crossing with the South Down, Leicester, and Merino, and with considerable success.

The Manx *garron* or pony.—The Manx ponies were all black and brown. Waldron says they were fleet, small, very hardy, never shoed, not eating corn, nor ever going into a stable. Formerly, Feltham remarks:

They are remarkable for their beauty, and much in request in England and Ireland, to run in carriages, but now their rumbers are much diminished, as larger horses are found more useful.

The *garrons* of the Western Islands and Skye,¶ like the Manx breed, were fed and reared, summer and winter, in the open air. With so much exposure their hair is very long, and they have altogether a very shaggy, weather beaten appearance. They were state their height. In Shetland they range 9 to 11 hands, and in the Orkneys 12 to 14 hands. *Gearran* in Irish is generally a hack horse, but in Donegal it means a horse.

Red Deer.—There was a small number in Sacheverall's time in existence in the Island, and plenty of goats and hares, and sufficient foxes for the sportsmen, and there is still the Lheim y chynney ('Foxleap') near the Sound to remind us of the Manx foxhunters of days gone by.

* *Account of the Isle of Man*, W. Sacheverell, 1707, p. 4.

† *A Tour through the Island of Man during 1797–8*, by John Feltham, p. 55.

‡ *The Sheep: their Breeding, Management, and Diet*, London, 1837; Baldwin & Cradock, p. 501.

§ During the sheep shearing season at Bradda Head in 1897, when I was present, the fleece produced 3 to 4 lb weight of wool, and the price was put down at 9d per lb.

¶ *Transactions of The Highland and Agricultural Society of Scotland*, vol. 4, 1872, p. 60.

46. LETTER FROM JACK JONES

Dear Sir,—I have read with much interest the various articles which have appeared in the *Examiner* on Manx, and also the Manx Notes and Queries. Re No. 34, I see in the names of fish that "Blockan" is given for Pollock. Whenever I have been out fishing in the Island I have always heard Pollock spoken of as "Kalleg."

I am much interested in the Celtic language revival movement, especially in the Manx. It seems to me, however, that one of the great needs is a reprint of Cregeen's *Dictionary* at a reasonable price; all the copies which are offered now for sale being at too high a figure for most would-be students to be able to purchase; and I would willingly subscribe for a copy if a new edition were decided on.

Wishing you every success in your efforts to awaken an interest in the Manx, and also wishing *Ollick ghennal as Clean feer vie.*

I am, yours truly,

JACK JONES.

London, 16th December, 1901.

47. THE OLD MANX BRAAINS

The Old Manx had two kinds of *braains*, the *braain laue* and the *braain vwillin*. The former are occasionally* turned up. The manipulation of these *braains* is illustrated in an interesting account in the *Hibernian Magazine*, December, 1793.† The writer says:

> They burn the straw of the sheaf to make the oats dry for meal and though the grain is black by the ashes and the meal coloured, yet it is not unpleasant to taste, and is thought to be very wholesome food. This, with most of their oatmeal, they grind on *braahs*, a kind of mill similar to the quern, but made of harder stone, and

grind on *braahs*, a kind of mill similar to the quern, but made of harder stone, and of the same magnitude with quern millstones. being about three feet in diameter, and four to five inches thick. The uppermost stone is turned round by the hand of one or two women, who grind as much meal, evening and morning, as to serve for the day.

The Irish name for it is *bro* (gen. *bron*, for which we have in Welsh *breuan*, Cornish *bron*, Breton *breon*) = *hand mill*, *quern*, and Professor Zimmer thinks that probably the word signified originally only the stone with which by the help of the hand the grain was ground.‡

* Instances: Cregneish, Ballastole, Lonan, Slieu Whallin, Bradda.

† *Of the Genius, Custom, Manners, and Dress of the Western Hebrideans*, pp. 304–505.

‡ See Prof. Zimmer, *Zeitschrift für celtische Philologie*, Band i, 1896, page 86.

48. THE MANX CARRANES

The Manx *carránes*, or *kerránes*, have really nothing particularly Manx about them, and we must dismiss the popular idea that they were peculiar only to Mona. In the Shetlands* the common shoes in which they travelled, called *rivilings*, were a kind of sandal made of cow's or seal's hide, dried. The flesh side is put to the foot, and tied above the ankles. *Logan*† informs us that the *cuáran* reached higher than the *broque*, which simply covered the foot, both being fastened with laces of thong. The *cuaran*, he says, worn in Mann and throughout the whole Highlands, was an oval piece of raw cow or horse hide, drawn neatly round the foot by thongs of the same material by means of holes in the margin. The hair was often kept inside for warmth, they were perfectly flexible and pierced with small holes for the purpose of allowing the water received in crossing rivers and morasses to escape. In Irish we have *cuáran* = sock, bandage, and *cuarog* = a shoe or brogue made of untanned leather; and in Welsh we meet with *cyran* = boot or boskin. To carry the enquiry a little further, in Dumfries they had the *screa* or *scrae* = an old shrivelled shoe; in Norwegian we meet *skraa* or *skrae*, for an old shoe; and the Icelandic presents us with its equivalent, *skor*, pl. *skuar* for the word shoe, probably derived from *skra* = dry skin.

* See Caton, p. 103; see also Rev. Dr M'Allum's *Excursion to the Shetlands*, 1829. There shoes are of untanned bull hides fastened with thongs.

† See James Logan, *The Scottish Gael*, vol i, p. 251.

49. FRAGMENT OF AN OLD SONG

Fragment of an old song which used to be sung to the children:

Nagh ren mee my lhiabbee,
As hie mee gys fea?
As haink mitchoor stiagh.
As cha s'aym quoi ve.

Nagh ren mee my lhiabbee,
As hie mee dy lhie?
As tra dirree mee moghrey,
Va'n lhiabbee fud thie.

Did I not make my bed,
And went to my rest?
A rogue came in,
I know not who he was.

Did I not make my bed,
And then lay down?
When I rose in the morning,
My bed was scattered over the house.

And then there was the chorus:
Yn cadley kiune er y beggan vree,
Ny mooar y nhee haink orrym!

Oh! the calm sleep of weakness,
Whatever came over me!

50. THE USHAG VEG RUY (ANOTHER VERSION)

Ushag veg ruy ny moanee doo,
Cre'd chaddil oo riyr s'yn oie?
Nagh chaddil mish riyr er baare yn dress,
Tra va'n gheay sheidey gymmyrkey lesh.

Ushag veg ruy ny moanee doo,
Cre'd chaddil oo riyr s'yn oie?
Nagh chaddil mish riyr er baare y thooane,
Myr shimmey mac dooinney te'r chadley ayn roym.

Ushag veg ruy ny moanee doo,
Cre'd chaddil oo riyr s'yn oie?
Nagh chadill mish riyr er baare y crouw,
Lesh fliaghey tuittym er daghcheü.

It will be seen that this rendering differs from the one given in the *Manx Ballads and Music* by A.W. Moore, p. 43. It is by far better and more rational, and should be substituted instead for accompaniment of the music.

51. SONG (FRAGMENT)

Mooinjir yn jiass ta bunnys roit ass,
Lesh gleck noi geay as tidey,
Ta'n jough cheet stiagh, yn argid goll magh,
As Neddy Gawne* yn eirey.

The men of the South are nearly driven out,
With striving against wind and tide,
Ale comes in and money goes out,
And Ned Gawne is the heir.

* Ned Gawne was the great brewer.

52. YN POOSEY BEG FANNAG, OR THE CROW'S LITTLE WEDDING

A wedding with none of the bride's relatives was called a "crow's wedding," and we have the following rhyme:

Poosey beg fannag
Hie shiar yn bayr,
Gyn mummig ny jyssig,
Ny shuyr ny braar.

The little wedding of the crow
Went over the road,
Without mother and father,
Or sister and brother.

53. SAYING

Dy neeagh by fee ny fannagyn,
As ny fannagyn ny fee,
Cha beagh unnane er-mayrn,
Dy ee convayrt erbee.

If the raven would eat the crows,
And the crows eat the raven,
There would not be one alive,
To eat any carcase at all.

54. THE CAT AND THE MOUSE

Old women used to say this rhyme to the baby about the cat and the mouse:

Lugh va sneeu er queeyl yn mwyllin,
Haink yn kayt as yeeagh e urree;
Cre'n red t'ou jannoo my ven ainshter?
Sneeu sheeidy as srol* da ben y ree.

Roish my jig bishaght ayns bainney ny baa,
Beem's kiart dy liooar my jig yn laa.

A mouse was spinning on the mill wheel,
Up came the cat and looked upon her;
What are you doing my landlady?
Spinning silk and gauze for the wife of the king.
Before the milk of the cows increases,
I'll be even with you before those days.

We have a somewhat similiar rhyme in Aberdeenshire, beginning:
A cattie at a mill door sat spinnin', spinnin',
Fin by comes a mousie, rinnin', rinnin',
Says the mousie t' the cattie,
Faht are ye deeing, my winsome laidie? &c, &c.

See Gregor, *Folklore of N.E. Scotland*, p. 125.

* New to the Manx Dictionary.

55. PROVERBS AND SAYINGS (1)
Ta saynt shiaght saggyrtyn ayns dhooinney dyn chloan, as ta saynt shiaght eirinnee ayns, dychooilley haggyrt.

There is the greed of seven parsons in a man without children, and greed of seven farmers in every parson.

56. PROVERBS AND SAYINGS (2)
I have heard a man, when fishing *bollans* at the rocks, saying:
Bollan beg ny feacklyn croï,
Cur uss rach, as veryms rach dt'oï.

Little *bollan* with sharp teeth,
Give me a rip, and I will rip against thee.

57. PROVERBS AND SAYINGS (3)
Er coonlagh ta arroo,
Cha vel veg er renniaght;
Ayns jiuys ta therr,
Cha vel veg ayns darragh;
Ayns dorrys ta treiney,
Ayns kurn ta jough.

On straw is corn,
On fern is none;

In fir is tar,
In oak is none;
In door is nail,
In can is ale.

58. PART OF A NURSERY SONG
Part of a nursery song:
> Vuddee veg, vuddee veg, cur mysh dty vraagyn,
> Gow dy reih Balladool, ny Ballakeigyn.

> Little damsel, little damsel, put on your shoes,
> Either Balladool, or Ballakeggan choose.

59. WEATHER RULES: VA'N SHEN SHEIH GRA
> Yn geay voish yn niar as yn fliaghey voish yn neear,
> Cha vel fastee rish cleigh ny thammag.
> Kiune dy bra, geay jiass s'niessey da;
> Tra ta bwoaillee er yn ghrian yow mayd sterrym as fliaghey.
> Tra ta yn gheay shiedey ta yn muir radey.
> Tra ta shag getlagh harrish yn thalloo,
> Dy row eh doora* fliaghey.

> The wind from the east and the rain from the west,
> There is no shelter by a hedge or bush.
> When it is very calm, south wind will come next;
> When there is a circle round the sun, we will get rain and storm.
> When the wind blows the sea stirs,
> When a cormorant flies over the land,
> It was a sign of rain.

This is complete—only fragments have been given so far.

* "Dearbhadh" in Gaelic = proof, evidence. This word is not noted in the Manx Dictionary. The nearest manx is *jaroo*, adj. *jarrooagh*.

60. WEATHER
The weather the old Manx used to wish was:
> Geurey roiagh as arragh keyagh.
> (A frosty winter and foggy spring.)

> Tra ta ny kirree goaill fastee,
> Cha bee eh agh frass, agh tra t'as gyndyr ayns y fliaghey,
> Bee eh ceau son traa lianyr.

(When the sheep shelter in rain, it will be only a shower,
But when they browse in the rain, it will rain a power.)

It is just now (July) what the old fishermen used to call—when there was a calm sea:
Kiunid villish nagh dug rieau straiu ayns craue dhooinney.
(Sweet calm that never sprained a man's bone.)

61. PROVERBS

Nagh ghow gys dty obbyr laa fegooish brishey dy hrostey.
(Don't go to your day-work without breaking your fast.)

Doonaght sheeidey, shiaghtin kennipey.
(A silken Sunday, a hempen week.)

Myr's moo ny cheayney,
Myr s'moo ny mooin.

(The greater the crying,
The greater the *mooin*.)

"I never heard talk of the toothache among the old people, and I believe that tea and sugar are the cause in many cases. I heard of a very old man in Cregnaish that said to someone enquiring about his teeth, that his teeth were as sharp yet as a young pup's teeth, and *myr s'doo, s'graihagh*—'the blacker, the lovelier.'"

62. PROVERBS AND SAYINGS

My vac, my vac gys yow eh ben,
Agh my inneen, my inneen aeg ny shenn.

(My son, is my son till he gets a wife,
But my daughter is my daughter all the days of her life.)

Ta dhooinney ny gha leaystey yn clean,
Nagh vel yn lhannoo bentyn da hene.

(Many a man is rocking the cradle,
The child was not his own.)

Baase mie mraane as aigh vie keyrragh
Ta er yannoo deiney ny ga berchagh.

(The death of wives and good luck for sheep
Has made many men rich.)

Ta'n dooinney creeney smooinaghtyn ooilley ny ta gra,
Agh ta'n ommidan gra ooilley ny ta smooinaghtyn.

(The wise man thinks that all he says,
But the fool says all that he thinks.)

Raad ta mranne ta pleat,
Raad ta guoiee ta keck,
Raad ta thalhearyn ta thollagyn,
As raad ta seyir ta spollagyn.

(Where there are women there is talk,
Where there are geese there is *keck*,
Where there are tailors there are crabs,
Where there are carpenters, there are chips.)

This is given only fragmentarily in Moore's *Folk Lore of the Isle of Man*, see page 183.

Ta un read cur lesh elley cordail rish shenn raa.
(One thing brings another as old as the old proverb says.)

Te ny share goll dy lhie accryssagh ny gholl dy lhie lesh bolg laare.
(It is better to go to bed hungry than to go to bed with a full belly.)

Ta charrey 'sy chooyrt ny share ny ping 'sy sporran.
(A friend in court in better than a penny in the purse.)

63. PROVERBS

Ta y aigney hene ec dooinney, agh ta y raad hene ee ben.
(Man has his own will, but woman has her own way.)

Yn dooinney ta jeeaghyn dy mie lurg y obbyr hene ta palchey ec eh dy yannoo.
(The man who minds his own business well has always enough to do.)

Lhag-laueys mergys ny annym.
(Idleness is the rust of the soul.)

Quoi erbee ta jeeaghyn son charrey fegooish foiljyn cha jean eh dy bragh geddyn shen ny te shirrey er y hon. Ta shin graihagh orryn hene lesh ooilley nyn voiljyn as lhissagh shin ve graihagh er nyn jaarjyn er yn aght cheddin.

(Whoever looks for a friend without fault will never get what he seeks, we love ourselves with all our faults and we ought to love our friends in like manner.)

Ta jeih thousanyn jeh ny voiljyn smoo ta ayns nyn nabooyn jeh ny sloo dy vadyr dooin ny yn foill sloo ta ayn-in-hene.

(Ten thousand of the greatest faults in our neighbours is of less consequence than the smallest of our own.)

Dooinney ta poost ta e hreishteil roit ass,
Te kiart goll-rish muc lesh teidd er y chass.

(A man that is married has lost all his hopes,
He is just like a pig with her leg in a rope.)

Sollan, sollan, sailley blass dy chooilley vee.
(Salt, salt, bring tastes to every meat.)
was a proverb among the people, they liked plenty of salt in everything.

64. CHILDREN'S RHYMES

As I went up on yonder hill,
I met my father in good will,
He had jewels, he had rings,
He had very fine things;
He had a hammer, working nails,
He had a kitten with ten tails;
Up Jack, down Tom,
Blow the bellows, old man.

The schoolboys used to say over a bargain:
Ring fingers, bottle bell,
Tell a lie and go to hell.

The boys and girls when they wanted some sweets from one that had some, shut their eyes and held out their hands, saying:
Fill the can, fill the can,
Fill the blind man's hand.

"The black spot on the teeth was observed among the school children. I remember when I was at school, if anyone was telling a tale, if the others did not believe it, the tale teller had to show his teeth, and if there was a blackspot on one of the teeth, it was thought he had told a lie; but if there was no black speck it was thought he had spoken the truth. The scholars would be very often shewing their teeth when telling anything."

Mothers, when dangling the baby on their knees, used to say:
Ding, dong, bell, the cat is in the well,
Who put it in? Little Johnny Tim,
Who took it out? Little Willy Sprout.

The school children had the following rhyme:
As I went up a sandy hill,
And sandy hill was dirty,
I met a little girl and she

Made me a courtesy.
I gave her ale, I gave her wine,
I gave her sugar candy,
And after that, the dirty slut,
She called me Jack the Dandy.

Hip, hip, hurrah!
My daddy is gone away,
He'll not be home till morning
Before the break of day.
Hip, hip, hurrah!
We'll kick the bobbies' asses,
We'll break the jugs and glasses
And send them off to Ireland,
Among the bugs and fleas.

65. THE NEW MOON

It was thought unlucky to see the new moon through glass:
    To see the new moon through glass,
    Trouble and care while it will last.

It was unlucky to be without some coins in your pocket, and some of the women turned the other side of their aprons outside.

Ta mee er chlashtyn ad gra fakin yn eayst noa yn chied cheayrt:
    Dy bannee Yee yn eayst noa,
    Dy bannee Yee mish troor cheayrtyn,
    Nagh doghan erbee cheet orroo
    Choud as veagh yn eayst shen ayn.

I have heard them say on seeing the new moon for the first time:
    God bless the new moon,
    God bless me three times,
    That no disease would all upon them
    As long as the moon was in.
That was a charm to keep them without an accident, and to keep from gathering hands and fingers while the moon lasted.

66. THE MOCK SUN, ETC.

Is called a "dog" by the fishermen; it was often a sign of bad weather; and a small ring round the moon is called a "cock's eye," and a sign of unsettled weather.

67. SNOW

When it was snowing big flakes of snow the old men said—"that they were plucking geese in Scotland."

68. DUST

Dust flying over the high roads was a sign of rain.

[Nos 64–68, "All from Cregneish"]

69. MANX NAMES OF FISH, ETC.

J. J. K. in Note 34 gives a list of Manx names of fish. He seems to be unaware that many years ago Mr J.C. Crellin, M.A., has drawn up already a very careful and scientific *List of Fish of the Isle of Mann*, for the *Isle of Mann Natural History and Antiquarian Society*, the arrangement and nomenclature revised by F. Day, F.L.S., author of *Fishes of Great Britain*, where he will find also the corresponding Manx names. In the same journal, edited by Mr P.M.C. Kermode, vol. iii, part xi, 1901, he will also find a *List of Birds of the Isle of Man, with Notes*, by Messrs P.M.C. Kermode and P.G. Ralfe, with the Manx names of the various birds. Mr Kermode has already done the same for the *animals* in the same journal.

It shows how little Manxmen really avail themselves of these ready and open channels of Insular information. The above society exists now for many years, and has regularly published its annual volumes; and done splendid work in connection with Manx antiquities, history, folk-lore, and the whole field of natural history; and Mr Kermode has laboured, as few, in that direction. It appears that the number of Insular members is very small and poor indeed in proportion to the population. The subscription is small and but nominal, the work turned out is excellent, and it is regrettable that this society is so little supported, which it, however, so well deserves. Every Manxman interested in the history and traditions of the Island, and in its natural history, should join and contribute to its vigorous maintenance, for want of which it is greatly crippled, and has to curtail publication of much valuable matter the society has, and is still carefully storing up and collecting. Their Archæological and Natural History collections at their Museum in Ramsey are of the highest Insular importance, but few Manxmen seem to be cognizant of the many Insular riches it contains.

I trust Manxmen will not leave things in that deplorable state, and not rest till they have a proper central Museum in Douglas, specially devoted to its history, antiquities, *etc.*, and it is to be hoped that the matter will be taken up at last in the House of Keys; the credit, moreover, of the Island being greatly concerned in it. Our towns in Lancashire all have their municipal museums. Why should the Isle of Man lag behind so long? It is an important Insular question, and sure to foster true Insular pride and interest in their history and development; and it would add to the delight and instruction ot the enormous flood of annual visitors flocking to the Island, and demonstrate to them the wonderful changes in ancient times the Island has passed through, which have helped so much to build up its foundation and constitution.

70. THE MANXMAN

To fully understand the "making" of the present Manxman it is necessary to trace the various forces which have been at work in the course of centuries, instrumental in building up the "physical" man, and shaping and adjusting his character and mental bent. A little sketch which reflects him, as he was known to Bishop Merrick (1577), Speed (1627), Blundell (1648), and Chaloner (1653), at the latter end of the 16th, and in the 17th century, will help us in our task. We are speaking, of course, of the broad country population.

The peasantry is represented as tall, of strenuous build, heavy and homely, and of surly temper. Blundell says he cannot parallel the Manxman with any so well and so fitly as the Hollander in the time of Elizabeth. He is rather given to incontinence of body from their general diet of fish which is of flatuous nature. They are a tall, gray-eyed race of men, the major part wearing black beards. They are characterised as civil, laborious, charitable to the poor and hospitable to strangers. Their diet is sparing and simple, their drink water and buttermilk; their meat consists of herrings, salt, butter, and oatcakes, thin as paper leaves, yet as broad and large as those of Wales. Beer and ale they only take in the market. The meal of servants consists of two boiled herrings, one entire oat cake, butter, with milk and water to drink. They are long-lived, ordinarily living to four score and even one hundred years. Their women are fruitful and hard-working, and they wear blankets of woollen and linen (the so-called winding sheet has to be exploded), a habit taken up from the Irish. Their bedding, hay and straw; the houses low-built, they live in little huts of stone and clay, and broom thatch, full of smoke; they have only one room, in this single room the whole family lodges, the meaner sort are forced to place their cows in a corner of the room at the bed feet, the geese and ducks under the bed, and cocks and hens over their heads. Few speak the English tongue, but more like the Welsh do— that is in raised voice. They are generally much addicted to the "musick of the violyne" and dancing, so that "there is scarce a family in the Island but more or less can play it, but as they are ill composers, so they are bad players and singers," and their musical sense has not developed since, or made to be cultivated. Their genius is apt for studies of humanity, or divinity, and they are ingenuous. The nation for the most part are mariners and fishermen, and the Island has always been a fine nursery for seamen. Until the reign of Charles I they merchandized by racking, exchange, and bartering of commodities. The English, Scotch, and Irish, and more almost of any other nation, drive the greatest trade in the towns. The wealthier sort imitate the people of Lancashire, both in their honest carriage and housekeeping; the common sort of people, both in language and manner, "come nighest unto the Irish, although they somewhat relish and savour of the qualities of the Norwegians"; all their officers and retinue are Lancashire men. In 1586 only six families of note were left in the whole Island, specially the Christians and Cannels, in former times there were several noblemen.

The population is spoken of as indifferent, neither now (1648), nor at any time heretofore, was it found to abound with numerous natives. Vigfuson estimates their number in the 10th century between 4,000 to 5,000 souls. Godred and Olave "equipped many ships, and in them brought great numbers from Ireland; out of the Islands of the Hebrides were brought the greatest number. In the year 1228 all the South of Man was wasted by Allan, Lord of Galloway, who spoiled the churches, and slew all the men he could lay hold of, so as the South of Man was laid in a manner desolate." Allan left his bailiffs in Man to gather for him all the tributes of the Country. The cessation of the Norwegian line of kings which, as a result, led to the inroads of the Somerled's, had a baneful effect on the population of Man, it was a time of oppression, extortion, and usurpation, and well might Manxmen moan and sing:*

Then came in Quinney and then Quaill,
With greater taxes and the rent
Which will be always demanded.
For the blessed Island they were the worst,
At making each bad law in her;
Then came great Ollister—he made most havoc.
O Scotchman, it thou were worthy,
Why didst thou not rule as did
The son of Norway's king?

We have also the Macleods of Cadboll, and the Macleods of Lewis (who quarter the Manx *trie cassyn*). They took and ousted the natives from their land and possessions, so did the MacGilbert who became seized of great possessions in the Island. It brought in the Quinneys (Clan Siol Cuinm), and the Quaills of the Ballad, and the Gannols, of the Clan MacDonald,† all of the house of Somerled, and their followers and bailiffs. The effect is even seen in the composition of the House of Keys in 1422–29, where we have the following Gilberts: Gilbert Reed, M'Allister, M'Callen (Allan), M'Quayle, M'Isaacs, M'Andrews, Gilbert M'Killey, Cubbon M'Cubon Cleark, Gubon M'Quandy, Quark, M'Martin, M'Cundrie (= Andreas). And to make it clearer on analysis, out of 28 members of the House of Keys, we have:

45 per cent. Scandio.-Gaelic names, representing comers from the Western Isles.

24 p. ct. from the Scottish borderland. (Or 69 per cent. Low and Island Scotch.)

14 p. ct *pure* Manx names.

10 p. ct. Irish.

2 p. ct. Icelandic, and

5 p. ct. undetermined.

We have to speak now of their political temper. Blundell (1648) remarks, the natives are not apt, or prompt, suddenly to be set on fire, not quick to complain of pressure, or desiring innovation: for during the reign of former kings they had many provocations, yet only once or twice avenged themselves of strangers and tyrants. For about 240 years—which brings it back to 1408—they preserved in their loyalty, and have been constant idolators of the Stanleys, who never forced but rather courted their consent to any new laws and impositions. It formed a landmark in the history of the Island. The reign of the Stanleys introduced everlasting security, peace, and a more fixed tenure, love for their rulers and their benevolent, paternal government. The Stanleys were beloved by the people and their influence played an important part in the final shape of the Manx character and temperament. With the influx of the Lancashire race, largely recruited from the Fylde, which began with the incoming of the Stanleys in 1407, Douglas, Castletown, and Peel became the great centres which transfused the Island with Lancashire blood, manners, customs habits, and ways; the computur of 1541–46, of the tenantry of Ballasalla, German, Sulby, Skynscowe, shows them to be made up of 50 Lancashire and 34 Manx families; and it may truly be said what Lancashire has lost in folklore can be restituted from the Manx peasantry, whose folklore, as it exists now, is largely of Lancashire origin; their songs, children's games, and music even have been absorbed by the Manx country people, and are found to have penetrate into the most secluded hill and upland villages. The Lancashire rule came as a blessing, and softened the hatred of foreign yoke which had sunk deep into the heart of the Manx, their aversion and apathy for anything Irish, Low or Highland Scotch, became proverbial and simmered on for centuries.

But the picture would not be complete without alluding to a few other points. Their agriculture, in consequence of unceasing wars, alien occupations and unfixed tenure, and Insular poverty, has naturally been slow, many remained crofter fishermen. In 1577 we find three free schools in the Island, at Castletown, Peel, and Douglas for the town people; the country people were mostly left without the boon of any secular instruction, and so illiterate that writing and reading ever was a thing unknown; in Cregneish, for instance within the last 60 years, there was only one person who could write and read, and had to be the scribe of the countryside. The Catholic clergy did nothing for lifting them from their ignorance, their main business was to extract tithe and boons, and their greed became proverbial:

There is the greed of seven parsons in a man without children,

And the greed of seven farmers (= landlords) in every parson.

They taxed the very rocks in the sea where fish or crab nibbled, and these rocks are known to place-name collectors in the Island as tithe rocks, or Cregyn jaghee, and were abandoned. In religious matters, the stern and paralyzing church discipline of Bishop Wilson did not mend matters much, and only with Wesley's appearance the peasantry woke up to new life, producing a succession of earnest and eloquent farmer-preachers, and the best metrical Manx version of spiritual hymns. The Wesleyan movement has left a lasting impression on the religious character of the Manx peasantry. We have to lament the total absence of the development of national poetry and ballad in the Island, in which it differs so much from Scotland, Ireland, and Wales, and which may be considered almost as a unique feature in its history. But it is due again to the peculiar fate that Mann unfortunately has suffered: a constant prey to abrupt domination by Irish, Viking, Scotch, and English invaders, without the blessing of Insular seminaries of culture, its poverty, and the suppression of national aspirations and ambition; ruled by the clergy, foreign kings, or their deputies, as they have been for long, untold centuries. All these factors have to be considered and we cannot expect wonders, or be surprised at the results.

The contending forces which have been busy in shaping the life and mental calibre and character of the Manxmen have provided, however, a co-efficient which may be indicated by his patience, prudence, and thriftiness. He is a solid and intelligent man, good at argument and discourse, with a proclivity for litigation, sober and reliable, and they class among best seamen in the British navy.

* "Little Mannanan" (see *Manx Ballads*).

† I give but a few noble families and chiefs, the Irish, Scandio.-Gaelic list of ancient clans in the Island might be built up again by the examination of old "Balla" names and a careful dissection of the old Surnames.

71. THE MANX COWREE

If you ask me the three things the old Manx worshipped above all things, from an epicurean point of view, I may whisper in your ear: *skeddan* (herring), *prinjeig* (haggis), and *cowree* (sowans or flummery)—a triad which used to form the time-honoured relish of a Manxman's culinary aspirations; but if you press, and furthermore ask me, *sub rosa*, which of above dainties—and the mere innocent mention of which made his eyelid twinkle, or caused his heart to flatter, or quicken his pulse a little above normal point, not to notice certain unsteady movements of his pedals— let me utter, in a low voice, the magic little bi-syllable: *cowree*. You cannot possibly, as a *Manninagh dooie*, dissociate or separate *cowree* from fairy; they have grown up together like foster-brothers, and nursed and reared in the same cradle, and, try as you may, you dare not sunder their ties.

How often have I cowered with my kind hosts in the nook of their lone mountain cabins, in the gloaming of a golden-streaked, mellow summer night, with just a few sparks glowing and crackling up from the sweet peat fire, to listen to the tales of the droll and wonderful doings and cranks of "the little people" of fairy realm that used to hover around their cots, in their nightly rambles ever cronk and glen.

Woe to the man, or household, however, who neglected the gentle and hospitable office of showing due courtesy and good manners to the *mooinjer ny gione veggey* or,—*Yee marin!*—omitting to leave for their supper a bowl, or wooden trencher of enticing *cowree*, neatly and properly served, before retiring to take their worldly rest. You had scarcely closed your eyes, softly "the crowd" lifted the latch, you could hear their little feet, trip, trap, scarcely touching the floor, and such a spectacle! There they are, bright in crimson-burning caps, and a raven feather inter-twined, sheathed in Lincoln green mantle and hose, then sitting down to their banquet, smacking their lips, and finishing up with an airy jig and roundelay, the silver moon brightening the gaudy display of their fluttering dresses; rollicking and gambolling in wild revel and orgie till the grey peep of day. Yes, often enough "the old man and woman" were compelled, from their loft above, with bated breath and tremor, to harken to the soft tunes rising up, when at last the old fairy fiddler clicked up his rebec in good I earnest; the little pairs gyrating and whirling in glee and merriment indescribable, and king, queen, and court attending; and then, oh, for Cruikshank's pencil! But, alas! it seems *cowree* and fairies have gone out of the land with the disappearance of the old stock, and dyspeptic tea and sodden potatoes and muffins, and sticky and nasty pies, have taken the room of a dish once the staple of every honest household. And the crisp, thin-leaved, tasty *bonnags*—where are they? Banished, too, from the Isle?

The *cowree*, as the little people would have it, and insisted upon, was thus (I filched their receipt):

> Steep the husk of the oats in water for some time, and some dust of oat meal, run the water through a sieve, to remove the husk; then it is like white water. Now fiil the biggest pot you have in the house with it, stir it with a pot-stick all the time it is on the fire, until it becomes thick and solid Then empty it into dishes and boil the milk with the *cowree* when it is quite cold, and serve it.

This is the royal way, and *probatum est*, and no other make or counterfeit accepted.

And if you ask to know what in the world *cowree* means, certainly and surely not the *cowry* gathered from the shore I invite you to an invisible ride into the Highlands, across the deep waters (we bestride our fairy horse—the stalk of the golden cushag—and put our tarn cap on, in haste),* there on nearing the mainland of Argyle-shire, we already discern the old folk busy pegging away at full swing in their cabins. How the plates fly, and they, like their Manx cousins, call it *cowry;* but it also bears a bit longer and a bit more melodious name: *cabhruich*, or *cabhrig* these, singly and all, again but contractions of the roots:

Càth-bhruich (the aspirated *bruich*), and
Càth-bhrig.

derived from the Gaelic:

càth = seeds, husks of corn; and
bruich = seething, simmering;

which exactly describes the art and mystery in a very comprehensive manner. It has also another name: *Càth-lagan,* and is defined in the books as a kind of food much used by the Gaelic and Lowland Scotch (the *sowans* of the latter), and made by boiling the acidulated juice of oat seeds to the consistency of a thick jelly.

But it quickly crept down to the North country and Lancashire homesteads. It formed a desirable dish in the Fylde district, and Tim Bobbin, the old Lancashire lad, has much to say about *flummery, sewl,* or *sowans,* all ugly Saxon names for *cowree.*

So we see what a fine mess it must have been, times out of mind—did not Esau barter his birthright for it? *It* was, I know, *not* for lentils: so fine, indeed, that the partakers of the dish were the fierce and generous Gael, and the stolid and spiteful Sausenachs, who, however, for once shared the same camp in brotherhood, and both crouched down peacefully together in co-worship of the seething cauldron that kept rocking from the *slouree,* bubbling and singing the while old mysterious runes over the blazing peat fire; the war axe is buried anon for the iron ladle, for a friendly and congenial onslaught on the preparing pottage.

And in tearing myself away from this pleasant meal—which they are just enjoying—I express the parting wish that my Manx friends—both, of the country and the town—may, too, make an experiment, provided their palate is still undegenerated for the trial, and maybe—wonders and miracles never cease—if they will but bring the dish again on the table board, in the old fashioned way, before joining Morpheus, and fill it brimful with good old solid *cowree*—who knows but it may tempt the Manx fairy tribe of yore to rise up again from their long Rip Van Winkle sleep, or revisit the Island anew, and, like my gipsy cowpanions, beat up again their familar nooks and quarters; and, perhaps, all bring back, by main force, or coaxing, laurel crowned *Mainshter Waldron,*† to tell us again or continue his sparkling Manx-Arabian Night stories, to the great joy and delight of all the sweet and true maidens and rose-buds of fair an ever lovely Mannin veg veen!

* In Irish Manx Folklore the fairies transformed the *cushag,* or ragwort into horses to ride on.

† See *Description of Isle of Man,* by George Waldron, 1726. He resided in the Island from 1710–30, and treats in his delightful book "on the Antiquities, History, Laws, Customs, Religious Manners of the inhabitant, likewise many comical and entertaining stories of the pranks played by fairies, *etc.,* the whole carefully collected from original papers and personal knowedge during 20 years residence there." It is a book which should be reprinted, and put in the hand of every Manxman—published at a popular price.

72. MANX ETHNOGRAPHY

In a treatment of folklore of such composite character as that of Mann it is, of course, absolutely necessary to enquire into the various races of people to whom it is due. Fortunately the investigations of Beddoe* and Moore† throw the clearest light on this important and interesting question. We must consider the Manxman in his anthropological aspect. The Manx face is usually long, and either scutiform or oval; the former is the outline most prevalent among the Scandinavian. The nose is almost always of good length, in outline oftener straight, less often sinuous than among the Highlanders and Irish. The influence of the Norwegian cross is shown also in the colour of the hair. Red hair is not frequent, fair and light-brown hair very common, the index of negrescence decidedly lower than in most parts of the Highlands or of Ireland. The distribution and combination of colour resembles more to such districts as Wexford, Waterford, some of the Islands off the coast of Argyle, and perhaps the Lewis. But the exact proportion of hair colour together with the greatest frequency of neutral eyes are not produced elsewhere. Blue eyes are less common than grey, and dark shades of grey, varying toward green and brown, very frequent. "Black" eyes are rare. The hair is pretty copious, straight or wavy, seldom strongly curled or very brightly coloured. Their average weight is 155 lbs, and the Manxman is certainly tall and large.

The fishermen and sailors average 5 feet 8.2 inches in height.

The miners, for the most part tall and dark, average 5 feet 10 inches.

The farmers average 5 feet 11.3 inches.

The Jurby, Ballaugh, and Michael people are the fairest and tall, and show preponderance of Norse blood, the St Patrick people being the tallest. The Peel people have dark eyes and fair hair, and are the smallest. It is a mixed population, like Castletown and Douglas, with large infusion of Lancashire and more recently Irish blood. The dark complexion prevails most in Malew and German parish. Gary (Garbh = the rough, rocky country), which contains the parishes of Maughold and Lonan, has the maximum of dark hair, all but the maximum of light eyes, and its population is largely Gaelic. The island has the largest percentage of light eyes. The eyes in the South are darker than in the North; the North hair is darker than in the South.

Principal Rhys gathers‡ that in the 11th and 12th centuries the Norsemen were in the habit of largely recruiting their fleet in Shetland and the Orkneys, not merely with thralls, but with men of a higher position, They infused thus a certain amount of Pictish blood into the Island the Shetland bind-Oghams distributed over the island, in such places as Braddan, Jurby, Michael, Onchan, and Bride, with names such as Cunaas, Eabs, Froca, Neaci, Ufaac, Onon, Ucifat, and Truian are sufficient proof. But there was a more primitive population in pre-historic times in the Island. The Picts spread through the whole of North Britain, through Wales, the Eastern Scotch Lowlands, Cumberland, and North Ireland; and it also postulates their presence in Man long before the 11th century. Beddoe found evidence of distinct Turanian types of the bronze race, of the pure Iberian race in Cregneish and elsewhere, and we see, when dealing with the analysis of the Insular folklore in detail through these pages how often we stumble on evidence of these older races.

* "Physical Anthropology of the Isle of Man," by John Beddoe, *Manx Notebook*, vol 3, 1887, pp. 21–33.

† "Physical Anthropology of the Isle of Man," by A.W. Moore, 1897.

‡ See "Inscriptions and Language of the Northern Picts," by J. Rhys, *Scotch Antiq. Soc.*, vol 26, p. 303.

73. THE MANX-GAELIC LANGUAGE

The Manx Gaelic.—For the exposition of the growth and development of the native idiom I refer to Principal Rhys' labours. I shall only allude to some few historical points. There cannot be any doubt whatever that the first impulse reached from Ireland. The Ogham inscriptions at Ballaqueeney connect it with Munster, which may possibly go back to the 6th century. In the middle of the 7th century, Senchan Torpeist, chief poet of Ireland, visited Mann. He found there a poetess from Connaught, which would mean a community of literature.* Earlier than this we find the religious contentions between St Patrick (died 461) and the Druidic Mannanan Mac Leir. We have Lonan and Brigit (438–508), to be followed by Columba (504–80). He named a parish, which also bears the alternative name of Arbory.† Against the end of the 6th century we have the Culdees. We have the Ogham inscription at Arbory of Magleog, probably falling within the 10th and 12th centuries, which again connects it with Ulster, Connaught, and Iona. Mann belonged to the Goidelic Kings of Ireland in early times, and was conquered by Aidan in 581, passing then away from the Irish connection.‡ Later on, in the 9th century, it was ruled by the independent Dana-Irish King of Dublin. During the whole of this century the relation between the Danes in Dublin and those of Mann appears most close, and the sovereignities of Dublin and Mann were often held, either by the same person, or members of the family, and forming an appanage to the Scandinavian kingdom of Dublin.‡

Sufficient has been said to show that the Manx-Gaelic had its rise from Ireland, and must have been nourished from various counties and channels of that kingdom. When finally the Norwegian Vikings became the masters of Mann a fresh current made itself visible. The Irish influence disappears in the background; contact was broken with its literature and pure speech and thought. The Dairiadic dialect of the Western Islands, and particularly of Lewis, Skye, and Galloway, say from 890–1270, took its place; its phonology suffered a change from the lips of the Hebridean and Northumbrian Gaels, who largely replaced the Manx blood which was drained by unremitting warfare and extirpation. It was further diluted by the arrival of the Stanleys and the Lancashire people. To trace the precise stages historically and phonologically the Manx language has undergone by the leavening with Norwegian, Galiovian, Lowland Scotch, and English invaders is a task which still awaits a careful investigator.

* See his *Outlines of the Phonology of Manx Gaelic*, 1894, pp. 1–183.

† See *Sodor and Man* by A. W. Moore, 1893, p. 25.

‡ See *Encyclopædia Britannica*, Ireland, p. 252.

74. ANGLO-MANX DIALECT

Anglo-Manx Dialect.—The Ethnography of the Island is further illustrated by the study of the Anglo-Manx Dialect. The subject has already been treated in a cursory way by Ellis,* sufficient, however, to assign its proper place. It belongs to his D23, Variation ii, and his tests have been procured from Lezayre, Peel, and Rushen.

Variation i forms the borderland at the extreme North of the Midland division, adjoining the South of the North division in Lancashire. It occupies Mid-Lancashire, the whole of the hundred of Amounderness, and probably that part of Blackburn Hundred which lies North of the Ribble. The main part comprehends the district known as the Fylde. The Manx variation differs from it only in few minor details, which I merely pass over.

The Manx dialect contains, however, some elements which must be referred to other sources. We may say that the English language was already introduced in the time of the Abbott of Furness, who got a portion of land in 1134 for his palace; later we have the arrival of the Prior of Whithorn and St. Bede. In 1246 the monks of Furness obtained all kinds of mines in Man and some land near St. Trinian's, and finally the inflow in 1409 of the Lancashire race, mostly recruited, as shown before, from the Fylde district, which supplied Stanley's officers, retinue, crafts, and tradesmen. There are certain differences of dialect in the North and South of the Island, and it is time, before it will be too late, to collect all the phrases and words from the various Sheadings.

The grammatical structure follows largely the idiosyncracies of the Goidelic tongue, to exhibit which I can recommend no better book than Rydings† *Manx Tales*, than which there is nothing superior to illustrate the Manx peasantry.

Scotch.—Traces of former Scotch occupation are afforded in the retention of *qhu* for *wh*, as in *qu*hole, *qu*hen, &c., which even affects the Manx language, compare: *quail, quiggel, quaillag, qhweel* = court, distaff, fly, wheel.

Irish.—We know that the Island swarmed with Irish refugees in the time of William III, and Irish beggars have been the bane of the Island even in the 16th century. In 1561 "the Irish women are commanded forth of the Isle"; indications in the dialect of their presence are frequent, phrases like "*bad cess* to him," and the Irish endearments—*the lamb millish, O the chree, the chree; the bogh millish, Mrs Kelly, a chree;*† the excessive use—*to the fore*.

Orkney and Shetland.—Then we have the use of Ellis' (*t*) specially before *r*, in the North and middle of the Island, while the South retains the regular *th*; as in *thrown, thread, three,* &c., an alveolar *t* which is formed with the tip of the tongue against the gums, and an *r* which is trilled, the tip of the tongue advancing quite to the gum during the flap. We have the same (*t*) again in *thick, thing* in the North, and these, as Ellis remarks, are in some respect comparable with Orkney and Shetland habits.

Norse and Cumberland.—The Gaelic-Manx has also influenced the pronunciation of words like *girl*, which is uttered *gjel;* in *again*—*agjen*, as in Lezayre, Peel, and Rushen, just as they pronounce Manx *kione* = *kjodn*, ard even *jodn* without *k*, &c., and traceable to Norse pronunciation; for *over, safe, alive, if,* they say *ober, sabe, alibe, ob,* as in Cumberland; compare *ebemin* = *evening, eleeben* = *eleven, seeben* = *seven*, &c., &c.

The traces of middle-English have been treated by Moore,‡ to which I refer. We thus see how even the dialect is a faithful mirror of the history of the Island, and how folklore, ethnography, and dialect unite to illustrate each other.

The Norwegian Language.—It may be said that it was spoken practically from 890–1270; it was introduced by the Shetland and Orkney men, and from Norway, with which connection was kept up, as shown by the grammatical structure of the Runic stones in the Island, which fall between 1170–1230. It was only the language of the rulers, and used at Thing and Hall resembling in this the old Norman barons and their courts in King William the Conqueror's time. It never took hold upon Manx soil, a bi-linguality may have, and is likely to have existed in the better classes of the natives, but the children learned, and were nursed up in Manx tongue. It was a foreign plant on the soil, and with the disappearance of the Norwegian vestige in 1230 died a natural death. The spirit of the Norseman only lives in the legal constitution of the Government, an inheritance that produced a free Parliament; and particularly in its place-names; the sea-fringe with its hundreds of Norse-rocks, creeks, fore-lands, and caves have left imperishable evidence of the mighty old sea-farers, the track they took, and the commingling and fusion they underwent in blood and speech in their voyages from the Shetlands and Western Isles to Man. Their language itself is so completely forgotten, that the dictionary has not even retained a good root for a word of common parlance.

* *English Dialect*, by Alex. J. Ellis, 1890, pp. 82–85. *Early English Pronunciation*, part v, Alex J. Ellis, pp. 360–61.

† *Manx Tales*, by Egbert Rydings, Manchester, 1896.

‡ *Lioar Manninagh*, vol. iii, part ii, pp. 59–64.

75. SUNDRIES

Itch in the Nose. When there was itch in the nose, it was thought there was some person talking of you, and people used to put a spit on the palm of the left hand, and hit it with the side of the right hand, and whatever side the spit went that was the direction the people were talking about you.

Sharp Objects. It was accounted unlucky to make a present of any sharp instrument, as it cut love, they said.

Signs of Death. "I have seen the old people watching the children when playing on the green; sometimes they would be singing and marching about, carrying a stool, or a stick on their shoulders, or something of that sort. The old folks said it was a sign of a funeral, and seemed to be concerned about it, and firmly believed it predicted a death in the village shortly. I recollect two little boys once walking about in that fashion, and the people took notice of them, and actually one of the little boys that was carrying the stool died soon after. I remember some other instances, but gave little heed to such things."

Eel. The skin of a fresh-water eel was held to be a cure for a sprained wrist or ankle.

Haddock. It is said by some that the Devil it was that took a haddock between his finger and thumb and burnt the black spots on the haddocks' shoulders, also that they are the marks left by the finger and thumb of Peter when he opened the fish's mouth to take out the piece of money to pay the tax for the temple's service for his Master and himself (the latter is also current in Scotland).

Ass. "Passed round the back and belly of an ass was thought to prevent whooping cough here. I remember myself being put through the drill by two women, the one was putting me half-way round, then the other was putting me round the other half."

Moths. When a moth was flying about a young woman or a young man, it was said that their sweethearts were thinking of them.

The "Herring" Moth (*Lhemeen y Sceddan*). I have seen a very large moth sometimes come in the house late in the evening, when the weather was fine, and it was called the "herring moth." When one was seen going about in the house they said there would be good herring fishing that night.

Bees. "The old fishermen thought it very lucky to catch the first bee they happened to see in April. It was the sign of a good herring season, they said. I have seen men chasing the first bee they saw for a long way, and if they caught her, they kept her in their purse, but if they did not catch her, it was a sign that their earning would be light. I knew a man that was born with a caul, and he took it with him in the boat, and I have heard some of the fishermen say it was half filled with dead bees. He was catching the first bee he saw for many years, and keeping them in the caul, and he was very fortunate when fishing herrings. Whether the caul and bees made him lucky or not I cannot tell."

Raven. If a raven lighted on the roof of a house or went flying round it, it was considered a sure sign of the death of some one of the family.

Seagull. If a seagull alights on the chimney of a house they say that stormy weather is near.

Thellog-faiyr. The *thellog-faiyr* or tit-mouse was reckoned to be a very bad thing for cattle. If one happened to come underneath a cow's mouth the cow would not eat, but snuff and shake her head, and continue in that state until some feather was got and burnt under her nose, after that she would eat again.

Cats. Cats were not allowed to go near the baby in the cradle in the Island, neither when it was young they did not think of the cat sucking the breath of the baby, but that its breath was poisonous to come on a baby's face.

Magpie. To see a magpie hopping on the road before you was consideredby some old folks very unlucky, and if going on business you were not not likely to succeed.

Hen-Cock. The crowing of a hen was the sure sign of death or bad luck here. The crowing of a cock on the roost before midnight was something the same in Scotland. If his feet were cold, it was supposed to be the sign that some of the family would be buried in a short time, but if warm, it signified a wedding.

Frogs. If they spawned in the deep water, it was an indication of a dry summer; if it was near the side it was the sign of a wet summer.

Spider. A spider running over our clothes was regarded as a sign of getting new clothes.

Salmon. When we saw a salmon jumping high out of the water at sea the men said it was the sign of a breeze of wind.

76. CHILDREN'S RHYMES (CREGNEISH)

I had a little pony,
His name was Dapple Gray,
I lent him to a lady
To ride a mile away:
She lashed him, she whipped him,
And drove him through the mire—
I would not give my pony
For all the ladies' hire.

*

Georgie, porgie, pudding, pie,
Kissed the girls and made them cry;
When the girls came out to play
Georgie, porgie, ran away.

*

Thread through your needle,
I owe you two shillings,
I'll pay you to-morrow.
Here comes a candle
To light you to bed,
Here comes a hatchet
To chop off your head.

Note.—When playing this "thread through the needle," two would be taking each others' hands, then all the rest were coming between them one by one, and they were catching one every time, and asking him "Which side are you on?' Then he would be standing on one side till all the rest would be caught, and then everyone on his own side. We had a tug-of-war, and the strongest side won the game.

*

There comes an old woman
From Dennis Land,
Five or six children
By the one hand—
One can knit, and another can spin,
Another can make a fine bed for a King.
Please, Mam, to take one in!—
They are all too black and too dirty,
To me ransom, dansom, decimal dance.
To me ransom, dansom, decimal dance.
We are well enough for you, Mam!
To me ransom, dansom, decimal dance.

Then the mother says:
Now my daughter, Jenny, is gone,
Without a farthing in her hand,
Nothing but a guinea-gold ring.
Good-bye, Jenny, good-bye.
As I went into my grandfather's garden,
I found an Irish farthing;
I gave it to my mother,
To buy an Irish brother.
The brother was so cross,
I put him on a horse;
The horse too much a dandy,
I gave him a glass of brandy;
The brandy was too strong,
I put him in the pond;
The pond was far too deep;
I put him in the cradle,
And rocked him fast asleep.

*

Man of war, man of deed,
Set a garden full of seed;

48

*

Man of war, man of deed,
Set a garden full of seed;
When the seed began to grow,
Like a garden full of snow;
When the snow began to melt,
Like a garden full of hemp;
When the hemp began to peel,
Like a garden full of steel;
When the steel began to canker,
Like a ship without an anchor;
When the ship began to sail,
Like a cock without a tail;
When the cock began to fly,
Like an eagle in the sky;
When the cock began to fall,
Like an egg on the wall;
When the egg began to spill,
Like a fairy on the hill,
When the fairy began to run,
Like a man on the drum;
When the drum began to sound,
Like a cow in the pound;
When the cow began to jump,
Like the water in the pump;
When the pump was running o'er,
And the Lion began to roar,
Success to ye all, bonny bairns.

*

Dittle, dittle, dumpling.
Our little John
Went to bed with his stockings on,
One shoe off, and another shoe on.
Dittle, dittle, dumpling,
Our little John
Sitting on the mat
Eating raw potatoes—
What do you think of that?

*

One, two, three,
Mother caught a flea;
The flea died,
Poor mother cried.
One, two, three; out goes she.

*

I had a little donkey;
He would not go.
Would I beat him?
No, no, no!
Put him in the stable,
And give him some straw;
Gee, little donkey; whoa, whoa, whoa.

*

What's your name?
Butter and Cream.
Who gave you that name?
My Aunty Jane.
What is she doing?
Keeping a school.
How many scholars?
Twenty-four.
Shut up your mouth,
And say no more.

[They are supposed to finish at twenty-four, and if they said more, they received a blow.]

*

What for are you scraping?
For a needle.
What for is the needle?
To sew a bag.
What for is the bag?
To carry some coals?
What for is the coals?
To light the fire.
What for is the water?
To scald the knives.

What for is the knives?
To cut the head of the chickens that's scraping the corn.

[Then the children would be running away.]

*

Matthew, Mark, Luke, and John,
Take a stick and lather on.

77. WEDDINGS

The bride and bridegroom did not go hand in hand to invite the wedding guests, but the bride went to invite her own friends and the bridegroom his, two or three days before the day appointed for the wedding, that the guests might have time to prepare for it if they wanted to get any new clothes, that they might have time to get them made. To be invited one day before the wedding day was a "fiddler's invitation," and no one that was invited one day before the wedding would accept the invitation, they thought it an insult. I was at a wedding once, and there were 48 in the company, and there was a fiddler coming with us from the church to Port St. Mary, and they were halting sometimes on the road to dance.

When a "walking wedding" was on the way to church, the first person they met had to turn back and go with them a little distance, and the best man gave him a silver piece when he let him go. They did not like a woman to be *qualtagh,* that was unlucky. None of the company was allowed to call the bride or the bridegroom by their Christian names after they came out of church, but the married man and the married woman alone, and to be called only *yn dooinney poost, as yn ven poost.* If any man happened to forget himself and call them by their Christian name, he had to pay for a round for the company—so that made them very careful.

78. SPONSORS

The people of this Isle did not allow a woman with child to stand sponsor for a baby, as they said something would happen.

79. JACULATORY PRAYERS

The old people, when going out of the house at a late hour, used to say: "*Shee yee dy ron maryn*" = 'The peace of God be with me'; and going along the road if they got "fearful" and feeling as if they walked in the air, not feeling the ground under their feet, without seeing or hearing anything, the old folk used to say: "*Dy bee Jee eddyr ayms as dy-chooilley ghrogh red*" = 'God between me and all evil things.' When a baby sneezed it was the custom for the mother or some other woman present to say: "*Dy banney Jee eh (ish)*" = 'God bless him or her'; and that is kept up still more or less by most of the country women in the Island.

80. CHARMS

"The people used to be afraid to bring new milk out of the house at night without putting a little drop of water in it, or a grain or two of salt, and flesh meat had to get a little salt on it to be carried out of the house at night—to keep the *glashtins* and fairies away."

81. CHURNING

The people of the Island used to churn the milk with a staff, the same as the Scotch, and they had a custom if a neighbour happened to come in the house at churning time, they had to take a spell of working the staff. Sometimes the milk would keep nearly all day before they could get the butter, and it was thought that some witch had her hand in it. And if a black cat came in the house while the women were churning and commenced to lick up the drops of milk sprinkled on the floor, it was a witch sure enough! They used to put the poker in the fire, and when it was red hot, try to shove it into the black cat, but I never saw any one that could manage to hit the cat, but I have heard of some one that stuck the red-hot poker in the cat and killed it, and it turned out to be an old witch that was killed, and that was the cause of trying to kill the black cat. I never heard of a black cat being unlucky only at churning time.

82. GAMES: PLAYING "BUTT THURRAN," OR "TIP THURRAN"

We used to be playing, when I was a boy, in the farmer's haggart, running among and around the corn stacks. We called it *butt thurran.* One was putting his head against the stack, and the rest getting away among the other stacks, and then the one that was lying was coming out and trying to tip some one and make him lie in his stead, and if he chased one to a certain distance from his own stack, whoever would catch him, then he had to ride them back to his stand again. We used to spend moonlight evenings in the winter at that game.

Stag yn ree.—There was another game we called *stag yn ree.* There would be about twenty of us gathering on moonlight evenings in winter, in a field, and casting lots who would be the *stag,* and whoever was the one he had ground marked out, and if he came beyond his boundaries, whoever would get behind and get hold of him, he had to ride him back to his stand; and if the stag could tip one of the rest first, they had both to be stags and hold each other's hands, and everyone they could tip had to join hands with them until they were all tipped; but the one at each end had authority to tip another, and when there would be a lot of them holding one another's hands, those that were free used to make a race at the middle of the line and burst through, and when the line would be broken, all the free ones would be catching hold of one and getting a ride on his back to the stand. If any of them could get to the stand without being caught, they had to ride no one. They had to continue until all were in the line, and then the first that had been caught by the first stag had to be stag himself for the next game.

Stag, stag yn Ree,
Who'll catch me.

Then one would say:

Run, run away,
Let's have a run,
Just for fun.

83. SCAAYN GOANLYSAGH (MALICIOUS SPIRITS)

Spirits of living people haunting those they had any spite to. There are several stories of such on record in the Island, and of psychological interest. I give them in the same form as related to me by my old Manx friend:

"I knew a man myself that had been haunted by another man, a living man, for a long time. The spirit came to him when he was alone and in the dark. Sometimes it put something like a small rope round his body, and almost squeezed him to death, sometimes it pinched parts of his body and jostled him about while alone walking on the road, as soon as it was dark, and he could see in the dark the form of the man until at last he knew him. It was a man he had offended once, and it appears he was a very malicious man. When Patrick, which was the name of the haunted man, knew who It was, be called out his name, and he departed from him for a time, and he got two men to go with him to the man's house, and gave him warning before the two witnesses to desist, but I don't know did that keep him away or not, however he got rid of him some way."

"There was a woman about my own age (70) talking about those things the other day, and she said that her mother, when she was young and courting, was haunted by another young woman. They both loved the same young man, but her mother was his favourite, and the other young woman had a spite to her in consequence. She would be coming in the dead of the night to her mother's bed, and squeeze her throat and nearly strangle her. When she got to know who it was that haunted her, the young man went with witnesses and gave her warning, but she derided him only. Her mother got advice, however, from some wise woman to put two sickles, or reaping hooks, across behind the front door, and she did not molest her afterwards."

"I have heard some stories about the spirits of the dead haunting some people, and they had to get a Catholic priest to banish the malicious spirits to the Red Sea for seven years, and at the end of it the ghost came back again, and if the person it haunted was not dead, the ghost haunted him again, and was more outrageous than ever, and the priest had to banish him again for seven years, at the termination of which it came back in great fury, and the priest had to banish it again, but if the person was not dead when it came the third time, the priest could do no more for him."

"Well I remember a public-house myself, and the publican murdered his wife. She was found dead in the house in the morning with the kitchen poker down her throat. The authorities were not so strict then as they are at present to investigate such things, and as there were no witnesses the man was not committed for trial, and I have heard the folks say many times over that the dead woman's ghost haunted until the priest sent the spirit away to the Red Sea. I have heard the fishermen reckoning when the time would be up to come back again, and I have seen the man, too, he was always in liquor. He would not lie in bed without a light in his bedroom. I remember hearing the man saying that the ghost came back on some night and the priest had to banish it again. I think he was dead before she was at liberty to return the third time, and she returned no more."

"I have heard of a young woman in Glen Meay that was haunted, and she was getting tormented every night until she was nearly dead. She was getting a man to lie the floor side of her in the bed, but all was of no use until the schoolmaster of the village, who was a very learned man, undertook to spend a night with her. He made a circle round the bed, and then sat on a chair in the circle. He had a good fire, and a candle burning. About twelve o'clock the room door was opened, and a big monster came in, something like an ox, it immediately extinguished the candle, and the fire got as black as night. The schoolmaster said: "This is the living and not the dead." When he said that the fire blazed up, and the candle was lighted again; and whatever the schoolmaster said or had done to it, gave it a stop, for it never haunted her afterwards."

"My father told me about some man that was haunted by another, and the spirit was in the form of a very large bladder. As soon as the sun was set the big bladder was upon him, and he could not get done with it, and he did not know who it was; but one evening, while sitting at the fire, the bladder was tumbling on the floor and bouncing upon him. He put the kitchen poker in the fire until it was red hot, and watched his opportunity. He thrust with all his might the poker into the bladder, and it immediately disappeared, and the first news he heard next morning was that one of his neighbours had got a wound in his side and not expected to live; but he got better after a long time, I think, but never haunted his neighbour again."

"The woman that told me about her mother being haunted, said she was acquainted with a woman that knew two men, and one haunted the other. The clerk of the parish had died, and those two men had their names put in as candidates for the office; one was successful, and the other that was unsuccessful haunted him, and he was tormented with him. But he went to a priest and he banished the spirit to the Red Sea. And the man kept to his bed for the seven years, with only a little life left in him, just to show he was not quite dead. When the time of banishment was up the clerk was afraid that he would be haunted again and he resigned his office, and the other man got the billet after all. When his spirit came back he got well and got up again. The one that told the story said she was acquainted with both the men, and the story was true."

I have heard some strange stories about the spirits of living people—quite of a different class, coming home to see their friends when away at Crookhaven and Shetland:

"A young man was in a house in Strugan snail on business some time ago, before the boats came home from Crookhaven. He came out of the house—it was when the sun was shining—and he met a young man in the street, one of the family that was fishing at Crook at the time, with his sailor's clothes bag on his shoulder. 'Hallo,' said the young man to the sailor, 'how are you at home so soon?' but he got no answer; but he went on towards the back door. The young chap made all haste to come back soon, and have a yarn with the fisherman that had returned from Crook, but when he came back to the house he could not see him, and he enquired for him, but the whole family said they had seen no sight of him. The young man was surprised, for he would swear it was him he met in the street."

"A woman that I am acquainted with has a son steamer-sailing. She said she had heard him very often coming to the door when the night was stormy, and open the door and go upstairs to his bedroom, and sit down on the bedside with a sudden jerk that made the room tremble, but there was no sign of his being at home in the morning."

"There is a house pretty near to my own, and the grandmother slept in the parlour; and being old, had a light in a bedroom at night. The father and mother were in bed, and the door locked; they had a son fishing at Crook, and in the night the latter heard the front door opened, and the footsteps of their son coming upstairs, and opening his bedroom door, and turning the key, and locking the door. In the morning they went to his bedroom to see if there was anything the matter with their son, when he had come home so suddenly. But the door was locked on the inside, and they had to break the lock when I here was no answer from within. When the door was opened, there was nobody there, and they were wondering greatly; but the old grandmother said to them when they went to see her, that he was at home, for he came in to her in the night and stood beside her bed, and wrapped the bed clothes around her feet before he went upstairs. But he did not come home for more than a month after that himself in person."

"It appears when sailors are in a storm at sea, and in danger, that they are thinking of home and friends, and are wishing to be there again. It is supposed that their spirits come, as their bodies cannot come."

84. AN OLD MANX PROVERB

There is a very old Manx proverb, so very remote indeed that its meaning has become a puzzle to the present generation of Manxmen, it runs thus:

Tra ta'n gheay 'sy villey,

Yiow shiu magh yn glass-ghuilley.

or:

When the wind is in the tree.

Soon the lockman here will be.

The lockman is a sort of sheriff's officer who had charge of all prisoners and convicts, whom he kept under lock and key until their doom; his real name was *guilley glesh*, or *glass*, which, to suit the rhyme, is here reversed. We have similar proverbs and sayings in England. In *London Notes and Queries*, vol. 9, p. 494 (1857), we read:

> A labouring man in Grantham made the remark that in March and all seasons when the judge was on circuit, and when there are any criminals to be hanged, there are always winds and storms and roaring tempests.

Again, these ominous storms are alluded to in Cornwall, where there is a very popular notion that they unfailingly accompany Assize times, and there is a passage in Hollingworth's "Childe Erconwold":

Hast thou never read

When trees in calm air move, then speak the dead?

and in *Willis's Current Notes*, November, 1855, in a note on "Thunder Storms on Great Deaths," it says:

> When in 1658 the Protector Cromwell lay a-dying, there came a mad and ruthless storm suddenly. [...] "Behold," said his friend, "the rush of archangels to marshal into paradise my lord's illustrious soul!" "Mark," said his enemies, "how the demons of the air battle for the mastery of his spirit, and assemble to grasp it, when it glides away!"

We know that Odin, or Woden, was the god of both wind and storm and war. To him the temple in Upsala was erected, and the great treasures were kept there. Every nine years the people celebrated here a great festival in his honour, when human and animal sacrifices were made to him. It lasted nine days, and the victims consisted of 99 men, 99 horses, 99 cocks, and 99 hawks. With their blood Odin was propitiated. The grove and the trees on which the slaughtered bodies were suspended were held sacred, and it was death to him who disturbed its precincts.

The above proverb takes us back to these old Norse pagan rites, before the introduction of Christianity had rooted out these dire customs. The sacrifices were principally made to propitiate him in times of war, or to appease him. It was believed that when the wind and storm played in the trees, that the god clamoured for fresh victims. We see, then, how very old our Mann proverb is. The Mann executioner was the *fer chroghee* or *crogheyder*, and the old fashion to deal with the condemned was to hang him up on the tree, just as the pagan Norse priesthood did with their human and other victims in the sacred grove of Upsala and elsewhere.

85. YN DREAN (THE WREN)

Keayrt dy row va ny ushagyn chaglym dy hoiljaghey da y chooilley cre obbraghyn va'd son jannoo. Va'd loayrt unnane eck cheayrt, ginsh guoid dy eean va'd troggal, as cre cha mie va'd laboragh. Tra haink yn drean beg dy nish cre foddagh ee jannoo dooyrt ee:

Myr s'beg mee hene, myr keyl my chass,
Un eean jeig ver ym lesh ass.

The birds all met together once upon a time to tell of all the great things they could do. They were speaking one at a time, saying how many young they were rearing, and how good they were labouring. When the little wren came to tell what he could do, he said:

Though I am light, and my leg is small,
Eleven chicks I bring out for all.

That's what the old people were saying.

86. MANX SEA LORE

When going out fishing in the herring season, it would happen that some of the boats were lucky and got plenty of fish, while other boats caught nothing. The result often was that great rows arose among the fishermen about such things. Suppose one or two boats fished well, there would be some of the others going in the night and and pulling a few straws of thatch off their houses (the successful men's) and that took away all their luck with it.

DRIVING A WITCH OUT OF THE BOAT

How the fishermen were driving the witch out of their boats when they were unsuccessful in catching herrings and thinking some harm had been done by a witch: "In the evening when the nets were in the water, if it was calm, they got a lot of oakum and tied it on the end of a stick, then soaking it well with tar in the tar bucket, when the darkness set in they lighted the oakum and the tar, and the skipper took the torch and commenced at the stem-head, and the rest of the crew looking out for the witch. They were telling many lies over it, sometimes one would say he had seen the witch in this crevice, and another would say that she was in that crevice, and the skipper went with the torch to every place where they said the witch was, and put the burning torch in that place. Then the witch had to get away from the fire, and they kept on going from one place to another for a long time, until someone said the witch was gone aft. Then the skipper went aft with the torch, and put it in every crevice round the stern sheets until the witch was on the rudder head, he said, and then she had to get off that, too, from the torch, and jump into the sea. Then he threw the torch into the sea after her."

CHARMS FOR THE FISHING

"As for the fishing, I never knew of any charm used for anything, as any sensible man would ask for God's blessing; but if times went hard against some folks they would foolishly go to certain folks that lifted herbs for the purpose, and the herbs would be boiled and everyone would have to taste it, and the remains would be sprinkled over the nets in the hold before shooting them, or stretching them full length in the sea or tide—*beayn ny traie*—and some would give a herb tied bits in a paper, or a piece of cloth, and it was to be put in the tail buoy* (*mollag faman*), and sometimes if the next neighbour would know the trick he would steal the buoy."

* *Mollag*—is a dog's skin blown up as a bladder, and used to float the herring nets.

87. QUERY

Cregeen, in his valuable dictionary, says: "That the Manks had names of their own for the months is evident, as *Mee ny Mannan, Mee ny Meayllagh,* &c."

But here he stops, and whatever he knew about the matter has been lost to posterity. The former of these month names means "the Month of the Kid," and the latter might perhaps be translated "the Squally Month," or "the month that makes everything bare." To which months these names were applied it is hard to conjecture, probably March and April. July was sometimes called *Mee Vuigh*, or Yellow Month; March was called *Mee ny Mart* or *Mayrnt*, and November *Sauin* or *Mee Hauiney*. Can any reader give any further information upon this interesting subject, or has any reader ever heard *Mee ny Mannan* and *Mee ny Meayllagh* made use of in colloquial Manx?

SEAGHAN MAC NAOMHAIN.

88. MANX NOTES AND QUERIES, NO. 83

It appears that my recent note, No. 83, on "Malicious Spirits," and previous matter, has greatly vexed some of the good people in Cregneish whom I much esteem. I am really sorry to have unwillingly given cause for raising any bad feeling, but I may assure them that I alone am responsible for the publication of these notes, which I have collected during the last six or eight years from a variety of old people in the neighbourhood. Unfortunately, the odium is cast on my old friend Mr Ed. Farquhar, who is absolutely free from any share: the information in question, along with many other items of folklore from that place, was given me at various times from a worthy old man now dead some years. But there is really no personal reflection intended or expressed on any one, and I trust those who feel aggravated will accept my assurance, and desist from venting their ire on Mr Farquhar, who has nothing at all to do with the matter, and who suffers greatly by the general animus against him, which I sincerely hope will cease after the explanation I have given, and that the former good relations will be established.

C. ROEDER.

89. WITCHCRAFT, ETC.

In any treatment of witchcraft and magic we have, of course, to go back to Druidism and the Druids, of which the Island had its full share. The Druids practised incantation of various kind, auguries by heavenly bodies, wind, clouds, smoke, birds' flight, they announced the geese, or things unlucky for chief or tribe, and finally their power became so intolerant that in the sixth century it was proposed to banish them from Ireland but for the protection of Coluincille. Armstrong observes that all the principal families or clans in the Hebrides had their *diuidh*, adepts in divination and medicine, who foretold the future events, decided all causes, civil and ecclesiastical, and who besides devoted themselves to philosophy, astronomy, education, and the study of nature. In Gaelic, seunadair and geasadair, he adds, correspond to druids. From these spring our Manx *fer obbagh, faaishneyder, bouch-chrout, fer ysseree*, and the whole tribe of *buitch* and *cailleach*, or in more modern terms, the men and women in Man versed in leechcraft, "be-speaking," witching, fore-telling, and cursing or destroying. They have, however, dwindled down in our times to mere herb-doctors, bone-setters, magnetisers, and hypnotisers; traces in the Island of actual belief in buitching or bewitching and the effect of the evil eye are still abundant, and have repeatedly come under my personal observation. The charms, of which there are many forms in constant use, are handed down from father to daughter, and from daughter to son; the art is hereditary, only a few families possess the secret which descends from family to family; they consist of written slips or formulas, whispered over the patient, and preparations of simple herbs, or powders, &c. The fairy doctors, as they are also called, pretend to encounter great difficulties when operating. Great darkness or horrid noises surround them when lifting the herb, their life and soul is in danger when they dispense their charms or work upon you. They generally work themselves into a state of excitement, the body shivering, and their muscles contracted, their eyes glaring and the face flushed and perspiring.*

I will cite a few cases of *fir obbee* and *buitches* known in the Island:

1638. Jony Tear,† accused for administering strange herbs, Ballaugh.

1659. Jane Cesar, Kirk Malew, bewitching.

1690 Gilbert Moore, John Steon, Picking herbs to forget, to blind, to obtain property, and strike people unknowingly

1712. Alice Knakell, Kirk Lonan, burning earth to ashes and giving same to cattle to procure more milk; burning pieces of the petticoat to powder and give it for drink to get sleep.

1713. Alice Cowley, Ballaugh, a regular dealer in charms, dispenses mineral powders for procuring crops, remove barrenness, cure sick children, and selling love philters.

Coming nearer our own times the most striking personage was:

Teare† of Ballawhane, whose power was known throughout the length and breadth of the Island. He had, and arrogated to himself, unlimited power over the birds of the air, and the beasts of the field; he could cut off the fish; he blessed the seed, and the net, and plough; no farmer would begin his operations before calling him in He declared that by probing the secret springs of nature he could accelerate, return, or turn aside, at pleasure, the natural course of events. He could call evil spirits to his assistance.

On the other hand, he once declared in my presence, "he would not move from 12 o'clock at night till cock-crow for the love of his life or anything." He seems in his person to summarize the essence and nature of a very ancient druid.

Speaking of witches, it is still believed in the South and the North amongst unsophisticated farmers, that these old women can at pleasure transform themselves into hares, they can injure your person, cattle, farm produce, and health, upset your bargains, endanger your property; and you can only kill or shoot them with a crooked silver coin; and to escape their spells and evil eye—collect the dust and earth from under their sole, and burn it to ashes and throw it into the fire or water, or rub over the victim of their craft with the dust. "Fasting spittle" is another precious recipe used in cure.

The late Rev. T.E. Brown truly sings:

... ... these ould things
That's selling charms to sailors‡-rings,
Papers ... hung about the neck.
But there is odds of charms
A sort of blessin'; but some is a cuss
Most bither ... cussing
Plough and harra, stock and crop,
Nets and lines ...
And harbs!§ they picks them
The right time of the moon and they'll take and mix them.

Now of the Pishag, or charms, there is great variety, and most have been described by Mr Moore¶ and myself. We have them:

"To get blood, stop blood of men and horses, to cure toothache, elfshot, for scalding, straying, frightening, loosing, for the nightmare, the foot falling asleep, sciatica, erysipelas, king's evil, for warts, for obtaining a fresh tooth in lieu of the decayed one, &c.;" further:

"For bewitching the milk, horse, cow, pig, baby, against the fairies. the buggane, and evil spirit; for protecting the boat, stable, and house, and you put a curse on the smell even."

The Amulets are stitched in your clothes, such as a brooch, &c., or you wear‖ it on your person, such as the *rowan*, or tie it in the cow's tail, or hang it over your door, &c. Holed stones, or beads, were worn round your neck, and some of the *Pishags* had to be consumed by fire or water, or were buried in the soil, or stuck in the hollow trees, or left abroad to decay, or were left with or transferred to the object to be operated upon; and consisted of bits of scrips, and written paper, rags, shells, stone, coin, pins, potsherds, blood, hair, spittle, clipping of the nail, bone, matter, or effinvia, of coral, or were communicated by touch, or effected by fascination of the eye, or images of wax or clay, and accompanied by the singing, or whispering and murmuring of spells, invocations, imprecations, and prayers, vows and oaths, such as *guesag, rhusag, sheean,* and *orradh,* and the *crosagh.*

The Manx *Pishags* belong to different periods, and have been derived from various sources, *viz.,* those which may be traced to very early times, such as:

1. "I will take the true spirit and cast from me the black spirit (*doo spyiryd*) ... and I shall never be the evil spirit (*drogh spyrryd*)." Moore, *Folklore,* p. 97.

2. "The black blood running ... I will take it and it shall be mine."—Moore, *Folklore.*

3. The Invocation to the Spirits of the Church Stiles, and the houghs (*ny Keimee as ny cughtee*).—Moore, *Folklore.*

4. The allusion to the "three young women who came over the water" (*three mraane aegey haink harrish yn ushtey*), which reminds us of the *deae matres,*** the cultus of which was brought over by the Teutonic auxiliary legions from the Rhine, and the sculptured altars of which frequently occur in Northumbria along the Roman wall.

5. The *Pishag* against *Elfshot:* "If it came out of the earth, or the air, from under the tide of the sea ... let it return back again."—My Folklore, part i, p. 169.
Some of which may go back to Druidical times.

The next batch, of which there are numerous instances, refers to those which are also commonly spread over ancient Northumbria, including East Scotland, Cumberland, Westmoreland, Lancashire, and Yorkshire, and of Norse and Anglo-Saxon origin, and those that fall within the sphere of mediæval and Catholic times. To analyse or enumerate the latter two classes specifically would take too much space. We see what great interest attaches to the collection of these charms, and how necessary it is to record even the least scraps, and particularly those relating to early Goidelic times in the Island. I have also added for comparative purposes, a list of the derivations which may help to throw some side-light on their formation.

* See also *Folklore of N.E. Scotland,* by Gregor.

† This seems to be the same family.

‡ In 1487 we read that the women in Man sell wind, closed under three knots of thread or more.

§ For instance, *vervain, wooishlyn, luss yn aacheoi, luss y chiolg, luss ny kiare duillag, bollan faaill eoin,* &c.; of the herbs which poison, blind, and make forget, we are of course in the dark.

¶ See *Folklore of the Isle of Man,* pp. 96–100; and My Folklore, parts i and ii; *Lioar Manninagh;* also *sub.* "Prayer," My Folklore, ii.

‖ The lucky or holy stone (a holed stone) was suspended to the tester of a bed-head to prevent the Nightmare (Ballacreggan); the lucky bone (in the form of a cross or Tau), taken from the sheep, was worn round the neck for good luck; the *bollan* bone was carried by the fishermen of the Island for the same purpose.

** The *matres* were also Celtic (note by Principal Rhys).

90. WITCHCRAFT (1)

Comparative list of derivations:

Drui, or *druai*, a druid, wizard, charmer; *Druiaghtagh*, enchanter, charmer, wizard; *Fer druiagh*, a wizard; *Druiaght*, the charm; *Laue druiaght*, chiromancy; *Marroo druiaght*, necromancy; also *Fer druiaght* (Deut. xviii. 11), for necromancer; *Cloagey druiagh*, the invisible cloak, rendering invisible at pleasure the person who wore it; *Cowrey druiagh*, amulet (*cowrey*, mark, sign, symbol); *Cohuleen druidh* (Irish), magic cap which makes the wearer invisible; *Gloine na druidh* (Gaelic) the druid's glass or the druid's egg.

We have also the following order of wizards, conjurers, *etc.*:

Fer obbagh (Manx), wizard, *m*, & *f*, (pl. *fer obbee* and *ben obbee*); see Lev. xix. 31; 1 Sam xxviii, 3; and *obbeeys*, witchcraft, Lev. xx. 6; *Ubag* (Gaelic), an enchantment, charm, incantation, spell; *Ubagaiche*, one who subdues by charms and philters; *Upadh* (Irish), sorcerer, witch; *Upaire*, charm-monger; *Upog*, witch; *Uptha*, charms, philters, sorcery, witchcraft.

Compare—*obair*, work; *oibrich*, to operate, work.

Then the Manx:

Buitch, witch; pl. *buitchyn*; *Bouch-chrout* (from English *craft*), conjurer; *Buitcheragh*, witchcraft (2 Chron. xxxiii. 6); *Buidseach*, *Buitseach* (Gaelic), *m*, and *f*, a witch, wizard; *Bana bhuidseach*, a she witch; *Buidseachd*, a charm, witchcraft; *Buitseachas* (Irish), witchcraft; *Cuir buitseachd*, to conjure.

Faaishneyder (Manx), wizard, juggler; and *Spyrrydyn faishnee* & *fir faishnee* (2 Kings xxi. 6); *Faaishnys*, charm; *Fiosaiche* (Gaelic), conjurer, and *ban fhiosaiche*; *Fiosachd*, sorcery, divination, fortune telling; *Faisdineagh* (Irish), wizard, soothsayer; *Cran faistire*, sorcery by casting lots; *Cranchar fiseogach*, magical divination.

Fer ysseree = *fer fysseree* (Manx), sorcerer.

*Cailleach** ny ghuesagh* (Manx), the hag or witch of spells; *Cailleach vear*,† sends destructive tempests; *Cailleach ny faitheag*, prophetess, witch.

Pisag,‡ spell, conjuration, amulet; *Piseach* (Gaelic), success, increase, good luck to you; *Piseach mhath ort*, good luck to you; *Piseagaiche*, sorcerer; *Piseog* (Irish), witchcraft; *Piosage*, sorcery, witchcraft, probably from:

Pios (Gaelic), a piece, bit, fragment, a splinter, morsel; *Piseag*, a rag, fragment of cloth, whether old or new. (Armstrong's *Gaelic-English Dictionary*.)

Then we have the Manx:

Guesag, spell, charm; *Giseag* (Gaelic), charm; *geasag*, *Gisreag* and *gis* or *geis*, enchantment, vow, prayer; *Geasan*, an oath, charm, sorcery; *Geis* (Irish), incantation, charm, a custom; *Geasa*, divination, religious vow,§ oath, charm, guess; *Geasan*, oath, vow; *Geas*, conjuration, prayer; Compare: *geis*, to divine, guess. German, *wissen*. *gradh ghiseag* (Gaelic), philter.

Also:

Rhusagh (Manx), amulet; *Rosad, Rosachd* (Gaelic), enchantment, charm, mischance, fatuity; *Raidseachas*, enchantment, prating; *Raidseach*, chief witch; *Rossachd* (Irish), charm, enchantment.

Compare:

raidse (Gaelic), a prater; *raite*, gibberish; *Duilgarnee, Doalgaarhee* (Manx), a charm, a darkness cast upon the eyes by witchcraft or to see everything double; *Dallaran* (Gaelic), a bewildered person; and *dolbh*, witchcraft; *dall*, dazzle, to blind; *doille*, blindness.

* *Cailleach* originally meant a devotee, but afterwards a female disciple or nun, and finally descended in meaning to an old woman.

† See Stewart, p. 542.

‡ See Douglas Hyde's *Beside the Fire*, 1890. Story of Bran, p. 17: "Who made a fawn of her? Oh, how do I know. It was with some of their *Pishtrogues*."

§ See ditto, "Tale of the King of Ireland's Son," p. 21. He put him under *gassa* and (mystic) obligations, *cur fuoi geasaibh* (Irish), *cuir fo gheasaibh* (Gaelic).

91. WITCHCRAFT (2)

We have another Manx charm:

A Charm against the Fairies.
Shee Yee as shee ghooinney,
Shee Yee er Columb-Killey,
Er dagh uinnag, er dagh ghorrys,
Er dagh howl goaill stiagh yn Re-hollys,
Er kiare corneillyn y thie,
Er y voayl ta mee my lhie,
As shee Yee orrym-pene.

Peace of God and peace of man,
Peace of God on Columb Killey,
On each window and each door,
On every hole admitting moonlight,
On the four corners of the house,
On the place of my rest,
And the peace of God on myself.

The above charm seems to be long forgotten, not remembered by the oldest people in Island. It is, of course, not confined to Isle of Man; we have it mentioned in *Guy Manering* in another form. Meg Merrilies, at the birth of the hero, breaks out, singing:

Trefoil, vervain, John's wort, dill,
Hinders witches of their will,
Weel is them that weel may
Fast upon St Andrew's Day.

Saint Bride and her brat,
Saint Colme and his cat,
Saint Michael and his spear,
Keep the house frae reif and wear.

Also in the *Songs of Scotland*, by Allan Cunningham, 1825, vol. i, p. 139, we have the spell:

Who sains the house to-night?
They that said it ilka night,
Saint Bryde and her brat,
Saint Colme and his bat,
Saint Michael and his spear,
Keep this house from the weir.

And on New Year's Eve (*Oidehe Challuin*) of which see description in my *Manx Folk Lore*, i, p. 180.* Macgregor gives the rhyme in. Gaelic and English that was sung on that occasion:

Mor phiseach air an tigh.
Piseach air an teaghlach.
Piseach air gach cabar is air gach ni saoghalt' ann
Piseach air eich a's crodh.
Piseach air na caoraich.
Piseach air h'uile ni.
S'piseach air ar maoin uil.'
Piseach air beann an tighe.
Piseach air na paistean.
Piseach air gach caraide.
Mor phiseach agus slaint d'huibh.

Good luck to the house.
Good luck to the family.
Good luck to every rafter to every worldly thing in it.
Good luck to horse and cattle.
Good luck to the sheep.
Good luck to everything.

Good luck to all your means.
Good luck to the good wife.
Good luck to the children
Good luck to every friend
Good fortune and health to all.

Which approaches the Manx wish very closely in substance; perhaps the rhyme may have been sung in Man in olden times at a similar occasion and accompanied by the same ceremonies as described by Macgregor in his *Highland Superstitions*.

* *Yn Lioar Manninagh*, 1897.

92. AMULETS, ETC.

Comparative list of derivations:

Sheean (Manx), a charm, fortune; *Seun Sian* (Gaelic), amulet, charm to make a warrior invulnerable, good luck, prosperity; *Scun* (Irish), a charm for protection, prosperity; *Swyn* (Welsh), a charm remedy, cure, medicine; *Swyno*, to charm, bless; *Sweyn serch*, a love charm; *Sion cloch buaidh* (Gaelic), stone of virtue, power, a germ, charm.

Compare—*Seinn* (Gaelic), chant, warble; and *Sian*, to raise one's voice gradually; *Sion*, a scream, roar, voice; incantation, invocation.

Orradh (Gaelic), a superstitious charm; *Orraidheachd*, superstitious ceremonies, enchantment (Armstrong); *Orra*, amulet; *Orraghan* (Irish), charms, enchantment.

Compare also Irish: *Urra*, strength, power; *Ortha*, prayer, charm.

Compare—*Oraid*, prayer.

The amulet was worn round the neck or stitched in plaid or shirt and hose, or attached to the bonnet or cap

In Gaelic* we have the *Orra graidh*, an amulet to provoke unlawful love; *Orra chomais*, an amulet to deprive virility, &c.

And lastly, the Manx: *Croshag* (the cross), the great Christian Talisman against Heathenism with all its evil spirits and powers.

The above comparison and analysis will help to follow the evolution of the various contrivances in the working of the charms.

* See *M'Alpine's Gaelic-English Dictionary* for a long and curious enumeration of these charms.

93. PRAYERS

Gregor* informs us that "there was a class of people whose curses, or as they were commonly called, prayers, were much dreaded, and every one used the greatest caution lest they might call forth their displeasure. To do so was to bring down their prayers, and disaster of some kind or other soon fell on those who had been so unfortunate as to fall under their anger, according to the nature of the prayer." A parallel to this is afforded in the Manx *guee*, which not only means to pray, intreat, but also to imprecate and to curse; they piously differentiate the latter, however, by writing it *gwee*. In Gaelic we have *guidhe* = entreaty, curse, and the verb *guidh* to pray and imprecate; and to distinguish the prayer from the curse, they have *daoch guidhe* = (bad prayer) = imprecation. There was malevolent and benevolent praying, and as Principal Rhys well puts it:† "The fact that a curse is a species of prayer, a prayer for evil to follow, is well exemplified in Manx by *gwee*, meaning both kinds of prayer; and Kelly thinks he has done a fine thing by printing *guee*, 'prayer,' and *gwee*, 'cursing.'" In Welsh we also find *gweddio* for pray, &c.

* See *Folklore of North East of Scotland*, p. 35.
† See *Folklore*, March, 1892: "Manx Folklore," by Prof. Rhys, p. 86.

94. CHARMS

Ghaw Ving.—Between Fleshwick Bay and Bradda Head there is a "Castle" Rock, called Cashtal Rackley, or Beckley, and at its outside is a cave, Ghaw Ving, so named on account of the echo that it produces. I have no doubt that it has been a place where the old Manx repeated charms. When an infant was sick, and thinking it would die, they used to go to the Ghaw Ving for it, and repeat:

Ghaw ving, Ghaw ving,
Cur jeed yn troo;
Va'n lhiannoo ching jea,
As bee eh ny share jiu.

Ghaw ving, Ghaw ving,
Put off the envy;
The child was sick yesterday,
And it will be better to-day.

We have a similar account from the old fishing village of Runswick, in the North Riding of Yorkshire, near Whitby. There one of the Hobs is still said to haunt a cave, called the Hobcave. Anxious and superstitious mothers brought their ailing little ones, and as they stood at the mouth of the caves, cried:

Hob, my bairn's gettent kinkcough,
Takkt oft, takkt off!

It is evidently of Norse origin. The Manx *cughtagh* is an evil spirit "whose abode was in caves by the sea, and whose voice was the coughing and whispering of the wavelets." It seems to me that the Manx charm was addressed to this *cughtagh*, which apparently corresponds to the Yorkshire *hob*. In Gaelic *cogair* = to whisper, listen, and *coig* = a secret, mystery, council, advice. In the Scottish we have *cow* or *kow** = bugbear, hobgoblin; hence *bu-kow* and *cowman* = devil.

* See *Jamieson's Scottish Dictionary*.

95. CREAMING THE WELL

In the first part of My Folklore (vol. iii, part iv, pp. 162–63) I gave a short note about a witch going to a running stream and muttering a charm, *"Bainney as eem yn dooinney shoh doys,"* to increase her supply of milk and butter. Gregor* gives an account of a similar procedure from Aberdeenshire, which seems to supplement and amplifiy the Manx version. He says:

> Such as were envious of their neighbour's success, and wished to draw away their prosperity, creamed the well they drew water from. This act was believed to be particularly efficacious in ensuring a rich supply of milk and butter to the one who had cows, and performed the act on the well of those who also owned cows. All the utensils used in the dairy were washed with part of the cream of the well, and the cows received the remainder to drink. It was gone through in some districts on the last night of the year. In a fishing village a handful of grass was plucked and thrown into the pail containing the water.

In the Isle of Man the woman dipped a *cushag* in the stream, and sprinkled herself and all around her with water.

* See *Notes on Folklore of the North-East of Scotland*, by Rev. W. Gregor, Lond., 1881, p. 159.

96. TO THE EDITOR

Dear Sir,—I note that some people say some of the nursery rhymes mentioned by me from Cregneish are also found in English nursery rhyme books. That is true enough, still I must mention them, as they have found a permanent soil in the Island, and it illustrates simply how much the Manx have borrowed from the Lancashire race and adopted their ways. The comparative folklorist requires these references for showing the distribution of this lore outside England. I have not given anything which is superfluous. The people who spoke to you don't know what the point is; besides, I have finished the nursery rhymes. I have also to constantly illustrate Manx matter with similar lore outside the Isle of Man. The Island is simply a link, and has nothing which can be claimed as being only of Manx original growth, and comparative method illuminates the matter considerably, and also makes it more instructive. It is done moreover to show Manx collectors how and what to collect to help the science of Insular Folklore.

Yours, &c.

C. ROEDER.

97. THE FAIRY DOCTRESS

There used to be a wise old woman living near St John's, who was making charms against witchcraft, and curing many things with herbs and charms. There was a couple that had been married many years, but had no family, and they were getting old at the time when a young couple went to live with them. When their first baby was born, the young wife was nearly out of her mind, for she saw this childless woman coming to the bedside times in the night, and pulling the baby away from her. She got her husband to lie the floor side but she was little better; so the man consulted this wise old woman, and she went to gather some herbs, and when she came back she said it was the woman living in the house with them, and that she did not wish them any harm, but that she coveted the baby, that was the cause of her spirit coming in the night, when her body was asleep, and she did not know anything about it. The fairy woman gave him some herbs, and told him to boil them a certain time, and wash the baby in some of the water, and to sprinkle the mother and the bed with some of the water, and then to empty the whole of the water and herbs that remained in a running stream, and he did all she told him to do and the mother and child got on very well, and she never saw the woman coming to the bedside nor pulling the baby away after that.

98. CHARM TO PROTECT HORSE AND PLOUGH

The old farmers—now very long ago—the first day they were taking the horses out to plough, used to get a bucket of *chemerly* (*chamberlye*, or *mooin*), and put some hen's dung in it, and stir it for some time, and then sprinkle the horses and the plough with it. That was the charm against witchcraft and the evil eye.

99. THE CABBYL USHTEY

The *Cabbyl Ushtey*, or Water Kelpie, or Water Wraith, and the *Each Uisge* of the Western Highlands, was a creature that was thought to be of an amphibious nature, inhabiting deep pools, rivers, and lakes, and believed to be the "foul thief" himself. At times he appears to the belated traveller on the lonesome road, and invites him by various allurements to mount him, when he rushes off into the curraghs, or stream, and carries the rider to his death. To catch and overpower him you have to cast over his head a bridle, as Harper* sings:

Stout Samson hands the magic tether,
Stuck round wi' sprigs o' holy Yarrow,
Woodbine, an' rawntree, an' rosemary;
Wi' hern-fern frae the ditches,
Emetics dire for deils and witches;
And now they draw a circle round him,
And wi' some potent speeches sound him.

In Scotland he turned into an old man with long grey hair and beard.† In the Island he is known besides as the night horse (*cabbyl ny hoie*), and appears invariably in the shape of a gray colt or horse. It is this colour which has led the Manx to call him also the *Glashtin*, derived from *glas* = gray. In consequence he is often confused with the *Glashan*, who has absolutely *nothing* to do with the water horse. Here are some of his reported lurking-places:

At Surby, where be generally makes for the Curraghs, his supposed headquarters.

At Ballure Glen, near Ramsey.

His transformation into a gray man or woman, as in Scotland, has not been noticed in the Island, and further local instances of his occurrence are very desirable.

In Sweden, the vulgar are afraid of his power. There he is called the *Nekr*, or *Vatna Hestr*, and ferrymen warn those who are crossing dangerous places in some rivers never to so much as mention his name, lest they should meet with a storm and be in danger of losing their lives. In these places formerly, during the times of paganism, those who sailed, worshipped *Nekr*, their sea deity, as it were, with a sacred silence for the reasons already given, for he exercised his dominion over the wind and waves.‡ This I may remark, in passing, may account for the absolute interdiction observed by the Manx fishermen to whistle while out at sea.

A bit of Norse folklore in the Island seems to be found near Laxey, on the Ballacowin stream, where we have a haunted dub or pool, called Nigison or Nikison, probably the residence of a water *nixie*.

* *Fruits of Solitary Hours*, by Alex. Harper, Aberdeen, 1852, p. 62.

† Gregor, *Folklore of N.E. Scotland*, p. 66.

‡ See *Jamieson's Scot. Dictionary, sub nomen.*

100. LHIANNAN SHEE

It is translated in the Manx Bible (Deut. xviii. 11) as 'familiar spirit.' We have it also in the Highlands and Ireland, and it occurs under three headings; a "familiar or guardian angel," as "sweetheart and love," and as "nightmare." We have the former on record in Man:

The *Lhiannan shee* of Ballafletcher (Kirk Braddan), the cup which the family held was dedicated to her, to break it would be deemed a catastrophe to the owner. It is the same as the legend of the famous Luck of Edenhall.

As a fairy wife we find her:

In Glendowin, where a man lived with her.

In Struan dy snail, in the shape of a white woman.

Near Port Erin Chapel, going up the gate to the mountain.

At Surby, where she is chasing a man in the shape of his wife.

At Kentraugh Bridge, where the man only gets rid of her by saying: "If you don't tell me who you are I'll make a sacrifice of you, by God," when she grins and is gone like a flash of lightning.

At Ballahick, near Ballasalla, where she follows the man over land and sea.

101. THE DOOINNEY OIE, OR NIGHTMAN,

Of the Manx peasantry constitutes a kind of tutelar spirit, attached to certain families, and the fore-warner of coming ill-fortune or calamity. McAlpine speaks of a Highland caointeach (from *caoin* = wail, cry), a female water kelpie, who gives warning to her favourite clans of the approach of death in the family by weeping and wailing, opposite the kitchen door. It is to be hoped that further instances of the *dooinney oie* may be put on record in the Island, along with his precise haunts.

102. THE TARROO USHTEY

Is a harmless creature, which mixes and breeds with the farmer's cattle, known by its sparkling eyes and short ears. It prefers swampy places and streams. It has been noticed formerly:

At Ramsey, in a pool now occupied by the Promenade.

At Slegaby.

Ballakilpherick.

Cregneish.

and should be found to abound in other places over the Island.

In the Highlands McAlpine* notices a fairy bull, called *Corc*, and the *laogh corcach*, "a calf, having small ears like his father the *Corc*." It seems derived from *corcach*, Gaelic and Irish = a moor, marsh, English car—their usual habitat. Perhaps it may point to an ancient wild and indigenous race of cattle.

* See *Gaelic-English Dictionary*, 1877.

103. THE BUGGANE

The Buggane is a creature of which the Manx peasantry stood always in great fear and trepidation. It was scarcely safe to venture abroad by night, for he strolled about the lonely lanes, roads, cross roads, stiles, and churchyards at the outskirts, and hillsides. He would chase, obstruct, and threaten the traveller, and timely flight, an ejaculatory prayer, or retreat across the hedge-banks, where his power apparently ceased, was one's only salvation. The shock he gave to the victim was such that generally it prostrated him for months, or even caused the person's death; occasionally it permanently unsettled his disturbed mind. He and the *good people* made their lives very uncomfortable. The belief is not quite died out yet in the more secluded parts. The *Bugganes* have suffered the same secular fate as the *Glashtins* and *Glashans, etc.*, and have become considerably mixed up. They are of different complexion, and have to be separated, to introduce clearness:

(1) We have the *Buggane* connected with the old keeils and chapels; their chief occupation at these Christian places of worship is to obstruct their erection, or to remove the material, and pull down over-night what has been built up by day, as:

The *Buggane of Keeil Pharick y drummagh* * who is a demon with a big head, long arms, big body, sharp claws and cloven feet. Saint Patrick made this devil ride across from Ireland with the timber, when the timber and the walls were put up, he pulled it down again, also:

The *Buggane of Keeil Saint Trinian* (or Ringian), who was as black as ebony, and covered with wrinkles, alluded to already by Grosse in 1774. He also tossed the roof off, as soon as it was on, with a loud fiendish laugh of satisfaction. He had, as at Keeil Pharick, an encounter with a tailor† who dared him. The latter seated himself in the chancel and began a pair of breeches, in which situation the "old chap" found him when he paid his regular obstructive visit. The tailor kept his eyes close to his work and escaped with his life. At the end the Buggane lifts his great head from his body and hurls it after him.

The whole host of these boggles march, run, and jump, or hang about cairns, tumuli, stone circles, churchyards, stiles, cross roads and lanes, *etc.*

(2) We have *Bugganes* connected with the sea-caves, as at the Ghaw ny Spyrryd, near the Sound of the Calf; his head is like a big pot, with three great horns. The *Buggane y Chione dhoo*, at Black Head; his head is like a big horse, his eyes like pewter plate.

And these Manx *bugganes*, now described, go about, galloping, clanging, making all sorts of unearthly noises, rattling chains, howling, roaring, wearing horns, and with their glaring, blazing eyes, goggling and frightening you to death.

To make a little advance in our notions of the nature and origin of the Buggane we must go a little further into the examination of the roots. We have the:

Gaelic: *Bochdainn* ‡ = *Old Nick*, as in the phrase *tha bhochdainn ort* = the devil is in you; gun gabh a bhochdainn = plague take you. Also *bochdan* = apparition, hobgoblin; *bocan* = ghost, bogle.

Irish: *bocan, boc, poc* = he-goat, buck, spirit.

Welsh: *bwgan, bwg* = bock, hobgoblin; *pwca* = fiend.

Compare the strange looking man with the Welsh *y gwr drwg* = the bad man, or evil one; and the *yr ysbryd drwg;* the Manx *drog spyrryd*, and *noid ny hanmey* = the evil spirit, and the enemy of the soul.

And let us remember also that the early Christian missionaries, who were familiar with the Pagan semi-human *satyrs* (half-goat, half-abhorred imp), the better to oppose heathenish rites and creeds, connected and presented the devil with, and in the shape of, a cloven-footed, horned, and black shaggy, goggle-eyed he-goat.

The evolution of the *Buggane* has a historical background, he is a reality: but we have to go back to a much earlier stage of religious development; and a comparison with the ceremonies and rites of modern savages, and their medicine men, *etc.*, will facilitate our comprehension.

At all great and particular occasions, the chief, the medicine-doctor, and the great men *etc.*, of the tribe, appeared in "full gala," dressed in gorgeous, imposing style; assuming animal garb and form, with moveable counterfeits super-imposed;§ shouting, howling, singing, and dancing the while. The Goidels and Teutons were no exception—names only changed, and the Druids and their privileged corporations continued the same observances, and the mediæval mummeries, morris dancings, and our modern pantomimes and carnival are but relics of a by-gone religious phase.

The Manx *bugganes* come out clearer into view at the dawn of Christianity, when they came into violent clash with a new set of religious ideas; here it was a struggle between Druidism and Rome. We see them do quite the same thing as the old medicine-men, *etc.*, the old *Buggane* (Druid) of *Keeil Pharick* and *Trinian* pulls his head off in a rage, he has cloven feet and horns, he roars and shouts. All the *Bugganes* swarm, and move about, assuming the shape of animals; ever growing larger and larger (an old trick); they are painted to increase terror and frighten Christian converts and proselytes; and to heighten the effect they bang and shout most unearthly. We naturally find them mostly in the neighbourhood of old *keeils*, cairns, churchyards, cross-roads, stone circles and tumuli.

The second class are the *cave-bugganes*, and *felches* or *ghosts*, of which the Island has many tales. These are the *detached* ghosts which appear after death. There are various reasons assigned for their appearance. Murdered persons come again to haunt their murderers, persons who had hid any treasures were doomed to haunt the place where it was concealed, and those who died with any heavy crimes on the conscience, not confessed. These latter of course, although popularly classified with the buggane proper, are compounds.

* See My Folklore, part i, p. 140

† Why the tailor was held in fear and dislike: He made the clothes which the savage men despised, clad as they were in skin and fur; they did not desire to be domesticated, which made them forfeit their liberty and roving life.

‡ See Armstrongs *Gaelic-English Dictionary.*

§ On the last day of Yule, the *Laare vane*, or white mare mummery, was performed in the island, even within recent years. This was a horse's head, and so contrived that the person who had charge of it and concealed under a white sheet, was able to snap the mouth at the guests. In Scotland the man dressed himself, however, in a cow's hide on New Year's Day, and went from house to house, saying: "God bless this house, and the cattle, stones, and timber belonging to it." Each neighbour then pulled off a piece of the hide and burnt it for driving away disease! The magical druid-medicine man again! changed into a *buggane.*

104. QUERY

The undersigned desires to be informed where the old spinning wheels were manufactured: also whether any of these picturesque household machines are at present in practical use in the Island, and if so—where?

A. CANNAN.

105. THE GLASHAN, OR MANX BROWNIE

Of these we seem to have in the Island two distinct sets, the semi-domesticated and the roaming or wild *Glashan*. The former attaches himself to the farmer and his stead, and good-naturally assists him, for little, in his labour; while the other, more sullen and intractable, and a rather savage specimen, roams at large, haunting and preferring the lonely glens, caves, and moorland shelters. Both have this in common that they are big powerful men, very hairy and shaggy, and dark complexioned, who disdain (for they wear, of course, skins, and grow long hair) the offer of cap, coat, shirt, and breeches. Of their local distribution our information is yet very meagre and limited. Of the first class we may mention:

The Glashans of North Barrule, who gather and drive in the straggling sheep.

The Glashans of Ballachrink, who thresh.

The Glashans of Bradda, who dry the grain in the kiln.

The Glashans of Cregneish, who dry the grain in the kiln.

And of the latter order I may name:

The Glashans in the North, savage women snatchers.

The Glashans in Glen Narradale, big, silent unclad fellows who, dog-like, follow the farmer.

The Glashans at Ballachrink, where the local Glashans are thrown into contact with a number of alien Glashans.

There were *he* and *she* Glashans. The domesticated sort were attached and grateful, but considered very stupid and clumsy. In the Highlands we have:

The *Glaislich*, a she and he giant that haunt the hilly coast of Invernesshire.*

Another *Brownie* was:

The *Gruaghach*, who haunted Skipness Castle—a supernatural female, doing jobs about the house for the maids, and living in the ruins until driven away by the offer of a cap and coat,† and the *Gruagach* = the hairy, uncouth fellow in Argyleshire who repeated a rhyme over the clothes;† furthermore the female brownie, to which the Highland dairymaids made frequent libations of milk.‡ The Irish *Gruagach* = a giant enchanter; otherwise *Browny*, a hairy,§ alluded to also by Kennedy as the *Gruagach* (*Graoch* in Breton) from *gruag* = the hair of the head; Manx, *gruag*.

Meg Mullach, the hairy Meg, a diminutive brownie, a hairy creature in the family of Grant of Tullochgorum.

The *Mailleachan*, the young brownie of the Irish and Highlanders.

The *Uruisg*, a brownie (*brunaidh*) that haunted lonely dells, moorland lakes and waterfalls. At harvest time he hovered at farm yards, stables, and houses, and especially the dairy; every manor and family had its *uruisg*, and in the kitchen was a seat left unoccupied for him. He performed many exploits in kitchen, barn, and stable without reward, and if offered any, left.

Then we have the:

Shetland domestic *Trow*, or *Brownie*, who attended on almost every family, and who during the night would thresh, brew, churn, grind corn, or milk, or sweep the house; but it was requisite to offer for each night's work a little wort or cream, *etc.* This would ensure good ale and butter, and preserve the stacks in the storm, *etc.*¶

And corresponding to these:

The *Hob-thrust* of Rayscar, in the Fylde, who housed the grain and got the horses ready for the farmer.

The *Hob* of the Gorge of Cliviger, a savage hirsute being.

The North Lancashire *Throb-thrush*, a domesticated brownie, who left, on receiving a coat and hood;‖ and the *Throb-thrush* of Millom, in Westmoreland,** a brownie who had his regular range of farmhouses. His only reward was a quart of milk porridge. He sheaved the grain, and did all the farm work. He left when "throb-thrush," as he sang, "had got a new coat and a new hood, and he'll never do more good."

The *Glashan* seems to have derived his name from the root *glass*†† = grey or pale, as in the Manx *neeal ghlass* = a pale complexion; a description which is also applied to the *Glashtin* or water-horse (from its grey colour), hence the confusion which has arisen between the two. We know that the Manx *Glashan* had black shaggy hair and a pale complexion, and was a muscular, tall fellow. All these comparative examples point, no doubt, to the existence of an older prehistoric race of people, scattered across the country long before the intrusive historic Celt or Saxon arrived! representing a rude, uncouth, fur or skin-clad, and physically strong people, which still survived in small numbers in the more inaccessible upland and moorland districts, dwellers of the glens and eaves, and lingering by tarn and stream; a view already urged by Campbell (see *Tales of the Western Islands*, vol. i, 101), who groups the *Gruagach, Glashan, Bucan, bodach*, and *fuath* as survivals of half-tamed savages, that hung about the pastoral homesteads. They were naturally enough looked upon as giants, enchanters, evil spirits, apparitions, and supernatural beings.

* *Highland Superstitions*, by Stewart, 1825, p. 542.

† *Popular Tales of the West Highlands*, by J.F. Campbell, 1860, vol. i, p. 23.

‡ Armstrong, *Gaelic-English Dictionary*.

§ O'Reilly, *Irish-English Dictionary*.

¶ See Caton, *The History and Description of Shetland Islands*, 1838, p. 115.

‖ See *Goblin Tales of Lancashire*, by James Bowker, London, n.d.

** *Westmoreland as it was* by J. Briggs, 1825.

†† In German folklore we have also the *Graumännel* (= *grey* little men).

106. THE FINNODDEREE

The *Finnodderee* has to be kept distinct from the *Glashan*, or Manx *Brownie*. He has a strange and wonderful pedigree of his own, unequalled in the folk-history of the Island, and has been the puzzle and despair of Manx folklorists. In order to get at him we must dissect the most reliable accounts. The preciscest description is related by Cumming:*

A farmer who was erecting a homestead on the mountains had determined on possessing (1) a large quartz block lying on a neighbouring shore which resisted all his efforts at removal. The *Finnodderee* conveyed it one night to the desired spot.

To reward him the farmer caused a few articles of clothing to be laid for him in his usual haunt at Ballathoar, in Ballaugh. The hairy sprite took up the garments, one by one, and thus expressed his wounded feelings:

(2) Cap for the head—alas poor head,
Coat for the back—alas poor back,
Breeches for the breech—alas poor breech,
If these be all thine, thine cannot be
(5) The merry Glen of Rushen.
    (Between South Barrule and Dalby mountains.)

Quiggin (*Guide to the Isle of Man*):
(3) He is covered like a he-goat with shaggy hair, (4) he has been known to mow the grass of a large meadow in a single night; (1) he has carried huge stones of many tons weight from the bottom of the lowest valleys to the top of the highest hills, and placed them as corner stones to mansions about to be erected.

Quiggin (a later edition):
The Big Boggane or Finnodderee (3) has thick hair as black as India rubber, he can (5) lie in the dark caves of South Barrule (and Snaefell) without bed, he would (4) thrash out the whole stack of the farmer in a single night, if by misfortune it had remained unthrashed until Candlemas; if left by laziness, be would scatter it to the winds.

Moore (*Folklore*, pp. 55–56):
A gentleman wanting to build a large house, a little above the base of Snaefell mountain, at a place called Tholt-e-Will, had the stone quarried on the beach, but (1) one immense block of white stone he wanted, could not be moved from the spot. To his surprise, not only this block, but likewise the whole of the quarried stones of more than a hundred cart loads were in one night conveyed to the site by the Finnodderee.

He also (4) cut down and gathered meadow grass which would have been injured by the coming storm. Once a farmer complaining he had not cut it close enough, the following year the farmer cut it himself, but the Finnodderee went after him, stubbing up the roots so fast that the farmer scarcely escaped having his legs cut of by the angry Finn at St. Trinian's Church, Marown.

It is said (4) he borrowed a sickle and cut down two fields of corn in the parish of Bride in one night.

In an old Manx song:
    The Finnodderee went to the meadow,
    To lift the dew at gray cock-crow,
    The maidenhair, and the cattle herb,
    He stamped them under both his feet.
    The scythe he had was cutting everything,

Skimming the meadow to the sods;
And if a leaf was left standing
He stamped it down with his heels.

A pendant to (4) is found in the *Popular Rhymes of Berwickshire*,† it says:

Crawshaws in Berwickshire was once the abode of an industrious Brownie, who both saved the corn and thrashed it for several seasons. At length, after one harvest, some person thoughtlessly remarked the corn was not well mowed, or piled up in the barn. He took offence, and the next night threw the whole of the corn over the Raven Crag, a precipice about two miles off, muttering:

It's no weel mowed! it's no weel mowed!
Then it's ne'er be mowed by me again.
I'll scatter it o'er the Raven stone,
And they'll hae some wark ere its mowed again.

Now we have to split up the *Finnodderee* into his component parts, and by

(1) He is a powerful, strong giant, who can lift and transport immense rocks and huge blocks of stone from the valley to the highest mountain top.

(2) He deserts the farmer when he is offered a reward cap, coat, and breeches.

(3) He is covered, like a he-goat, with shaggy, thick, black hair.

(4) He cuts down and gathers the meadow grass for the farmer, but if the latter finds fault with him, in his rage and fury he scatters the crop to the winds, or stamps it down; he also lifts the dew at gray cock-crow and the maiden-hair and the cattle-herb (*luss ny ollee*); the latter useful for sores in the mouth of cattle and thickening of the milk; robbing the farmer of his curative and useful herbs, and collecting the dew at gray cock-crow for some charm for evil.

(5) He lies in the dark eaves of South Barrule, in the merry Glen of Rushen (the pass to South Barrule), and also on Snaefell mountain, on the upland hills—the home of the giant; or he is seen in the valleys and flat-lands hanging about farms; at Ballathoar and near churches, in the round field close to St. Trinian's Church.

The *Finnodderee* is called occasionally *Finn* in the South of the Island; the *Finn* is also a giant in Norway:‡

The Manx Bible translators (see Isaiah xiii. 21, and xxxiv. 14) in their attempt to coin a suitable and good Manx equivalent for the *Satyr*, apply the term *Finnodderee* (they give it in the fanciful form of *Phynnodderee*); while the Irish translation for want of a substitute retains *Saitir*, and the Gaelic gives us *daoine fiadhaich* = wild men; and Luther in his German version uses *Feldgeister* and *Kobold* = field boggles and hobgoblins.

The bearing of all this, the next chapter will show.

* See *Guide to the Isle of Man*, by the Rev. J.G. Cumming, London, 1861, p. 23.
† Quoted in *The Goblin Tales of Lancashire*, by James Bowker, London, p. 247.
‡ See *History of Christian Names*, by Miss Younge, 1863, p. 71.

107. WHO THE FINNODDEREE REALLY WAS, AND WHAT BECAME OF HIM IN AFTER-LIFE

We are enabled now to perceive what composite being he really is:

(1) shows him to be a powerful giant.

(2) Our old friend the *Glashan*, the good natured and hard working Brownie, who loves to hover about the farmstead, and for whom—the half-civilized creature—the farmer has a great partiality.

(3) Proves him to partake of the *Buggane* or *Satyr.*

(4) Is another genus of the Brownie group, more erratic in his habits, a cross-grained, ill-tempered fellow, uncontrollable in his rage and spitefulness, and more closely related to the Scandinavian *troll,* and little brought under the domination of civilization.

But who is the powerful giant?

He is the same giant mentioned in the legend of the enchanted Manx king, where in the devil's den, at the foot of South Barrule, he keeps bound, by magic spells, a great prince, and is one of the giants inhabiting Castle Rushen "till the days of Merlin'; he is transformed by tradition into *Goddard Crovan,** who, it runs, lived with his termagent wife in a great castle on the top of Barrule, and down in the valley of St Mark's lies the famous granite boulder, weighing 20 to 30 tons, which be hurled after her in his temper, when he could bear her tongue no longer. The same giant keeps spell-bound in his castle at Rushen no other than Godred Crovan (1095), as I shall show later on. But this is not all: he turns out to be Finn's cook, Eaoeh, who with his witch-wife, Ada, dwelt in Fin's Castle on the top of Barrule, and the two Osianic Manx legends of Finn and Ossian declare him to belong to the heroic race of the mighty Finns—great Norwegian Vikings and freebooters—he is, what must be perfectly clear now, Gorree, or Finn Gorree himself, the mischievous destroyer of Brugh Farola, who set fire to the castle, and shutting in all the women of the lions, thus extirpating the clan—a thing not wholly unknown in the history of the Highlands. He is executed with the magic sword, Mac an Luinn.

Passing to the analysis of the word itself, is it composed of the two roots Finn and Gudrodar, which finally crumbled down to Godrod, Godrod, Gareth, Gorree, and Orry. In Manx phonology and mutation the word, of course, became *Finn-Odderree*. We can follow now the stages through which Gorree passed:

(1) A member of the Fions living in their Castle of Barrule.

(2) A *Glashan.*

(3) A *Buggane.*

(4) A *Troll.*

(5) Falling into the handsof the Bible translators, a good makeshift for *Satyr;* and thrust into a shaggy he-goat, with glowing eyes, two horns and a tail, to serve the devout congregation—*sic transit gloria mundi!* And lastly we see him merged with Mannanan, Mac Leir, the great Island magician, who ruled on Barrule, wrapped in

mist and mystery, ages before him, and whose power in spells and charms tradition has lent to the Finnodderree subsequently.

 * In the legend of Goddard Crovan's Stone.

108. WHAT CAUSED THE DECOMPOSITION OF THE LEGEND
I think we can follow the various stages of transformation the conception of the *Finnodderree* underwent in the course of the succeeding centuries.

We have to consider the:

Norwegian rule (890–1270) for 380 years.

Scottish conquest (1271–1344) for 73 years.

English change of hands (1345–1406) for 65 years.

Lancashire or Stanley government and influence (1407–1765) for 360 years.

The story of the Finns and King Godred, their bold adventures and heroic feats and performance were to the Scandio-Manx household tales, during the early rule of the Viking race, forming the topic of entertainment many an evening at their hearth. With the baneful invasion of the Scotch and English contenders for the next 138 years, which was a time of oppression and extirpation, and being an alien people indifferent to insular traditions and institutions, the vestiges of the old folklore dwindled into oblivion, or became dimmed and confused, their vividness crumbling quickly away. Gorree became a misty giant and wizard, and was turned into a *Troll,* and *Glashan.* With the influx of the Lancashire men, 500 years after the Norseman set foot on the Isle, the trituration and dilutation of the legend had robbed it of its very essence, and produced a blurred counterfeit into which their *boggart* and the Manx *buggane* largely entered; but although he has been stripped of his original features, Celtic tenacity still clings to this day to the old Manx word of 1,000 years ago—his memory is still fresh in Manxland.

The legend entered clearly into Man from the North with the Norse who landed at the Lake, Lhane Mooar;* it left traces at Ballathoar (in Ballaugh); it firmly fixed itself on South Barrule; and we follow it finally to Castle Rushen.

 * In the North we have besides *Cashtal Ree Gorree.*

FOLKLORE FROM TOWNLEY'S JOURNAL (1791)
109. WEATHER RULE
There is an observation here, that when Mona's mountains wear dirty night caps in a morning, you may expect plenty of rain to wash them clean before night (p. 23, vol. i.).

110. BURNING THE WITCHES OUT
I took a walk up to the Head (Douglas) about eleven; the whole hill side was covered with nets, spread out to dry, and also to be mended. The dog fish (*gobbag*) had made terrible havoc the night before. Some of the men were industriously employed in

repairing the monstrous breaches made by that voracious species, some few were pulling dry ling, to exorcise their boats with, or burn the witches out of them. Their mode of doing it is as follows:

They set fire to a part of the heather, in the centre of the boat; then make wisps of the rest, and light them; one going to the bead, another to the stern, others along the sides, so that every part may be touched by the flame (15th Sept., 1789, vol. i, p. 197).

There was another burning of the witches out of an unsuccessful boat (last night) off Bank's How. The flames were very visible, to the top of the bay. Those witches that are so very mischievous, and play so many wayward tricks with poor fishermen, are undoubtedly desended from the famous Mannanan Mac Leir, *etc.* (25th Sept., 1789, vol. i, p. 207).

III. TREATING THE FAIRIES (1)
At every baking, and every churning, a bit of dough, and a bit of butter, is stuck upon the wall for the little folks. This custom still prevails very much amongst the country folks especially up in the mountains.

112. HUNTING THE WREN
St. Stephen's Day is distinguished here by a very strange custom: the hunting of the wren. Numbers assemble by daybreak, with long staffs, with which they beat the hedges and bushes, till they start one of those smart little birds from its evening retreat. They then pursue it with great shoutings, from bush to bush, till the little creature is so tired as to be taken by the hand or knocked down by the stick of one of its barbarous pursuers. It is then fixed upon the top of a long pole, to which is suspended a red handkerchief, by the way of a banner, and in that manner it is carried round the town in triumph—which serves as a pretext for begging money, or liquor, from the inhabitants.

If they can catch or kill the poor wren before sun-rising, they firmly believe that it ensures a good herring fishing the next season (26th Sept., 1789, vol. i, p. 311).

113. TREATING THE FAIRIES (2)
Whenever they eat anything, a small bit is always thrown away for the little fairies (1797). See *Journal of a Tour through North Wales and Isle of Man*, by the Duke and Duchess of Rutland, pub. 1805, p. 252.

114. A FOX-DAY
Observing upon the uncommon fineness and pleasantness of the day, for the month of January, to a farmer, he replied: "Yes, but he feared it would be only another fox-day; for there was a great hoar upon the ground, early in the morning, though very little frost." A fox-day is a very common expression in the Island, and by it, I believe,

they mean a single fair day, that is sure to be closely pursued by a rainy one (Townley, vol. ii, p. 50).

115. MURDERED WITCH

About two miles from Peel on the further side of the river, is an uncultivated hill, still haunted by the spirit of a murdered witch. She does not appear to mortal eyes, but every night joins her lamentations to the howling of the wind (*Wood's Isle of Man*, p. 159, 1808).

116. FAIRIES

While waiting at Port Erin for the departure of a herring boat, which was to convey me to the Calf, a fisherman introduced himself by warning me to take care of the fairies which I should meet there, tell me that he "had charms against their power." Another fisherman, who that morning had very civilly walked two miles out of his way to shew me the road, pretended to laugh at his companion, but upon being questioned seriously upon the subject, confessed his firm belief in them, He said his father once met with a crowd of them, and he was not a man to tell a lie (*Wood's Isle of Man*, p. 140).

117. ANNEXATION OF ISLE OF MAN, 1765

Saturday, June 1, 1765. The English colours were hoisted on the Castle in the Isle of Man, the sovereignity of that Island being now annexed to the Crown of Great Britain, and the inhabitants in every respect subjected to the laws, customs, and privileges of their fellow subjects.—*Gentlemen's Magazine.*

118. GREAT CATCH OF HERRING, 1765

"They write from the Isle of Man that they had on those coasts the greatest take of herrings that has been known for many years past, so that upwards of 20,000 barrels have been exported to foreign parts."—*Universal Magazine*, Feb. 8, 1765.

119. MANX-NAMED INNS IN LANCASHIRE, ETC.

The mention of the following inns is made in *Whitworth's Manchester Magazine*, February 18, 1755:

"To be lett, The Old Leggs of Man Inn, in Prescott, in Lancashire, lately kept by Mr Dumbell, and now in the hands of his widow."

March 15, 1757.—"The Sign of the Leggs of Man, in Prescott, the house of Henry Hatton."

May 17, 1787.—"The Legs of Man Inn, in the Market-place, Wigan" (*Manchester Mercury*).

The Three Legs Inn, in Leeds (June 24, 1766).

120. THOMAS HORTON, A FORMER GOVERNOR

Manchester, March, 22, 1757.—"On Friday, Thomas Horton, Esq., suddenly died at his house in Deansgate. He was formerly Governor of the Isle of Man, and has been many years in the Commission of the Peace, and one of the feoffees of the (Cheetham) College" (same paper).

121. SMUGGLING—APPLICATION TO PARLIAMENT IN 1757 TO STOP IT

Dublin, Nov. 29.—"We are credibly informed that application will be made to Parliament to have all smuggled teas, India goods, and spirits coming from the Isle of Man to be burned, spilled, and destroyed, as well as all ships, barges, wherries, and other craft; that our custom-house officers, informer, or any other person whatever, shall be allowed to dispose of any goods thus bought; but that on the contrary, no merchandise whatever that is smuggled, shall be exposed to sale; but that the officers, or the informer, shall be allowed 2s 6d in the pound for green tea and 1s 6d for Bohoa, that all shall be run or smuggled into this kingdom; and that no person whatever residing in the Isle of Man shall be at liberty to sue for any sum or sums of money, or upon any contract whatever that shall be made or agreed upon in the Isle of Man."—(*Whitworth's Manchester Advertiser*, 13th Dec., 1757.)

122. CAPTURE OF MANX VESSEL (DURING THE WAR BETWEEN ENGLAND AND FRANCE)

Liverpool, March 11, 1757.—"The Annondale, Ths. Dury, belonging to the Isle of Man, bound from Chester to this port, was taken within the limits of the harbour (Naples) by a French privateer; but is ordered to be cleared by the Government of Naples, and is now in quarantine."—(*Manchester Magazine.*)

123. FAIRIES

The Manx fairies are both big and small, have little eyes, and are agile and vindictive, if annoyed. They are generally dressed in green jackets, and red caps, but sometimes wear leather caps; they dislike evil smells such as *mooin*, and live in green hill sides, in the mountains, and forests, under human habitations, and sometimes in the tumuli. They are fond of hunting, and also fish in the glens and on the sea, and great lovers of music and dancing. Sometimes, if they can manage, they use men for their horses, into which they can change them. They kidnap and snatch human children and women, and are particular eager to capture fiddlers, whom they keep in their subterranean dwellings for their entertainments. They visit farmers at night time, and to keep them at peace and on friendly terms, every household has to leave them broken bread and victuals, *cowree* and clean water. They talk foreign languages. On the Mull a little fairy man, seen by a farmer, measured five to six inches high, without beard, he had a little pale face, and his ears were not larger than a shirt button. They also sport in the *trammon* trees, of which tree they are very partial, they have been seen banqueting, and at their musical festivals, and in stormy nights they have claimed the hospitality of the peasant. Although they are generally good natured and kind hearted people, still there are also very bad ones, whom one has to guard against with charms, as a preventive from their mischief and malice. Amongst these the most potent are: salt, iron, the cross, the Bible, iron tongues and knives, certain herbs and flowers, particular of yellow or blue and red colour, spread at the door and floor, and particularly so on Midsummer Eve. The *rowan* is also a great preservative, and affixed to the cottage, and so is the horseshoe; a red thread round the neck, secures the safety of the child, and a "God bless me," or "God preserve me," makes them helpless and powerless. They dislike the ringing of church bells. The Island has produced a rich store of fairy tales, and I have collected personally a great number, some of them perfect gems, and there is sufficient material waiting to make a splendid book, especially if well illustrated, of *Manx Fairy Tales*. The Manx call the fairies now mostly by the English name, *Ferrishyn*. The Lancashire word is *feorin*; of the dwarfs, distinguished as such, the Island knows nothing. The Norse or Danish word, *troll* has vanished. Neither have we in the Island any indication of the little *Clurican* of Co. Cork, or the *Lurigadaun* of Tipperary, and the *Leprechan* of Leinster. The tailor and "Beggar man," who used to travel from house to house, are our great story tellers of adventures and fairy tales in Mann, we often come across them in our tales.

124. A LITTLE FAIRY

It was in the last harvest time, two young chaps went about sunset to get the cows home. The cows were in a field near the mountain, and when they were driving them along the road they saw a little man, five or six inches high, walking before the cows' feet, and they hollowed to him to keep out of the way of the cows, but he took no notice, and kept going on just before the cows' feet. He was very small, and had no beard and a little pale face, and his ears were only as big as a shirt button, and they were a little bit afraid of him, little as he was. He was dressed in blue, and could walk as fast as the cows, but when he had come along before the cows, they got courageous, and proposed they would try to catch him, but when they were just going to lay hold of him, he spread the wings of his little coat, and rose up to the clouds, and was out of sight in a moment. He had very little feet and shoes, they said, and left no footprints on the dust of the road.

125. FAIRIES SPORTING IN THE TREES OF LHINGOWL

An old woman was telling me she and her daughter went down to the place in Ballachrink river, called Lhingowl, one fine summer evening to get the cows home, and the sun was not quite gone down, but was shining on the tops of the trees, and they heard a lot of folks talking in the trees. She could distinguish between young and old, beside the voices of children, and they seemed to have some sport, but she could not understand one word. They went to the spot where they were hearing the talk to try and get a sight of them, but when they got there they would hear them in another place, and they went to five or six different places, but never got a peep at them. When they got to the place where they were hearing the sport, the sport would be in the spot they had just left. And she said to her daughter that they had better drive the cows home, and get away as soon as possible, for it must be the fairies; and they got away, but could still hear them. She said she never liked to go down near Lhingowl again after that.

126. FAIRIES BANQUETING AND CUTTING UP BEEF

There is a house in Glenchass, which has the name of being haunted. The man who lived in it—an old sailor and a bachelor—one night, when sleeping in the cockloft, was awakened by a great noise in the kitchen. He got out of bed, and had at them, and saw a great many people there, and a great number of candles burning, and they had a long bench with a fine beef laid upon, and they were busy cutting the beef up, chopping with cleavers, and sawing with saws: but he did not say a word, but got into bed again. He was expecting all the furniture to be all smashed with the row they made, but everything was as he left them, and all the beef was taken away, and there was not even a stain of blood nor trace of their butchering to be seen.

127. FAIRY HUNTING PARTY

The fairies were hunting in Glenchass hill one fine night, and a man saw a great crowd coming over the cronk, and the dogs were coming in front, and when the dogs came to the stream of water, always running in the glen, they had a drink before crossing, and then the hunting party followed on horses, and some on foot, and they had all red hats on, but they could not tell whether their coats were black or green.

128. CALLING ON THE FAIRIES

A woman had a little baby, and he was very cross in the night, and one night he was crying she lifted him up and said: "Here fairies, take him"—to frighten him, and in a moment the bed was struck with some great club, which shook herself and husband and frightened them very much.

129. FAIRY VISITORS

The man that lived in the cottage in the heather up the Mull, had the fairies often coming in the house when the wife and himself were in bed, and playing, and dancing about the room, but they were not talking but very little when they were awake. They were very little people, but they could jump well. He was awake one night when they came in, and there was one big chap with them that night, and he saw the big fellow coming towards the bed, and he closed his eyes, and feigned to be asleep, and the fairy bent over him. Then he said to the company in Manx: "Ta'n ghenn chellagh ny chadley er aght erbee" ('The old cock is asleep anyway').

130. FAIRY VISITORS AGAIN

A man who was living in a house not far from the Chasms—but the house is taken away to mend hedges for some twenty years now said the fairies were coming in at the door in the evenings about sunset, as the wife and himself were sitting at the fire: they were like little boys about seven years of age, and they had leather caps on, they would be coming in and going out again, and some of them would come quite near to them at the fire, but they never did any mischief about his premises, and so he never molested them, but let them dance and jump as much as they pleased.

131. GOING WITH THE FAIRIES

It was said of a young chap that lived in Fistard, that he was going with the fairies every night, and coming home in the morning. He was going out at night, and coming home in the morning. He was going out at night, and they could not keep him in the house; he would sometimes tell them of the sports he had with the fairies, and that they were turning him to a horse and riding on his back, and telling about the nice whips the fairies had, and how sharply they cracked. He was going that way for years, but he died before he was twenty. The front teeth in his mouth grew very big, and he was a terror to look at.

132. FAIRIES RIDING IN THE ELDER TREES

The fairies have deserted the haunted house; there were great noises every night, but they have left it for some reason; there used to be very large elder trees growing about it, but they are all decayed, and there is no proper branch to ride on, but whether that is the reason or not, there is no one able to tell, and it seems that Glenchass cronk was a favourite haunt of the fairies.

133. FAIRIES, IMAGE-MAKING

A woman at Glenchass has been confined and was in bed, and a light burning in her room: her husband was lying the wall side of her, fast asleep, and she saw a good many of the fairies peeping in at the door, and in a short time they ventured in, and commenced to make an image. She did not know whether it was herself or the baby they intended to take, as they were making the image so big. And she was trying all the time to awaken her husband, but he was very hard to get him to move, but before the form they were making was quite finished, she got him roused, and as soon as they heard his voice they were off as fast as possible, and they were dragging the image after them; she could hear it bumping on the stairs as they were running down; they seemed to have big heads, for their ears, she affirmed, were the size and shape like wine bottles.

134. FAIRIES AT WORK

A woman related that on a calm evening and the sky was clear and cloudless, and not a breath of wind there arose a smoke out of the garden, and a great white cloud going up straight towards the sky, as thick as the chimney of a house, and was rising at a great rate. The cloud of smoke was cut even with the top of the trees, and went away like a bank of white fog over the fields, but there was nothing burnt in the garden, neither could they smell fire or smoke, but since the big elder tress are taken away, and the cow-house, and the garden, there is nothing to be seen or heard ever since, so it appears the fairies left the place when there was no shelter or trees to ride on. At one time the fairies began to beat the wall of the old cowhouse with something like a sledge hammer, but she could not see, but could hear the blows, and felt the ground trembling under her at every blow.

135. A FAIRY LOVE HAUNTING A MAN (LHIANNAN SHEE)

There is a story about Ballahick, a farmhouse near Ballasalla. It was about a young Scotchman, and he was coming home late at night and saw a light in Ballahick house, and he knew it was not inhabited at the time, but he thought there was some tenant come to live there, and he would go to the house to see the new inhabitants. When he came to the gate there were two young ladies standing there, and he asked them if there was some family come to Ballahick, and they said there was, and asked him to go up with them and see. He went in the house, where there was a great company, two or three pairs on the floor dancing, but there was no face that he knew among them all. The company made him very welcome, and one of the young ladies he met at the gate kept very near him, and it appears he made free with her. When the dancing was over they were leaving the house, and he came away with the rest, but his fairy love followed him home and haunted him ever afterward. He went abroad thinking to leave her behind, but she followed him wherever he went—over sea and land. It is supposed he must have kissed her, and that gave her power to haunt him, and to go across the ocean with him.

136. FAIRY FIRES AND FOREIGN FAIRIES

A man once saw a bonfire on Glenshass but there was no sign of fire in the morning, and he had seen many times Perwick Brows on fire in the night, but there was no trace there next morning; and he was coming home from the *Oie'l Verree* at Christmas and it was late, after twelve o'clock and he heard great talking at the house when he came near, but could not understand one word. He expected his people up for him, and that the house was full of his companions, but when he got into the house all were in bed fast asleep.

137. A BIG STACK OF FIRE

Some men were going home from Port St. Mary about one o'clock on Saturday night, and saw a great big stack of fire coming in from sea, and they heard some drunken fellows quarrelling and fighting at the four roads at the time, and this stack of fire went towards the place where they were fighting and disappeared, and the row was over.

138. A STORY OF A FAIRY CHILD IN FOXDALE

There was an old man from Foxdale telling about a changeling in Foxdale. He said it was a true story, for he knew the man and woman and the house, and he had seen the fairy child many times. The father was a miner. At the time the child was changed, on that evening he was later than usual. The wife was looking out for him, and she heard a great bustle outside as if a great crowd of people were going about the house, and she opened the door, and looked out, but saw nothing. When she came in again the baby was screaming in the cradle, and she went to give it the breast, but was surprised to see her own fair child changed into a dark little child with only skin and bones. They could do nothing but keep the little fairy as well as they could, but she could not get him quiet, but he always was crying. If they put him to sit on the mantlepiece, or on one of the shelves of the dresser, he would not fall but was helpless when in their arms, and could not sit up at all. The neighbour woman was trying to persuade them it was a fairy, and wanted her to let them have him to try some experiment on him, but she was for a long time very unwilling. At length she allowed them, and they got a lot of dry gorse and laid it in a circle, and put the child on some dry straw in the middle of the circle, and set fire to the gorse. so he lay quiet until the straw began to burn, then he commenced to tumble and tumble and tumble out of the ring in a place where the fire had not kindled, and the place where they intended to burn him was on the bank of a river, so he tumbled out of the ring, and went on rolling down the hill toward the river, but just before he tumbled into the water the mother ran, picked him up, and she had to deal with him for many years afterwards, but he faded away to a skeleton, and at last seemed to be dead, and they got a coffin and shut him in, and buried him, and that was the end of all their trouble with him. Perhaps if she had allowed him to get into the river he would have floated back again to fairyland, and sent her own child back again, but her own baby never returned.

139. ANOTHER STORY OF A FAIRY CHILD FROM THE NORTH OF THE ISLAND

There was a travelling tailor once serving in a house in the north of the Island, and the farmer's wife had a fairy child crying and yelling in the cradle. Her own child had been exchanged. And the tailor was a great fiddler and always took his fiddle with him, and was playing it when not sewing at meal times. The farmer's wife went out to milk the cows in the morning, and when the tailor was left alone with the child, he took the fiddle, and began to play some new tune he had been practising when, to his surprise, the baby leapt out of the cradle, and began to dance, and jump like a mad thing, but when he heard the footsteps of the farmer's wife, he got into the cradle again, and was crying as usual. The tailor said nothing about it for some days, but whenever the house was clear he took the fiddle, and began to play, and the baby was on the floor in a moment dancing like a juggler, but when the tailor had nearly finished his work, he told the farmer's wife about it, and that the child was a fairy. Then they made a great fire, and were intending to put it in the fire, but when the fire was ready he was gone, and their own baby was sleeping in the cradle.

140. FAIRIES PULLING A BOAT ASHORE

An old man was telling about one time they came into Perwick in a boat which they had for carrying lintels from Spanish Head, and the boat was too heavy for them to pull her up above the high water mark, and it came on to blow in the night, and he got up out of bed to look after the boat, and it was rather dark; as he was coming down the cliff he heard great shouting where the boat was, and he was hurrying to help, as he thought they were people drawing the boat. He saw a great company of people, with an anchor set up in the cliff, and hauling a boat up, and they were shouting in Manx: "*Ooilley cooidjagh*" ('All together'); but when he came to them they all disappeared, and the boat was not moved out of her place. While he was there they commenced to haul up a boat in another place, and were shouting like the old fishermen used to be when the herring season was over, and pulling their boats up on dry land for the winter. One would be shouting and the others pulling: "Hurrah, hurrah, launch away, a long pull, and a strong pull, and a pull altogether." He did not go near them any more, but left them to draw their boats in peace.

141. A WOMAN NEAR KING WILLIAMS'S COLLEGE

A man was once going from Castletown to Derbyhaven a little after one o'clock in the morning, and when near King Williams's College he saw a woman coming towards him with an old-fashioned cloak on, and the hood over her head, like the old women used to wear them. He made for the other side of the road to allow her to pass, but she came right in front of him; he then made for the other side of the road, and she did the same, and he had to hold up his hand to keep her face away from him, and they shifted across the road many times, but he cried out: "In the name of the Almighty, what is it?" and she slipped past and immediately disappeared.

Many others had been telling him since that they had met with something in the same place, and they believed it was a murder that had been committed in that place, and that it was the spirit of the murdered person that was haunting the place. It is supposed by the Manx people that when the time of their natural death has come that the spirit goes to its rest, and hence it is that the *bugganes* are all gone away, as there are no murders in the Island now that the murderers have not been found out and punished.

142. A WOMAN NEAR FOXDALE

There were some young men going across the mountains between Foxdale and St John's one night, and one of them lingered behind the rest for about five minutes, and when he began to walk again he saw a very tall woman walking beside him. He did not like to speak to her for some time, but when he saw that she was coming with him he ventured to say some words to her but got no answer, and then he began to suspect she could not be a natural woman. And he spoke to her again, mentioning the name of the Almighty, and she disappeared in the twinkling of an eye, and he took a great fright at it, and when he came to his companions they might have wrung the perspiration out of his clothes, and it affected him for a long time afterwards.

143. A WOMAN IN WHITE

A man went to one of his fields in Glenchass to get the cows home about sunset, and he met a woman dressed in white, coming up the hedge. She was very tall, but he said not a word, neither did she, and ever afterward as long as he lived he would not go in that field after sunset.

144. AN INVISIBLE COMPANION

I went over the Cronk one fine night, and there was some young men standing at the foot of the hill, and they immediately stopped their sport when I made my appearance on the top of the hill: they all said they saw some person beside me dressed in white, but I did not believe them, although they all affirmed it was the truth; and Glenshass is a likely place for fairies, with its deep glens and running streams.

I recollect the men tell about a lady they were seeing somewhere on the Douglas road walking on a hill by the side of the road; she was often seen on moonlight.

145. AN OLD GRINNING HAG AT THE FISTARD

There was a young man living in Fistard, and he was in Glenchass lodge one night until it was late. It was a fine clear night, but rather windy, and he made across a little field in front of the house, and he saw something black beside the hedge, and thinking it some article of clothing that had fallen on the bushes, he went toward it to lift it on again, but the thing got up of itself, and was in the form of an old woman, and came towards him grinning fearfully and opening her mouth wide enough to swallow him, and he ran home as fast as he could, and was very bad for six to seven months after that.

146. CARRIAGE AND HORSES

It is said there was a carriage with four black horses drawing seen many times going through Port St Mary after twelve o'clock at night. There were two men standing in the street one night, and the carriage drove past them. They saw the driver sitting in his place, but the wheels made no noise, neither the horses hoofs, and it went along Lime-street, and towards the Point, but no one knows where it goes to, and what it is, and where it comes from.

Another version.—There is a carriage coming through Port St Mary about two or three times a year with a pair of grey horses going toward the breakwater, but it has not ever been coming back.

Another.—The people on Port St Mary have heard the sound of a carriage many times after twelve at night passing towards the pier, it had four black horses, but they could not see no driver, and no one has seen it coming back.

147. TWO LITTLE GIRLS, FOUR PONIES, AND A LADY IN A CARRIAGE

About two years ago a young fellow had been seeing his young woman, and left her rather too early. When he was on his way back there was a corner on the road, and before going round the corner he met two little ladies about a foot and a half high, very nice little things, but he did not feel any fear of the little ones until he heard the rumbling of carriage wheels, and when round the corner he met a carriage with a pair of small white ponies, about the size of dogs, and the carriage itself was very low, and a woman driving, and it was going at a great rate where the road was very rough. He said he knew they were not human, but he got home all right.

Another account.—A young man one night last September had been walking on the shore about twelve o'clock, and he was coming through a lonely place where there were no houses, and there came two little girls and walked on each side of him, so small they only reached his hips, and each had an umbrella. They looked up in his face, but he could not hear the noise of their feet. As they passed on before him there were four ponies came after them, two had harness on, and two had none, and they went after that there was a carriage came past and a lady sitting in it, and she was as high sitting down as he would have been if he had been standing on his feet. She was the tallest woman he ever saw in his life.

148. DREAD TO PASS KING ORRY'S GRAVE IN THE NIGHT

"Superstition is rife throughout the Island, and a very remarkable instance of its force came under my own observation. Near some lead mines, in a retired spot on the road from Douglas to Ramsey, is a place known as King Orry's Grave, who is reported by tradition to have been murdered at this place and buried. Being at Ramsey rather late one evening on business, and exceedingly anxious to return home to Douglas, we made application to every car proprietor in the town, but neither bribe nor persuasion were of the slightest avail in securing the fulfilment of our object. It was approaching midnight, and at that hour no Manxman, if possible, will dare to invade the precincts of the royal sanctuary. There was no help for it, and so at some considerable expense and inconvience, we were obliged to remain in Ramsey for the night." (See *My Sketch Book*, Hy C. Robinson, Gloucester, 1853, p. 109.)

149. TWO LADIES AT THE SUGAR LOAF

A man one morning in summer was pulling heather with his hook near the Chasms, when the sun was rising in the east, and he saw two ladies in white coming up the cliff, near the Sugar Loaf, dressed very fine, and they came towards him, and he was near the end of the cliff. They passed him, but did not speak. They rambled about until the sun got a bit warm, and then went to the perpendicular precipice, and walked over so the man got very timorous, and ran home as fast as his legs could carry him, for no mortal creature could come up or down in that place, but the birds, and he was taken ill through fright for some time afterwards.

A fisherman that has spent most of his time fishing about the Calf Island and the Sound, said he was on his way to Port St. Mary one evening in his boat, and another man was with him. The sun was just going behind the mountains, and when they were just past the Sugar Loaf they saw two ladies going up the perpendicular cliff, walking quite leisurely, and one one had a red dress on, and they were running about like if they had been in a green field. The sun was not set, but just behind the hill, and they kept running about for a long time. They could see them when crossing Perwick Bay. He said he was sure they were not human beings, but spirits.

Another old fisherman in Port St. Mary said he was going to the Calf to fish in a boat alone one evening about sunset. He had a lug sail on his little boat, and was sitting in the stern steering when he was near the Sugar Loaf. There was little wind, and the sail was flapping about once when a little breeze came off the land, and the sail spread, and there was a lady sitting in the bow of the boat, but he could not see her face, and was afraid to speak to her or to sit, so he was going on steering for Port St Mary, and the lady looking out until it got calm again, and the sail hid her from him. When the breeze sprang up again, she was gone, and he saw no more of her, but he would not go to the fishing alone after that.

150. BRIGHT LIGHTS

Some men were passing Spanish Head in a fishing boat in the middle of the night, and saw a light in the middle of the cliff, and it went along to the Sugar Loaf and up the Chasms, and disappeared. They were also passing Glen Wither another night and saw a light there, but it stopped in the same spot, and there was a man fell down some time afterwards and was killed—they allowed it was the sign of his death.

There was a nice green hollow at the foot of Cronk ny Irree Laa, at the bottom of the cliff, and there are the ruins of an ancient church or chapel there yet, and they call the place Lhag ny Killey. I have heard many of the old fishermen saying they often have seen a very bright light there, many times while going past late at night, about twelve o'clock, in their boats. It was supposed by the old folk the chapel was a druidical temple.

A man had been at Ballakilpheric at Christmas, and was a bit late coming home. At Ballacreggan he saw a fire in the middle of the road and when he was near the fire went over the hedge, and the hedge was very high where it went over but he climbed up and saw it still burning behind the hedge, and he could see it burning away in the road when at the top of Ballacreggan hill.

151. DARKNESS ARISING

There was a man coming home from Port St Mary to Cregneish, and when he was just at his own house he got into some darkness, and could not see where he was until he found himself at the Smelt, right against the big mill door, and his cap was lost, so he started home and found his cap just at the house in the morning.

A fisherman said he came out of the house in Limestreet in Port St Mary one night, he wished to have a look at the vessel before retiring, and he was on his way towards the pier when he all at once came into some darkness. He could see nothing, but felt as if he had been in the midst of a crowd, but could feel nothing with his hands but was carried back with the throng until he came to a small opening between two houses, and he got in there and the crowd went by, and it was light again. He met another man coming, as he came out of the darkness, nor feel anything—he was of opinion it was a sign of death.

152. HAUNTED HOUSES (1)

I have often heard talk of Ballacurry House that it was haunted. One night there were some young men in with the farmer's daughters, and the maids and they were all sitting quietly in the kitchen, and the backdoor was locked, but the door opened and a very big man came in, and walked upstairs, and made a great noise in the rooms and they got into another room and their sport ended for that night.

153. HAUNTED HOUSES (2)

A farm labourer said that in the farm house he lived, they were hearing something going upstairs. When they were in bed they were hearing it often, dragging the chairs about the kitchen, but they said nothing about it. One night an old tradesman doing some job for the master was sleeping in the house, and the man was very deaf. Well, he felt unwell and could not sleep, so he got up again and went down to the kitchen, lit the fire and warmed himself. But deaf as he was, he could hear the chairs dragging about, but could see nobody. At last he heard something by his side, and a voice said: "Go to bed." Well, he did not mind that, he though it was one of the men sleeping upstairs that called him to go to bed. And he sat still, and the chairs were kept going through their performance as before. At last a very coarse voice said: "Go to bed out of this!" But he did not go to bed after all, thinking it was one of the servants, but they were all asleep in bed.

154. NOISES AND BLOODY BLOTCHES IN AN OLD HOUSE AT PORT ERIN

There is an old house in Port Erin on the hill above the chapel. It has been without a roof for many years. A man lived in it, they called him Captain, and the old house "the Ship." There was a school mistress once keeping school in that house, said a woman, when she was a young girl, and often there was some noise on the kitchen loft like if a person lay on his back and beat the floor with his heels. The missus, she said sent her up to wash the floor one day, and it was all over blood at the bedside, and under the bed was all covered, and looked as fresh as if it had been spilt that day, and they cut the boards away many times and put new ones in their places, but the blood was on the new boards the same as the old ones. I suppose the ghosts of the murdered persons were howling for revenge until the time of their natural life was expired, and then they seemed to be at rest, or perhaps the murderer had died and they had their revenge.

155. BLESSING THE DEAD

I have heard the old people, especially the women, say that it was right to bless the dead, whenever they were mentioned, and I have often heard them saying, when talking of the dead "*My vannaght lesh ny merriu*" ('My blessing with the dead'): and if one person was spoken of: "*My vannaght lesh yn varroo.*" Also when a baby was born the old women would say: "*Dy bannee Jee yn lhiannoo*" ('May God bless the child').

156. UNBAPTISED CHILDREN

It is said of children dying without being baptised that their ghosts used to be lamenting in the churchyard in the dead of the night, I have heard them tell about some man that was passing the churchyard, and he heard a little voice saying:

"*Lhiannoo dyn ennym mee, lhannoo dyn ennym mee.*"

and the man said:

"*My she gilley oo, ta mee bashtey oo Juan, as my she inneen oo ta mee bashtey oo Joney.*"

'If thou art a boy I christen thee John, and if thou art a girl I christen thee Joney.'

Myr shen va yn scaah shen eck shee.

therefore that ghost was at rest.

It is the custom yet to bury a stillborn child at dead of night, as they are not allowed to be buried in consecrated ground.

157. AN ENCHANTRESS CHANGING INTO A BAT, AND HER PALFREY INTO A PORPOISE

An enchantress who rode on a milk white palfrey, led her train of lovers to a deep river, and when they were all a good way in it, she caused a sudden wind to rise which, driving the waters up, swallowed them all. She changed after into a bat and flew off, and the palfrey turned into a sea hog or porpoise, and plunged itself to the bottom of the stream.

* See Waldron's *History of the Isle of Man*, 1726, p. 75. I have re-stated these to bring them again into eminence.

158. A SPECTRE IN THE SHAPE OF A WOLF

On a wild common near Kirk German an appearance was seen which assumed the shape of a wolf, and filled the air with most terrible howlings.

* Waldron's *History of the Isle of Man*, 1726, p. 37.

159. SPECTRE HUNTSMEN

A man was going over a pretty high mountain, coming from Douglas on his way to his sister in Kirk Malew in the night, when he heard the noise of horses and the halloo of a huntsman, and the finest horn in the world. He counted thirteen in number, all dressed in green and gallantly mounted.

* Waldron's *History of the Isle of Man*, 1726, p. 33.

160. THE UIRCEAN-SONNEY, OR LUCKY LITTLE PIG

I have heard of some little white animal, like a young pig. They called it the *uircean sonny*, or the lucky or plentiful little pig. The old people used to say if you caught it you would be very fortunate; that you always find a piece of silver in your pocket when you are in need of it. A woman once said that she was walking one night, and came across some little white thing, but she did not catch it, nor try to catch it, but for some time afterwards she always found a silver piece in her pocket, when she needed it, and put her hand into her pocket, not thinking to find it. And this continued for some time but she told one of her friends about it, and she did not get any more—the bank was closed. It is wrongly mixed up with the Manx *eairkan* or Gaelic *adharean* = lapwing but it is really derived from *uireean* or *oircein*, Gaelic = little pig; the diminutive word of *eairk* = pig, is short in the Manx dictionary.

161. DISTURBING OLD FOUNDATIONS

I heard a man tell about one time he went with his father-in-law to mend a hedge, and there had been the ruins of some old building near the place. And they were digging up some of the foundation stones for the purpose of mending the hedge, and he had made a hole down, and was pulling some stones out with his hands, and as he had one stone nearly out, it was pulled in again with a sudden pull, and that was repeated again, and it was pulled out of his hand, and something like a shock went through his body, and he refused to touch it any more. But his father-in-law made fun of him, and went to try it himself, but he was electrified himself, and fell upon the ground. And they shut up the hole again, and left it, and he never liked to go near the place since.

There was an old house on Mull mountain, and they brought some long stones from it to put for flags in the floor of another cottage, and while they were in the floor the people had no rest at night, but great noises in the house all night, and knocking and thumping on the stones, and the man had to take them up and send them back to the old ruin again; and there was no more noise in the house after that.

There was a man living at Ballakilpheric, in a small farm called Kirkle, and he got blind when he was about 35 years of age. There was a graveyard on his farm, an uncultivated spot, and he took it in hand to cultivate, and he worked very hard digging it up with a pick, and there were many human skeletons. His father often was telling him something would happen to him, for disturbing the dead, and in a short time afterwards he got stone blind.

Gregor tells us that in the North-East of Scotland (page 115) that druidical circles and monoliths (as in Man), were looked upon with awe, and when disturbed disease fell on cattle, and there was no peace for man or beast till the stone was put in its old place.

162. THOMAS BUSHELL (1594–1674), AND HIS SECLUSION ON THE CALF OF MAN (1628–1630)

The Calf of Man towers out like a large sentinel, detached from the mainland of the Island by the little Sound, facing distant Ireland. Manx tradition connects its vicinity with the heroic feats of Finn Mac Cooil, and Kettel is said to have hunted here the elk, and leaping the Sound with his spear. It is now the goal of the seeker after nature, and a favourite haunt of the artist and Izaak Walton's disciples. Its lights and tints, ever playing and moving about its greyish-brown cliffs and crags, hung with heather bloom and sea pink, rising from a sea, now purple or emerald, or merged into a surging mass of molten gold, spanning against the soft summer sky form a picture of unfading attraction and beauty. To study its varying moods, view it at the first blush of the morn, when the rays just delicately strike the Calf, or when it is glorying in the wild dance of the snowy curling spray of the breakers; at sunset, when the main heaves and burns in the mellowness of myriads of gorgeous colours; by night when the silver sickle or the full orb of the moon diffuses her magic light over its serene face, hushed into dreamy silence.

The Calf, held variously by the Earl of Derby, the Stephensons of Balladoole, the Duke of Atholl, and the Careys, has been rarely resorted to by visitors, but has recently been more opened up to free and easy access by a syndicate at Port Erin.

In Feltham's time (1797), and centuries before him, boats to the Calf were launched from Bradda Head; "you require," he says, "four hands, as the strong tides at the Sound require; the Calf," he continues, "is about five miles round, sheep abounds, but no part is in tillage, fern, heath, and short herbage variegate the surface. On the west side the rocks are stupendous, and the quantity of birds, called *muirs*, *etc.*, are incredible, whether sitting on the rocks with their young, floating on the surface of the sea, or filling the immediate air—they give variety to the scene, and their shrill voices arrest attention, and pleases from its novelty." Chaloner (1652), at a much earlier period, speaks of its plentifulness of sea fowl, particularly puffins, of its falcons, red deer, "of some ayries of mettled faulcons that built in the rock, of the great stores of conies, and in some time (he adds) there arrive out of Ireland and the western parts of Scotland many of the small hawks called *merlyns*."

You would land then a little east of Kitterland, at a point now called Grant's Harbour, or Purt ny vaatey—the port of the boats—on the north-east part of the Calf, and a track led you along the western side to a little farm-stead. Near that stupendous precipice, the Ooir Vooar—the great rock rim—you behold yet the traces of an ancient chapel and burial ground, erected on the highest point of the Calf—421 feet above the sea—and close by are to be seen the ruins and site of a place called Thie Vushell, or Bushell's house. This little hut has quite a romantic history, and faint memories are still afloat at Cregneish. It once harboured a man who played a not un-important part in the fortunes of King Charles I. The original structure, slight and frail, was composed of a single room with a narrow entrance to it, and shows at one side a recess, measuring about three feet wide and six feet deep— probably the dormitory.

Thomas Bushell, the tenant of this little hermitage, was born 1594 at Cleve Prior, in Worcestershire, and when 15 years old entered the household of the great Lord Chancellor, Francis Bacon. He showed a natural genius for natural philosophy and experiment, and his master, who also became his instructor, "imparted to him many secrets in discovering and extracting minerals," and his own subsequent mining processes were the natural outcome of Bacon's theories. On the disgrace of the Lord Chancellor he went first to the Isle of Wight, where he lived for some time as a fisherman. He after retired to London, and some years after Bacon's death (1626) crossed to the Isle of Man. He narrates the reasons of his retirement hither: "The embrions of my mines proving abortive by the sudden fall and death of my late Lord Chancellor Bacon, in King James's reign, were the motives which persuaded my pensive retirement to a three years unsociable solitude in a desolate Island, called the Calf of Man, where, in obedience to my dead lord's philosophic advice, I resolved to make a perfect experiment upon myself for the obtaining of a long and healthy life, most necessary for such a repentance, as my former debauchedness required, by a parsimonious diet of herbs, oil, mustard, and honey, with water sufficient, most like to that our long-lived fathers before the flood, as was conceived by that lord, which I most strictly observed, as if obliged by a religious vow, till Divine Providence called me to a more active life."

Blundell (1648), further alludes to Bushell's stay: "All Mann glorieth in its Calf, and do still retain the memory of that vast wit for inventions where he late had a hermetical life in the cave of a hollow rock in the Island, and do still talk of his pendant bed (such as the hammock in a ship) and strange diet."

It may be asked: What allured him to particularly select the Isle of Man for his voluntary self-banishment from the metropolis and the court? That question may be satisfactorily answered as we have the clue.

We know Edward Christian was appointed by James, the seventh Earl of Derby, and King of the Island, as Governor of Man, in 1628, which office he held till 1635. The Earl, in a passage of a letter to his son, says: "I was newly got acquainted with Capt. Christian, whom I perceived to have abilities enough to do me services; I was told he made a good fortune in the Indies, and that he was a Manxman born. He is excellent good company, as rude as a sea captain should be, but refined as one that has civilised himself half a year at court, when he served the Duke of Buckingham."

Chaloner (1652) adds that "he was employed in command at sea by the East Indy Company, and sometimes under King James in one of his Royall ships."

Edward Christian then, as we see, was one of the suite of the famous Duke of Buckingham, who was likewise the great patron of Lord Chancellor Bacon, who on the occasion of his elevation to his office wrote an eloquent letter of thanks "for the influence he had exerted in his behalf for the obtention of his appointment." It was thus that Bushell and Christian were intimately thrown together as members of Bacon's and the Duke's retinue. It was Christian who entertained him of his native Island and the Calf, and when Bushell had fully decided on his retirement, Christian no doubt urged and invited him to come to Man for that purpose. Castletown, the seat of the government, would be his first destination, as a guest of Christian, who also, no doubt, conducted him to Port Erin. His stay in the Island coincided thus with the elevation of Christian as Governor of the Isle in 1628.

Bushell's solitary residence in the Calf, and his reasons for such a strange step, must have naturally puzzled the natives. Blundell observes: "Neither himself (Bushell) is truly understood, nor his diet related by the Manksmen." Although he lived cut off from direct intercourse, his seclusion must by no means be considered as perfect and complete. It was no doubt varied by occasional visits of and to Christian, to talk and converse about their former life in London, and to discuss with him future plans and schemes. The Isle offered also a favourite field for his following investigations into the nature of veins and their distribution. That he must have examined minutely the character of the strata of the vicinity appears clear. In the little creek of Cabbyl Ghaw, at the east side of the Parade, in the Sound, where the Cregneish fishermen throw their boats, is still an old, disused mining shaft, where some rotten timbering and traces of former mining operations in search of ore have been discovered, and Chaloner informs us, moreover, that Edward Christian found the rocks at Mine hough (Bradda Head) contained much silver; that "ore of lead is near unto the sea crag at Mine hough and has been experimented by Edward Christian to hold much silver, and that the veins of this mine by its brightness may be plainly discovered in the rock towards sea." Christian himself was not versed in mining matters directly, and probably the knowledge of the existence of ore here must have been imparted to him by his friend Bushell, whose practised eye soon had found evidence of it at Bradda, Spaldrick Bay, from whence the boats plied regularly between the mainland and the Calf.

His necessities of life, and such things as honey, oil, mustard, *etc.*, were procured from Castletown. Beehives were then more extensively kept in the Island for the honey and wax. Here then he lived for three consecutive years, engaged in study and speculation, and maturing his ideas. The bracing sea air, and the quiet and tranquil course of his life, his regular habits and diet, invigorated his shattered frame. He laid by a good stock of bodily and mental vigour and self-reliance, which conduced to the development of great energy and longevity, for he reached the good age of eighty. When he took possession of the little hut on the Calf he was in the hey day of his life, and about 34 years old. Had he there kept a diary—as Hall Caine makes his hero do, when banished by the Bishop of Man, his father—or written his personal recollections, while in constant contact for 16 years with his great master, what wonderful glimpses might he have afforded us into the inner and outward life, and the various traits and habits of that great personality!

163. THOMAS BUSHELL (1594–1674), AND HIS SECLUSION ON THE CALF OF MAN (1628–1630) (2)

He left the Calf in the course of 1630 for Road Enstone, near Woodstock, where he had an stablishment and constructed some curious and ingenious water-works, which greatly pleased Charles I, who visited him when in the neighbourhood. He next occupied himself with perfecting a new method of soap-making which, in 1635, he secured the exclusive right. But his great opportunity came in 1636, when the King made him a grant to work the royal mines of Cardiganshire, in Wales, by indenture,* stating that many hopeful mines discovered upon the mountains in Wales, wherein were great quantities of silver, were lost by the unskilful working of these mines, therefore his Majesty, by securing the same to Thomas Bushell, and for encouraging the poor miners by a more timely and speedy pay out of their own labours, thought fit the said Thomas Bushell should erect a mint in the Castle of Aberystwyth, with officers and workmen necessary for the coining of all such bullion only as should be drawn out of the mines within the Principality; and that the monies there made should be stamped with feathers on both sides, *etc.* The mines were last farmed by Sir Hugh Myddleton, at the low annual sum of £400, whose efficient management effected so great an alteration that his monthly profit from

Cwmsymlog alone has been estimated at £2,000. Bushell, on his installation, recovered the inundated mines, and employed new and more expeditious methods of mining. He became warden and master-worker of the mint, occupying 500 families and spending £7,000 before reaping the fruit of his indefatigable labours. It took him four years to recover the decayed mines, and he discovered also some old mines, wrought by the Romans. The coins struck by him were, as authorised by this deed, half-crown, shilling, sixpenny, great, half-great, threepenny, penny, and halfpenny pieces, and bear date between 1638 and 1642, when the mint was removed to Shrewsbury in consequence of the distractions arising out of the Civil War. When the King was pressed by the Parliament forces, Bushell made a noble acknowledgment to his royal master by raising a regiment among his miners, and clothing his whole army, besides supplying him with £40,000 in his necessity towards the payment of his troops. He proved a most devoted Royalist, and with unexampled self-abnegation, used all his entire resources and powers in support of the cause of his royal patron; "he converted," says Thomas Fuller, "the mattocks of his miners into spears, and their shovels into shields, formed them into a regiment, and commanded them in person, in defence of a cause too desperate for recovery." The King, in touching language, acknowledged his great obligations to him in an autograph letter, in which he speaks of the:

> Manie true services actually done in these times of trying a subject's loyalty as in raiseing us the Darbyshire minors for our lifeguard at our first entrance to this ware for our owne defence, supplyinge us at Shrewsbury and Oxford with your mint for for payment of our armye, your charging the dollar wee paid our soldjers at 6/- a piece when the malignant partie cried them down at ffive, your stopping the mutinie in Shropshire, your providing us 100 tonnes of lead shot for our armye with mony, your helping us to 26 pieces of ordinance, your cloathing of our life guard and three regiments more with suites, stockings, shoes, and mounterees when wee were readie to march in the ffield; your contractinge with merchants beyond the seas, for providing good quantities of powder, pistol, carabine, muskett, and bullen, in exchange for your own commodities: with diverse other services.

Speaking of his later career, Mr W. Wroth† says:

> He held Lundy Island for the King, and in 1647 surrendered it and went into hiding. In 1652 he gave securities to the Council of State for his future good behaviour, and obtained from the Protector a renewal of his lease of the royal mines and confirmation of his grant for coining the silver there extracted. These were confirmed in 1658 by Richard Cromwell, who also protected and encouraged him in his operations in the lead mines in the Mendip. His mining schemes in Somersetshire also received the sanction of Charles.

He seems to have been overtaken by great adversity and impecuniousness pressing on him in his old age, for in 1663 there is the petition of Ths. Bushell, master-worker of the royal mines, praying the King for a royal protection for arrest for two years, having contracted great debts in the service of the late King, which he hopes to repay in time from his mineral proceeds. Nothing more definite is known of him after this, and he then silently drops out of ken; but his splendid services were fittingly acknowledged, for on his death in April, 1674, he was buried in the cloisters of Westminster Abbey. His wife was Anne, widow of Sir William Waad, Lieutenant of the Tower.

Such is the eventful history of the recluse; and the visitor, on bending his steps to the crumbled pile of Thie Vushell, will approach it, not in curiosity alone, but with a fuller knowledge and sense of the deep interest that is bound up with it and the lone dreamer who while in occupied the sea-girdled rearing heights of this sparkling diadem of Mona—the Calf of Man.

* See *New Guide to Aberystwith*, by Thomas Owen Morgan, barrister, Aberystwith, 1864, pp. 43–44 and 57–58.

† See article: Thomas Bushell, *Dictionary of National Biography*, vol. viii, 1886; written by Warwick Wroth.

164. ENCHANTED ISLANDS
Another account.—The old people said there was an enchanted island south-west of the Calf of Man, and it was seen once in seven years, when old May Day was on Sunday. Someone of the name of *Oany Vadrill* was the last one that saw it; but it is often cloudy in the mornings in May, and the people used to be up looking for it for many years. A Peel man said they had the same old tradition in Peel, but it was off Jurby their island was seen.

165. GIANTS
Lheim y chenney (Fox-leap) is the perpendicular cliff adjoining the Bowyn Purt Chiarn in Bay Fine, and Slieau ynnyd my chassyn (the mountain of the place of my feet), is situated quite near to it and about a hundred yards from the cliff. Tradition says that the rock bears the marks of a giant who jumped over from Ireland and you can see his club foot sunk into the rock

There was a man who once found a barrel of olive oil on the shore, and there were four of them went in the night to get some of the oil, and as they were coming up the cliff the man that was behind said: "Boys, keep all together"; and they all stood in a group, and there came a big man past them as big as one of Gulliver's giants and went down the cliff.

Some years ago a man was walking in the mountain near the Chasms one foggy afternoon, and as he was coming across the field next the slieau he saw a man sitting by a hedge with a top hat on him, and he thought it was one of his neighbours, and he went towards him: when he was just at him, the man stood up, and he said he was about twelve feet high; he was afraid to look at him, but when he did look again the tall man had disappeared, and he could not see him anywhere.

166. HEADLESS MEN

There was a man one night, and it was moonlight, he went on the pier to have a walk. When he came to the watch-house he met a headless man, who passed him as near that he would have put his hand on him, but he did not speak a word. He also said he had seen the fairies many times, playing in the boats, and climbing up the riggings and laughing when the crews were gone home.

GHOSTS

The old folk believed that every ghost came back with a peep at the house and its inmates the third night after burial.

167. THE GHOST OF PAT NY KEYLLEY

The people used to talk about some man they called *Pat ny Keylley* ('Pat of the Forest'). He was an old beggar-man, and after he died his ghost was coming to some house, where the people had offended him some time when he was travelling about. He seemed to be haunting the house, and was coming into the bedrooms and taking hold of the bedposts and shaking the bed, and the people in it, at a great rate. I never heard how they got clear of him.

168. THE GHOST OF A MAN SEEN ON A STEAMER

There was a man sailing in a steamer which was lost in the winter with all hands. When this man was sailing in her he had seen a man on the bridge in the night, when there was no one but himself there, and all the crew below, and he was afraid to sail in her. He left her on reaching their destination. On her next voyage she foundered with all hands, and he was glad he left her, as he believed she was haunted by some evil spirit, and was sure something would come of it.

169. A GHOST OF A SUICIDE

A man was once going to Douglas to hear a great preacher. He left Surby soon after twelve o'clock on Saturday night, and as he was just going to cross the river near Ballasalla, he heard a gruff voice, saying: "Ha, thou art early though" and he looked round, and saw a big man standing by the side of the bridge, and he said he knew the man, he committed suicide some time before drowning himself in the river.

170. A DEAD WOMAN SEEN

There was a man once saw a woman in the way before him, a woman he was well acquainted with, and she was looking at him very hard, and her face looked very pale. He hurried up to her to have a talk with her, but when he came near her she disappeared, and he was greatly surprised. When he came home again the first news he heard was that this woman was dead.

171. THE GHOSTS OF SOME TWIN CHILDREN

An old woman from Ballakilpheric was telling about some one that had twins in the neighbourhood, and both died when they were beginning to walk about, and one night after they were buried she heard something at the door and went and opened it, and there were two little white lambs at the door, and she was greatly surprised, as it was in the dead of winter, before there were any lambs to be seen, and they seemed to be looking under the door steps. She shut the door again, and next morning she went to look under the steps and found a pair of scissors in a hole, that were missing some time and given up for lost. But it was her belief that the little ones had put the scissors there, and that the two little lambs were their spirits coming there to see them, according to the old superstitions about ghosts.

172. DEATH OMEN

A man who was following a pair of horses for another farmer, was coming home one fine evening in May, and as he was nearing the gate leading to the farm, he intended to dismount to open it, but at that time it was half-past six o'clock he saw the mistress, the farmer's wife, coming from the house towards the gate, and she opened it and passed by him, but did not speak nor take any notice of him. He turned round and looked after her until a turn in the road hid her from him. He was surprised she did not speak, as she so often was giving him a word. He drove the horses to the stable, and one of the servants came to him, and said the mistress was dead, suddenly, that she had complained about half an hour ago, and that she died a few minutes ago, and it was at that time the spirit left the body.

173. A HORSE SEEING A GHOST

There was an old woman, called "*Sarah yn varron,*" who kept a small farm, and she was in the habit of going to Douglas on Saturdays with butter and eggs, on horseback. One night she was coming home from market at a late hour, when the horse saw a ghost, and would not go forward. She used the whip to him, and he made a great leap and threw her off, and galloped away leaving her lying in the ditch. She had fainted with the fall, and when she came to herself again, the ghost was standing over her and sucking his lips, and saying: "What a pity, what a pity," until the night was nearly over, and then he went away and left her, and she had to make the best of her way home on foot, but the horse was at home before her.

[In Manx Folklore horses and dogs can see ghosts.]

174. TWO MEN AND A WOMAN

A man was coming up from the Howe one night, and when he was between the Craggans, and just past the top, he saw two men and a woman coming down off the Mull towards him, and he thought the woman was going to fly, her clothes were all in shreds flying with the wind. He was very fearful when they were coming near him and could not feel the ground beneath, and he repeated some good words and immediately they turned round and went up the Mull again. He was so frightened he had scarce strength to get home, but saw nothing more of them.

BUGGANES

175. YN GHOAYR HAITTAGH (OR HADDAGH)

There is something the old people called the *ghoayr haddagh* (the antic goat), shouting in the Island of a calm night. His voice resembled that of a goat, but much larger, like laughter, *ha, ha, ha*, for a minute or two, as if it was a goat with the ague. Many people have been frightened by it. It seems to live in bogs and marshy places, and people passing those places in the night and hearing his *ha, ha, ha*, on a sudden, were often terrified.

176. A COCK AND A CLOUD OF SMOKE

There was a lot of young fellows who once went for a walk on a fine Sunday morning. When they were at the Chasms they heard a cock crowing very loud down in one of the holes, and after a while they rolled a big stone down in the Chasms and they heard no more crowing, but there was a cloud of smoke came up. I suppose the stone must have fallen on the fire and spilt the fairies' big pot and spoilt the broth for them, when the steam came up so quickly.

177. MEETING A MONSTER

A man in Ballakilpheric was going to the fishing to Douglas, at ten o'clock on Sunday night, and coming down the Chapel, when he met some monster and it tumbled and bruised him, yet the man could not see anything at all.

Coming home at a late hour one night, a man, as he was passing a gap in one of the hedges that was shut up with gorse, saw the gorse was shaking, and he went to it, and gave it a shake, but saw nothing, but at last saw a great black monster coming behind him, and he ran home as fast as he could, but the black monster followed him to the door, and made a great noise for hours.

178. TWO WHITE MONSTERS LIKE SERPENTS AT THE HOWE

Some fishermen coming home from Port St. Mary at a late hour, and when nearing the farm house in the Howe, there saw two white monsters, like serpents, crossing the road and going down the steps leading to the house. The men said they were like white congers of an enormous size; they disappeared behind the garden wall, and when the men got to the cart road at the other end of the garden, the white congers came up again, and went up the hill before them at great speed, and the men were terrified, and waited until they were out of sight, and they saw them no more.

179. [MEETING THE BUGGANE]

A man was coming home from Port St. Mary station one night, long before the railway was proposed, and he saw some little black thing in the road. He walked up to it, and tried to give it a kick, but could not touch it, and in a moment it grew as big as a horse and though he was so courageous, he had to retreat, walking backwards with his knife open, until he came to a house near Ballacreggan. He burst the door open and got inside but the boggane did not follow and stayed outside until morning.

A man was telling about a great monster he saw. When he was a young man, he had been at a chris'ning, and went home with one of the young ladies in the evening, as is the fashion yet in the Island. The young men go to see their young ladies at bed time, and if they are in bed, they knock at her bedroom window, and the girl gets up and dresses herself again, and comes downstairs and opens the door for the young man, and they sit at the fire until morning talking about love and housekeeping. They did, however, not agree so well, and he went away soon after twelve o'clock. He had a cross road to go home, and when he was near home, he saw a great monster standing in the road, and he could not get past, and had to turn back and walk home on the high road. It was like a round tack of corn, he said, and his arms resting on the hedge each side.

A man was returning from the harbour, and when coming up the Howe, he saw some curious animal in the road leaping very high but he managed to get past and left him jumping. He said it must have been something supernatural, as no creature of earth could have leapt so high.

180. [CHASED BY A MONSTER AT NIGHT]

There was a man telling he was coming home from Port St. Mary, and it was a bright night. In a field beside the road he heard a great noise, and he thought the mountains had opened, or split asunder, and he saw something like a bear going round the field, as fast as if it had been flying, and it was shouting, and he thought it was echoing in Fleshwick, and in a moment it stood in the road before him, and he was standing by the hedge. The monster put his paws on the hedge, one each side of him, and his open mouth before his eyes, and he could see his big teeth ready to gobble him. He put his hand into his pocket to get his knife out, but he could not get it or his hand out, and there he was standing trembling, expecting to be devoured every moment. And the monster opened his mouth big enough to swallow him up, and he began to pray and in a moment it was gone like a flash of lightning.

A woman was coming home one night, and when between the station in Port St. Mary and Ballacreggan, she heard a great noise, and saw a great monster in the road, but she passed by it very courageously. When she was past the farm house she heard some great noise coming behind, and turning, saw a great monster following at a little distance. She could not tell what it was like, it had no shape nor form, but was like a stack, or like one of the turf stacks the old men used to make, and it followed her to the top of the plantation hill, but not further.

181. HARE GROWING BIGGER AND BIGGER

I have heard of different men getting a start on the beach at the top of the harbour at Port St. Mary. Two men came down the beach at a late hour to go on board of their boat, which was in the middle of the harbour and as the tide was out they intended to walk to her. But when they came on the beach they saw a little animal like a hare running about, and one said to the other, let us try to catch him; so when he heard that, he came towards them, and at every jump he was growing bigger, until he grew so big that they got frightened, and ran to the nearest boat and climbed on boards, got down in the forecastle and made the door fast inside, and in a moment he was on boards, too, and the vessel was shivering until they were afraid she would fall in pieces, sometimes shoving against the bulkhead until it was bending, and they were both standing at the door with the hatchet and the poker ready to defend themselves if he would burst in the door, and they were kept in suspense for about three hours, and then he went away.

182. CALVES

A man told me that one morning he had been seeing his girl in Surby, and was coming to Port St Mary in the dawn of a fine summer morning. When he was near the place where the station is, he saw two animals, something like young calves, but they did not seem to be calves neither; so he got over the hedge, and went across the field towards the plantation road, and when he got to the road again, the two calves were standing before him once more. He went across another field, and when he came over the hedge at Miller's hotel they were there again, but he managed to get past and into a yard, and they did not follow him there, but went down toward the Port; so he waited till the sun arose and they had disappeared, and he saw no more of them.

183. A BULL

Some fishermen were going to Port Erin to dig for sand eels, and as they were coming along Ballaphurt road they saw a little white thing in the way before them, and it got into a briar bush by the hedge, and one of them put his knife in the bush after him, so that made the little pig angry and it came out again, and grew as big as a bull, and they had all to do to defend themselves with their knives and retreat as well as they could until they came home and burst the door and got inside.

184. THE DEVIL IN THE SHAPE OF A BIG BULL

Many years ago there was a great revival of religion in the Howe Chapel, and there were a good many young people in the chapel every evening and sometimes they were late coming out, but one night in particular it was after twelve o'clock, and the company was going up the road singing. A young woman who had joined the party was a distance behind them, and she could hear the clanking of iron chains, as if a horse were galloping with chains fast to his feet, and she could hear him going up behind the hedge at a little distance from the singers; but it appears he got enraged and came away galloping past her where the hedge was low, but he was leaping in fury, and she was sure it was the devil, he was like a monstrous big bull, and she was ready to drop with fear, until one of the young men thought about her and came back to look after her, and the monster went away. She thought it was the devil, angry and raging, because the young men and girls were singing and praising God.

185. A LARGE PIG

Three of us went for a walk one Sunday night, and when we were crossing the Four Roads at Ballacreggan, we met a very big pig in a great hurry, and every corner we passed afterwards we met the pig coming at full speed. We met her in many places in Surby and Bradda, and in Port Erin, as we came through, and at Strugan snail she began to follow us, and at last we had to jump over the hedge and go home across the fields. She stood at the hedge where we jumped over, and was looking up at us, but I cannot tell where she went afterwards.

186. A GREYHOUND

A young man was telling about a fairy he came across. He was going towards the Plantation Hill about eleven o'clock, and it was very bright moonlight. He saw a great monster crossing the road, and going towards an old gate, and right through it without opening it, and it stood in the field. It was some thing like a greyhound, but very high, he said, and he went to look at the gate in daylight, and there was not a hole in it that he could get his own arm through.

187. FAIRY DOGS

A fellow was coming home late one night, and met the fairy dogs. They were very small and the road was full of them, and he was obliged to get on the hedge to get out of their way, and they kept going for a long time, until he was very angry with them, but at last they were all gone by, and it appears he said something to them that did not please them, for when he got home he was taken ill, and did not get up for six months.

188. A LITTLE DOG GOING AWAY IN A FLASH OF FIRE

About six or seven years ago there were two men in a small boat fishing round the Calf, and in the evening about sunset they were pulling along the south east side of the Calf, and they saw a little dog upon the rock near the water, and it was the prettiest little thing they ever met, and they went to get it, and one went on shore, but when he was just in the act of taking hold of the dog he went away in a flash of fire and disappeared, and both of the men were sick after for a long time.

189. A LARGE DOG AND A TALL LADY

There was a man who said that one night, when he was young, he was getting ready to go to Castletown on Saturday evening. The sky was clear, and the full moon shining. And there came to the door a very large dog, and stood there till he came out, and went along with him nearly to town, but disappeared at the old Windmill. He was some time in the town, and it was late when he was coming on his way home. At the old Windmill, where the dog vanished, there was a very tall lady standing, and she came up, and walked beside him, but he was afraid to speak to her, and they came together until they reached Balladoole lodge, and she went towards the stile that was near the gate. Then he took courage, and turned back to have a look at her, and she turned round and grinned upon him, and he said he never saw such big teeth in any animal as she had; but she did not follow him, and he did not see her again. I have heard of many people seeing her at the gate at different times. There was a Primitive Methodist minister preaching in St. Catherine's Chapel in Port Erin, and he was going home to Castletown after the service, and at this gate he saw the lady standing, and he spoke to her, but she gave him no answer, and only turned round grinning and showing her big teeth, and he was glad to leave her behind.

190. MEETING A LADY AND A CHASE

Formerly there was no highroad to the Sound but only a path across the field. A young man was going towards it one moonlight night at a late hour, and as he was crossing a field a very fine big lady stepped up to him and walked by his side, so he was afraid and began to run, but she kept beside him still; when he was jumping over the hedge, she was jumping over beside him, but as noiseless as a cat. He ran all the way home, and the lady with him until he jumped across a stream, and it appears she could not get over the water.

There was another man came home late one night, and stood at the gate of the house to have a look before going in, and he heard a sharp whistle at some distance, and he whistled too, and in a moment there was a score of little dogs about him and all the hunters after them. He managed to get in the house some way and shut the door, and the chase went away towards Spanish Head. The men are all gone and dead now. The house was left standing, but it is taken away over twenty years.

191. MEETING A CAT AND DARKNESS OVERTAKING A MAN

A young man was coming from the Howe one night, and there was something like a cat coming alongside until they came to a gate, and the cat went in at the gate, and the next night he was coming up the cat came up with him again, but the third night he made up his mind that he would try and catch him, so he had to wait for some time; at last he came, and he made an attempt to catch him, but he jumped over the gate, and the man could not find the gate; it got so dark that he had to come away without finding it.

192. THE ROYAL VISIT TO RAMSEY IN 1847

We have a very interesting account of the event preserved in *A Handbook for Visitors to the Isle of Man, being a Pictorial Guide to the Picturesque Scenery and Beauties of Mona*, London, Kent & Richards, 1852, and in *Leech's New Illustrated Tourist's Guide to the Isle of Man: Its Scenery, History, Popular Customs, &c.*, Ramsey, F. Leech, and in *Backwell's Handbook for Visitors to the Isle of Man*, edited and revised by James Burman, Esq., F.R.A.S., Douglas, which deserves a permanent record in your valuable columns. It says, putting the various information together:

At the back of Ramsey, immediately under the base of the mountain, are the estates of Ballure and Claughbane, two of the sweetest properties in the Island. Around by these under the mountain cliffs is a favourite walk which for picturesque beauty surpasses any other the public have access to; from thence the town below, and plain beyond, are to be seen at great advantage. The mountain overhanging Ballure and Claughbane was called Lhergy Frizzel, but has lately been named Albert Hill, and the glen below Victoria Glen, from the occasion of Prince Albert having ascended its summit on the 20th September, 1847, the Royal Squadron being at anchor in Ramsey Bay on their way from Scotland. The Prince availed himself of the opportunity, went on shore and ascended the hill. His Royal Highness expressed enthusiastic admiration of the scenery from this spot, yet remembered with a natural pride by the loyal inhabitants of Ramsey. Meanwhile Her Majesty the Queen surveyed the town and the green uplands from the deck of the Royal yacht, and graciously received a deputation composed of some of the most respectable townspeople. On Easter Monday, 24th April, 1848, the foundation stone of the Albert Tower was laid by the lady of the Hon. and Rev. Bishop of the Diocese, in the presence of a vast multitude of people from all parts of the Island. The day was kept as a holiday, the shops in Ramsey being all shut. The various clubs of the northern parishes attended on the occasion, with bands playing, and banners flying, and formed an imposing procession from St. Paul's Square, and marched in order to the hill, where having arrived, the Rev. Wm. Kermode, chaplain of St. Paul's, offered up a most appropriate and impressive prayer. The inscription, which is engrossed in Manx and English, and deposited in a hermetically sealed glass bottle, is as follows:

The first stone of a tower erected by the loyal lieges of the Isle of Man, to commemorate the auspicious visit of Her Most Gracious Majesty, Queen Victoria, to the shores of this Island, and the landing of His Royal Highness the Prince Consort Albert, at Ramsey, on the 20th day of September, 1847, was laid by Mrs Eden, the Lady of the Honorable and Right Reverend Robert John Eden, D.D., Lord Bishop o f Sodor and Man, on the 24th day of April, 1848.

Several speeches were delivered on the occasion. The procession then re-formed, and returned to the town in the same order. Thus ended one of the most interesting ceremonies, one the most cordially united in by all classes of the community, that ever took place in the Island. It is a subject for congratulation that the Island possesses so neat and substantial a memorial of this noble and deservedly beloved prince.

The anniversary of the day on which the Royal personages first visited Mona is still kept in remembrance by those who had the pleasure of witnessing this most interesting event. The Albert Tower is a neat substantial square structure, built of granite, with machicolated battlements, to which visitors are admitted on payment of a small gratuity.

About six miles off may be seen the solitary lightship, warning the passing mariner from the dangers of the Bahama Bank, which, although never uncovered, is rendered thus the more dangerous to navigation. This ship was placed in her position soon after the Royal visit, the result of Her Majesty's inquiries while anchored in the bay.

A pair of tailless kittens, male and female, were sent to Windsor Castle on the occasion of Her Majesty's coronation, by a gentleman of Douglas, a compliment which was acknowledged and handsomely rewarded.

It seems that the name of Victoria Glen loyally given in 1847 to Ballure Glen, has not survived. In commemoration of the second Royal visit perhaps Ramsey may be glad to christen it now Alexandra Glen, to perpetuate the present occasion, a suggestion which, I am sure, will meet the united assent of the people of Ramsey and the Town Commissioners.

No allusion to the above visit is made in Broadbent's interesting little book, *Visit of the King and Queen to the Isle of Man, August, 1902*—which forms a real and valuable record—and I have no doubt Manx people will be pleased with having the memories of 1847 revived. It may be also new to many to know that to Queen Victoria is due the placing of the lightship at Bahama Bank.

193. A GRAY HORSE AT THE STILE GOING AWAY IN A FLASH OF FIRE, AND A LITTLE STAR

When I was a little boy, going to the Howe Chapel, I heard once an old Methodist preacher in the Howe, called Jemmy Brew. He belonged to Kirk Lonan, and was blind at the time. He read the lesson, pointing with his forefingers to the palm of his hand, as if it had a book, and read verse after verse as the congregation sung them, yet I do think he could not read nor write when he had his eyesight. They had heard him telling from the pulpit many times about a young woman in his neighbourhood that was very ill and near death, and he was very anxious about her soul, and after his day's work was going to see her in the evenings to speak to her about her soul and prey with her, but she was not able to trust in God, and the last night he went to see her he was crossing a field, as he always had been, and had to go over a stile, but this night when he came to the stile there was a very big gray horse, and would not allow him to go over; the horse was rearing and opening his mouth, as if intending to devour him, and made thunder and lightning in a frightful manner, but the old man knelt down and began to pray, and the horse went away in a flash of fire, and he saw him no more; so he got over the stile and came to the house where the young woman was, and he saw she was very near her end of life, and spoke to her, and God saved her, and she trusted in Jesus, but she died that night before Mr Brew left, and as he was still doubtful about her salvation, be asked her to come back and tell him if she was saved, and she said that she would, and died very soon after she had promised. Some days after the funeral he was coming from his work in the evening, and he saw a little star in the sky, and was surprised to see a star before the sun was set, and stood looking at it, and it seemed to be coming down towards him, and it came down to the place where he stood, and immediately the young woman stood before him. He had his pocket handkerchief in his hand, and he put his hand on her and he felt she was not a shadow, but a substance that could be felt. She told him she was saved and happy, but never to ask anyone again to come back to tell anything, for she said her companions that went with her had gone on and she could not overtake them in all eternity, but she only told him very little, and was gone again. His opinion was that the gray horse was the devil, and that he knew the young woman would trust Christ, and therefore came to stop him from going there, that she would not have anyone to point out to her the way of salvation, and to accept the gift of God.

194. THE DEVIL DANCING TO THE FIDDLE
There was a man once lived at the Sound. He was a very decent old man, and he used to play the fiddle, and the neighbours coming to dance. So he was fiddling away in the dark one evening before the candle was lit and the fire, and all was dark, but the fire blazed up suddenly and he saw the devil or some of his imps on the floor dancing; he threw the fiddle out of his hand and never played a fiddle again.

195. A BIG WHEEL OF FIRE
A man, when he was young, was seeing the girls home late in the night, and when coming to the end of Beyr yn clagh glass (the grey stone road), he heard a great noise, and he looked in every direction, but could see nothing, and the noise was coming nearer. He did not know what to do, so he got over the hedge, but the noise was just

over him, and he looked up and saw a thing like a big wheel of fire. It was going round at a great speed, and went towards Ballacurry and when it was near that place it vanished, and he saw no more of it.

Second Account.—A man was coming along the grey stone road in Ballakillowey, and he met a big wheel of fire, going around at a fearful rate, but remaining in the same place, and he could not get past, so he went back and took another road, but he met the wheel again at the next opening, and he went across the fields to shun it, but when be came to the high road the wheel was there again, but he ventured to pass it and got away. It made a great noise with whirling round.

196. BUTCHED AT A STILE, UNABLE TO PASS THE STILE

A young woman at the Howe Chapel was going home. Her road was across a field or two, but the night was fine and light, and she was not afraid to cross the little field alone. She walked along the road right enough until she went over the stile into the field and along the path towards the other stile, but when she came to the hedge where the stile was, she could find no stile, and the hedge was so high that she could not climb over it, so she was going round by the hedge looking for the stile, but she could find none, nor any spot in the fence that she could climb. At last she was weary, and thought to sit down and rest herself, but there seemed to be something urging her to walk, and there she kept walking around the field for the whole of the long wintry night until she was so tired that she could hardly drag her feet. But day dawned at last, and she found herself in the little field next her own house, and the stile in the same spot where it used to be, and the hedge low enough to get over anywhere.

197. CROSH MOLLEY MOOAR AND POYLL VILL

These two places-the former meaning the "great deceiving cross," and the latter the "honey pool," are situated a little south of the stone circle on the Mull, up the way to Cregneish. The stone circle itself is called in Manx, Lhiack ny virragh = a sharply pointed pile of stones. I was very anxious to obtain the proper spelling and sounding of the name, and examined a great number of old men from the Darrag, Ballahowe, and Cregneish, and I am perfectly satisfied that the above rendering is the only correct one, which exactly describes the place. In the paper "The Excavation of the Neolithic Stone Circles on the Meayll Hill," 1894, by Prof. Herdman and Mr P.M.C. Kermode, it quite wrongly given as Lhag ny Boirey = the hollow of trouble(!)* The legends which cluster round Crosh molley and Poyll vill, taken in conjunction with the stone circle that crowns the height of the cronk, are of great importance—the spring just above, called Chibbyr ny gabbyl—not Chibbyr ny garval—or the horse well, is also haunted by fairies. (See my "Contribution to the Folklore of the Isle of Man," vol. iii, part iv, page 166.) The Crosh molley may have stood as the first of the big upright monoliths forming the long avenue running from west to east outside on the south side of the Circle; the Crosh has disappeared, but the traditions are still known to the old Mull people.

* The name in the mouths of the Mull people is variously Yack y veddach and Yack y verrach, the *d* is often in common parlance used for *r*. We have also such Manx place-names as Gob *birragh*, Balla-*birragh*, Lag *birragh*, the *Berragh* = sharp, pointed.

198. CROSH MOLLEY MOOAR

I never knew why it was called so nor ever heard of any settlement, but there are traces of ruins near to it. It was said the fairies called it so. There was another man of our gathering, from Surby, telling one time he was coming to Cregneish up Port Erin way at a late hour one fine bright night to see his sweetheart, and when he was coming up at Crosh molley mooar, he heard great laughing and sport up near Poyll vill, and as he got near the company he saw a great crowd of gentlemen and ladies dancing in rings, and others playing "kiss in the ring," and others jumping, and they were all dressed very fine. He stood for some time to get a good view of them, and they kept dancing, and jumping, and laughing, and shouting away; they did not seem to take any notice of him. So he came on his way to Cregneish and they got on with their merriment until he was out of hearing.

There was an old man on the Mull. He was on his way home from Port Erin, and when he came to Crosh molley there was a great crowd there, and they took hold of him, and he was obliged to go with them, and when they came to Pooyl vill they met a very big man, and he found fault with them for taking the man away with them. "Let the decent man go," said he, "right before the wind." So they let him go, and he got away before the wind as fast as he could. Many of the old people used to see fairy crowds at Cosh molley when the were near it, but on arriving there they had vanished, and I fancy that Crosh molley took its name from that, because the "crowds" always disappeared and they were deceived or disappointed.

Returning from Port Erin—it was one night in the winter—we got on very well till we came to Crosh molley mooar, and we could not tell where we had got to, and could see nothing. We were climbing precipices on our hands and knees, and more than once we walked into deep pools of water, taking us up to our knees. But after a little while we saw a bright light and made towards it, and found it to be our own. If we were on the Mull all the time it was very strange how we had to climb such places and walk into such deep pools of water.

I was coming home from Port Erin alone one night, about thirty years ago, and it was moonlight, with a full moon in the sky. When I came out on the gate that leads to the Mull I could see the road very plain before me going towards Crosh molley, but I went on walking for a long time, but could not find Crosh molley at all, and could not tell where I was going, but all of a sudden I found myself at the gate again, and started towards Crosh molley again, and got past it without any difficulty.

199. POYLL VILL

A man from the Mull was coming from Port Erin at a late hour, and when he was near Poyll vill he heard a hand bell tolling just beside him at a great rate, and he stood to listen and look about to see who it was, but he did not see anyone, and the ringing ceased, but as soon as he began to walk again the bell ringer commenced to ring again, sometimes at his right side and sometimes at his left, and it kept on until he was very near Cregneish, but he never saw anybody.

Seventy years ago some of the men got a new yawl built at Port St. Mary, and they carried her in a cart to Cregneish. She was a boat to fish in the Sound of the Calf; they put her down in the mountain above some house until it would be fine to take her to the Sound to fish. She lay there more than a week, and the people that were passing Poyll vill in the night were saying that the fairies had her in Poyll vill every night sailing away. I suppose they were not getting many fish in the Pool, but I have heard of an old man that was engaging a crew in the public-house to go with him to fish *penprock* in Poyll vill. I think they are called crayfish in English.

A young woman was coming from Port Erin. It was Pancake Night, and she was going to the farm-house in the Sound to make pancakes. She was coming at Poyll vill, and some darkness came over her, and she did not know where she was going, but walking all night and did not see or feel a hedge; but she must have gone over hedges, for when daylight came she was in Ballahowe mountain, in the middle of the cliff above Ghaw ny mooar.

200. BALLAQUEENEY IN RUSHEN

Ballaqueeney is too important a place in Manx archaeology to be passed over. It is connected with pre-Christian times, and has many features to single it out specially from other places. In 1874, in cutting the railway, an ancient burial ground and a superconstructed keeill was discovered, at a former little eminence called Cronk Ballaqueeney. The keeill displayed remains of foundations, chiefly built of stone, the walls were erected without mortar. The keeill, which stood in the centre, had a number of graves round it, forming tangents to the centre which it formed. They had slabs over them, the interior lined with flags; two bodies were found in the same grave. Close to the remains of the keeill was found an old paved platform, with a lot of charcoal scattered about, pointing to a previous occupation by pre-Christian peoples. The now famous two Ogham-inscribed slabs (re-used for the later graves) in memory of a *Bivaicunas maqui Droata mucoi cunava*, and of *Dooaidona magui Droata* (son of the Druid), bring the place certainly back to at least the fifth or the sixth century, beyond that we cannot go at present; the fire-burial or cremation place it, however, into pre-Christian times. The Druids were certainly in possession of the place, and in early times it must have attracted the eye of Columba as a rich field for conversion. The parish is called after him, Carbory (Corbbri's name is also found on an Ogham stone in Mayo), and we have already seen that it drew a goodly number of Culdees to the locality, attested by the copious numbers of keeills; besides it was very accessible and the district inviting by its greater fertility and situation. Flint implements also have been found in great number, in the hollows particularly, all through Port St. Mary, Ballacreggan, and Ballaqueeney by my old friend Cowell, late of Ballacreggan, who searched the district attentively for me, many years ago. Close by at Ballacreggan we have a square stone near the middle of the field, twenty tons in weight, with a hole on the top, and said to mark a place of worship. Another one of the so-called "giant quoiting stones," 7 to 8 ft. high, exists near the place, also supposed by tradition to have been a place of ancient worship, at the Four-roads. In the night-time many *bugganes*, and a very large pig, two calves, and a great monster, as big as a turf stack, hang about the place to frighten off the traveller; all this, taken in conjunction, shows the early pre-Christian existence of the place. That this centre must have continued in importance is shown by the former existence of a runic cross, originally standing in the Magher clagh ard (of the 12th century). Up to that time it appears that Ogham writing was probably even practised there—witness the Ogham stone Macleog (at Arbory); and the additional discovery of coins in the graves dating from Edmund (946), Edred (955), Edwy (958), and Charles III, the Simple, of France (893–924), serves us as a good finger post during the course of the troubled occupation in the 10th century by the Scandinavian Kings of Dublin.

201. BALLAQUEENEY AND THE STONE CIRCLE ON THE MULL

After finishing my preceding observations, some additional information supplied to me by a very old Manx fisherman, of Surby, extends my views about the prevalence of Druidism in the South. The fact that we find evidence of Ogam inscriptions only in this part, *viz.*, at Ballaqueeney and Arbory (the Kirk Michael inscriptions stand on a different and independent basis) will strike everyone as a noteworthy thing. No other locality in the Island has yielded Ogam stones, in spite of Mr Kermode's ardent searches for many years.

I mentioned Port Erin as a probable port at which early Irish missionaries, such as Carbery, Columba, or St. Patrick's followers, and many Ouldees might have originally landed, from thence penetrating into the Parish of Rushen, and Arbory in their efforts of the conversion of a rather dense native pagan population.

My informant, in replying to a query of mine: whether Port Erin had any other name, answered that it was also called Port Casherick, or the Holy Port. It is just what I might have expected, for Erin here means clearly Ireland, as I have already shown elsewhere. It was, no doubt, the port, *par excellence*, to which these holy men flocked from the Emerald Isle to the southern parts of the Island.

There appears to be a historical thread from the time of Bivaicunas and Dovaidona, in the 5th or 6th century down to the 12th century, connected with and indicative of the unconverted and converted native Manx and the later intrusive Norse settler.

The Mull Circle (Lhiaek ny virragh).—That it must have been a place of very ancient worship cannot be doubted. It had a long and grand avenue leading up to it from the west, and at its lower end was the Crosh molley and the Poyll mill.

We gather from the legend already given that:

(1) There is always a great crowd to be seen at the Crosh and Poyll.

(2) A big man is here met and asks the crowd not to molest the stranger, but send him before the wind.

(3) The crowds when you draw near the place, vanish and disappear.

(4) Or darkness suddenly and generally sets in, and you completely lose your way, and land from where you have started first.

(5) Great laughing, sporting is going on, a great crowd of gentlemen and ladies is seen, dancing in ring, others jumping, others playing "kiss-in-the-ring," and all dressed very fine.

(6) When coming to the Poyll a hand-bell is heard, tolling at a great rate, without seeing any one on looking, after passing it the bellringing begins again, sometimes at the right side, sometimes to the left.

And perhaps we may also venture to weave this up into a slight picture.

There is the great crowd of pagan worshippers wending their way to the avenue, and up the stone circle—their solemn place of rites. The big man is the Druid who sets the arrested intruder off again "before the wind." We see them forming themselves into a ceremonial ring, dancing and singing, the Druid in the centre; afterwards they have their rejoicings, dressed very fine in their robes. When they are disturbed in their ceremonies they break up and disappear, or the Druid casts his magical spells and darkness suddenly is spreading over the hill and circle;* intruders lose their way. At the Poyll there is to be heard the tolling at a great rate. The Poyll vill is the honey poyll, the sweet and blessed water poyll, used first by the Druid for his rites; but when the power of Druidism is slowly broken up, and the missionary comes to invade the very fountainhead on the Mull, and firmly sets his foot on Druidism, the poyll becomes a blessed vehicle for baptism and consecration—the holy water for wetting finger and forehead, and the Crosh molley mooar, planted firmly now at the entrance to the avenue, the symbol of the cross, becomes the breaker of heathenism; to the pagan worshippers it meant the great deceiving cross.

We seem to perceive the missionaries ascending and winding up in procession, with banner and cross, the silver bell ringing out over hill and mountain, chaunting and solemnly approaching the poyll with their triumphant Christian stone-cross planted beside, preaching and anathematizing druidic creeds and spirits, which the sweet tinkle of the bell and the chaunt of the psalter drives away. And thus the connection between Ballaqueeney, Arbory, and many other now forgotten places, and the Mull, seems to come out clearer. Of course, we have no direct demonstration for the picture I have introduced; but it may not be improbable in certain aspects.

* The Druids were accredited with the power to produce and spread mists over the place to make it invisible—perhaps by some dense fumes.

202. THE CORONATION OF KING GEORGE IV. AND THE DUKE OF ATHOL'S FEUDATORY PRESENTMENT OF TWO MANX PEREGRINE FALCONS

It is curious that King Edward should have paid his interesting visit to the Isle of Man so shortly after his crowning in Westminster Abbey. At one time a very curious connection existed between the Island and the ceremony of the Coronation. Man, as everyone knows, was formerly a kingdom all by itself, and then came the Stanleys, who continued to hold the lordship "of the isle and Castle of Pelham (Peelholme) and their serviory and dominions" for many a year. The conditions attached to this office simply consisted in the presentation of a nest of Falcons to the English Kings on their Coronation Day. The Stanleys, as Earls of Derby, retained their position until the eighteenth century, when Man passed by marriage to the Duke of Athol who sold his sovereign rights to the Crown in 1784. He still however, retained the actual territory on the same curious tenures. The last occasion on which this quaint condition was fulfilled was at George IV's coronation, at which we learn that "Amongst the feudal services, the two falcons from the Isle of Man were conspicuous. Seated on the wrist of his Grace's hawking gauntlet, the beautiful peregrine falcons appeared with their usual ornaments. The birds sat perfectly tame on the arm of his Grace, completely hooded and furnished with bells. The King descended from his chair of state and the ladies of the Court pressed round to caress and examine the noble birds." (See *Manchester Guardian*, column: London correspondent, August 28th, 1902).

203. ON CRONK NY ARREY LHAA AND MANX WATCH HILLS IN PARTICULAR

Mr Moore, in his *Surnames and Placenames of the Isle of Man*, says this eminent hill forms one of the series of ancient watch hills, he spells and translates it: "The Hill of the Day Watch." According to the ancient statutes, constant Watch and Ward had to be kept throughout the Island; "the night watch shall come at sun-setting and not depart before the sun-rising, and the day watch, shall come at the sun-rising and not depart before the sun-setting." Now we have (I give the spelling of the Ordnance Survey):

1. Cronk ny arrey lhaa, 1,449 feet above the level of the sea, between Niarbyl Bay and Fleshwick.

2. Cronk ny irey lea, 34 feet above the sea, near Point Cranstal.

3. Cronk arrey lhaa, 96 feet above the sea, a tumulus in Jurby, south of Sartfield.

4. Cronk ny Harrey (= Arrey) 430 feet above the sea, on the Mull, south of Cregneish.

There were officers in each parish appointed to look to the strict observance of day and night watch of the coast and ports. The burning faggot passed from parish to parish. Archallagan, in Patrick, is known to have been a watch hill, and so was certainly the one above Cregneish and Cronk ny Watch, near Scarlet.

When we come, however, to the Cronks Nos 1 to 3, we meet with certain difficulties in accepting Mr Moore's interpretation of the Manx name. Why, if they were watch hills, should they be qualified as arrey *lhaa, viz.*, of the *day* watch? Why should we, on that basis, not also have hills known as of the *night* watch? The night watch was perhaps even more important than the day watch. Have 2 and 3 been also used formerly as watch hills?

I believe the correct spelling to be really Cronk ny *irree* lhaa, the hill of the *rising* day, for reasons I shall now give.

A Manx friend of mine, an aged fisherman, when talking about this topic, once told me that he thought the old fishermen gave the hill that name in old times. The fishing and the herrings then followed much nearer the land, and when at the foot of Cronk ny irree lhaa (No. 1), they always saw the sun rising over that hill. He also mentioned, which is of significance for my contention, that some called it Cronk *brishey* yn lhaa, or daybreak hill, for the dawn is in a direct line behind that hill. Some of the characteristic points near the coast, amongst them Cronk ny irree lhaa (No. 1), were also often used as landmarks at sea.

It would be really interesting if Mr Kneen, or the grand old custodian of Peel Castle, would draw up and supply a full list of all the known ancient Manx beacon hills. It has been done for Lancashire and Cheshire in a very attractive and instructive form.

I regret to see so extremely few Manxmen assisting the *Manx Notes and Queries*, their help would preserve many valuable and now perishing traits, and besides a little support in many other directions—biographical and domestic—descriptive of the old peasantry and their habits and life, indoors and outdoors, would increase the value of the columns considerably. I hope my appeal will fructify, and then we may gradually obtain a more faithful mirror of the old customs, habits, and life in Man during days gone by.

Note.—"For whosoever fails any night in his ward forfeiteth a wether to the warden, and to the warden the second night a calve, and the third night life and lymb." (See Statutes 1411 and 1594.)

204. THE SODORIAN ISLES

While the more immediate descendants of Sumerled possessed the Sodorian Isle with a kind of royal jurisdiction, the Nordureys, or the Isles to the North of Ardnamurchan, were governed by the viceroys sent thither by the Kings of Man. These viceroys or governors were generally the sons, or brothers, of kinsmen of the reigning princes. Of one of those lieutenants are descended the Mac Leod; a family once very powerful in the Northern division of the Ebudes. Their descent from the Kings of Man appears not only from tradition, and the genealogical tables of the

Sennacbies, but likewise from the arms of the family; one branch of the two into which it has been divided, about five centuries back retaining the three united legs, and the other ship with its sails furled (page 306).

The promontory in Argyllshire, which is called the Point of Ardnamurchan, was the boundary which separated the Sudereys and Nordureys of former times from each other.

To the South of that promontory lies Man, Arran, Bute, Cumra, Avon, Gid, Fla, Colensa Fura, Scarba, Mull, Yona, Tiree, Coll, Ulva, and many other isles of inferior note.

To the North of Ardnamurchan are Muck, Egg, Rum, Canna, Sky, Rasay, Barra, South Uist, Benbicula, North Uist and the Lewis, including Harris, together with a vast number of small isles.

All these when joined together, and subject to the same Prince (Hakon), made up the whole kingdom of Man and the Isles.

The Southern division of the Ebudes was reckoned more considerable than the Northern. The seat of empire was fixed in the former the kings kept their courts in the Isle of Man and sent deputies into the Nordureys, who resided either in Sky (Ealand Skianach, or the Cloudy Island; Sky in the Norse language signifying a cloud), or in the Lewis (Logos or Lodhus, *ie*, a marshy country, more fit for pasturage than tillage) page 282-3.

(See *Critical Dissertations an the Origin, Antiquities, Language, Government, Manners and Religion of the Ancient Caledonians, &c.*, by John Macpherson, D.D., Minister of Slate in the Isle of Skye.—4to, London, 1768.)

205. THE FRASERS OF LOVAT, THANES OF THE ISLE OF MAN

Before coming to the Bield and the Crook Inns, we pass the site of Oliver Castle, on the left bank of the stream (Talla), the foundations of which are now so much gone as to render it difficult to discover the precise site where it stood. This was the ancient seat of the Frasers of Lovat, who, coming originally from France, at a very early period of history, were thanes of the Isle of Man, and afterwards became possessed of large territories in the South of Scotland, especially in Tweeddale. They were high sheriffs of the County of Peebles, and in the reigns of Alexander the II and III, and during the minority of the Queen, Sir Simon Fraser, Lord of Oliver Castle, with the assistance of the Cummin, and with an army of 10,000 Scots, in one day, gave three successive and complete defeats to different bodies of Edward the First's army, amounting in all to no less than 30,000 men, near Roslin, on the 27th February, 1303. This hero was the Wallace of his time; and as his heroism and patriotism were not inferior to those of that celebrated Scottish champion, so his services to his country met with the same reward, for he was given into the hands of Edward, and died a martyr to his country's wrongs.

(See *Scottish Rivers*, by Sir Thomas Dick Lauder, Tait's *Edbro' Mag.*, 1847, *The Tweed*, p. 339.)

206. ARRAN AS CAAJEY, BREAD AND CHEESE

If any woman in the Island was near her confinement they would be saying: "There will be bread and cheese in such a house in a short time"; and when a man's wife that had no cow of his own was near the event. he bought a cheese for the occasion, and provided plenty of oaten bread. The confinement in Manx was called *arran as caajey*, and by some also merely *caajey*, it was likewise called *ayns y cornaill* ('in the corner'), or *ayns ny straueyn* ('in the straws'). The Manx cheese was made of milk with the whey squeezed out, and had plenty of salt in it.

It was customary from the birth of the child till after it was baptised, to keep in the room where the woman was confined a peck or wooden hoop (*dollan*), three or four inches deep, and 20 inches diameter, covered with a sheep skin, which was heaped with cakes and cheese, of which the gossips freely partook, and small pieces of bread and cheese, called *blithe meat*, was scattered in and about the house for the fairies.

When the child was taken to church to be baptised, the woman who carried it also carried some bread and cheese, and the first person met (*qualtagh*) received of it likewise, in order to preserve her charge from evil influence.

In Scott's *Gay Mannering*, on occasion of the hero's birth, the *groaning malt* was brewed, and the *ken-no*, our Manx *caajey*, or the Highland *kebbock*, was presented after the good-wife's safe delivery, and Meg Merrilies descends to the kitchen to secure her share of it. The custom was universal in Scotland and England. In Lancashire we also meet with the *lady in the straw*, and it was also the habit for the husband to provide a large cheese and cake against the birth of the child. Here it was called the groaning cheese and cake, and the first cut of the sick wife's cheese was taken and laid under the pillow of young women to cause them to dream of their lovers. In a ms. journal of 1706, we read: "John Leigh brought my wife a groaning cheese."*

In Fargher's *Annals of the Isle of Man* occurs the following interesting entry:

1730 Lying-in expenses of a natural baby. An account of the costs and charges of Margaret Mylrea:

	£		
To the Midwife	£ 0	5	10
To a man and horse	0	2	4
To liquor when ill, and sugar, also ale	0	3	6
To pound of candles and 1 ıb. of cheese	0	1	7
To dinner to gossips, and ale	0	5	0
To woman attending me night and day during a week	0	8	2
To clothes for child when born	0	3	6
	£ 1	9	11

* See *Lancashire Folklore*, by Harland and Wilkinson, 1867, pp. 260–61.

207. JOAN MERE'S HOUSE AND WELL

"Under the Chasms, on the shore, is a well, near the sea. The salt water comes into it at high tide, but when it is ebbing the fresh water spring drives the salt water out of it, and the water is very good. The old men called this well "Joan Mere's House." The place is covered with very great rocks, and is something like a cave, and they called it "Joan Mere's house," instead of "Joan Mere's well" perhaps the mermaids were sleeping in it at night. Well, there were two men, but both are dead now, sir, and they used to tell about the mermaids they had seen, near this place. One of them saw them on a rock in the west corner of this bay, and the other in the east corner, which, he said, was a male; the female in the west corner had very long hair, and her skin was white, she had very large breasts, and when she saw them coming too near, she slid down from the rock. She dragged herself along with her hands until she got into deep water, and immediately disappeared. The male, who had his hair and beard like a man, used to swim about the rocks, and once was seen, by one of the fishermen, swimming through the opening between the Sugarloaf and the mainland, and was turning round and watching every object until he got some distance off the land, and then he dived and disappeared."

208. A DEAD MERMAID

"I have heard from a man from Ballakilpherick that once, when going down one morning in search of shipwreck, as there is sometimes floating timber coming on shore near the hollow of the church, they found a dead mermaid on the strand, and they went home and got a spade and made a grave, and buried her in Lhag ny Killey."

209. THE MERMAID'S GREEN

Between Bow Veg and Glen Wither, on the coast north the Sound, is a place called Lhiondaig Pohllinag, or the Mermaid's Green, or Garden, and the tradition is that the mermaids haunted it and sported about, basking themselves there.

210. SHENN LAA CHIBBYR USHTEY

The old fishermen used to mark the twelve days after the fifth day of January, each day representing a month, and they wrote down what *airt* ('quarter') the wind was at, and whether it was wet or dry, and allowed that each month would be like the day that stood for it, more or less, and farmers are keeping it up still. Those that mind it, and mark the days, say it is always coming true.

This is in Manx the *Shenn laa chibbyr ushtey* ('Old feast of the water well') of Bishop Phillip's time, or twelfth day, and was the last day of Yule in the Northern Calendar. Formerly it was a day of revelling and called *Laa giense* ('Day of dancing');

no fire was allowed to be lent then and there were many performances, such as "Cutting off the fiddler's head" and the *laare bane* ('white mare'). It was a time of "best wishes," feasting, and merry-making, with lots of mummery, and the season for divination.

211. THE USE OF SEA SHELLS FOR DRINKING AND OTHER PURPOSES

Waldron (1726) tells us that in his time and, of course, long before him, the Manx at their marriage feasts sent up broth in wooden piggins. This they sup with shells called *sligs* he adds, very much like our mussel shells, but larger. But it is the scollop shell, the *Pecten maximus*, which entered so largely at their festival occasions. Turning to Kelly's *Manx Dictionary*, we find mention made of the *shlig raucan*, or the scollop shell, which was formerly used for a drinking cup.

The custom of drinking out of shells is of great antiquity, and was very common among the ancient Gaels. Thence the expression so often met with in the Fingalian poets: The hall of shells, the chief of shells, the shell and the song. The scallop shell is still used in drinking strong liquors at the tables of those gentlemen who are desirous to preserve the usage of their ancestors.* Macpherson says: "After the feast, when the Hebridean chiefs returned home after a successful expedition [...] the harp was then touched, the song was raised, and the *sliga-crechin*, or the drinking shell, went round."(1) Flintoff observes: "The culinary utensils of the old Britons were earthenware, the shells of risk, and sometimes wooden bowls."(2)

Whitney, in his *Century Dictionary, sub nomen* scallop, says:

The shell of *Pecten maximus* is often used for scalloping oysters. Scallop now in culinary terminology, is a small shallow pan, in which fish, oysters, mince meat, *etc.*, are cooked, or are finally browned after being cooked. This was originally a large scollop shell; it sometimes is so still, or is made in the exact form of such a shell. Scalloped oysters were at first done literally in distinct scallop shells.

Shell: Icelandic, *scel;* Swedish, *skal;* Danish, *skaal;* Old Saxon and Frisian, *scale, skal* (3) stand for a bowl to drink from, a cup, a pot, and point to the same use in Teutonic lands.

The Irish name for a scallop shell or a cup is *Creach,* and *creachan. Creachan* in Gaelic means also a rock, a hard rocky surface, a scollop shell, a cup.

In Gaelic it is *slige chreachainn;* and in Manx *shlig raucan*, where the *c* (or *ch*) is eclipsed. *Shlig,* or *slige,* in Gaelic and Irish, itself means shell.

We see that the Manx name for scollop, which occurs in Kelly's and Cregeen's Dictionaries, as *roagan* and *raucan,* has no real existence, and should be replaced by the proper word *creachan,* to make sense of it!

Then we have in Manx the *shlig screebey*—a large mussel shell, which the country people used to scrape their sowen pots with.

The scollop shell was also used by the Manx fishermen for a lamp. They put the rush in, which was hanging out from the edge, and the former was filled with cod oil. It is also called *tan rogan* (from *teine* and *creachan*) by them.

The maritime Laplander during the night uses a lamp. A sea shell holds the oil which supplies the wick, made of a kind of rush, and thus is the constant light of a lamp readily procured from materials near at hand. It exactly resembles the Manx *tan-rogan!* (4)

* See Armstrong's *Gaelic Dictionary*, 1825.

(1) *The Ancient Caledonians, etc.*, by John Macpherson, D.D., Minister of Slate, in Isle of Skye. London, 1768: 4to., page 328.

(2) *The Rise of Progress of the Laws of England and Wales*, by Owen Flintoff. London, 1840.

(3) *Skal* in Manx, is a flat dish, a saucer; *skaaley*, a flat wooden dish used in wort (Cregeen).

(4) See *Travels to Sweden, Finland, Lapland to the North Cape*, 1798–9, by Jos. Acerbi. London, 1802: Vol. 2, page 190.

212. RANGE OF WELSH TRADITIONS IN THE ISLAND

We have no precise evidence of any Welsh rule in Man, although Cumming alludes to it in definite terms. According to him, the Welsh dynasty extended from 650 to 888. It is thought that both Cynan and Howel lived and fought for the supremacy in Man, that finally Howel was driven out, and that it was then held by Cynan, who died in 816. His daughter, Etthil, is said to have married Merveyn Vreich, her father-in-law being Goriad, that she had a son, Guriad, who was slain by the Saxons in 877.

An inscription, running *Crux Guriat*, was discovered in 1896 by Mr Kermode, on a stone by the roadside at Port-y-Vullin, one and a half miles S.E. of Ramsey, which stood originally within the burial ground of the old keeill on Ballaterson Treen.

There is a very distinct tradition that the cairn of the Cloven Stones, at Laxey Bay, is the grave of a Welsh prince, who invaded the Island, and, having landed at Laxey, was slain in the first engagement with the natives and interred where he fell. In the genealogies of the men of Cumbria and Strathclyde the name of Guriad (877) is mentioned, and some "Gwryat, son of Gwryan in the North," according to the Triads, was one of the Kings of the Welsh who were of servile origin. As the inscription and the tradition current at Laxey occur on the eastern side of the Island, it would show that any contact must have come from Cumbria or Strathclyde, but even then their influence can only have been very slight and transitory. There are no traces left of any Cymric place-names, or lore. In the south of the Island we have a hill called Cronk-y-Vretney Veg and Vooar, above the Struggan on the Mull, and another near Castletown, which, as I am told, had their names from the fact that Wales could be discerned from them.

Principal Rhys informs me: "That the story of 'Welsh rule over Man' is due mostly to confusing Mona = Anglesey, with Man. Howel and Cynan's contests were for Anglesey, and in Anglesey, and the beaten one seems to have escaped to Man."

213.   THE LEGEND OF CRONK NY MOOAR IN RUSHEN

In Part i of my "Folk-lore" (see *Lioar Manninagh*, vol. xi, p. 144), I stated that this mound is still variously called by the people Cronk How Mooar. To show the great plasticity of tradition, it is interesting to find that Quiggin, in his *Guide of the Isle of Man*, 6th edition, while speaking of this "fairy hill," says: "The natives supposed that it was formerly the palace of the Fairy King. In some of their tales of wonder yet related by the upland peasantry, the fame of a Glastin musician, called *Hom Mooar*, has reached our time, who had, by the melody of his music, decoyed many a wandering wight into the hallowed precincts, from which few ever returned. One of *Hom Mooar's* achievements is related by Waldron."

This remark has reference to the tale of the Fairy Cup of Kirk Malew, the substance of which shows certain variations and omissions from my own recovered version, and contains some of the details of my legend: Dancing twelve months with fairies (see my "Folk-lore," pp. 146–47).

Waldron collected his legends in and before 1726, and it not only proves the tenacity with which these old traditions live on, nearly 200 years having passed since, but also confirms the veracity and genuineness of his often doubted legends, of which, however, alas! he has only preserved for us a comparatively small number, merely touching the surface.

We have a similar tale in the Altar Cup, in Aagerup, a village in Zealand. The tale of the Fairy Cup of Malew seems derived from a Norse origin, and may go back to the 10th or 11th century.

SEA-LORE

214.   SEA-LORE (1)

Dr. J. Jakobsen, who lately made a prolonged stay in Shetland to investigate the traces of the Scandinavian language, published his results in 1897 (1). It offers many points to stimulate research in the Island. I must especially refer to the vocabulary used by Shetland fishermen when at sea. The number of words that are tabooed is, indeed, large. He says (page 23): "As is well known to all Shetlanders, the Shetland fishermen before this day, like the fishermen in Faroe and Norway, had a great number of lucky words that they would use only at the *haaf*, or deep sea fishing. *Haf* is the old Norse word for ocean. The origin of this custom is not easily explained, but the custom itself is very, very old, and deeply rooted in Pagan time. The likely explanation seems to be that before the introduction and spread of Christianity, and also long after that period, the people, and especially the fishermen, believed themselves surrounded by sea-spirits, whom they could not see, and who watched their doings. In the Pagan time, people believed in the sea god, and he had his attendant minor spirits, who watched intruders upon his element. The feeling of the fishermen was one of mysterious dread. They considered the sea a foreign element on which there were infringers, and, in consequence, the sea spirits hostile to them. They had, therefore, when at the fishing, to be careful what they did, and it became to them very important to have a number of mystic names, to a great extent agreed upon among themselves, although derived from words common in the Norse language. The oldest portion of *haaf*-words seem to have been originally worship words. The *haaf* terms extend much further. All the domestic animals, for instance, got separate names at the *haaf.* For the ocean they had *ljoag, yube, maar;* they had special words for sun, moon, horse, wind, fire—these of a poetical character." He continues: "A sufficient proof that the custom of using lucky words at the *haaf* was rooted in the Pagan times, is to be found in the fact that the minister and the church were on no account to be mentioned by their right names at sea."

Persons, animals, and things are named according to some striking characteristics about them.

The cat, for example, was called *foodin, kisert, poosi, raami, voaler,* and *skaavin,* and *skavnashi,* the latter means the shaver, the nose-shaver, for the cat's habit of washing itself up around the lugs and down over the nose.

There were special names for the cow, otter, seal, whale, halibut, ling, dog, horse, limpet-bait, the staff to strike the fish with, the boat, mast, sail, the sharpening-stone. There was a word for cutting the fish-bait, the fishing lodge, the fire tongs, the kettle, the end of the fishing line, the wife, &c.

Catton (2) speaking of the ancient inhabitants of Orkney and Shetland, says: "They also believed in a God Shupitter that presided over all waters, and who used to assume the shape of a Shetland pony. This deity, or water trow, is the same as is referred to in the Edda, and which recommends prayer to him for success in navigation, fishing, and hunting. The mermaids had the power of entering the skin of some animal capable of existing in the sea. The most favourable form was the large seal. Each merman and mermaid possesses but one seal skin, and if they lose it while visiting the abode of man, they either must perish in the ocean or become an inhabitant of our earth." He also quotes Dr. Edmondstone respecting their superstitions. From knots in the bottom boards of a boat they can foretell whether it will be lucky to fish or not. When they go fishing they carefully avoid meeting any person unless it be one who has long enjoyed the reputation of being lucky. Nor when the boat has been floated is it deemed safe to turn it but with the sun. They also observe omens. When at sea they seldom call things by their usual names, but by Norwegian. Certain names must not be mentioned while setting their lines, especially the minister and the cat.

(1) See the *Dialect and Place Names of Shetland,* by Dr. Jakob Jakobsen, Lerwick, T.J. Monson, pp. 125–1897.

(2) *The History and Description of the Shetland Islands*, by the Rev Jas. Catton, Wainfleet, 1838, pp. 14 & 114.

215. SEA-LORE (2)

In the Orkneys a notion formerly prevailed that drowned people were changed into seals. Old women still retain an unaccountable aversion to turbot, and avoid naming this excellent fish when crossing sounds and bays in boats. Some people also deem it unlucky to call things by their proper names at particular times, and there is a strange prejudice against turning a boat "widdershins," or contrary to the sun, at the beginning of a voyage. So late as 1814, an old beldame in Stromneys, named Bessie Miller, sold favourable wind to mariners at the charge of sixpence (1).

Let us now go to Aberdeenshire (2). When at sea the words *minister, kirk, swine, salmon, trout, dog, hare, rat,* and certain family names were interdicted. A white stone would not be used as ballast. To meet one of the family of Whyte when going to sea, was held unlucky. A horseshoe was nailed to the mast of the boat. It was disastrous to ask a fisherman, on proceeding to sea, where he was going. It was believed fish could be taken away. It was unlawful to point with a finger to the boat at sea, nor must the boats there be counted; neither must any gathering of men, women, or children be numbered. To pronounce the word *sow*, or *swine*, or *pig*, when the line was baited, was sure to cause its loss. If it is mentioned, the fishermen cry out: "Cold iron"; even in the church, when the same words are uttered by the clergyman, this is done, &c., &c

The salmon was called *so and so's fish*, or the *beast*, or *spey codlin*.

At Flamborough (3) a fisherman, 30 or 40 years ago, would not go to sea if a hare or rabbit crossed his path. As late as three years ago, they would not go out if anyone mentioned a pig in any way when they were baiting their lines; and they had a great fear if rabbits or eggs were spoken of. It was considered very unlucky for a woman to walk over the nets, or any of the fishing tackle, although the women take a very active part in collecting bait, and helping their husbands to bait their lines. It was considered a most unlucky thing for a clergyman to enter a cottage when the "gude mon" was baiting his lines, or to meet one on his way to the beach. "I'd as soon meet the devil as the parson" they would say. A few years ago no fisherman would go out to sea on Old Christmas Day, it being considered heathenish to do so. At Preston Pans (4) if the fishermen, on their way to their boats meet a pig, they at once turn back and defer their embarkation. The event bodes ill for their fishery. It is a favourite custom to set sail on the Sunday for the fishing grounds. A clergyman of the town is said to pray against this Sabbath-breaking, and to prevent any injury accruing from his prayers, the fishermen make a small image of rags and burn it on the top of their chimneys.

Impelled by Jakobsen's labours, and with a view to discover, if possible, traces of a corresponding character in the Island, I have for the last few years paid particular attention to this most interesting subject. Unfortunately, the number of old conservative Manx fishermen is on the decrease, and even these have only retained fragmentary recollections of old "sea ways." However, enough has been preserved to prove the close relation of these ancient customs between Man, the Shetlands, Orkneys, and the North-East coast of Scotland and Yorkshire.

Isle of Man.—To begin with, the proper old Manx word for the sea was, as in the Shetlands, *mooir* or *muir*, not *faarkey* or *keayn*. It was also called *Joan gorrym* ('Blue Jane'). Near the chasms *Joan muir* or *mere* had her house and well.

The *merman* (and also the *mermaid)* was on land *pohllinagh*, but it was not allowed at sea to call him so, but *gilley beg*,* ('little young fellow'). Just as the fairies were called *mooinjer veggey* by the peasants for safety, when mention was made.

It was not allowed, at sea, to mention any animal with hair on, by its proper name. A hare was called *fer yn cleaysh wooar* ('the man of the big ear'); the mouse, *lonag* at sea, and *lugh* on land; the rat, even to this day, *sackots*, also *uncle*; the rabbits, were known by the name of *pommits*; the cat is *scraaverrey, scraavrey* or *scraper*, and there is a place between Bradda Head and Fleshwick Bay, called among the fishermen *scraavrey Harry*, or *Harry's cat;* it is noteworthy that, according to Dr. Jakobsen, the cat is called by the same word in the Shetlands. The pig is *swoiney;* the dog, *moddey*, is called sometimes *choll* in a boat; nor was the horse allowed to be mentioned when on board (*haaf*-name lost). It was, of course, also unlucky to carry a cat, or hare, &c., on board, and if anyone mentioned the name of these tabooed animals, a fine of a shilling was inflicted.

(1) See *Summers and Winters in the Orkneys*, by Daniel Gorrie, 1868.
(2) See *Notes on the Folklore of the North-East of Scotland*, by the Rev W. Gregor, 1881, pp. 197–202 and p. 129.
(3) See *London Notes and Queries*, 13th April, 1875.
(4) See *London Notes and Queries*, v, p. 5, 1852.
* In Gaelic, *gille fioun* is the small white periwinkle; in Manx, *gille purn* is the devil fish.

216. SEA-LORE (3)

When the young men were leaving home to go to the herring fishing, if the first person they met was a woman they thought it a bad sign. If a boat comes to another boat for the loan of salt, they refuse it. They also reckoned it unlucky to turn the boat round against the sun at going out of harbour, and a great many of the fishermen will take a lot of trouble to turn the boats round with the sun even now. The third boat going out of harbour is supposed to be unlucky. They don't care to make a start on a Friday. On St. Columba's Day (21st June) the fishermen always expected gale and bad weather. Black pigs see the wind ("*Muckyn doo ta faakin yn geay.*") I have heard of an old woman shutting the black cat in the cupboard to make stormy weather, and I was likewise told that a family that kept a black cat without a speck of any other colour would never have anyone drowned at sea. For a child to be born at low water when it was *roayrt*, or spring tide, was very bad, as it would never prosper. It was also unlucky to take white stones as ballast. It was time for the fishermen to look for land when a merman whistled at sea. "When I went first to sea, the old fishermen did not allow anyone to whistle at sea, as they had some superstitions that whistling was bothering the wind, and made it blow; and I don't like it myself, although I have no belief it will make more wind to come." To ward off any ill they used to scratch the mast. Sailors don't like to carry a dead corpse in the boat, as it was held to be unlucky. "I was with a skipper some years ago, and he would rather go back to port again than to go to sea if anyone mentioned a bishop or a priest." There was a parson in Rushen some years ago, called *Lhergy*, when they talked about him on board the boat. There is some place in the North they call Lhergy Grawe, where the sheep-stealers used to steal sheep, and the parson was born somewhere near the place. (Lhergy is a gorsy hillside.)

"Yn 'nhee' bwoirrinagh" was at sea *chunnag*. There was a boat called so, but her proper name was "Diamond." The Sun they called sometimes, when rising above the sea, *Gloyr yn seihll* ('Glory of the world') and *Ree yn laa* ('King of the day'), and the moon *Ben-rein ny hoie* ('Queen of the night').

"The old fishermen, when leaving their crofts to prepare their boats for the herring season, I have heard, could tell whether the season would be good or bad by the kind of fairies they saw on their way home in the evening." They had some old notions about herring bones, and did not allow to burn them in the fire, for it was thought that if his bones were burnt in the fire the herring could feel it. In eating the herring, when coming to the bone, it must be taken away before eating the other side, for it was believed to turn the herring was to overturn the boat in which it was taken at sea, if they happened to be out fishing. They considered it unlucky for anyone to ask for one of the herrings which they are usually carrying on a string for their own consumption from the boat, unless they first put salt on it, so that no harm could be done. To ask a man on his way to fish "where he was going," is held to be very unlucky, some even, if asked, would turn back for fear it might put a spell on them. As charms they carry: The crossbone of the *bollan* fish as a good protection at sea for not straying; a horse shoe is nailed to the mast, and the *rowan* is also used; and the witches are burnt out of the boat before going to the fishing grounds.

Some charms also were used to secure luck in fishing, as sweeping the dust off the steps of the lucky skippers houses, and putting it in a bag to sprinkle on the nets. They also used to go to old Ballayeigh, the witch doctor, who would take out in his garden a small bunch of *vervaine*, which had to be boiled in a little water in the boat's pot, and when shooting, some of the water had to be sprinkled on each net as it went over the vessel's side. It was sure to bring up the nets brimful with herring, while the scoffers of these charms earned nothing but *gobbacks* (dogfish) and torn nets. Sometimes the vervaine was put in the buoys (*mollagyn*) which floated the nets.

Every man at sea is supposed to give a civil answer to every question, and cursing each other is prohibited.

When at sea they call each other by nicknames, or slightly alter their surname on purpose. On a certain fishing boat, I am informed, the skipper was called *Billey Yemmy*, and another man whose Christian name was Tom, was called *Joe* by some, and *Butters* by others. Another was called *Meseff*, and the cook *garron* (= pony). For another boat they called the skipper Thomas *Nickey*, and others called him *Gaaue garroo* (or 'coarse Smith'), there was Jem *Fayle* (Jim *Gale* was his proper name), and others called him *Tabernacle*, another was *Jonny Yoan Bet* or *Polly beg* (= 'Little Parrot'), another *Clim, Danny, Jenny, Tom, Etty, Nick*.

217. SEA-LORE (4)

Answers and replies, having reference to any operations or occurrences while engaged at sea, were rendered in certain phrases or jargon, perfectly known and understood by the initiated, but unintelligible to other people. This slang is very curious, and I will give now some examples:

When one of the boats heave to, the other boats run for him, and ask him *"if he had seen any signs."* He is supposed to tell what he has seen. I have heard them ask: *"Did you see the hog?"* and heard them answer sometimes *"Have you lost one?"* And when fishing off Douglas the boats sailing about speak to the boats lying by their nets asking: *"if they were proving?"*—if they had been, they said: *"Yes, boy."* *"Then what did you see?"* *"So many casts or hundred";* and if no herrings, the answer was: *"Water, boy; what store have you?"* and the answer would be if we had a good fishing: *"Thirty or forty mease";* and sometimes they would say *"A child,"* *"What is the age of the child"?* *"Fifteen or sixteen years";* and sometimes I have heard them say: *"This cook is getting rough"* (if there was near twenty mease), that would be the answer. They would be asking *"what, strap they had,"* because we used to sound the water before shooting our nets, and sink them to the bottom. I have heard them answer: *"Salt water,"* and the other would tell.

To pick out only a few items from this mass of information we find: In the Shetlands the sea god called *Shupitter*, changing himself at will into a pony. Drowned people are changed into seals; mermen and maids are possessed of a seal skin, which they don at pleasure.

The names bishop, priest, minister, parson, kirk, or church must not be mentioned; to prevent injury if the former has been spoken of, at Preston Pans a small image of rags was made, and burnt on the top of the chimney; if church was mentioned, "cold iron" was called out immediately.

Black cats brew strong winds and storm, if shut up in a cupboard (the cats are old witches).

Of land animals, the swine, sow, pig, hare, rabbit, rat, mouse, cat, cow, and horse, were tabooed, which belonged to a different element.

Of sea animals, the seal, whale, halibut, ling, salmon, otter, turbot, and trout, must be left unnamed, or only indicated by their haafword. The merman and maid were called at sea by another word, *Gille beg*, and *Yoan gorrym*.

The belongings of the fishers and sailors, such as boat, mast, and sail, bad *haaf-* names; also their wives, the bait, the fish staff, spear, and sharpening stone; so had wind, fire, firetongs, and kettle; nor must the boats or men be counted.

The men were not allowed to whistle on sea; the mast was scratched to ward off ill (stroking, an act agreeable to both mortals and gods).

The loan of salt must be refused.

No white stones were allowed as ballast; and anything white, and even the surname of White, was objectionable. May it have been a reminder of the priest's Alba?

The boats must not be turned widdershins.

On Columba's Day the Manx expected gale (he was a Christian missionary).

The fishermen must not divulge where they went to (the sea god has to be kept ignorant). The sounding at sea, the result of their catch of fish, is only communicated in unintelligible speech, or he may understand it.

The fishermen have to assume nick-names, or make a slight change of their real name. Even the shape of the boats originally were in form of a sea snake, dolphin, or water-horse, &c., and the keel bore the image of mermaids, sea animals, or the figure of Neptune, to impose on the inimical sea gods.

The sea even had to be called by other names, as *ljoag, gube, mooir*.

The leading feature of these various observances is the constant and conscious terror and dread of the sea spirits and deities they express—beings to be cajoled, deceived, mystified, propitiated, and humoured, while encroaching on their element, on which the fisherman appears as a timid poacher and intruder who proceeds but stealthily, and with a knowledge of the danger of his trespass and thieving.

That mighty ruler of the seas and winds and waters was Neptune. We find him again as the Celtic *Nudd, Nodens, Nudens*, as the *Huikudar, Nyker*. He was the most powerful deity of a ship, and sea-faring nation, and also the great war god, and worshipped as such by the pagan Goidels. To break his power in the eyes of the pagan worshipper, the church degraded him finally into "Old Nick."

The above list exhibits various forms and stages of early cults, but it is not my intention to develop the matter further. We see the Goidels and Norse, as they pass gradually through various cycles of conception and belief; and we watch the contact points of incipient christianism, so largely permeated and tinctured with pagan colour.

218. PEEL SEA LORE (1)

It brings ill-luck to mention a whistle, or to whistle on board a boat, as it might be confused with the merman's whistle. The merman's whistle was a notice for all hands to go on shore, rough weather being at hand, and it is always heard before a gale. (It may be that the fishermen mistook for a merman's whistle the whistling sound often made by the *carrag-cooar*, or Great Northern Diver, before a storm.)

It is lucky if a Roman Catholic priest comes on board, but a clergyman of any other denomination was very strongly objected to. The first herring caught on a fishing boat in the season was always split open to see whether it had a roe or a milt: the roe herring being the lucky herring, and the milt herring foretelling a bad season.

It was a common practice for farmers to buy two or three mease of herring for winter stock. When the herring was brought home to be gutted, there was always green fern put under them on the ground, and no other thing would do. The reason for this was that the fern was supposed to be the fairies' plant, and that this little attention would please them.

A Peel vessel, bound from Liverpool to Peel, became becalmed some miles off Douglas. One of the crew suggested to the informant that they ought to stick a knife in the main mast to raise the wind. A knife was accordingly stuck into the mast, immediately a gentle wind rose up, and increased into a stiff breeze which continued until the vessel was off Contrary Head, about a mile off Peel, when it was decided to take the knife out of the mast.

This was done, and at once the wind fell to a dead calm, and it took the men all their time by towing and rowing with the small boat to get their vessel into the harbour that tide. (I have forgotten to mention that the boat was thought to be becalmed by reason of three women—wives of some of the crew—being on board.)

On Old Xmas Day, the fishermen could tell by the way the wind blew and the sun shone on Peel Hill, whether the coming herring season would be a good or bad one, and where the greatest bulk of the herring could be caught, whether in the Big Bay towards the South, or off Maughold Head, or on the West. This sign is still looked for on this day and believed in.

The herring caught on the West, though small, were considered particularly sweet and good, but were best eaten quite fresh, as they more liable to fray (?) or black gut than those caught elsewhere. There is still heard a saying that "*Skeddan beg er y hayrit*" ('Best herring ever caught'); but when the time came to buy the winter stock of herring, herring men liked best the larger and firmer herring from off the South.

When herring were prepared for breakfast on board, the cook always threw a few overboard, for luck, to the merman for his breakfast.

The Fairy Fleet. It used to be a common ocurrence for the fairies to put to sea from Peel in their fairy fleet, and fish in the Big Bay which is that part of the sea that lies between Niarbyl Point and Bradda Head. Their lights would be so numerous that they sometimes even deceived the fishermen. The fleet, being so clear to sight that their floats were even seen on their nets, but if the real boats came among them the lights would go out. When the morning dawned no boats or nets would be seen. These lights were always seen where the herring was most numerous.

Fairy Coopers. Down at the sea shore, under Cronk-ny-Irree-Laa, there is a cave known as *Ooig-ny-Sieyr* (= 'Cooper's Cave'). Here the fairy coopers used to be heard making barrels to hold herring. If they were heard making barrels in the month of May, it was a sure sign that there would be a good herring season that year.

219. PEEL SEA LORE (2)

After hauling in the nets, and when the herrings are shaken out, some salt is taken and thrown over both herrings and crew, while one of them says the following:

"Ashes to ashes, and dust to dust,

To keep all evil eyes from looking at us."

No one but the man that pulls the end of the net is allowed to look over the side of the boat into the water.

The first herring taken out of the nets the first shot of the season, is always put aside and boiled whole to mark it from the others in the pot. Then when it is cooked every man on board must come and take a pick of it, so as to share and share alike through the season.

There are fishermen yet on the quay on Monday morning who will not give you a match if they were asked one. If they had to, they would break it in two pieces, and keep a part.

If you had a good fishing, and a man outside your own crew walked across the deck, it would have to be swept after him, or else some of your luck would go with him.

To raise the wind, it was common to stick the knife in the main mast. It must be put in the side of the mast according to the *airt* ('direction') from which you, wish the wind to blow.

220. THE ANCIENT ROAD OF THE TWENTY-FOUR KEYS AT MAUGHOLD

Perhaps in the whole range of ecclesiastical history, in early times, there is no more venerable spot in Man than what is now the quaint little parish church which clusters at the sheltered slope of Maughold Head. In summer time the old kirk offers an unparalleled view against the delicate sea line; while North Barrule gives a bold touch to the surrounding scenery. When we approach its tiny porch we almost forget that it once was the cradle, and a great centre of an early Manx Christian mission. Here, in the sixth century, driven in his frail *curragh* of wicker-work, its hull wrapped up in a cowhide, Marcuil reached its creek from Ireland, and in a hollow built his little *keeill* of sods and stones. He became in course of time a powerful influence, gathering round him a crowd of devoted followers, and ceaselessly employed in fervid prayer and conversion. The stream of religious life runs uninterruptedly onward till, like a river that has divided its strength in many channels, it was shorn of its ancient lustre, and finally, when the dissolution of the hierarchic church swept over the land, its ultimate sequestration and stripping brought about its utter decay.

It only flickered on as a modest parochial wayside church—its work was done. Its early numerous sepulchral crosses, so precious as a telling record of its past history, exhibit the influence of four distinct schools—the Irish, Anglican (derived from Cumbria), Cymric and Norse, extending from the 6th to the 13th century. It is particularly mentioned in 1231 as the Exclesia Sancti Maughaldi, and for many centuries had the privilege of a sanctuary.

The Northern part of the Island, during the 10th and 11th century, stands out as the great and memorable battle-ground on which the Scandinavian earls and kings fought for supremacy in Man. In 1079 a hot contest was fought at Sky Hill by Godred Crovan; another in 1142, when Godred II met Olaf in Ramsey harbour; and again in 1164, on Godred coming from Norway. Until the Scandinavians firmly settled down, and prior to their acceptance of Christianity, probably effected about the beginning of the 11th century, the little valiant Christian centre at Maughold, which had weathered so many storms, cannot have escaped the throes and pangs of wholesale pillage and destruction from the hands of the heathen warriors who had occupied Ramsey and the neighbourhood. On the conquest of the Western Islands and Man in 1098, by Magnus Barefoot, a union took place of the two Sees of Sodor and Man, and about 1050 Roolner (Hrolfo), a Scandinavian, held the Bishop's staff in Maughold. He was buried here, and an elaborate cross in the church commemorates his name, and is referred to by the distinguished Ramsey antiquarian, Mr P.M.C. Kermode. Hrolfo was an ambulatory bishop attached to the king's court.

Up Maughold Head, which rises to a height of 600 feet, there is a zig-zag path, ascending a grassy hollow, which is known as the *Raad Kiare as feed,** or the Road of the Twenty-four. Tradition says that here the original twenty-four Keys first landed.

It would seem from this that at the period of the Godred dynasty, when the Keys were instituted, the "sixteen free Houlders in the land of Man," probably met the eight *taxiaxi* of "the Out Isles" on their bi-annual visit to the Island, where the king resided, for attending the customary Thing, being received in ceremony by the bishop previous to their united out-set to the Tynwald, held anciently at Cronk y Keeill or Cronk Rule, in Baldwin; either by taking ship to Douglas, or following the King's highroad along the coast, which, starting from Ramsey, joined a by-road from Maughold, and passing Laxey, the Stad of the Salmon River, terminates half-way between Douglas and Conchan. The assembly would probably proceed thence to Kirk Braddan, a nucleus teeming with Scandinavian life, as attested by its rich Runic crosses. Here Bishop St. Brandinus held sway in 1025. After holding their Thing at Cronk Rule, they would pass across the mountain path via Baldwin, Ulican, Injebreck, to Kirk Michael, situate at the north-western coast, a place no less conspicuous for its Norse ascent and strength. Here the Thing was held at the Hill of Reneurling, also called Cronk Urley.

These Things were primarily held ambulatorily, and as circumstances or requirements would dictate, for we have a distinct declaration of the Deemsters and the Twenty-four in 1422, made to Sir John Stanley, King of Man, that "the Lord or his Lieutenant may hold a Court or Tinwald wherever he pleaseth him," and in fact we find in 1422 a Court held at the "Hill of Rencurling"; 1419 at Castle Rushen; 1429 at Tinwald (and before this) "in the last Tynwald at Killabane."

It would appear as if originally the Deemsters were on circuit in the north-western and north-eastern parts (Killabane and Rencurling)—of the South, or visits to it separately, we have no indication—and that in much later times, for better despatch and concentration, St. John's Tynwald was fixed upon, and the spheres of Deemsters re-adjusted, *viz.*, into complete jurisdiction extending over the whole territorial North and South halves of the Island.

* See *Backwell's Handbook for Visitors to the Isle of Man*, edited and revised by James Burman, Esq., R.R.A.S., Douglas (1862).

221. SOUTH BARRULE

Hoary, indeed, is the history of South Barrule, and unique its position in Manx legendary. We are taken back to the mysterious wizard-King of the Island, Manannan Macy Leir, to whom:

> The rent each paid out of his hand
> Was a bundle of green rushes every year,
> And that was on them as a tax
> Throughout the country each John's Eve (= *Oie feaill Eoin*).

> Some went up with the rushes to
> The great mountain up at Barrule,
> Others would leave the grass below
> With Mannanan, above the Keamool (= (?) *Kione Bhuile*)

who, warrior, trader, navigator, magician, all in one, shrouded Himself in its silver mist.

Although supposed to be a Celtic god and hero, the tribute, strange enough, was laid on Midsummer Eve, the celebration of which was of Scandinavian origin, and not particularly observed by the ancient Goidels, whose great time was really May Day Eve (*Oie Voaldyn)* and *Laa Boaldyn*—the *Beltaine*. The festival of both the Celtic and Scandinavian commemorations was performed in the same manner: Fires were lit, blazing wheels were rolled down from the summit of the hills (Mannanan used to roll down as fast as the wind, like a wheel, from Barrule), the mugwort was gathered and woven into a chaplet, and made into a belt to be worn as a protection against witches and evil spirits, for then, of any period, the fairies and old hags were abroad, and on the next day the great Scandinavian Tinwald Court was held.

By the time the Vikings had planted themselves firmly on Manx ground, his memory must have become already mixed up, for his tax-collecting was deferred for a month—or may be, after all, there might have been true Norse blood in his veins, streaking his pedigree.

In the 9th or 10th century, we find the mighty Fionns already in possession of Barrule, their castle on its summit. In Dingwaall it was a vitrified fort, called traditionally Knock Ferril, in Argylshire, Farola, in Islay, Farabhuil—equivalent to the Manx Barrule. In Gaelic, Barra Mull, or Far bhall, stands for a bartizan battlement. All these are connected with the Gorree Legend. They had also a supply of water on the mountain, for tradition says there is a well on the top of South Barrule with very fine water. When you had found it, and drunk of it, and went a few yards away, you lost sight of it, and could not discover it again that day.

There also King Godred Crovan (1095)* is said to slumber, in the Devil's Den— since the last 800 years—spellbound, and waiting to be called to succour and free the Manx nation; and giants and *bugganes* hang about the skirts of its height, to frighten the peasant when the sun sinks glowing down to his western rest. Here, too, the Manx were routed in 1316 by the Irish freebooters, led by Mandeville, letting loose on them their Irish war-whoops, still dimly revealed, it seems, in the legend of the two fairy armies that met on Barrule, ready to begin fighting on the ringing of a bell.

And latter, we have a view of James Lord Strange (1637–51), leisurely making his way from his castle at Rushen up to Barrule where he fondly tarried to survey his lovely Island-realm from its lofty eminence: "When turning me round," he breaks out, "I see England, Scotland, Ireland, and Wales [...] Which no place, I think, can afford such a prospect."

Barrule, with its mountain passes, was an important strategical key to the possession of the North, and a natural shelter to retire to with their cattle on the landing of an enemy, and at large camp is visible yet on its height. We see, then, of what interest Barrule is, and always must be, to the Manx people. It was one of the last climbs of the aged poet-patriot, T.E. Brown, who loved that towering mountain so much, an attempt that so heavily taxed his yielding strength.

* See Moore's *Manx Folklore*, 1891, p. 58, another fragmentary corruption of this legend; also Harrison's "Old Man" in same work, p. 64.

222. THE ENCHANTED GIANTS AT CASTLE RUSHEN

We possess the following legends:

(1) Castle Rushen has long been famous for its subterranean passages and there are individuals amongst the Islanders who still believe that they lead to a beautiful country underneath, inhabited by giants. Amongst the many tales they relate is one that, several attempts being made to explore the passages, a number of daring fellows agreed to attempt the enterprise. Having armed themselves with staves, *etc.*, and procuring torches, they descended. After proceeding a little way, they found an old man, of great size, with a long beard, and blind, sitting on a rock, as if fixed there. He, hearing them approach, enquired of them as to the state of the Island, and at last asked one of them to put forth his hand, on which one of them gave him a ploughshare which he had, when the old giant squeezed the iron together with the

greatest ease, exclaiming at the same time: "Then there are yet men in the Isle of Man."

(2) Waldron: They tell that the Castle of Rushen was at first inhabited by fairies and afterwards by giants, till the days of Merlin, who by magic dislodged the greatest part of them, and bound the rest in spells. Waldron then gives the same account of exploration by some enterprising men: They come at length to a very large and magnificent house, illuminated with a great many candles [...] and to another house, more magnificent yet, the windows all open, and numberless lamps burning in all rooms. They beheld a vast table in the middle of the room, and on it at full length a monster, or giant, at least fourteen feet long, who lay sleeping, with his head on a book and a sword by him; terror-struck, they retreated. They were told by the servant of the first house, on returning, if they had knocked at the second house they would have seen company enough, but never could have returned. Desiring to know what place it was and by whom possessed, he replied these things were not to be revealed.

(See *Denham's Tracts*, the *Greater Mona*, 1850, also Waldron's version of the Sleeping Giant of Castle Rushen.)

A corruption of No. 1 is found in my Manx Folklore, part i, page 139, where a man once going to Peel on the mountains, seeks shelter in a cave against a great shower of rain. Shortly after, the *Buggane* (a *Fynnodderee* * in another place) comes to the mouth of the cave asking him if he could tell him three words of truth. If he could he would let him go free. The man gave him some stupid answer, the Buggane says he knew that himself. Well the man had the sock of his plough with him for the smithy, and the Buggane wanted to shake hands with him; and the man slyly gave him the end of the sock, where three prongs were on, and the Buggane squeezed them all into one, and said to the man: "There are some strong Manxmen in the world yet."

* See Moore's *Manx Folklore*, 1891, p. 58, another fragmentary corruption of this legend; also Harrison's Old Man in same work, p. 64.

223. THE ENCHANTED PRINCE IN THE DEVIL'S DEN, BARRULE

It is related by Waldron:

"About a League and a half from Barrule, at the foot of the mountain, is a hole called the Devil's (or Wizard's) Den. It contains now a very great prince who never knew death but has for the space of 600 years (according to the tradition of the peasantry) been bound by magic spells. A little beyond the Den is a small lake, in the midst of which is a large stone on which formerly stood a cross; round the lake the fairies are said to celebrate the obsequies of any good person."

Waldron wrote his legends in 1726, and the latter would bring us back, say, to the end of the 11th century, and seems to refer to the traditional Gorree, who is said to have brought order and law into Man. This king has been shown by Vigfusson to be no other than Godred Crowan, who died in 1095. He is the most popular king, and cherished in the old legends. The close parallelism of the giant legends of Castle Rushen points to one and the same source. The legends fall into the same line as the Old Wizard of the Edge, at Alderley, Cheshire, King Arthur, Frederic Barbarossa of Kuffhäuser, and we have many similar traditions elsewhere. These centre round an old national or mythical great hero or king, but are to be traced back beyond, to a Sun-hero, round which as a nucleus they formed and grew up. In Man the sun-myth is absorbed in the great national regenerator Gorree.

224. THE ISLE OF MAN IN 1761

The Isle of Man has for its principal towns Rushen and Peel, though Douglas is the principal port, which is much frequented by smugglers, because the duties of importation and exportation were not extended to this Island until very lately: though the soil produces corn, in which their exports consist, as well as in wool, hides, and tallow.

King Edward IV granted the regality of this Island to the Earl of Derby and his heirs; but on the death of the last Earl, it devolved to the Duke of Athol. This alienation of the Island from the British Government has occasioned more disadvantages than all the royalties and jurisdictions of Scotland, because the Isle of Man is the great magazine for the French to deposit their wines and brandies, teas, and other commodities in, till opportunity offers of smuggling them on the coasts of England, Scotland, Ireland, and Wales, whereby the loss to the British nation, and the gains to the French, were inexpressibly great; who in the case of the sovereignity of Bellisle, formerly in possession of the family of the famous duke of that name, plainly shew that they would not suffer such sovereignity and jurisdiction to remain on their coasts. Besides, the Isle of Man creates a prodigious expense to the British Government, in maintaining so many officers and cruizers to guard against the illicit and pernicious trade; not to mention the notorious frauds committed in the Customs, together with the perjuries always attending them; with the entry of certain goods for exportation, receiving a drawback or debenture; though these goods are landed in the Isle of Man, and then run back again upon the British coasts. Therefore, and as the whole revenue of the Island belonging to the noble proprietor is reported not to exceed £3,000 or £4,000 annually, it could be a cheap exchange to the public if he was paid 40, 50, or 60 years' purchase for his property therein.

(See *A History of Trade and Commerce*, by Rolt, London, 1761, folio.)

225. A MANX PROVERB

The following unpublished Manx proverb was sent me by the late Rev. T.E. Brown. Has anyone the exact Manx equivalent? I do not suggest a translation, as thereby it might lose some of its original flavour:

"Never marry a woman unless you can see the smoke of her father's chimney from your midden."

Mr Brown's comment was: "Isn't that good and characteristic?"

G.W. Wood, Streatham.

226. THE HERRING MEASURE, OR MEASE

It is of interest to trace the origin of the mease.

In old Irish *mias* stands for a plate, a dish, a charger, a table; and *mias* in Matthew xiv. 8, expresses the charger on which the Baptist's head is placed. In old Cornish *muis* or *moys* = a table.

Principal Rhys says: "As the ancient Brytbons, like the Irish, and presumably the Norsemen, had no table in the Roman sense of the word, the borrowed word not only served to denote the borrowed idea of the table, but it was also partly applied to that of the native substitute for a table, namely, a dish, or platter."

In Gaelic *mias*, likewise, means a plate, a dish, as *geal mhias mhor* = a large white plate. Compare also the English *mess*, for a dish.

But we must not think here of the modern plates, platters, and dishes of wood, china, or pewter, but of a period much anterior; and the Welsh word *mwys* points clearly to that earlier stage, for it is equivalent to a kind of basket, pannier, or hamper. These no doubt were originally made of rushes or osier, and sometimes sheepskin spread over it, such as the Manx *dollan*, and used for containing food, *etc.*, and either shallow or raised. The Welsh *mwys bura* was a basket to carry bread.

It was also used for the reception of fish, such as herring, and in course of time this basket or hamper, from being a mere receptacle, became gradually the fixed measure for the quantity of fish it contained.

In the Isle of Man there are five long score (= six ordinary) and four herring to a hundred (= 124), and a mease, or maze, Manx = *meaish*, make consequently 620 fish.

The herrings are counted into baskets, and it always takes two men to count a basket. They are counted by warps. When 40 warps are counted in, you sing out "Forty warps" (= 120), the other man will then cast in another warp (= 3) and a herring over (= 1), saying "Warp, tally." The basket is then finished.

The Welsh also have the *mwys o ysgadan* = the herring mease, of five long score, or 620 fish (see Owen's *Welsh-English Dictionary*), while the English herring fishers, according to Rolt (see *A New Dictionary of Trade and Commerce*, London, by Rolt, 1761), as their measure, had six scores to the hundred (= 120), *without* the warp and ally; 1,200 = a barrel; and 12 barrels = a last.

We see, therefore, that the meaning of the word *mias* spread out in various directions: Originally it was the hamper, basket, pannier; then partly became, and denoted: the dish, plate, and the table itself; and, finally, the measure of a certain quantity contained in the receptacle.

227. THE STORY OF THE BODDAGH YN COOIT LAATCHAGH, OR THE CHURL WITH THE LACING COAT

This is an old fireside story, and of a type that used to be in vogue in former centuries. It is interesting as it comes from the Island. I find that a version running on similar lines is found in the *Irish Penny Journal*, vol. i, 1810, page 130–133, called *Bodach an chota lachtna*, or the clown with the grey coat. It is supposed that the Boddagh yn cooit laatchagh was the wizard chief of the Island who rolled into the sea at Jurby Point. And now to the story:

It was about a great champion called Iron Bones; he was a great warrior and a great runner. I don't know what was his proper name, or whether he was a king or a prince. It is so long ago since I heard my father telling it that I can recollect but very little of it. But this Iron Bones was visiting all countries in Europe, and when he landed in any country he went at once to the king's palace, and challenged the king to get any man in his kingdom that could fight and conquer him, or beat him at running. If he found any man that could beat him in fighting or running he soon left the country, but if there was no man in the country that could beat him, he made that country pay tribute to him.

It appears that he was not meeting with any one that could beat him in any country, and at last he came to Ireland and went to the palace. He was admitted to the king's presence, and he told the king that he was the great champion called Iron Bones, and if the king had any man in Ireland that could fight him or beat him in a race, he (the king) must get the man as fast as possible.

The king said he did not think he had any man in his kingdom that would like to fight with him, but he thought he could get one to have a race with him. So he told the king to go and get the runner, and he would wait until next morning to run against him. So the king called his prime minister, and enquired of him where he could find a good runner. So the prime minister told him that Kitt McKeelens, the man of swiftness, was the best man.

The king set out at once to go to Kitt's house. He was the swiftest man in Ireland, and it appears that Kitt's house was not very distant, for the king was running on foot. He came to a grove of trees, and he thought he would be at Kitt's house sooner by crossing the wood. He had but just entered the wood when he met a very big man, almost as big as a giant with a big coat down to his heels, and big broags on his feet as large as little boats, and, as the weather was wet and the roads very mucky, the big man threw about a barrowful of muck off his heels at every stride. The King felt nervous when he saw the big man, and the big man's face was very yellow, and seemed to be well greased.

"Where art thou going in such a hurry?' said the big man to the king, but the king was desirous to get away from him as fast as possible, but he caught hold of the king, and he could not get out of his grasp. So the king told him about Iron Bones, and that he was going to Kitt McKeelens to get him to have a race with Iron Bones.

"Thou need'st not go no further," said the Big fellow. "I will race with him in the morning, and go back and tell him so."

Then the king went home again, and they were all surprised that he was returned from Kitt's House in so short a time. But, the king told them that he met a man in the wood that was willing to have a run with Iron Bones, and that he would be ready to start whenever Iron Bones thought proper.

So Iron Bones was desirous to see the man that was to have it race with him, and the King took him to the wood where the big man was. When Iron Bones saw the big fellow, he asked him what was his name. "*Boddagh yn cooit laatchagh*, or the body with the lacing coat, in English."

Iron Bones said he objected to run with such a big, ugly greasy *boddagh* as that, but the *boddagh* told him he was only a man, and if he would not run with him he must depart out of the country at once. Then Iron Bones consented to have a race in the morning. They were to run forty or fifty miles, I forget which. So in the evening Iron Bones went to the wood. They were to start from the wood at daybreak. The *boddagh* began to cut branches of trees to build a shed to sleep in for the night, and he was not long in making one. He invited Iron Bones to come and share the hut with him, but Iron Bones refused, and went and laid down underneath the end of a rock. He was not very long lying there until he was startled by a great noise. He got up to see what was up, and he saw the *boddagh* in chase of a wild hog.

He soon caught the hog and killed him and lit a fire and roasted the hog while he was away somewhere looking for ale. He soon came back with a barrel of ale under each arm. He came to Iron Bones and invited him to come and have supper with him, but Iron Bones refused. The *boddagh* devoured half the hog and drank one of the ale barrels; then he lay down to sleep.

When Iron Bones awoke at the dawn he awoke the *boddagh*. The *boddagh* told Iron Bones that he had better start, because he wanted his breakfast before he started. So he ate the other half of the hog and emptied the other barrel of ale. Then he started to run after Iron Bones. He was not very long until he overtook Iron Bones and passed him. He ran on until he came to a place where the blackberries were very plentiful, as they always are in Ireland unto the present season. The *boddagh* began to gather blackberries and eat them, and what he could not eat be put them in the pockets of his big coat, while Iron Bones passed him, and left him out of sight gathering blackberries.

When the pockets were full, the *boddagh* started to run again, and overtook Iron Bones and passed him a long way. Then he began to run at leisure, until he put his hand into one of his coat pockets to get some blackberries to eat, but there was no pocket. He put the other band in his pocket then, and that pocket was also gone: the weight of the blackberries had torn the pockets out of his coat while running, but he did not know that the pockets were lost until he put his hands into them. Then he went back again to look for his pockets, and after a while he met Iron Bones, and he asked if he had seen his pockets on the road.

"No," said Iron Bones, but I seen a couple of sacks about four miles behind me."

"That was my pockets," said the *boddagh*, and hurried black to get them. When he found them he had to carry them under his arms; so he commenced to run again, and overtook Iron Bones and passed him, and did not stop until he was in Dublin which was the end of the race. He got a sack of groats and mixed the groats among the blackberries, and began to eat it as fast as he could. He had all devoured to the last handful when Iron Bones arrived; the *boddagh* was often looking towards Iron Bones as he was nearing him. So the *boddagh* threw the last handful of groats and blackberries at Iron Bones, which turned him quite round about.

The *boddagh* bade Iron Bones go on board his ship and go away, and when, the ship's head was turned out to sea the *boddagh* put his foot against the ship's stern and gave her a shove, and it was said the skip went five miles with the shore from the boddagh's foot.

This *boddagh*, according to Manx tradition, lived somewhere in the North of the Island. He was supposed to live in Ireland after he rolled into the sea at Jurby; Mannanan Beg Mac Leir was his name in the Island, but he gave himself the name of *Boddagh yn cooit laatchagh* when he was going to run a race with Iron Bones in Ireland.

228. THE HERRING MEASE

A few more words about the subject. The mease as a measure of herring is already mentioned: 14, Henry III (*viz.*, 1230), see the *New Law Dictionary*, Giles Jacob, London, 1745. In Rider's *English-Latin Dictionary*, London, 1626, it is rendered in Neo-Latin, *Alestergium;* and an interesting account of the manner of counting herring by the Yarmouth fishermen is given in *The Food of London*, by Geo. Dodd, London, 1856; he says, page 345:

> The Yarmouth arithmetic is very strange in the numbering of fish: 4 herrings make a warp; 33 warps, or 132 herrings, make a "hundred'; and 100 hundred, or 13,200, make a last. Practically the fishermen and salesmen do not count a last, for they employ a basket, called a swill, which will contain just about five long hundreds (660) average herrings; and 20 of these basketfuls are deemed to make a last.

The Manx *meaish* contains 620 herrings, while the Yarmouth *swill* is 660 herrings; the Welsh *mwys* is also given as 630. There is, therefore, a little variation in local custom.

THE CYCLE OF THE MANX OSSIANIC LEGENDS

229. FINN MAC COOIL (1)

The preservation of the following Ossianic legend will add to the traditional treasures of the Island. It is of the soil and bears the native stamp. It has some similarity with "Finn Mac Cooil and the Scotch Giant," given by Kennedy in his *Legendary Fictions of the Irish Celts* (pp. 179–81). Mac Cooil lives there in a great fort in the Bog of Alher, and one day the great Scotch giant of Far Rua, is coming over the big stepping stones that lead from Ireland to Scotland (the Giant's Causeway) to have a fight with him. He had heard of the great Mac Cooil, he says, and wants to see who is the best man. "Oh, ho!" says Finn, "I hear that the Far Rua is three feet taller than me, and I'm three foot taller than the tallest man in Ireland. I must speak to Grainne, the vanithee *etc.*"

Our Manx Finn Mac Cooil dwells at the Sound, and the big giant, who lives on South Barrule, and thought himself the strongest man in the Island, hearing of one of Mac Cooil's great feats, comes over to the Sound one day, to have a wrestle with him to see which of them is the stronger. Finn's nimble brain is quite a match for the Goliath of Man, and his ruses, and daring challenges are quite delightful; the poor, credulous, and simple minded giant gets so panic-struck that he makes off as fast as he can back to his mountains, of course to the great relief of Finn.

230. FINN MAC COOIL OF THE SOUND CHALLENGED BY THE GIANT OF SOUTH BARRULE (2)

I heard a story about Finn Mac Cooil. They say he lived at the Sound, and there are ruins of three houses on the Burrow Ned. I suppose they were his dwelling-house and stable and barn. I heard them say that he was a very strong man, and he was coming along the road and cattle to some men trying to get a horse out of a ditch, and they could not get him out. When Mac Cooil came up he told them to leave the horse for him, and he took the horse by the tail and drew it up on the road, and nine men could not do it.

There was a giant that lived on South Barrule and he was very powerful, and thought himself the strongest man in the Island. When he heard of Finn Mac Cooil taking a horse out of a ditch by the tail, he came to the Sound one day to have a wrestle with Finn to see which of them was strongest.

And Finn was outside the house, when he saw the giant coming across the fields. There was no highway to the Sound in those days. (I remember when the Sound road was made myself.) So Finn went in the house when he seen the giant coming, he lay down in the cradle, and told his mother not to tell the giant who he was. The giant came in and asked if Mr Mac Cooil was at home. His mother said he was not at home at present, but she expected him soon. So the giant, thought to have a walk in the field while waiting for Mac Cooil to come home, but he had a look in the cradle and asked the old woman who was in the cradle. "Finn Mac Cooil's eldest son," said the mother. "He have a very strong beard for a young chap," said the giant, and he went out to have a walk in the fields.

Finn got out at the back door, and was in the field with the cows when the giant came to him. "Who are you?" said the giant to Finn. "I am Mr Mac Cooil's cowboy," said Finn. So the giant began to question him abort his master: how big he was, and how much beef could he eat at a meal. He told him a great yarn about Finn, how strong he was and what wonders he had done, and that he could eat a cow at a meal. He intended to frighten the giant and to get him away, but the giant did not mean to go away that soft, without having a wrestle with Finn. So he thought he would take away one of the cows to try if he could eat the whole of it; and he took hold of the cow by a horn, and intended to pull the cow after him, but Finn took hold of the other horn, and they pulled the horns off the cow. The giant thought then that Mac Cooil must be a great man when his cowboy was so strong.

Then he left the cowboy and went walking, and Finn went home to the house and told his mother that the giant was to lodge at their house that night, and she was to make two cakes of oatmeal for their supper, to make his cake pretty soft, he said, and to put the griddle in the middle of the giant's cake,

So the mother did as he told her, and when the giant came back from his ramble in the fields, Finn went to meet him and told him he was Finn Mac Cooil, that he had just got home off his journey, and that he would have to wait until the morning to try their strength, as he was tired and wanted a night of rest. So the giant was agreeable to wait till the morning. Then Finn invited him to supper, and Finn's mother laid out the supper for them. I don't think it was tea, for there was no tea in Europe in Finn's day. I suppose it would be bread and milk. So they sat down to supper, and Finn was able to chew his cake easy enough, but the giant could not get his teeth through it, and he thought it was a wonderful thing that Finn could chew his cake so easy and he could not chew it at all. "Mac Cooil," thought he, "must be stronger than myself. He is a wonderful man. I think it would be better to make the best of my way home again, but that would be cowardly in a big man like myself to be afraid of a little man like Mac Cooil. So I will lodge here for the night and have a go at him in the morning." So the old lady made a shakedown for the giant in the barn.

When the morning came it was very warm, and Finn said they would have a wrestle after breakfast; but the poor giant could eat no breakfast, and be refused to take anything for fear of Mac Cooil seeing that he could not chew his bread. When Finn was ready, he said to the giant that the day was very warm and that they had better take a swim to freshen them before the wrestle. "With all my heart," said the giant.

Then Finn said to his mother: "Put all the bread in the house in my wallet, and a small crock of butter, and a cheese or two." The giant stood by wondering. He said at last: "And what would Mac Cooil be after doing with all that?" "For provision for its while we are swimming," said Mac Cooil, "for we may be hungry; a long swim sharpens my appetite." "I thought we were only going to swim in a river or pond," said the giant. "Ah, no!" said Finn, "we are going to swim in the sea, as there is plenty of room for a race. I often go as far as Wales."

The giant said no more, but got out of the house as fast as possible, and got home again fast as he could. And Mac Cooil got clear of him, for he was afraid to come again, that he would not be shamed.

231. FINN MAC COOIL AND GORREE

The story of Finn Mac Cooil, who lived at the Sound, and who was challenged by the Manx giant of Barrule, seems to shed additional light on the Ossianic Island legends, and assumes an interest even beyond the limits of Man. Before going more fully into it, and to make it easier to follow the thread of my subsequent excursions, I must reproduce the legend of Olave Goddardson and the Sword Macabuin, as reproduced in Moore's Manx Folklore, page 27–29:

OLAVE GODDARDSON AND THE SWORD MACABUIN

According to tradition, there resided in Man, in the days of Olave Goddardson, a great Norman baron, named Kitter, who was so fond of the chase that he extirpated all the bisons and elks with which the Island abounded at the time of his arrival, to the utter dismay of the people, who dreading that he might likewise deprive them of the cattle, and even of their purrs in the mountains, had recourse to witchcraft to prevent such a disaster. When this Nimrod of the North had destroyed all the wild animals of the chase in Man, he one day extended his havoc to the red deer of the Calf, leaving at his castle, on the brow of Barrule, only the cook, whose name was Eaoch (which signifies a person who can cry aloud), to dress the provisions intended for his dinner. Eaoch happened to fall asleep at his work in the kitchen. The famous witch-wife Ada caused the fat accumulated at the lee side of the boiling pot to bubble over into the fire, which set the house in a blaze. The astonished cook immediately exerted his characteristic powers to such an extent that he alarmed the hunters in the Calf, a distance of nearly ten miles.

Kitter, hearing the cries of his cook, and seeing his castle in flames, made to the beach with all possible speed, and embarked in a small currach for Man, accompanied by nearly all his attendants. When about half way, the frail bark struck on a rock (which, from that circumstance, has since been called Kitterland), and all on board perished.

The fate of the great baron, and the destruction of his boat, caused the surviving Norwegians to believe that Eaoch the cook was in league with the witches of the Island, to extirpate the Norwegians then in Man; and on this charge he was brought to trial, and sentenced to suffer death. The unfortunate cook heard his doom pronounced with great composure; but claimed the privilege, at that time allowed to criminals in Norway, of choosing the place and manner of passing from time to eternity. This was readily granted by the king. "Then," said the cook, with a loud voice, "I wish my head to be laid across one of your majesty's legs, and there cut off by your majesty's sword Macabuin, which was made by Loan Maclibuin, the Dark Smith of Drontheim."

It being generally known that the king's scimitar could sever even a mountain of granite if brought into immediate contact with its edge it was the wish of everyone present that he would not comply with the subtle artifice of such a low varlet as Eaoch the cook; but his majesty would not retract the permission so recently given, and therefore gave orders that the execution should take place in the manner desired.

Although the unflinching integrity of Olave was admired by his subjects, they sympathised deeply for the personal injury to which he exposed himself, rather than deviate from the path of rectitude. But Ada, the witch, was at hand: she ordered toads' skins, twigs of the rowan tree, and adders eggs, each to the number of nine times nine, to be placed between the king's leg and the cook's head, to which he assented.

All these things being properly adjusted, the great sword Macabuin, made by Loan Maclibuin the Dark Smith of Drontheim, was lifted with the greatest caution by one of the king's most trusty servants, and laid gently on the neck of the cook; but ere its downward course could be stayed, it severed the head from the body of Eaoch, and cut all the preventives asunder except the last, thereby saving the king's leg from harm.

When the Dark Smith of Drontheim heard of the stratagem submitted to by Olave to thwart the efficacy of the sword Macabuin, he was so highly offended that he despatched his hammer-man, Hiallus-nan-urd, who had only one leg having lost the other when assisting in making that great sword, to the Castle of Peel, to challenge King Olave or any of his people to walk with him to Dromtheim. Olave accepted the challenge, and set out to walk against the one-legged traveller from the Isle of Man to the smithy of Loan Maclibhun, in Drontheim.

"They walked o'er the land and they sail'd o'er the sea."

And so equal was the match that, when within sight of the smithy, Hiallus-nan-urd, who was first, called on Loan Maclibhun to open the door, and Olave called out to shut it. At that instant, pushing past he of the one leg, the king entered the smithy first, to the evident discomfiture of the swarthy smith and his assistant To show that he was not in the least fatigued, Olave lifted a large forge hammer, and under pretence of assisting the smith, struck the anvil with such force that he clove it not only from top to bottom, but also the block upon which it rested.

Emergaid, the daughter of Loan, seeing Olave perform such manly prowess, fell so deeply in love with him that during the time her father was replacing the block and the anvil, she found an opportunity of informing him that her father was only replacing the studdy to finish a sword be was making, and that he had decoyed him to that place for the purpose of destruction, as it had been prophesied that the sword would be tempered in royal blood, and in revenge for the affront of the cook's death by the sword Macabuin. "Is not your father the seventh son of old windy cap, King of Norway?" said Olave. "He is," replied Emergaid, as her father entered the smithy. "Then," cried the Kind of Man, as he drew the red steel from the fire, "the prophecy must be fulfilled." Emergaid was unable to stay his uplifted hand till he quenched the sword in the blood of her father, and afterwards pierced the heart of the one-legged hammerman, who he knew was in the plot of taking his life.

This tragical event was followed by one of a more agreeable nature. Olave, conscious that had it not been for the timely intervention of Emergaid, the sword of her father would indeed have been tempered in his blood, and knowing the irreparable loss which she had sustained at his hands, made her his queen, and from her were descended all succeeding kings of Man down to Magnus, the last of the race of Goddard Crovan the Conqueror.

232. A DEMON'S TRICKS FROM THE OLIO, BY F. GROSE, 1792

The Rev. Mr Wood, of Douglas, told me the following story of a Mr Cosnan (minister of Kirk Santon) which his father had from his own mouth: "This gentleman's house was haunted by a ludicrous demon, who played a thousand monkey tricks, such as scribbling upon a newly-plastered wall; and once at noon-day, Mr Stanton throwing a stone across a river, it was returned to him by an invisible hand, and that an hundred times successively; that he might not be mistaken, he had the precaution to mark it. This story making a noise, several substantial farmers called in to enquire tide truth of it. One among them doubting it, and in displaying his eloquence striking his hand on the table, a stone suddenly fell from the ceiling near his hand and stuck in the table, to the great astonishment of the whole company."

G.W. WOOD, Streatham.

233. THE LEGEND OF FIN GORREE

The legend of Olave Goddardson, as recounted in my last note, is in reality a compound made up of a group of distinct sub-legends, which age, it seems, has thrown indiscriminately into a common melting pot, but which, by analysis can easily be decomposed into its various elements, and thus he compared with the traditional tales derived from other sources, and so restored.

Let me now take up the thread again:

There lived in Man in the times of Olave Goddardson, our Manx tradition says, a great baron, named Kitter, who, was fond of the chase and extirpated all the bisons and elks in the Island. One day he extented his havoc to the red deer of the Calf, or Kitterland (Kitterland is, of course, *Kittel* or *Kettel*-land and so pronounced in common parlance by the Manx fisher-people. I have come across with, and Kettel is the same as Fin Kettel and the name of a Norseman who yielded great influence in

Ireland and Man about the middle of the ninth century.) He left at his castle on the brow of Barrule his cook only, called Eaoch to dress provisions. This is, as we have seen in our legend of Finn Mac Cooill and the Giant of Barrule, no other than the giant of Barrule who again is to be equated with the Orree of the subsequent Manx legend of *Fin as Oshin*, to which I shall return. His witch-wife Ada, the legend continues, caused the fat to bubble over into the fire, which set the castle in a blaze (in *Fin and Oshin* it is Orree who sets the castle on fire). The cook(!) alarms the hunters in the Calf a distance of nearly ten miles. Kitter, seeing the castle in flames, made to the beach with all possible speed in a small currach, for Man, accompanied by nearly all his attendants. When about halfway the bark struck on a rock (since called Kitterland) and all perished. The fate of Kitter and the destruction of his boat caused the surviving Norwegians to believe that Eaoch (= Orree, the cook, the Barrule Giant) was in league with the Island witches (= the unthinking wives of the Fians who bound and jeered Gorree) to extirpate the Norwegians then in Man, and was brought, to trial and sentenced to suffer death. He heard his doom with great composure, but claimed the privilege to choose the manner of his death. He said, "I wish my head to be laid across one of your majesty's legs, and there cut off by your majesty's sword Macabuin (= Mac an Luinn), which was made by Loan Maclibuin, the "Dark Smith of Drontheim." It being generally known that the King's scimitar could sever even a mountain ot granite if brought into immediate contact with its edge, it was the wish of everyone present that he would not comply with the subtle artifice of such a low vaglet as Eaoch (= Gorree, who was considered the weakest and lowest of the Fians and held in contempt by the women); but he would not retract the permission given, and gave orders to have the execution in the manner desired. But Ada, the witch, was at hand; she ordered toads skins, twigs of the rowan tree, and adders eggs, each to the number of nine times nine, to be placed between the king's leg and the cook's head, to which he assented. All these things being properly adjusted, the great sword Macabuin was lifted and gently laid on the neck of the cook, but ere its downward course could be stayed it severed the head from the body of Eaoch, and cut all the preventives asunder except the last, thereby saving the king's leg from harm.

In the legend of *Fin as Oshin*, which was rescued from a Manx woman in the year 1762 by Deemster Heywood, the full details and cause of the destruction of the castle, due to the revenge of Orree or Gorree, are particularly attended to, and this poem presents an important and precious supplement to the later legend of Olave Goddardson. I must, therefore reproduce it for a proper comparison with the Gaelic parallels which will form my next note.

FIN AS OSHIN

Hie Fin as Oshin magh dy helg,
Lesh sheshaght trean as moddee elg,
Cha row un dooinney sloo ny keead,

Coshee cha bieau cha row ny lheid,
Lesh feedyn coo eisht hie ad magh,
Trooid slieau as coan dy yannoo cragh,
Quoi daag ad ec y thie agh Orree beg
Cadley dy kiune fo scadoo'n creg!
Slane three feed qualliau aeg gyn unnane sloo,
Lesh three feed cailleeyn dy yeeaghyn moo,
—Dooyrt inneen Fin ayns craid as corree,
"Kys yiow mayd nish cooilleen er Orree?'
Dooyrt inneen Oshin; "kiangle mayd eh,
Lesh folt y ching chionn gys y clea,
As chur mayd aile gys y cass cha bieau."
Clysht tappee eisht hug Orree ass,
Tra dennee'n smuir roie ass e chiass,
Loo Mollaght Mynney ad dy stroie,
Va er n'yannoo craid er mac y ree,
Dy farbagh breearrey ry ghrian as eayst,
Dy losht ad hene as thieyn neesht,
—Hie Orree beg magh dys ny sleityn,
As speih mooar connee er e geayltyn,
Hoght bart mooar trome hug eh lesh cart,
Hoght kionnanyn currit ayns dagh bart.
Hoght deiney lheid's sy theihll nish t'ayn,
Cha droggagh bart jeh shoh ny v'ayn
Ayns dagh uinnag hug eh bart as ayns dagh dorrys,
Agh mean y thie mooar hene yn bart mooar sollys.
—Va Fin as Oshin nish shelg dy chionn,
Lesh ooilley nyn treanee ayns ollish as loan,
Yaagh wooar ren sheeyney ass y glion, neear,
Troggal ayns bodjallyn agglagh myr rere;
Roie Fin as roie Oshin derrey d'aase Oshin skee,
Agh she Fin mooar hene chum sodjey nish roie;
Eisht dyllee Fin huggey lesh coraa trome,
"Cha vel faagit ain nish agh tholtanyn lhome,
Quoi ren yn assee shoh nagh re Orree beg?'
V'an chosney voue chelleerid gys ooig fo yn creg,
Raad plooghit lesh yaagh hayrn ad magh ery cass.

Fin and Oshin went out to hunt, (1)
With a noble train of men and dogs,
Not less in number than one hundred men,
So swift of foot and keen, none were their like;

With scores of Bandogs fierce they sallied forth,
O'er Hill and Dale, much Havock for to make.
—Whom left they then at home, but youthfull Orree!
Who slept secure beneath the shadowy rock;
Full three score Greyhounds, with their whelps they left,
(With three score lovely maidens, young and fair,)
As many old dames to attend the young.
Says Fin's fair Daughter, in Disdain and Scorn,
How on young Orree shall we be revenged?
—Says Oshin's Daughter
Fast to the Harrows we will tie his Hair,
And to his nimble feet, we'll set a train of Fire.
Then up starts Orree, with a nimble Spring;
Feeling his Feet a broiling with the heat.
With curses direful, vowing to destroy,
Those who presum'd t' affront a King, his Son!
Swearing most bitterly by Sun and Moon.
To burn themselves and all their habitations;
—Then to the Mountain hies he fast away,
His heavy Gorse-hack poized upon his shoulder,
Eight pond'rous Burthens thence he carried off,
And eight large Faggots cram'd in ilka Burthen.
Not eight such Men as in the world are now
Could from the Ground one of these Burthen's raise.
Into each Window, he a Burthen thrust.
Into each Door, a Burthen of the same,
But, the grand blazing Burthen, on the Floor,
Of the great Hall he laid, and set on Fire (2).
—Meanwhile, our Heroes, Fin and Oshin hight,
They and their hardy men pursued the chase,
Eager, in sweat and dust, all cover'd o'er.
—Vast clouds full floating from the west
Were seen like Billows dreadful, as I ween.
—Then Fin he ran, and Oshin also ran,
Till faint, and out of breath, he sat him down:
But Fin, the hardy chief, still held it out,
Then lift he up his lamentable Voice,
"We've nothing left but rueful, ruin'd walls!"
—"This mischief who has done?" Who but young Orree,
Who fled, and in a rocky Cavern bid himself,
—Then choak'd with Smoke, they drag him by the heels,

(And tore him Limb from Limb (they say) with Horses wild.)

(1) Kitter going to hunt on the Calf

(2) Fin Orree = the cook = the Barrule giant setting fire to the castle.

234. THE DESTRUCTION OF THE CASTLE OF THE FIONS BY FIN GORREE (= ORREE), AND THE CONSEQUENT DESTRUCTION OF THE WHOLE TRIBE

In my last I have given the Manx version, and now proceed to the traditions derived from and current in the Highlands and the Isles.

In Hugh Miller's legend (1), the castle is on the summit of Knock Ferril, near Dingwall, forming the remains of one of the vitrified forts, constructed, as tradition says, by a gigantic tribe of Fians for the protection of their wives and children, when engaged in hunting. Garry, not much more than 15 feet in height, falling behind the hunting party, returned to the castle; he was no favourite with the women, and the butt of their many teasing jokes. On seeing that he had fallen asleep, they fastened his long hair with pegs to the grass, and awakened him with their shouts and laughter. Infuriated, he wrenched up his head, leaving half his locks behind him. He set fire to the stronghold into which they had rushed for shelter. The flames rose till they mounted over the roof, but Garry held fast the door until all was silent, when he fled into the remote highlands toward the west. The males of the tribe, who were meanwhile engaged in hunting on the part of the Northern Sutor, alarmed by the vast column of smoke, came pressing on to the Firth of Cromarty and, leaping across on their hunting spears, they hurried home. They arrived too late; wild with rage they tracked him into a nameless glen, known ever since as Glen Garry, and tore him to pieces. And, as all the women of the tribe perished in the flames, the race of the Fians died out.

In the Argyleshire version (2), the Fians leave big Garry, the son of Morna, behind them to find out what secret means of nourishment the women had—they lived on the leaves of trees, the roots of heather, and the tops of hazel. While watching, he fell asleep beside an old log, or the seven sticks of wood, which, like tether-pins, they drove into the ground, tying seven plies of his hair to the sticks.

Then they raised the war-cry of the Fians. It was heard over five-fifths of Ireland, and Garry, on hearing it, leapt up, leaving the seven plies of hair sticking to the log. He set the dwelling of Brugh Farola on fire. The Fians seeing the smoke and the dwelling blazing high, leapt across the Sound that separated Skye from the mainland. He was caught in the cave and put to death, and allowed to choose the manner of his own death.

In the Islay legend (3), it is Farabhuil where the wives of the Feinns (Fians) lived, at the foot; of Farabhein, in Ardnamurachan, and Conan here takes the place of Garry (= Gorry, Orree, Finn Gorree). His strength lay in his hair, which was kept cropped to keep him weak, for, if it grew, every single hair gave him the strength of a single man, and he was so cross that if it would grow he would kill them all.—The story runs on in the same style as the preceding ones.—When the castle was seen in flames, the Feinns were on the other side of Caol Readhin (Kyle Pay); they leapt the strait, but one Mac an Reaidhinn, in the attempt, fell into it and was drowned, and since that day the name of Reaidhinn's Strait has stuck to it. The Feinns were in great fury against Conan, and he asked, as a favour, to have his head taken off with Mac an Luinne, the sword of Fionn Mac Dhuil, that would not leave a shred behind, and that his own son Garbh, (Garry) should smite him on the thigh of Finn. They put seven grey hides, and seven bundles of twisted twigs, and seven feet of marshy soil on Finn's thigh:

And quicker than dew upon a daisy
Were heads of arteries cut into Fionn's knee.
Fion died, and the whole Fian race suffered loss.

We have here an amplification of the Manx version of *Fin and Oshin*, first from Cromarty, and the Isle of Skye, and from Islay. The Cromarty and Skye parallels ran remarkably close to *Fin and Oshin*. The latter is complete in itself. There has been much romancing about its nature and history in the Island (4). In the Goddardson legend the Orree tradition forms the introductory part, and is joined on to the independent legend of the Lay of the Smithy and the Sword Mac an Luinn, of which more hereafter.

(1) See: *Scenes and Legends, the Traditional History of Cromarty*, by Hughes Miller, 1829–1832; page 38 to 39.

(2) See: *Waifs and Strays of Celtic Tradition, Argyleshire Series*, no. iv, The Fians, by J. Gregorson Campbell, London, 1891; page 165; see also pages 12 and 13.

(3) *Tales of the Western Highlands* by Campbell, vol. iii; page 108.

(4) See preface xi, *Manx Ballads and Music*, edited by A.W. Moore, 1896.

235. THE LAY OF THE SMITHY (DUAN NA CEARDACH)

We have seen from the first part of the legend of Olave Goddardson the doom that awaited Orree for the ruthless destruction of the castle of Barrule. The ballad of Brugh Farola tells us that Garry was the son of Molum, and his head was severed with Finn's celebrated sword Mac an Lubin, which "never left a shred of the flesh of man."

The second part of our Manx legend alludes to the journey of Fionn to the smithy at Drontheim, where he forged his magic sword. I will give now the Manx rendering, broken up as it is, which will be better understood from a comparison with the Gaelic parallels:

When the dark smith of Drontheim heard of the stratagem to thwart the efficiency of the sword Macabuin, he despatched his hammerman Hiallus-nan-urd (= Nial of the hammers), who had only one leg, having lost the other one in making the sword, to the castle of Peel to challenge King Olave, or any of his people, to walk to Drontheim. Olave (= Finn) accepted it and set out to walk against the one-legged traveller from the Isle of Man to the smithy of Loan Maclibhuin (= Lori Mao Liobhann).

"They walked o'er the land, and they sailed o'er the sea."

So equal was the match that, when within sight of the smithy, Hiallus, who was first, called to Loan to open the door, and Olave called out to shut it. At that instant, pushing past Iliafus, Olave entered the smithy first, to the evident discomfiture of the swarthy smith and his assistant. To show that he was not afraid, Olave lifted the large forge hammer, and under pretence of assisting the smith, struck the anvil with such force that he clove it through, and also the block on which it rested. Emergaid(!), the daughter of Loan (in the Gaelic version it is Fionn's mother), seeing Olave perform such prowess, fell deeply in love with him, and during the time her father replaced the block and anvil, found means to tell him her father only replaced them to finish a sword he was making, that he decoyed him to the place for destroying him, as it had been prophesied the sword would be tempered in royal blood in revenue for the affront of the cook's death by the sword Macabuin. "Is not your father the seventh son of the old windy cap, King of Norway?" said Olave; "he is," replied Emergaid, as the father entered the smithy. "Then," Olave cried, as he drew the red steel from the fire, "the prophesy must be fulfilled." Emergaid was unable to stay his uplifted hand till he quenched the sword in the blood of her father, and afterward, pierced the heart of the one-legged hammersmith who was in the plot.

Olave made her his queen, and from her descended all the succeeding kings of the Isle Man down to Magnus (1219), the last of the race of Goddard Crovan.

The prose tale from Gortean Taoit, in Ile (1), as given by Campbell, runs as follows:

On a day when Finn and his set of men were out hunting in Haslainn, they saw coming to meet them an unhandsome man, with a shaggy eye in front of his face. He was running with might, and making right for Fionn MacDhuil. When he met these he asked them to follow him to the door of the smithy. Said Fionn: "Where stripling is the smithy? or shall we be the better for seeing it?" "My smithy," said the fairy smith, is not to be found, and if I may, you shall not see it." The fairy smith and Daor Ghlas stretched out against the mountain breast, and they would but give the one step over each cold desert glen; there could but scarce be seen a glimpse of their clothes on their hips. On nearing the door of the smithy the heroes neared each other. "A little opening," said the fairy smith. "Tear it before thee," said Daor Ghlas. Then turned round the fairy smith, and he said: "Oh, king! that thou hast earned the name of Caoilte (slenderness), Daor Ghlas shall not be thy name from this time." It was then that they began at Mac an Luinn, and when they were at it the daughter of the fairy smith came in to the smithy and she asked:

"Who is the slender, grey, fearless man?"

'A shineadh a' pinah cruach?'

The maiden fell into weighty question with Daor Ghlas and she gave him notice that her father would say to him when the sword was ready: "What did it want now?" and that he should say: "It wants one little thing yet," and that he should seize the sword and thrust it through her father's body to temper it.

MacPhail, Scanliste (2) relates in addition:

That the arms required to be tempered in the blood of a living person; that the smith's daughter took a fancy to Fionn, who had a love spot which was Diarmaid's property), and that she told him unless he killed her father with the sword that her father would kill him. This Fionn accordingly did.

In the Lay of the Smithy, from Portree, Skye (3), and Breubhaig, Bara (4), which I have combined for my purpose, Finn is accompanied by Osein, Osgar, and Daorglilas, and:

There was seen coming from the hill (plain)
A long, dark man upon one leg
In his black, dusky, black skin mantle,
With his dusky head-gear so rusty red.
  Fionn spoke:
Where, smith, is your dwelling? Smith
  Smith:
Lon Mac Liobbann is my right name,
I was a while at the smith's mystery
With the King of Lochlann, at Spaoili (Upsala)
  also Meirbhe (Bergen?).
I am laying you under spells,
Since you are ambitious of seeing my smithy:
To be in a dark, dark grey, sickly glen
To-night westward from the doors of my smithy.
Then they set them to their travel
One band of these was the blacksmith,
Another band of them Daorghlas,
Another company was Derg, son of Druin,
Fionn was after them alone.
The smith would only take one step
Over every dark grey desert glen,
And they could not see, but with difficulty
A piece of his raiment over his haunches.
(Arrived now at the smithy)
"Open, open," said the smith—
A little delay, said the smith;
"Shut not before me," quoth Daorghlas.
They found then bellows to blow,

The workshop was scarcely found out
Four men were found of the King of Meirbhe,
Hammers striking, and smithy tongs,
To every smith there were seven hands,
Seven pincers light and substantial,
And the seven hammers that crushed them,
And no worse would it suit with Daorghlas.
Daorghlas who watched at the workshop
'Tis a certain tale that they fell out.
He was as red as a coal of the oaktree
Was his appearance from his labour.
Outspoke one of the blacksmiths:
Who is that dauntless, slender man
Who has spoiled for us our steel anvil?
  Outspoke Fionn:
His name was Daorghlas till this hour.
The heroes then forge their swords, and Finn wrought his Mae an Luinn (the son of the surge).

[The remaining strophes are not essential for comparison with our Manx version, and need not be referred to. The final episode between Finn and the smith's daughter, and Loan Maclibhuin's death, are not recorded in these two metrical versions.]

(1) *Popular Tales of the Western Highlands*, vol. 3, p. 110.
(2) Ditto, pages 390 and 394.
(3) *Ossianic Ballads*, Alfred Nutt, 1871.
(4) *Popular Tales of the Western Highlands*, p. 579.

236. THE LAY OF THE SMITHY

After having given the Manx and Gælic versions, it is also necessary to allude to the Irish Cuchnlainn* (= our Fionn) legend. It refers to his visits to the other world in quest of a wife.

The maiden's name was Emer (in the Manx tale it is Emergaid), daughter of Forgall Monach (Forgall the Tricky), who lived at a place called Luglochta Loga. In the Manx parallel he is Loan Mac Liobhann or Libhuin, the seventh son of the old windy cap, King of Norway, at his smithy in Drontheim; while the Gaelic ballads call him variously the King of Lochlin or Lochlann in Gilvin (Sheilbinn) at Spaoili (Upsala?), of Meirbhe (Bheirbe, Bergen?). Emer calls herself daughter of the coal-faced king, who is also stated to be the son of a sister of Tethra, King of the Fomori. Forgall discovers Cuchulain's inclinations for his daughter, and as he is against him, he resolves on his destruction. He therefore sets out in disguise to King Condrobar, his father's court. In the Manx tales he sends one of his hammermen, Hiallus-nan-urd; in the Gaelic versions it is Loan himself:

A long dark man upon one leg,
In his black, dusky black skin mantle,
With his dusky head-gear so rusty red,
One shaggy eye in his forehead.

He persuades him to have Cuchulainn trained by certain friends of his, from whom he expects him never to return alive. The first of these is living in Alban, and was called Domnall. Cuchulainn, having learned all he wanted, then leaves with his companions (= the Fianns) and comes to an island to the east of it, where Scathach (= the shadowy) lived. To get to her court he first passes through many dangerous adventures, crossing, amongst others, a frightful plain; one half of it was so cold that their feet would cleave to the ground, while the other half, grown with spear grass, cast them against their points. He crosses then a perilous glen, which was a terrible gulf, connected from cliff to cliff by only a slender cord. In the Barra version:

They set themselves to their travel
O'er the fifth of Munster in their hurrying speed
And on yellow glens about birch trees.

Hiallus or Loan, who accompanies him, in the Manx and Gaelic legends being a giant:

The blacksmith would cut but one step
On each lonely glen through the desert,
But scarcely his arms would reach to
A tuck of his clothes on his haunches
Ascending the ground of the corrie,
Descending the pass of the edges.

Again, in the serial Barra ballad:

He set off like the wind of the Springtime
Out of the dark mountains of the high grounds.
He would take but a single step
O'er each single cold glen of the desert.

At the end of his journey he was met by demons and phantoms, sent by Forgall to kill him. But he overcomes all these obstacles, and was received by Scathach with surprise. From her court he sets finally out to Luglochta Loga to carry away Emer, whom for a whole year be was unable to communicate with, owing to the close watch kept over her by his henchmen (the blacksmiths, Loan's hammermen). But he succeeds at last, and appears all of a sudden in the middle of the stronghold where he performs such marvels of valour (= Fiann and his companions' feats in the smithy) that Forgall lost his life, in leaping terror-stricken over his own walls. Then Cuchulainn makes his way out with Emer, *etc.* (In the Manx legend Fiann kills the king with his red hot sword, quenching it in his blood, and leaves then with Emergaid).

There is, however, another Icelandic story, found in a ms. of the 15th century, mentioned by Principal Rhys:

It relates how one of King Olaf's men landed in the fairy realm of Godmundr. His name was Thorsteinn. Godmundr tells the latter that he was on a dangerous journey to the court of a neighbouring king called Geirroedr, who claimed him as a tributary, and who had caused the death of Godmundr's father when he last went to Geirroedr's court to pay him his tribute. Thorstein asks to accompany him, but Godmundr being a giant, was amused at the small stature of Thorstein, though for a man he was a person of very powerful frame. He allows him, however, to accompany him, and rendered him valiant services in all his contests. Finally Thorstein (= the Fiann) killed Geirroedr (= Loan Mac Liobhann), and enables Godmundr to annex his kingdom; he also found himself a wife there called Godrun (= Emergaid, Emer).

Although variating in detail and local colour, we notice the general central idea which runs alike through all these legends of the Lay of the Smithy, found both in Ireland, Man, the Isles and the Highlands, and Iceland.

In my next note I shall refer shortly to the Irish and Welsh parallels of the Gorry Legend, and then show their relative connection with the mythical Sun Hero underlying the same.

* See *Celtic Heathendom*, John Rhys, London, 1888, pages 448–455–456.

237. IRISH PARALLEL OF THE GORREE LEGEND

It is given by Principal John Rhys in his *Celtic Heathendom*, pp. 98–99, he says:

The story may briefly be summarised thus: Finn and his men had set up their hunting booth in Tethby, Anglicized Teffia, a district in the modern counties of West Meath and Longford; and while Finn was busy with the chase, Lomna, called Finn's fool, lurked about here where he came one day across Cairbre, champion of the Lingui, with the Luiguian woman who was Finn's wife in that district. She entreated Lomna not to tell Finn what he had seen, but being unwilling to be a party to the disgracing of Finn, wrote an oglassi, which Finn on his return did not fail to interpret. The result was that Cairbre, coming again when Finn was away, cut off Lomna's head, and carried it away with him. Finn in the evening found a headless body in the booth, and was soon convinced that it was Lomna's; so the hounds were let loose, and Finn with his Fiann tracked the murderer and his party to an empty house, where they had been cooking fish on a stone, with Lomna's head on a spike by the fire. I will not extend the tale further, except adding that this decapitated head has the power of singing and prophesying, which may be compared to the Norse story of Mim's head (which likewise had been struck off) which would converse with Woden and tell him many secrets; and in the Welsh story of Brán, whose head is cut off too, we find the same power of speech and prophecy. In the Irish tale all the actors are subverted, while the sequence which relates the wonderful virtue and power of the severed head is lost in the Manx and Highland tales, which close with the mere decapitation of Gorree.

238. QUERY

Would you kindly tell me in the enquiry or "Notes and Queries" column of your *Examiner* if there are any notable interiors of churches in the Isle of Man, and also whether there are any ancient carved fonts?

EXPLORER.

239. AN OLD MANX BARD AND SOME TEMPERANCE HYMNS, TRANSLATED BY HIM INTO MANX

In *The Little Manx Nation*, Mr Hall Caine eloquently describes his visit to an "old Manx bard" who lived in a lonely glen in the mountain district near Foxdale. He says he "found the old man setting in the chimney nook, a little red shawl around his head and knotted under his chin. He was no hermit, but a farmer, and though nearly ninety years old had never been off the Island." In response to Mr Caine's invitation, "he took down his thumb-marked, greasy, discoloured poems from 'the lath' and read them aloud to him in his broad Manx dialect." He found "they were all startling and almost ghastly appeals to the sinner to shun his evil ways." The old bard was John Quirk of Carn y Greie. I knew of him, before reading this account, as the translator and versifier of some eight or nine old Manx ballads, which were printed in the volumes of the Manx Society, viz.: "The Fisherman's Ballad," "A Song on Farmers' Daughters," "The Herring Song," *etc.*

Mr A.W. Moore also gives a short account of him in his *Manx Worthies*, and describes him as "probably the last remaining specimen of the kind of men who composed the Manx carols." He gives an extract from one of Quirk's carols, in which the blind leaders of the blind are compared to frogs.

Staying in Peel a year or two after Mr Hall Caine's book appeared, I resolved if possible to see the old bard for myself, so accompanied by a "manninagh dooie," who had met him and knew something of the eerie district in which he lived, we, *ie*, my wife and I, set out to discover him. After traversing some miles of a steep and rugged mountain road we were directed to the house we sought. It was not, however, Carn y Greie. The bard had moved to another abode near by. We were admitted by his wife, now, as she proved to be, his widow, for she told us the object of our search was no more. He had been dead several years. She was pleased to see us, and seemed gratified at our desire to see him. She willingly sought out the old bard's books and papers to show us, and amongst them was his old ms. book of "Manx hymns or songs for the use of temperance meetings, and several pieces of poetry suitable on other occasions. Partly composed originally in Manx and partly translated from the English language, by John Quirk, parish of Patrick." Such is the title it bears on the cover. It had been kept in a damp place, and but for our timely rescue would soon have been illegible, or, indeed, have perished altogether. After drying it before the fire she generously offered it for my acceptance, of which offer, needless to say, I gladly availed myself. The book is now well cared for, and I have had all the pieces it contains carefully copied out. These number 69. Of the original compositions, a few have already been published, the best known of them being perhaps "Yn Jeirkagh meshtyllagh" ('The drunken beggar'). The others are Manx translations of English and American hymns. I have sought for some time to discover the originals of these, because no versified translation that could be made into English could be so satisfactory, and I wished to print them in both Manx and English. I have now succeeded in finding the source of a few in a little hymn book kindly lent me by Dr Julian, author of the *Dictionary of Hymnology*. With the editor's concurrence I purpose sending these for publication, when perhaps some of your Manx linguists will express their opinion upon the merits of the old bard's translations. To me the rhythm seems particularly pleasing and faithful to the original version.

It may not be inappropriate here to express regret that so few Manxmen are contributors to your "Notes and Queries" column. There must assuredly be many titbits of folk-lore and the like lurking in their memories. In a few years all that has not been committed to paper will certainly be blotted out. Much of what has already appeared, besides being valuable to the student, must have proved interesting (albeit sometimes amusing) to the general reader. After this brief digression I now give the first of the "Temperance Hymns," to be followed by others as opportunity offers for their insertion in the Examiner.

G.W. Wood

I LOVE A LITTLE SUP
The temperance cause I wish it well,
It cries "to help come up";
Help you that choose, but for myself
I love a little sup.

The noble effort I approve,
And ever cry it up,
But I'll not sign the pledge, because
I love a little sup.

The doctor says "it hastens death.
And why not quit the cup?"
And so I would, but—I know why—
I love a little sup.

The preacher urges next, "'tis sin,
And shames the church, give up";

My secret plea is stronger yet,
I love a little sup.

Ten thousand tortur'd wives cry out,
And beggar'd babes, "give up!"
I hear their cries, and pity, but-
I love a little sup.

The spirits lost in anguish shriek,
"O quit the poison'd cup";
I feel the terror strike, but still
I like a little sup.

All argument I can outbrave
That bids "the pledge take up";
This one is proof against their force,
I love a little sup.

Tho' groans and blood, and death, and hell
All cry "forsake the cup,"
I know 'twere best, but then—but then—
I love a little sup.

[American]

S'LIACK LHIAM BINE DY YOUGH
Lhig dauesyn saillin shassoo seose
Dy choadey'n stroialtagh,
Ta aigney mie sym hene da'n chooish,
Agh s'liack lhiam bine dy yough.

Neem kinjagh taggloo ass e lieh
Myr chooish feer ymmyrchagh,
Ny yeih cha, jeanym signal eh,
Son s'liack lhiam bine dy yough.

Fer-lhee ta gra dy vel e ghah
Cur naardey'n challin voght;
Lurg ooilley shoh cha dreigym eh,
Son s'liack lhiam bine dy yough.

Preachooryn neesht ta kinjagh ginsh
Jeh trimmid mooar e loght,
Agh mian my chree t'erskyrn dagh nhee,
Son s'liack lhiam bine dy yough.

Ta mraane as paitchyn geamagh noi
Fo gortey rooisht as boght,
Ta'd doostey chymmey ayns my chree,
Still s'liack lhiam bine dy yough.

Spyrrydyn caillt ayns torchagh geam
Noi chappan meshtyllagh,
Ec clashtyn jeu ta'n cree ercreau,
Agh s'liack lhiam bine dy yough.

Neem shassoo magh roish dagh argane
Ta noi jough veshtyllagh,
Ta shoh my oyr yn slane gansoor,
Still s'liack lhiam bine dy yough.

Brooghyn as fuill, toyrtmow as basse,
Ta loayrt feer atchimagh,
My chreenaght eisht dy scarrey rish,
Agh s'liack lhiam bine dy yough.

240. THE GORRY SAGA

I may now compare the leading features of the two stories, and first let me advert to Gorry.

In the Manx version, Kitter (= Kettel) on leaping the Sound is drowned, and Kitterland is named in memory of the occurrence; in Islay, Mac an Reaidhinn falls into the strait, and the Kyle is called Caol Readhin after him.

In the Manx tale, the destroyer of the Brugh on Barrule is little Orree or Gorree; in the ballad of Brugh Farola, it is big Garry, son of Morna; in Cromarty, Garry is called a little fellow, although only 15 feet high. In Islay, it is Conan who sets fire to the Brugh, and he is executed by his own son Garbh (= terrible), and Conan is kept cropped *(maol)* like the Gror Moel (= the bald man) of the Welsh Triad. He was the weakest of the Fions; he had but the strength of a man, but if his hair should get leave to grow, there was the strength of a man in him for every hair on his head. I may here also mention Goll, the one-eyed son of Morna, leader of the Clanna Morna, and one of the principal foes of Finn—so small and dwarfish at birth, and so powerful in after-life.

In the Islay account, the chase being very scarce at the time, Finn sets Conan watching to find out why, however, their wives kept so lusty, fair and comely, and he finds their meat is boiled hazel tops, and their drink the "bree." In the Farola tale, they live on the leaves of trees, roots of heather, tops of hazel.

Garry was no favourite of the women, and while asleep (in the Islay version) they fasten his hair to two sticks, which they drive into the earth on either side of his head, and he left part of it and of the side of his head on the sticks; in Farola they take seven sticks of wood and tie seven plies of his hair to them, and then raise the war cry of the Fions; in Cromarty they fasten his long hair with pegs to grass, and he wrenches his head off, leaving half his locks behind him.

He then burns the Brugh and the wives who are inside; in Cromarty, he then flees to the west; in Farola, Finn puts his finger under his knowledge-tooth, and he is discovered hiding in a cave. He is executed by the magic sword, Mac an Luinn; but in Islay, it is Conan who has his head severed by Garbh; in the other version, it is done by Finn himself.

In Islay, they lay first seven grey hides, seven faggots of firewood, and seven "tiruin" of grey bark over Finn's thigh for protection; in Skye, it is guarded by seven divots of lea ground of coarse fibre, but here, nevertheless, Finn is wounded in the act of striking; in the Manx version they employ toad skins, twigs of the rowan tree, and adder eggs, each to the number of nine times nine, as a charm.

In the Irish version, it is Lomma who has his head struck off, which thus brings it into relation with the story of Brán, Uthr Ben, and Mim's Head, all of which have the virtue to speak and prophesy.

241. KING GORREE, THE MYTHICAL KING OF MAN

At this point I must say a few words about the mythical King Gorree, who plays such an important part in the early history of Man.

According to Manx tradition, in the beginning of the 10th century Gorree, or Orry, a Dane, having conquered the Orcades and Hebrides, arrived on the shores of Man with a strong fleet and landed at the Lhane River in the North of the Island. The Lhane and Kalhane were the two rivers which drained the lakes on the westward side of the Great Curragh, and with those lakes cut off the Headland of Jurby, forming the Island called St. Patrick's Isle, or the Isle of St. Patrick, in Jurby.

The Manx received him at once, seemingly glad to place themselves under so powerful a leader. It is stated that when Orry landed he was asked whence he came, upon which, pointing to the milky way, he said: "That is the road to my country." Hence, to this day, the Manx name for the milky way is: *Raad mooar Ree Gorree*, or 'the great road of King Gorree.'* According to the *Orkneyinga Saga* † the vikings and sea kings derive their descent from Fornigot, King of Finland and Kvenland had three sons:

Hler (Aegir) who ruled over seas

Logi who ruled over fire

Kari ruled over winds, he was father of Yökull, the father of King Snow, whose children were:

Thorri, who had Norr who had the mainland, and Norway was called after him; Gorr who held the Isles for that he was called a sea king, and he is the mythical ancestor of Vikings and sea kings; daughter Goï.

Kari, from whom the sea kings claim descent, evidently corresponds with the Scandinavian Odinn or Woden, the storm and wind god, has also the eagle as his emblem; his hound receives the souls and takes them up the bow and the galaxy to the cloud waters. The Celtic Groydion comes under the same head, he is the son of Don, whose residence is Caer Groydion (the fort of Groydion), or the galaxy and Aneurin speaks of "the eagle of Groydion that hovers round the sky." He is supposed to preside in the air, or rather the starry region. His father, Don, dwells in Lhys Don (the court of Don) or the Cassiopeia, and his sister Arianrod, has her residence in Caer Arianrod, or the Corona Corealis, while Gorree, Groydion, has his abode in the milky way, called in Manx: *raad moor Ree Gorree;* the galaxy is the winter *gatan* of the Swedes, or the *heol y gwynt*—the street of the wind of the Welsh.

Groydion may be connected with the Aes Side, whose residence, in Irish mythology, in Caer Sidi, where neither disease nor old affects any one, and this land or home of gods is found again on Scandinavian ground in the Asgard, the realm of the Aesir, separated, and in another world, in Vanaheimr live the Wanes or Vanir. And compare this stage Finn Mac Cumaill (= the white of the sky), and Gwyn ab Nud (the white son of the mist). Gwydion is an enchanter of wonderful power. Gwyn ab Nud is a king of the other world, the god of death and darkness,who hunts with his fierce hound the souls of those that are dying, in which he resembles again Woden, the fierce hunter, who is seen, in folklore dashing and tearing along with his black dogs and huntsmen in his wild chase. Groyn is also the god of carnage, and king of the fairies. In close relation to Gwyn and Woden, no less stands Finn with his hound Bran, and his mighty hunters, all of them gifted with the power of knowledge, and the prediction of the future, and who were great warriors, huntsmen, especially poets and diviners.

* See *Guide to the Isle of Man,* by the Rev. J.G. Cumming, F.G.S., 1861.

† See vol. 3, pp. 1–3 and pp. 333–34.

242. GORRY

In the legend of the Brugh of Barrule, Brugh Farola and Knock Ferril (Brugh is a word applied to the dwelling of the Alf race), Gorry figures eminently as the great antagonist Finn and his sib. He belongs to the Clanna Morna, the chief of which, Goll, the one-eyed, is the principal foe of Finn, the head of the Clanna Baiscne. His name, big or little Gorry, or Garry (Gaelic: Garbh), ranges in legend from the extreme north-east side of Scotland, Cromarty, across Argyleshire, down Man on the west, or Scandio-Goidelic contact-points. In Ardnamurachan alone, Conan, Goll's grandson, takes his place, whose strength consists in his long hair, which consequently is diligently cropped. We find a parallel in the Semites Samson (a dark divinity), whom Dedilah deprives of his locks in his sleep. The women of Brugh Farola fasten Gorry's seven piles of his hair to seven logs. When he wakes, jumping up, he leaves seven piles of his hair behind. Garry is a turbulent and rough companion ("Garbh," Gaelic–rough), and not on good terms with the clan with which, as a hostage, he has been received. He reminds us, in his position, of Honir and his companion Mimir, and Njorder, who had been exchanged in like manner amongst the opposing Aesir and Vanir, after the conclusion of their great war. The Vanir, later on, cut off Mimir's head and sent it to Odinn; the same fate awaits Gorry, who is decapitated by Finn. The antagonistic Fenian clans, here represented by Finn and Gorry, seem, comparatively, to occupy the same ground as the Alfir, inferior elementary divinities, who were divided into two classes—the "white" Alfir, or elfs of light, related to the Aesir and Vanir (compare "fiann"–white, fair, splendent, and "vanum"–shining), and the "black" Alfir, or elfs of darkness, who dwell in caves and sally out at night. Finn, on these lines, appears as a light divinity, and Gorry as a dark divinity, but both rivals are sprung from the same power—the sun. They are, naturally, constantly fighting against each other for supremacy, and encroach upon each other's realms. The whole picture resolves itself finally into an old nature myth. Their existence is closely bound up with the annual course of the sun, which, increasing and decreasing, ascending and descending, his rays shortening or lengthening, produces the seasons; their opposing forces produce darkness and light, vegetation or decay, life and death, night and day, heart and frost. The sun divinity (here Fiann, the fair, splendent), whose power has been gradually falling off, succumbs to the powers of his enemies (Gorry—the divinity of darkness), the powers of darkness and winter. The beginning of the winter is indicated by the difficulty of Finn and his hunters to procure game in the chase, and their wives eke out their life with leaves, roots of heather, and hazel tops.

When Garry awakes, he regains the power over the summer, he destroys Finn's burgh, the blazing up suddenly disappears. Garry's power has begun, the sharp winter sets in. The lamentations of the frantic women and the blaze recall Finn and his party from their hunt, and them hurry forward. Gorry flees and hides himself in a cave, or tries to gain the west (darkness). He is captured at last, and his head struck off by Finn with his magic flaming sword. Although, in revenge, Finn severs his head, he cannot completely destroy Garry's power and vitality, for as we have seen in the case of Lomna, Bran, Mimir, and Uthr Ben, the decapitated head acquires unexpected new abilities: it speaks, sings, and prophesies. Mimir is the guardian of the Odrerir, the mead of the poets, which confers wisdom and knowledge, and he likewise guards the burn from which all waters spring.

Gorry is executed on Finn's thighs, but although protected by an old wondrous charm, covered with earth, and sods, and wood, still Finn receives a severe wound, from which he recovers only slowly. The sun lies level with the earth and is protected with sod and mould, and recovers only slowly his strength and vigour when he climbs up again in the spring. Finn and his companions are all summer giants, and they hunt with their spears, the long sun rays; when on their last hunt, at the beginning of winter, their power is already beginning to fade, and on leaping across the strait one of them falls in and is drowned, the sunbeam fails to hold out in their passage.

Another primitive idea breaks out in the Gorry legend. It is as if Gorry and Finn were conceived to be two distinct sun-divinities of lesser and greater power. The dark god (Gorry) is constantly kept cropped, and not allowed to strengthen: the sunbeams, his hair, are tied down; it ruffles him, but he has to submit to his fate. Here we see another indication of the winter sun; he runs to the west, when pursued, or to a cave: the darkness must be his home.

243. FINN

We come now to Finn's visit to the dark smith of Drontheim, the King of Lochlann, or Forgall—the coal-faced king of the Fomori, in Luglochta Loga, of the Irish legend,* where Cuchulainn apparently takes the place of our hero Finn. Both Forgall and the dark smith of Drontheim are intent on Finn's destruction. Finn sets out with his men, accompanied and conducted by a long, dark man, wrapped in a black, dusky skin mantle and dusky headgear; one shaggy eye in his forehead. We seem to recognise here Odinn, who is pictured in folklore as a cooled, one-eyed, tall old man, clad in a dark mantle, his hat slouched deep over his face. He is a mighty traveller and strider, and Finn and his followers can hardly keep pace with him. They are setting out of the dark mountains, under his spell, to the west, and have to pass over horrid plains, cold desert glens, and come to a perilous gulf, only spanned by a slender cord: the bridge of dread; and after untold perils and adventures, they at last arrive at their destination. Here Finn forces an entrance, and forges his famous sword with which be kills the dark smith of Drontbeim, or the coalfaced Forgall, and brings away his lovely daughter, thence returning home to his country.

We are here reminded of Odinn's ride to Niflheim (the mist world), where also he passes through the dark glens till he comes to the border-river Gjoll and, the golden bridge, guarded by the maiden Modgudr. Lochlann, before it came to mean the home of the Norsemen, denoted in Irish mythology a mysterious country in the lochs or the waves of the sea, or the under world.

Thus we see Finn, Cuchulainn, Arthur descending into Hades; great Odinn guides Finn in his perilous journey, and Finn, in his quality as a solar hero (it is the summer sun), where he invades the realm of the dark and ferocious god of the under-world slays him with the magic sword which he forges in the smithy; he also carries away the dark king's rosy daughter, Emergaid (the Dawn), of course, only after first having killed him. She rises after the night is gone.

Against Finn and the dark smith we may put, as a parallel, Siegfried and Wieland. What Finn is to the Goidelic people of Scotland, Man, and Ireland, is Arthur to the Cymric people of Wales. The Gorry legend, to put it short, represents the dark power, and the Finn legend the light power. Both are solar heroes.

CONCLUSION
There is a visible stratification to be noticed in the growth of the Fenian stories,
which in the earliest form are built on a few mythical heroes, such for instance as
embodied in the stories of Finn and Gorree. I pointed out the close relation existing
between the Vanir and the Fianna, or early Fenians. The chief point to be kept
constantly in view in considering the ultimate development of these stories is their
pervading antagonism, the deep hostility to each other, the white and black badge, if
I may say so, which distinguishes the contending champions. The early traditions did
not die away and burst into fresh flame and national meaning when the Goidelic
people were brought into keen clash with another foreign race, the early Norse
invaders, who fiercely overran Scotland, Ireland, and Man, slaying and sacking.
These were the historical men of Lochlann or Norway, the great antagonists of the
Goidelic stock. Many of the Vikings of the first invasion of the 8th century came
from Hardanger Fiord; they were the Finngheinte or Findgaill (fair strangers), men,
to the Celtic eye, of gigantic form and strength: fomori (Gaelic—*fomhair;* Manx—
faowr), like the mythological Fianna, and dubbed by the Goidels white men,
inconsequence of the invaders fair complexion. Their murderous mutual strife is only
a repetition of the inimical Clanna Morna and Baiscne, headed by Finn and Goll as
leaders.

We find already Kitter or Caittil Find introduced in the early legend of the Brugh
of Barrule, towards the end of the 9th century. Gorree, the mythical King of Man,
appears early in the 10th century. Finn and Gorry are to be met again in a duplicate
legend, referring to the time of Olave Goddardson (Olave Gudrodar), who ruled
Man in IIII; all the national attributes of Gorree, as legislator and regenerator of the
Manx race, are conferred later again on the historical Gudrod Crowan (1095), called
Manninagh, the founder of the House of Man. The pre-historic Gorree, as we have
seen, claimed a divine descent; he, like King Arthur, may have been a historical
personage, confounded with the mythical Gorree, who is said to have been a Dane
who conquered the Oroades and Hebrides and Man. What is of interest is to notice
Gorree, as the antagonist of Finn: he occurs both in the Cromarty, Argyleshire, and
Manx legends. He and Finnodderee = Fin Gudrodar (represented as the mighty
giant) are found together on the summit of Barrule; from here also Gudrot Crowan,
who dwelled here in a great castle, flung the great granite boulder after his termagent
wife, and he slumbers on in the Devil's Den. Gorree and Gudrod are rolled into one.
The Devil's Den reminds us of the cave of the legendary Gorree.

To sum up: the later and historical development or second stage of the Fenian
stories is largely leavened and coloured with Norse elements, and the immediate
outcome of the life and death strife existing between the contending two races, as we
clearly see from the Manx legends where distinct Norse figures, of both vikings and
kings are introduced. And, furthermore, we hear the distinct mention of Drontheim,
to which Olave Goddardson sets out from Peel to face the dark blacksmith evidently

a proof that the expansion of the legends from the 9th to 12th Century is due, at this point, to the existing close inter-relation and contact of the Scandio-Goidelic races, while the broad framework rests on prehistoric Goidelic elements with mythological solar heroes, such as we meet in Finn and Goll and Gorry. The latest product— romantic tales—form a luxuriant after-math, not unlike what we find in the subsequent treatment of the Arthurian legend.

* See *Celtic Heathendom,* J. Rhys: pp. 448–51, 456–57, 466–67 (chapter, "The Sun Hero").

244. THINGS UNLUCKY WHEN GOING TO SEA
It is not lucky to meet any barefooted persons, or to sell herrings without first sprinkling them with a handful of salt, or to bring them in sight of any person, outside the crew, before some salt is thrown on them, or to go to sea the first night without salt, or to put white stones in among the ballast. Some men, too, are noted for bringing ill-luck with them to whatever boat they may go to sea in, and many is the bad herring season put down to so-and-so's being on board.

245. THINGS LUCKY
To nail a horseshoe to the stern of the boat inside. To dip the end of the first net down into the water three times, before beginning to shoot all out.

246. OLD CUSTOM
When the old Manxmen started to get ready for the fishing, the first thing was to get a "kishen" apiece of ale, and after that to haul the boat alongside of the ballast; the skipper would be carrying a bottle of rum with him to give them "drops" at intervals. He did not work, but sat on the gunwale at the stern, with his claw-hammer coat on, the tails of which had to be a certain length. The men would put stones in the boat until the tails of the coat touched the water, when the skipper would sing out: "*Cum ort! patchey ayn jeh.*" ('Stop! there's plenty in her.')

247. FAIRIES BLEEDING A SERVANT UNDER HER BIG TOE
A company of fairies visited a farmhouse one night, after the good folk had gone to bed and were preparing to bake cakes, when they found there was no water in the crock to wet the dough; a great hubbub arose, as they all united to jaw the servant for her carelessness, and ended by going up to her bedroom and bleeding her under the big toe until they had enough to wet the dough and finish their baking. An old beggarwoman, who had been given a shakedown in the kitchen, heard and saw the whole performance, but went away in the morning without telling what she had seen. The servant was taken sick with some mysterious ailment that could not be cured, until the old beggar came to the house again, and hearing of the servant being sick, told what she had heard the fairies say on the night of her last visit, whereupon

the master went to a herb-doctor, and got herbs for her, after which she recovered all right.

[Nos 244–47, (All these notes come from Peel.)]

248. HERRING FISHING IN PEEL A HUNDRED YEARS AGO

The following extremely interesting and valuable account is due to a worthy old resident, who has passed the seventies. He went to sea since he was twelve. When for a boy on board first, most of the crew were men between 60 and 70 years of age, and as he can well remember the "yarns" they told him, it may be said that his memory of the fishing goes back over a hundred years. I think it is, in all respects, the best portraiture of the ways, habits, old customs, and manner of life of the genuine Manx fisherman of yore we possess, and I am sure these reminiscences will be highly appreciated.

"Of all the fishes in the sea,
 The herring is the king;
 And all the sellers of the grog
 Rejoice when he comes in."
 —(Old Manx Ballad.)

"In old times we used to build our boats in the country anywhere near trees; timber where the fairies were taken was right lucky to build them with. The boats we built then were not so big as they are now, nor so fancy. They would be about the size of the small nobbies now, and could carry about 100 mease of herring. There would be four or five of a crew going on them. A silver piece, or a bit of iron, would be put under the stern post for luck sometimes, same as they put money under foundation stones. When the boat was ready to be caulked, we would have to turn her over with the sun—a boat, must always go with the sun, going out to sea, specially, if you can came at it in the world, go out with the sun; if we were lying in the harbour with her bows up, we always turned her with the sun; it would be unlucky to go out any other way.

There used to be a law that you were not allowed to go to sea before midsummer. The old song that we would be singing on board often will tell you that, and all about the fishing, true enough it is, too:

"Barley sown and potatoes down,
 We'll get our boats in order;
 Midsummer Day and we are away,
 In earnest seeking herrings."

Each family had a croft of ground. The first thing on Monday morning, if you had forgotten no matter what at home, you must not turn back; if you turned back for a thing after once leaving the house, things would go against you all the week. But if you met a parson or a woman, you might as will turn back at once and stay at home for that day. Nobody can be more unlucky to meet than a parson. We were not allowed to mention his name on board—I always called them "blackcoats." Roman Catholic priests would be thought lucky enough, as they were supposed to have some sort of power over things of darkness, spirits and the like. It wasn't right, too, to say on sea the name of any land animal. We always had our own names on them at sea. A cat would be called a *scrayheyder* (a 'scratcher'), a hare *yn fer lesh cleaysh liauyr* ('the fellow with the long lugs'); but I disremember the names mostly now, as these sort of things were nearly gone out in my time. It you did happen to call unthinkingly anything by its shore name, "Cold iron" must be said and touched at once. A rat was a very bad thing to talk about. It is thought to be lucky enough, though, to talk about fairies at sea.

If your boat was doing well at the fishing, men on other boats would try to steal some thing of yours, so as to get some of the luck from you. If they could steal one of your herring baskets they were almost bound to be lucky; but the best and surest of all things to steal from you was the tally-stick. Some of the boys were right *debejagh* ('cussed') for this sort of thing They would be coming after you, too, asking for a match, may be, but you must on no account give fire or salt out of the boat—them two things in particular.

In the season we would be coming ashore early every morning for breakfast, carrying about half a hundred of fresh herrings with us. There was no fire in the boats in those days. We used to go to a public house for breakfast, and the woman there would take the herrings from us and scrape them as clean as clean, and then she would boil a potful for us. When they were done, we would shake the herring from the bone, into little brown dishes with yellow edges. These dishes were not as big as soup plates, more like the saucers you see under flower-pots now. We would fill them up with the herring broth, supping it with the herrings. Some of us, to make it more tasty, would sometimes put a scallion in the broth. We would have our own bread and butter to eat with us. Afterwards some would, may be, have a pint or two of *jough* ('ale'), and sometimes we would carry a jar of it on board with us. There was then no tea or coffee. Every Monday morning we would carry the week's grub from home with us in a wallet slung round our necks—something after the shape of a shepherd's purse. We would have about a pound of butter in a round wooden screw-capped box. Some would take oatcakes made in very thick quarters, and baked as hard as hard over the fire. My another would be giving me little *bonnags* made of barley meal and potatoes, kneaded well together. They would be about two inches high and from four to six inches across; she would clap two of these together to keep them moist, and they would be going a-baking in a pot oven. A pot oven baked as well on the top, as under it; the lid was made flat so as to hold fire on the top. Nothing in these days can cook a bit of meat so well and sweet. For *kitchen* (relish) fresh fish could be had in plenty on board. We would also carry from home with us a piece of cheese, or beef, or stockfish.

A big *mollag* (buoy) blown up tight would be made to do for a pillow, but we did not get much sleep on board in those days, for we would be pulling the nets with the mast up, a far harder job than pulling them in with it down, like they do now.

When the nets were being pulled up, no man was allowed to look over the side of the boats but the man who was pulling up. I have got many a *polt* in the head, when a lump, for keeking over.

On sea we would be watching for signs of herrings, such as gannets, perkins, and such like. But gulls were our best friends:

"The crews that would by fishing thrive,
  Steer to the spot where gulls and gannets dive."

That is why there is a law in that they must not be shot. The signs of the gulls were always minded. The best sign is to see them lying in a flock upon the waters, making a noise, and turning their heads about; then rising, flying, and settling down again. Young gulls are far keener for fish than old gulls.

"Of your approach if fishers want a test,
  They scale the rocks to seek the eagle's nest;
  There, if your fins, or scales, or bones appear,
  The signal's certain—all pronounce you near."

We would be watching the signs of the gulls on land, too, on Monday morning when coming down from the country to our boats. For the gulls would be going higher or lower on the hill as the fish shifted out off. But when they went up the river we knew it was time to go round for Douglas "back" (back fishing). Some of the men were putting these signs down making an almanack of them for the week. We could tell where to look for fish, and when to get it for, from the sitting of the gulls on the land. But the best of all the signs is to see the "lil silver felllas" themselves. On a dark night if you came over a body of herrings, the water would be all lit up with them, and you will see them shining and glittering underneath the waves quite plainly. We had a lot of fishing marks on sea, too; if we caught nothing off one mark, we would say let us try "Thie Jack" now, or "Gob-ny-clieau," as the case might be.

The first herring on board the first night out at sea would be boiled, whole. The other herrings in the pot would have their heads and tails cut off. We called the first herring *yn eirey* ('first son'). When it was cooked every man on board would have to come and take a pick of *yn eirey*. When putting nets on board, it is right to brush up off the quay any bits of roughness that may come off them. Nets are apt to gather bits of straw or leaves when out drying on the fields, and you must on no account leave so much as a leaf of this on the quay.

These were the times the good fishings were in. But sometimes, if we were not doing as well as the rest of the boats, I would be sent to old Charles Ballawhane for herbs. We would have to boil them in a pot, and every one of the crew would have to drink a drink out of it—mighty bitter stuff it was, too; then the rest of the liquor with the herbs in it would be thrown over the nets. Sometimes the luck (the herbs) would be tied to the tail net. Hemp cables were used at sea then, chain ones being unknown. Oilskins came into vogue only recently, and we wore at sea coat and trousers made of canvas. Some would tar their suits and others paint them to make them waterproof. which made them as hard as a coat of mail. If it was a fine morning the wherries would be out among us buying the fish.

> Now Phœbus ushers in the cheerful day,
> Now commences bustle in the busy quay;
> The cooper's adze, the carts' discordant tones,
> And herring barrels rolling on the stones.
> Now busy factors cure, and smoke, and dry;
> To distant chimes export the scaly fry.
> Hail, mystic myriads! Mona's pride and boast,
> From Arctic regions pour'd upon her coast,
> Whose annual visits since the world began
> Have cherished and enriched the sons of Man.
> Herring's the toast, through all the happy Isle,
> And when you meet a face—you meet a smile.*

* See "The Herring Fishery," a poem by a Manks lady, July, 1798: given in Feltham's *History of the Isle of Man*.

MANX SEA FISHING IN EARLY TIMES

249. MANX SEA FISHING IN EARLY TIMES (I)

In my notes on sea-lore, I have attempted, a general outline of the prevailing customs peculiar to the fisherman when out on sea, followed up in my last by a short sketch of his habits and style of life towards the end of the 18th century; and to-day I propose to discuss and trace the beginning and gradual growth of the sea fishery in general. There is indeed no subject equal in intrinsic interest or importance to a Manxman, or so directly interwoven with the fortunes and welfare of Man, as the exploitation of the deep sea, whose treasures piscatorial, for centuries untold, have been the very life of the Island, by contributing to its chief wealth and sustenance.

In prehistoric times, when the aborigines seem to have confined themselves more or less to the occupation of the literal fringe, of the Island, we meet with numerous distinct settlements pitched on the brooghs of the shore line, indicated by the remains of kitchen middens on the beach of Port St. Mary, where, amongst other objects, we have accumulated beds of shells of the limpet (*baarnagh*) interspersed with flint knives, scrapers, *etc*. The presence of the coast dwellers is seen again at Ronaldsway, the Sound, at Peel, Kirk Michael, Jurby, and Ramsey. Here, on the Mooragh, the great stores of flint implements of all kinds, fire-holes and pottery, attest their activity and local occupation. But so far, to my knowledge, no remains of bones of any sea fish such as the herring, mackerel, cod, plaice, *etc.*, have been discovered, as found in the kitchen-middens at Hastings.

The fishing was then, in all probability, carried on close to the shore, in the estuaries, the inlets and river courses where plenty of salmon, trout, and eel was to be had. They also fished, no doubt, the extensive lakes which were scattered broadcast over the Island, and particularly in the northern parts, such as the Lhen, the Curragh, Mirescough, and Lough Cranstall. Manufactories of flint implements have been found on the margins of all these lakes, and canoes of bog oak at Seafield (Santon), Tosaby (Malew), Ballajora (Maughold), and in German, a few miles off Peel. There is an absence of bronze or iron fish hooks in the finds, and the hooks (*clooan,* or *dubhan*) consisted probably of pointed chips of bog oak and flint which were attached to the line (*darragh;* later made of black hair, snooids), while the salmon (*braddan*) was caught with the fishing spear (*shleiy eastee*), as practised within recent times at Tromode, Port Skillion, Glen Maye, *etc.* When at last the early Manx more boldly ventured out into the open main it was in the frail wicker boat or *currach*, peculiar to the ancient Britons and Gauls. I may allude first to the testimony or the Greek and Roman writers:

Timaeus (352–256 A.C.) tells us: The Britons visited an island Mictis, at the distance of six days' sail for tin. They went there in osier-made boats, lined all round with hide.

Caesar (100–44 A.C.): The keels and kelsons of their long boats were formed of slight material, and the hull made of wicker, covered with raw hide.

Pliny the Elder (23–79 P.C.): The Britons make wicker boats, stitched round with leather, which they handle with great dexterity.

Solinus (about 238 P.C.): The commerce between Britain and Ireland, kept up on both sides, is by means of boats made of wattle and covered with skins, each end of the vessel terminated in a sharp beak, and it was rowed indiscriminately either way.

Procopius (beginning of the 6th century): they used oars for the most part, though they were not unacquainted with the sail.

Isidorus Hispaliensis (570–640) gives as the Latinized name for the boat: Carabus, a little skiff made of wicker and raw bullock hides.

It was in one of these tiny boats that at the end of the 5th century St. Maughold crossed from Ireland, and was cast up in the creek of Maughold Head. Aubrey, in 1696, makes mention of the boats on the Avon, which he describes as baskets of twigs, covered with an ox skin.

In the Western Islands of Scotland they were much in use, even long after the art of building boats of wood was introduced in these parts by the Norwegians. (1) Brever (2) informs us that in Ireland an the western coast, in a great part of the district, no other boats in comparatively recent times were used by the fishermen than the ancient canoes, of the Celtic tribes, consisting of a rude frame, covered with the hide of the horse or bullock, and that sea fishing was consequently restrained to a small distance from the land; and again in 1840 (3) we learn that the Irish in the south-west and went coast, especially in Valencia and Kenmore had for their boats the curragh, made of wicker and covered with a horse-skin or pitched canvas. And going to Wales, Richards (4) tells us that the natives availed themselves of the *coriog* or *cioragh*, which was of oval form, made of split rods or twigs interwoven, and on the part next to the water covered with pitched flannel, canvas, or horse skin, in which one man, being seated in the middle, will row himself with one hand, while with the other hand he manages his net or fishing tackle, and coming off the water he will take the light vessel on his back and carry it home. These wicker boats were plied on the Avon, Wye, Severn, Dee, *etc.*

In Gaul they were also used on the Garonne; and the *caraba*, or *carabela* in Galicia (Spain) is a long and narrow skiff wtih three sails, and also the name for the basket the women carry on their heads.

We see, then, that the ancient Celts had two kinds of wicker boats—a round or oval one, occupied and rowed by one man only, which was used on the rivers and estuaries, and particularly on the west side of Britain and Ireland; and a long wicker boat, each end terminating in a sharp beak, and rowed either way, and that they used also the sail. The latter type was run in the traffic between Ireland and Britain, and on the east and south-west of Britain, and along the sea borders.

The *currach* or *carabus* in its original form was nothing else but an enlarged wicker basket, which is thus the prototype of the wicker boat. To follow the steps of its evolution is highly interesting. The most ancient form was round, and then oval, until in course of time it was drawn out gradually into the long wicker boat which served for the reception of a small number of hands, and was fitted up with a sail. We can trace the root. Etymologically we have it again in the Latin form *corbis*, a pannier, a basket; in the German *korb;* the Scottish *corban* (a small wicker basket); in the French *corbeille* (from *corbicula*); and the Spanish *caraba* and *carabela*. The Manx word for the wicker boat has long since gone out of date, but a dim allusion is contained in the Manx word *currag* or *corrag* (see Cregeen) which means a bundle of osiers.

The habitat of the osier is in marshy, low lying, and fenny flat lands and lacustrine regions, and along the river courses, or lochs, with an outlet into the sea, inhabited by litoral tribes, who made fishing their chief occupation. The osier grew abundantly at hand and was easily obtained and worked up into wicker boats, baskets, and traps; and the absence of forests of fir and timber, in the first instance, determined its prevalent use among the Celtic Britons. They chiefly fished the rivers, lakes, and estuaries. It also, as a natural consequence, kept them backwards possessed alone; as they were of the frail wicker boats, from making any real progress in navigation, or following the sea fishery of any large scale. It was due to quite another set of natural surroundings, which places Scandinavia early in the forefront of powerful and daring navigators. The wonderful and inexhaustible wealth of their primeval pine and fir forests that descended and crept down to their fiords, glens, and lochs, and occupying their very sea rim, gave them the ready means and skill for building and launching their stout hulls and fleets, and, as a corollary, the early command of the sea. They naturally quickly developed into mighty sea-farers, great sea fishers and rulers. In very early times they sailed in vessels of a large size and substantial construction. The Suiones, or ancient Scandinavians, had their fleets in the days of Tacitus, before the time of the elder Pliny; they not only ventured out into the tempestuous sea of Norway, but even passed over to Thule. The British Celts were thus placed physically and economically at a great competitive disadvantage, and sea fishing to any large extent made but slow advance.

The Manx did not make any headway for many centuries. Their slight nutshells were too primitive to face the perils of the sea; the political conditions too precarious to venture much abroad, and, furthermore, the litoral population too poor and scanty for any maritime co-operation. When at last the Norwegians appeared on their shores, with the Goddards firmly settled as Kings of Man, in the 11th century, things, under Goddard Crovan, assumed a brighter view, and material: progress was made. The Norse, who were the great herring fishers—in the Edda they live on herring and porridge as their national food—introduced to and taught the Manx the art of boat building and sea fishing. The herring abounded on their favoured shore. and we soon see busy coast settlements springing up from Jurby, Kirk Michael, down to Dalby, the Calf, and Castletown. Peel formed then, as it always has been since, the great centre of the Manx herring fishery. The Norse blood and strain is in greatest evidence on this side of the Island, facing the Irish Sea, where the great wealth of the sea spread out before them. The names of the hundreds of headlands, creeks, rocks, cleats, and bogs bear all the imprint of the Norse tongue, and tell us even after a lapse of almost 900 years the silent tale of their journeys in their fishing smacks, along the indented heights of the southwest of the Island. It was the Norwegians who helped the Manx to become the brave sailors and fine herring fishers for which they are justly renowned.

(1) *Gaelic-English Dictionary*, by Armstrong, 1823.

(2) *The Beauties of Ireland*, by J.N. Brever; vol. i, c. lxiii; London, 1825.

(3) *Irish Penny Journal*, vol. l, p. 391, v. 40.

(4) *Welsh-English Dictionary*, by the Rev Thomas Richards, 1753.

(5) The Britons were famous in antiquity for their basket wicker work; the *bascuda* of the Romans (the Celtic *basgaid*).

250. MANX SEA FISHING IN EARLY TIMES (2)

Man, let us recollect, formed but a small part of the greater group of the Nordreys and Sudreys, ruled by the powerful earls of the Orkneys and Shetlands, long before Goddard Crovan possessed himself of the Island; the Gaels of the mainland of Scotland, the Hebrides, and the Southern Islands which had fallen under the sway of the Vikings, had already undergone then the process of a closer fusion and intermingling of blood with their foreign masters. There grew up, therefore, in course of time, amongst the Scandio-Gaelic coast population, a more uniform system of fishing; their fishing boats were built and managed much in the same fashion in Man, as by the men of Lewis, Ronaldsway, Wick, or Moray Firth.

On the west side we had a coast that rivalled in wealth of fish with the fiords and lochs of Norway; such as Loch Roag, Urn, Broom, Torridon, Carvon, Caroy, Loch Fyne—stretching from Lewis to Solway Firth and Man, rich in salmon and herring, and boasting of fishing grounds inexhaustible. Soliuns (240 P.C.) speaks already of the early inhabitants of the Hebrides (five in number) who lived on fish and milk. We have no positive knowledge of the style of wooden boats in use among the fishermen during the dominion of the Scandinavians, but some light is thrown on the subject in the Manx Statutes of 1610, which make us acquainted with two kinds of boats used for the herring fishery. It speaks of the (Manx) countrimen which have *small* boates, and those which have *scowtes* (1).

Vigfusson, in speaking of the Scandinavian war-vessels, the *skeids*, swift ships of the class *lang skip* (= long ship), mentions the *skuta*, a small cutter, a number of which used to accompany a fleet for use in rivers or the coast; these were of a large build, high prows and stems, and 80 feet long; but for the fishing, apparently a much smaller size was adopted; the Manx *scowte* is the same as the obsolete Scottish *scout* or *skoutt* (= the Swedish and Icelandic *skuta*, Danish *skude*, Dutch *schuit*, and the equivalent Irish and Gaelic *sgoth*, or *scoth*, translated: a small boat or skiff) which were also used for salmon fishing.

Another and similar boat was the *scow* or *skow* (2), a small, flat-bottomed boat of shallow draught. In Moray, it was a small boat made of willows, covered with skin (practically still a wicker-boat), while in Aberdeenshire we hear of "an auld herring scow."

Remembering that much of the fishing was done in the lochs and firths in very early times, exclusively, it is not surprising that both the *scowtes* and the cobles, of which I shall speak directly, were flat-bottomed, and have maintained this conservative feature up to our times in the north-eastern coast.

The other boat was the coble, so well known in Scotland, Northumberland, Durham, Yorkshire, and used in the salmon fishery, and for crossing rivers and lakes; it is a short flat-bottomed rowing boat. Another sort of coble for sea-fishing, also with a flat battom, open, or deckless, used in Scotland, Aberdeen, Kirkcudbright, Fife, Northumberland, *etc.*, having sharp prows and a flat sloping stern, without keel, but two bilge clogs in addition, and a very deep cut-water, is used for herring fishing (3); it was the herring coble proper. It is apparently of Scandinavian origin, even were we to argue on topographical grounds alone, and the word has been taken up by the Welsh and Bretons, who have it as *ceubal, ceubol, caubal.*

The construction with flat bottoms, let me repeat, clearly points back to a period when the fishing was confined to the lochs and estuarine rivers.

These Manx *scowtes* of which we have spoken, as the statute says: "ought every of them to be of the burthen of 4 tons," but in reality they were not more than of 2 tons even in the time of Bishop Wilson, in the beginning of the 17th century, and cost 30/- to 40/-, and therefore similar to the boats of the Orkney farmers, which are, in general, miserable cables between 1 and 2 tons burden, with four or five men in each boat, whereas the cod and ling fishery would require boats of at least 5 or six tons burden (4).

We read in the Saga of St. Olav that Sigurd Sir (about the year 1000) used to lend boats and fishing apparatus for catching herrings to his *traelle*, or slaves, to purchase their freedom from him, and he settled them upon his seaters, or uncleared waste lands, for which they after a time paid him yearly rents. Probably in Man it was not much different at the in-coming of their new task-masters.

(1) See *The Antient Ordinances and Statute Laws of the Isle of Man*, Wills' Edition, 1841, p. 501.

(2) See Prof. Wright's *English Dialect Dictionary, sub nomen.*

(3) See Prof. Wright's *English Dialect Dictionary* and Murray's *English Dictionary, sub nomen.*

(4) See *A Tour through the Orkneys and Shetlands* by Patrick Neill, A.M. Edbro', 1806, p. 61.

CHAPTERS ON THE MANX HERRING FISHERY

251. CHAPTERS ON THE MANX HERRING FISHERY (1)
Who'll buy my caller herrin?
They're no brought here without brave daring;
Buy my caller herrin!
Ye little ken their worth.

Who'll buy my caller herrin?
O ye may ca' them vulgar farin',
Wives and mithers maist despairing
Ca' them lives of men.

The Island presents a melancholy picture in the 10th century, it was literally weltering in blood, and the natives were groaning under the ceaseless ravages that went in columns of smoke through the length and breadth of the desolated land. It was plunged in the deepest misery and poverty, and its population seemed to ebb fast away. Vigfusson estimates it then between 4,000 and 5,000 souls, but that number must have contracted yet considerably in the next century. The battle on Scacafell (Sky Hill), in 1079, the internecine strife between the Northern and Southern Manx, which culminated in the engagement of Santwat in 1098, added another crimson chapter to the reduction of its native population. Goddard Crovan, and, after him, Olave I, in order to check this appalling depopulation, were obliged "to equip a great number from Ireland, and out of the islands were brought the greatest number." During these times the ruthless destruction of life and farmsteads, and the consequent neglect of the cultivation of the soil, left the country almost destitute, and it required some generations before the wretched conditions of life began to mend, and before things assumed a more favourable turn.

The establishment of the herring fishery, during the rule of Goddards, must, therefore, have come as a great national boon. Its prosperity and importance is vividly brought home to us by the peculiar wording of the oath imposed upon the Deemster and Water-Bailiff on the installation into office. They are: "To execute the laws of the Isle so indifferently as the herring back-bone does lie in the midst of the fish." This curious, time-honoured phrase, is still in full force in our own times, and forms one of the landmarks the Goddard dynasty has left on the statutes. The next glimpse we get is in 1291, when the church claimed tithe on all fish caught. The period occupied by the Scottish usurpers forms one of the blackest spots in the annals of the Island. Their particular business seems to have been confined to wholesale plunder, extortion and killing. The sea fishery, instead of gaining increased stability and encouragement, must have fallen altogether into rein and decay. Insecurity of life and property became a general and chronic disease. We read that in 1228 "all the South of Man was wasted by Alan, Lord of Galloway, who spoiled the churches and slew all the men he could lay hold of, so as the South of Man was laid in a manner desolate"; in 1275, King Alexander (Ollister) improved upon Alan, it made Manxmen more groan and cry out in distress in their old precious ballad—that golden heirloom:

Oh! Scotchman, if thou were worthy,
Why did'st thou not rule as did
The son of Norway's King?

—there were greater taxes, rents, and confiscation than ever.

In the battle at Ronaldsway he slew 527 Manx. When the Scotch vanished, came the Waldeboeufs, Montacutes, Scropes, and the Percies from 1344–1406; their only merit was an end of slaying, but the confusion continued the same with the various change of masters. The people only breathed up again with the advent of the Lancashire Stanleys, when, for one good thing, insular peace and order took the place of anarchy and chaos.

The Goddards, it must be granted, exerted a beneficial influence upon the Island on the whole, and during their reign the economical and political status underwent considerable improvement. The farmers again dared to stock their crops of oats, and to rear their cattle and sheep, which, more extensively introduced by the Scandinavians into the Island, formed the great part of the staple and wealth of the Manx. The salmon and trout fishing was as diligently followed as the herring and sea fishery. The Laxey river was one of the rivers particularly rich in salmon (*lax* = salmon), and at its embouchure the Norse settlers founded a little stad that bears its name.

A new and more conspicuous era begins with the investment of Sir John Stanley "as King and Lord of the same Land of Mann," in 1406, who, along with his successors, exercised all his great feudal powers. One of his first laws has reference to the herring fishery, it says:

Alsoe we give for Law that a Castle Maze be paid out of five Maze of Herrings in a Boate taken and Halfe a Maze out of two Maze and a Halfe in a Boate gotten, as oft as they go to Sea and gotten soe; and that is our Law by Custome and Usage; and the Lord to pay vid. for a Maze thereof, provided that the Bringers of the first Maze shall for the same have iii. iiiid. (3s. 4d.).

He claimed therefore 20 per cent. of all the herrings caught, and to pay 6d. a maze if the bringer of the first maze got 3s. 4d. The price of 3s. 4d. seems to have been founded on an old Statute of 22 Edward IV (1483):

That no herring be sold in any vessel but the barrel (= 600 herrings, or a maze) contains 32 gallons which must be well packed, and as good at the middle as the ends on pain of forfeiting 3s. 4d. a barrel."

In 1561 (see Mills' *Statutes*, p. 39) it is further ordered:

At every Herring Fishery upon the Coast of Mann all Manner of Person, whether they be Barrons, Officers, or Soldiers, to pay the Castle Maze and Customes as hath been heretofore used.

We come now to the "Spiritual Lawes and Customes belonging to the Isle of Mann" (see Mills, pp. 46, 50–51), and the additional privileges and exactions of the church:

First that the Bishops shall have their Herring Scoute and their fishing Boate, freely and franckly, without any Tythes paying, wheresoever they Land in the Isle. In like manner had the Abbot, the Priors, the Archdeacons. Alsoe, all Parsons, Viccars, of the Thirds or Pention instituted, shall always choose their Fishing Boate at Easter Time, and their Scoute at Herring Fishing Time, whether their Fishing be about this Land or elsewhere. Alsoe, every Master of every Fishing Boat shall cause all the Fish to be brought above the full Sea Mark, and there pay truely the Tyth. And if they will not truely pay, then the Master shall make five Shares of all his Fish and the Proctor shall appoint to be divided what share he will; the Master must divide: the Proctor shall choose in that Order, because it has no life.

Alsoe, when Herring Fishing is, the Proctor shall take his Tyth where the Boat doth ground and land; if the Boates land in another Parish than their own, they pay half Tyth there for the landing, except it be such Boates as are in the first article specified.

And if there be any Salmon Fishes taken, either in Salt Water or Fresh Water, the Tyth thereof is to be paid.

Alsoe, all those Boates that Fish, either in England or Ireland, either for Herring or Gray Fish, is to agree for half the Tyth at their coming home, with their own Parson, Viccar, or Proctor and in case they bring any Fresh Herrings, not having paid half Tyth there, they must pay whole Tyth here.

And we read in an Act of Tynwald, 1610 (see Mills, p. 503):

Also, the Water Bailiff shall have out of every Boat, as oft as they fish, a certain measure called a Kybbon full of Herring (probably from Keep = a large basket, or Kibble = a bucket, or tub), and whosoever refuseth to give the same, or Twelve Pence in Money in lieu thereof, shall be excluded from the Fleet (the price of a maze in 1678 was 5s, so that a Kybbon-full must have been a good hundred).

Besides this, if the fishermen went about rock fishing in their little skiffs round the coast, the parsons exacted their due share on the rock fishing, and these rocks were ill-known under the denomination *Creggyn Yaghee*, or tithe rocks, and the fishermen gave them a wide berth.

Now as to the *scoutes*. These were little boats of generally not more than two tons burden, with a short mast, and one sail of coarse cloth, built of Norway fir, and a keel of oak; only few had a proper rudder, and a short oar, or stuiri (as the Norwegians called it), was used instead by the master, when necessary. The seams were caulked with wool, dipped in tar. The crew consisted of four men, and the share was proportioned out (in 1648) into eight parts:

3 to the owner of the nets (who suffering great and serious damage, done by the *gobbags* and the *bock*, were well entitled to it).

1 to the owner of the boat.

4 to the men, *viz.*, 1 share each.

The supply of the nets for the herring fishery was compulsory by Statute, and "every farmer or tenant within the Island, whether Lord's or Barron's tenant, had to provide eight fathoms of netts furnished with buoys and corks ready for fishing, out of every quarter of ground, containing three deepings of nine score mashes upon the rope" (see Mills' *Acts of Tynwald*, 1610, p. 502).

The number of boats in 1670 was 200, with but an indifferent population; what it was in the 15th and 16th Century, with a much inferior density of population, it is impossible to say, but certainly not above that number. Blundell (1648) says neither now, nor at any time heretofore, was it found to abound with numerous natives. We see, therefore, that both the King and the Church, either in natures or money value, had their good pound of flesh out of the crofter-fishermen of Man: 20 per cent. had to go for the Lord, 20 per cent. to the Bishop, Abbot, the Priors, and the rest; the Water Bailiff had his modest share into the bargain, and there must have been little crumbs for official hangers-on, who now and then had to close an eye; and so fishermen, farmers and wives and daughters had to make their nets and build their boats and toil, good times or bad times, and 40–45 per cent. went like a flash in a frying pan before they could touch a single fish.

But there is already a black cloud which lurks threatening on the horizon: the periodical disappearance of the herring itself—the effect of which (with all their main strength bent and concentrated on one single point, to the exclusion of an equal and proportional attention to the cultivation of the soil) brought on the Island a long train of misfortunes which ripened into fuller fruit in the course of the 16th, 17th, and 18th centuries. The herring "famines" which were yet to break over the land in full force are already slightly foretold in the Spiritual Statutes, quoted: "All those Boates that fish either in England or Ireland, either for Herring or Gray Fish, is to agree for half the Tyth on their coming home"; and we can read it again between the lines without great difficulty in "The rates of the Customs at every Port within the Isle of Mann, given this 28th day of June, Anno Domini, 1577" (see Mills, p. 43), but of this I shall speak in my next note.

252. CHAPTERS ON THE MANX HERRING FISHERY (2)

The unsatisfactory prospects of the herring fishery towards the latter quarter of the 16th century are to be gathered from the Customs "ingates" of 1577, where we find the rate for:

Herrings, the maze,   1d.
  do. the tonn,   12d.
Fish, the tonn,   12d.

A very slight charge indeed, and a clear invitation to the strangers to bring their fish to the Island.

The import of salt is already mentioned, in 1523:

If it be a ship of Salt, the Merchants (in Man) are to have a Barrel of Salt out of every 20 Barrels; and when all is discharged, the Clearke of the Ship is to have half with the four Merchants, how many Barrels they have taken up.

And the tariff of 1577 runs:

Salt, the Tunn, 12d. Shipp with Salt, British or Portugal (bay salt), inward, shall pay a Quarter Tunn before the Mast, and another above the Mast, if it be 20 tunnes, or els the half.

It was employed principally for curing white herring. The natives were evidently unacquainted with the old process of curing red herring until late in the 18th century; Blundell* says in 1648:

I suppose it will be as strange for the reader as it was for me to observe it, that these Manx people who have traded in herrings, even aborigine and the poorer sort, making them all the year long their daily and constant food, notwithstanding so respectless are they of variety of dressing them, or to give them any other gust than their own taste, that they are so far from having any red herrings that they know not what they mean, neither do they desire or learn how to make them.

On the various items concerned in the construction of the fishing boats, the rates, levied in 1577, were as follows:

Oares, the hundred 3d. or 6d.

Oares of every Boat after the rate of paying for hundred 8d.

Oak timber or Sparrs, the hundred 3d., of either sort, or 6d.

Plancks, for shipps the hundred 3d. or 12d.

Tarr, for shipps the hundred 1d.

Pitch, for shipps the hundred 1d.

Nails, for shipps the thousand 1d.

Nails, for shipps the last 2/6.

Hayre ropes the dozen 1d.

Ropes British the hundred 6d.

The scarcity of herring, at the latter part of the 16th century, is to be inferred in addition, from "the examinations, in 1610, of fower anncyent men, *viz.*, Mallo Caloe, Willm Kerush, John Christin, and Willm Corran, who speak of themselves as 'Fishers driving for Hearring in the North of England with Mancks Boates.'"

We learn from another Act of Tynwald (24th June, 1613) that the existing law of the Custom herring of 1422 (called Castle Mazes) was a very heavy and deterring burden. Lady Elizabeth, Countess of Derby, was:

Advertized that because of the great imposition not onlie Strangers (who even then flocked to the Manx fishing grounds) have refrayned to come to the late Fisshinge of the Isle, but also the Islanders themselves being thereby discouraged did not shewe their willinge Minds, nor consequentlie use their industrious Paynes in and about the Fisshinge as otherwise they would have done, being reasonablie dealt withall for the said Castle Mazes.

She directs, therefore, that:

Out of every smalle boate whereof a Countriman is Owner, to be paid in Lieue of Custome Heyrings for all the Tyme of this next Fishinge, to the Lord two Maze, of the best Fish whensoever a Public Call for Payment and Delivrye thereof be given throughout the Fleete of Boates.

And every of the Countrimen which have Boates, called bcowles, to pay in the same Manner four Mazes for all their Custome during the tyme of fisshinge.

And out of everye small boate of the Stranger, one Maze for the first night that the same boate taketh any herrings; and so ever afterwards one Maze weeklie, while it continueth at the Fisshinge.

And in like Manner, out of every Scowte of the Stranger, two Mazes the first night, and then two Maze weeklie during the Fisshinge.

The time to begin to drive for heyring this present year is, by general Consent, to be upon the 15th Day of July next (1613).

Those Boates to bringe the said Custome Heyrings and deliver them, such fish:

From and betwixt St. Maughal Head and Douglas at Douglas. Between Douglas and the Calf of Man at Castletonne. Such as fish on the North Parte of the Isle at Peeletowne. Whosoever shall use any Draw Netts or Stake Netts during the tyme of the Fisshing shall forfeit 10s.

Blundell also writes (1648):

The Lord of the Island hath no duty paid unto him of any other fish but of the herring only, but the tithes are paid both of herrings and of any other fish that is taken, as of cod, ling, macarel, thornback, &c.; and he that brings the first herring caught in care to the Lord, at his castle at Rushen, by ancient custom, is to give him 3s. 4d.

The lord was more merciful than the Church which, more iron-handed, continued its exaction of the full old tithe and, be it noticed, it claimed fish-tithe on all descriptions of fish, both sweet water and salt water fish. We shall see how desperate the people fought, time after time, and century after century, though unsuccessfully, against this harsh and heavy infliction, a perennial grievance which was really only slowly settled at the end of the 18th century, and the cause of much misery and ill-feeling all over the Island.

* See Blundell's *History of Isle of Man* (1648–1656), Manx Society xxv, vol. i, p. 86.

253. CHAPTERS ON THE MANX HERRING FISHERY (1600–1700)

There must have been want and disease, to quote only from the Parish Registers of Kirk Michael (1), where in 1623, 1629 and 1639, the deaths were very numerous; in 1641 there seems to have been an increase in the indigent class, and great numbers of poor beggars were straying about the country (2); and things came to a climax in 1642-3, when the people carried on a tumultuous agitation, headed by Edward Christian, "newly begun betwixt the clergie and commonaltie about their matter of tythes. The counrey would pay no more tythes, and would feight and dye first." Only to enumerate some of these tithes. Besides the tithe on the fishery, of which I have already spoken, there was the tithe on corn, honey, cheese, milk, butter, lambs, purrs, calves, colts, geese, eggs, hens, wax, wool, milk sheep, milk goats, the Plough groat, the Clerk's silver, the Smoke penny, and the Corse presents or mortuarys, &c.; these impositions were keenly felt, for times were then very bad. The church, however, rode triumphant, and "the principle disturbers, together with Christian, were tried, fined, and imprisoned."

That the people had cause to revolt and complain is fully borne out by Blundell (1648) (3), who writes:

The fishermen complained much at my being present there, for of late years they have not taken half the quantity of herrings which they used to take in former time, and, moreover, within the memory of some of them, until of late, they have failed not to have great fishing for cods (this is the first allusion to the cod fishery) of which they were accustomed to take in such plentiful abundance, as that they were enforced to cut off their heads and to cast them away upon the shore, either for the poor or for any that would take them up, which they did, least their boat should be overladen and sink; and now this is otherwise.

As for the lord, he appears to have put the Castle maze on a new basis, and Blundell states:

If 5 meaze be caught by one boat they give the lord one meaze or 500, if 10 meaze, 2 meaze or 1,000. Then the lord can demand no more, for after the proportion being paid, they are free to take as many as they can without paying anymore to the lord, although they should afterwards catch 1,000 meaze; and except 5 meaze be caught by one boat the lord hath not any part at all.

We also learn from him how the people lived in 1648:

Their diet is sparing and simple; their drink-water and butter milk; their meat consists of herring, salt, butter and oatcakes. The meal of servants consists of two boiled herrings, one entire oatcake and butter, with milk and water to drink. Beer and ale they only take in the market.

Of "late years," then, both the herring and cod had seriously fallen off again; and to increase the misery and want, in 1649 there came "a time of great dearth and scarsitie," during which many of them died of starvation, the summers having been very wet, and to alleviate the famine to some degree the earl imported some corn from France (4). In addition to this, agriculture, all round, languished, in consequence of the precarious land tenure, and it continued in that state until the Magna Charta, or new Land Act of 1704 was wrung from the lord.

There was great rejoicing, however, in 1667, the *annus mirabilis;* an immense herring shoal, such as had never been witnessed before, arrived on the shores of Man. Bishop Wilson alluded to it in 1719 (5):

Formerly, he writes, herring were the great staple commodity, of which within the memory of some now living near 20,000 barrels have been exported in one year to France and other places.

Sacheverell (6) refers likewise to the prosperity of that year

Formerly (1667) they had such quantities that 500 have been sold for a groat, and yet the fishing worth £3,000 per annum.

According to Haining (7) there were 2,531 men between the ages of 16 to 60, and the total population was estimated 7,000 souls. By this time the ale-houses had already much increased, and in this year of great plenty (1667) (8) Bishop Barrow called the clergy to account for disgracing "their callinge [...] by vendinge ayle and beer and keeping victuallinge houses." The money and earnings went to the public houses for the *jough*, "many of the people became not only tipplers, but also infamous for sottishness and drunkenness," and so the profits of a good season were squandered away.

In 1670 (9) when a good fishing doeth fall, each boat paid to the lord:

Per 20 maze–2 maze, or 10s.

If 5 maze–1 maze or 5s.

If 2½ maze   ½ maze, or 2s. 6d.

There were then 200 boats employed in the fishing.

A sea disaster seems to have befallen the herring fleet in 1672, for we read that "this year the men was cast away at ye herring fishing Sept. 2nd"; in 1675 many died of flux.

By 1681 Douglas had become the place of "the greatest resort in the whole Island, because the haven is commodious—unto which the ffrench men and other fforaigners use to repair with their bay salt, having traffic again with the Islanders and buying of them leather, coarse wool, and powdered beefe."

There was a severe epidemic in Kirk Michael in 1684, and the smallpox which had broken out in Ramsey in 1685, carried many people away; about that time another serious herring famine, which lasted for 30 years, visited the Island. We cannot fix the exact year when the fish began to fail. Sacheverell says in 1693–4:

Since their herring fails [...] so that this want has reduced the Island to great extremitie.

It was just when these clouds hung over the Island, and when revenues, and the earnings of the fishermen and farmers had sunk to a very low ebb, that the Island became involved in the smuggling trade.

In 1681 the King (Charles II) "threatened the earl with a *quo warranto*, and sent custom-house officers out of Dublin to inspect their importation of merchandises," and in 1682 the Island is described "a magazine of all sorts of foreign goods as might thence be transported clandestinely into any part of the three kingdoms." The governors were only lukewarm in their endeavours to extirpate this new pest. It grew and prospered, and although it temporarily filled the exchequer of the Stanleys and Atholls, it reacted perniciously on the healthy development of the Island; it not only proved the death blow of the regime of the Atholls, but it also deteriorated the entire moral stamina of the population, and checked the growth of its agricultural resources, while the sea fishery, or what was left of it, was only followed in a half-hearted way. The smuggler and publican held the field.

(1) See *Yn Lioar Manninagh*, vol. I, 1889, p. 5.

(2) See Moore's *History of the Isle of Man* vol. I, pp. 237, 241, 260, 282.

(3) See Blundell, vol. xxv, vol. I, Manx Society, pp. 86 and 87.

(4) Moore's *History of the Isle of Man*, p, 283.

(5) See Bishop Wilson's *History of the Isle of Man*, vol. xviii, Manx Society, p. 104.

(6) See Manx Society, vol. I, p. 14.

(7) Haining, *Isle of Man Guide*, 1834, p. 81.

(8) Moore's *History of the Isle of Man*, p 405, vol. I, footnote.

(9) Moore's *History of the Isle of Man*, vol. II, p.942.

(10) *Yn Lioar Manninagh*, 1889, vol. I, p. 5.

254. CHAPTERS ON THE MANX HERRING FISHERY (1700–1750)

The new century was ushered in in sable garb—the failure of the herring lasted on to 1711; to make the situation more acute, there was an epidemic in 1704, and Bishop Wilson had a petition inserted in the Litany in 1705 (1) to be read in all the churches within the Isle, *viz.*: "That it may please God to restore and continue to us the blessings of the sea" (*As dy char erash as dy hannaghty dooin bannaghtyn ny marry*). The people were plunged in want and penury; in these hard times they turned their eyes to the Fylde district, with which they kept up an active smuggling intercourse. The potato had been cultivated there, at North Meols, Ormskirk, Kirkham, &c, as far back as the latter part of the 17th century, and from there was introduced into the Island, between 1706–7, and Waldron tells us in 1710 that oats and potatoes were the chief produce of the Manx, and Manx Earlys were early known for their good qualities. By some ingenious definition of a convocation held 1712 at Kirk Michael the clergy soon made them tithable. The people mainly subsisted then on fish and potatoes. In 1710, Lord Derby had an assessment of the commons made, and began enclosing some of the common lands and selling them, which caused another soreness. There was a fresh appeal in 1711 against the fish tithe, but it availed nothing. Smuggling became more rampant than ever, and the prevailing conditions made people still more desperate. At this time the fishery began to revive a little; the Lord's receipts from the herring fishing, which between 1702–10 were nil, rose in 1711 to £34. The smallpox was raging again in the Island in 1714, and the clergy for once made a surrender of the tithe in the next year. The revenues of the herring fishery are missing in 1717 and 1719, another indication of a bad sea-harvest, and about this time Bishop Wilson writes that the lord commuted the Castle maze for a money payment of 10s for every Manx boat (that took 10 maze, and with a smaller payment when the quantity was less). There was a fresh failure of herring between 1721–8, and in the Book of Common Prayer, in Manx, published 1727, the litany has the petition "to renew and continue the blessings of the sea," inserted anew. During that time, in 1724–5, there was another fierce outbreak of the smallpox, which killed one-tenth of the population of Ramsey, Maughold, German, and Peel. Disease and starvation went closely hand in hand. The fishing between 1729–1734 was only fair and fluctuating, during 1732–3 and 1737–40 many died of flux; there was a great scarcity of corn in 1734, and the new edition of the Common Prayer (1738) renews the old petition, for there was another bad fishing from 1735–1737, when the Lord's receipts are likewise missing again. The Statutes (see Mills, pp. 238–39), 1736, allude to this period:

Whereas the herring fishery in this Isle has for many years past been very uncertain, and yet severell strangers as well as natives have bought and transported fresh herrings before the country was supplied [...] and obliged to buy herrings from abroad at high prices, no persons be permitted, or suffer to buy up any herring for exportation from this Isle, or the coast thereof, before the country or communally be supplied, that is to say, as long as the herrings may be bought and sold at is 2d. per 100 (= 7s. a maze) or above, and the fishermen have a vent for the same at that price in the Island.

Drinking and smuggling meanwhile had increased at the same rapid pace, and the number of alehouses, which in 1734 was limited to 200, soon afterwards leapt up to 300; the statutes (see Mills, p. 226, 1734) say, "the great consumption in these houses often occasions a scarcity of corn and other provisions, necessitating the Island to supply it from abroad," nor was the drinking confined to beer and ale alone, but there was an alarming rise in the consumption of brandy, rum, gin, geneva, *etc.*

For many years the Island did not produce sufficient corn for supporting the population, and the scarcity was such, in 1740, that they had to procure it from Holland. To add to this confusion the smallpox and a contagious fever, equally deadly, visited the Island in 1741 and 1743. In 1740 lobster tithe was ordered to be paid (2). There is a steady growth in the Lord's receipts from the herring fishery, for while in 1734 it had been £44, it climbs up gradually in 1738 to £69 (3), then:

1739-40 to £86; or £43 average per year.
1741 to £92 (rising from thence)
1742-5 to £452, or £113 average, per year.
1746 to £114.
1747-8 to £222, or £111 average, per year.
1749 to £109.
1750 to £109.

This return gives us, of course, only a vague idea, for we don't know at all the number of boats employed; we have seen that since 1719 every boat paid 10s., instead of the former castle maze, and those which caught less than 10 maze paid a lesser sum, nor do we know the yearly value, extent, or price per maze of the catches made. But if we assume the number of boats to have been pretty constant during that time, the return gives us a fair general measure of the prevailing state of the fishery for the above period.

(1) Fargher's *Annals of the Isle of Man.*
(2) *Ibidem.*
(3) Moore's *History of the Isle of Man.*

255. CHAPTERS ON THE MANX HERRING FISHERY (1751–1765)

The return of the receipts for 1751 amounted to £109, or equal to the preceding year, while the total for 1752-9 was £1,080, or £135 average per year, indicating a further steady rise. We read that the herring fishery, in 1752, at Haverford West (Cardiganshire), consisting of 18 busses, caught 9,000 barrels, or 500 barrels each (1), and the Manx fishery in the same year must have been very good, too. The same paper informs us, in a letter dated October 2nd, 1754, from Douglas to a Manchester correspondent:

Every body here (Douglas) is busy curing herrings, more having been taken here within 6 weeks last past than in 6 years before. There has upwards of 500 tons been salted in bulk in this town and shipped off for Ireland, *etc.*, besides some thousands of barrels packed and cured for the West Indies. The weather has been the finest that ever was seen, which has occasioned this vast trade. 'Tis a charming sight to see the Whitehaven busses, about 50 Irish wherries, and 300 boats all upon the sea at one view.

It is a pretty picture.

In another letter, in the *Mercury,* dated October 1st, a little sidelight is thrown on frail human nature:

The Shannon, Lowther, Stephenson, and Despatch busses, under the command of Commodore Copeland, were returning from the Shetland fishery, and in returning have taken 210 barrels of herring in one night off the Isle of Man, where there appears an uncommon quantity of fish. They were to return thither on the 16th (September), and have taken proper precaution to prevent the people of the Island for cutting and destroying their nets, as some evil-minded persons did before.

It evidently was a splendid year, and the catches were made during the "back" fishing at Douglas.

It may also be of interest to mention that August 18, 1752, British pickled Shetland herrings were sold in Manchester at 2d per piece in retail, according to the Manchester paper.

In 1670 the Island employed 200 boats, and in 1754, or 84 years later, the number of the Manx boats had slowly increased to 300 boats, ranging from 3 to 8 ton burden, and consisting of *scowtes* and (the smaller) of "yawls."

The *Mercury* also gives us a regular weekly return, in its column, of the fresh herring shipments from the Island to Liverpool. I have made an analysis from 1756–1760.

In 1756, 38 boats were despatched to Liverpool with fresh herring cargoes, plying between 27th July to 19th October; some of them went from Douglas every fortnight. The boats were the *Dreadnought, Francis, John, Ellen, Endeavour, Two Brothers, Alice, Alexander, Swallow, Providence, Bull, Young Tom, Dolphin, Success, the Douglas Packet, Molly, Experiment.*

1757–12 boats were sent off from 26th July to 21st September.

1758–25 boats were sent off from 10th August to 6th October.

1759–12 boats were sent off from 6th July to 25th September.

1760–5 boats were sent off from 8th August to 3rd September.

This, of course, is to Liverpool alone, and the export of fresh fish to Dublin, *etc.*, has to be added; these exports argue good seasons. Feltham (2) gives us the lord's receipts for the next five years:

It shows for 1760 £121 19s, against an average of £135 for 1759, or a tangible decrease, which may also account for the slight shipments of fresh fish in 1760 to Liverpool. There is a quick drop in:

1761, £92 4s.

1762, £90 19s.

1763, £81 19s; the boats of Kirk Michael Parish already built are few in number (3).

1764, £60 9s. (there was a fresh epidemic in the Island, which seems to explain the drop).

1765, the return is omitted for this year—"none paid to his Grace's family" (the Island passing into the hands of the British Government).

1765 is, however, a "red letter" year, for the *Universal Magazine* says:

They write from the Isle of Man that they had on those coasts the greatest take of herring that has been known for many years past, so that upwards of 20,000 barrels have been exported to foreign parts.

The same year the Keys petitioned George III to grant them "the liberty and privilege" of curing fish on the coasts of Great Britain, together with a bounty. It was about this time that the Manx began to attempt—rather late in the day—to cure red herrings, the presentation to the world of the famous Manx kippers.—I am anticipating a little, occurring five years later (1772).

I have to descend now again to the early fifties.

Notwithstanding constant threats and remonstrances from the British Government, the smuggling had assumed gigantic strides, to the great injury of its fiscal revenues. Practically the Island had usurped the prerogatives and jurisdiction of the *mare clausum*. In 1753:

The captain of an English cruiser followed a valuable Dutch dogger into port and seized her; but the man found himself mistaken. Five of his men who had taken possession of the dogger were thrown into jail. The captain himself, with two men and a boy, narrowly escaped to Whitehaven. The loss to the revenues is calculated at least £200,000 a year (4).

This was a time when Captain Dick Hatterack, of the Youngfrauw of Hagenslaapen, could roar out in *Guy Mannering*:

I am all in the way of fair trade. Just loaded yonder at Douglas, in the Isle of Man, neat cognac, real byson, and sonchoug, and Mechlin laces, if you want any; we bumped ashore a hundred kegs last night.

Look at the inflow to the Island in the earlier smuggling times. The people of Douglas in 1730 (4) consisted of:

111 Manx families, headed by 14 Kellys (Hoy Kelly!), 13 Moores, 11 Christians, 8 Cannels, 7 Corlets, 64 English, and a few Irish families, representing 1050 souls, with 6 people to a family.

The population of the ports, such as:

	Peel	Castletown	Douglas	Ramsey
had grown in 1757 to	805	915	1814	882
from 1726	475	785	810	460
increase in 32 years	330	130*	1004	422
(depleted and attracted to Douglas).*				

demonstrating the excessive and abnormal influx of aliens that had flocked to the principal ports of the Island for mere purposes of smuggling and illegal trading. We read again in 1761:

The Isle of Man creates a prodigious expense to the British Government in maintaining so many officers and citizens to guard against the illicit and pernicious trade, not to mention the notorious frauds committed in the Customs.

The cup was brim full; and so we read in the *Gentlemen's Magazine*, Saturday, June 1st, 1765:

The English colours were hoisted on the Castle in the Isle of Man, the sovereignity of that island being now annexed to the Crown of Great Britain, and the inhabitants in every respect subjected to the laws, customs and privileges of their fellow subjects.

The independence of the Island, the little kingdom of yore of the old Stanleys, so full of stirring ups and downs, had crumbled to dust, and the Atholls packed, and sadly said good-bye.

It retained its curious insular flag, joined on the Union Jack, its Tynwald, and its House of Keys, and a new political era began for Man.

(1) See *Manchester Mercury*, November 14th, 1752.
(2) See Feltham's *History of the Isle of Man*, 1798, p. 1.
(3) See *Fargher's Annals of the Isle of Man*, May 7th, 1762.
(4) See *Postlewaite's Commercial Dictionary*, London, 1753, vol. 2, p. 67.
(5) See Transactions of Manx Society.

256. CHAPTERS ON THE MANX HERRING FISHING (1766–1800)

By an act of Parliament bounties were granted, in 1767, for the encouragement of the herring fishery, and the judgment of the Manx spiritual court in the same year, by which the fishermen were liable to pay full tithes for fish, even though sold at sea many leagues from the island, was confirmed by the Privy Council, in 1769. The fishermen, nevertheless, remained obstinate, and John Cannell, of Kerrooglass, Kirk Michael, boatmaster, to quote an instance, refused payment of the herring tithe, in arrear for 1768 to 1770, and therefore was ordered to be committed in 1771, "until he submits to law" (1). The clergy, at a convocation held 1772, resolved to vigorously defend the rights of the church with respect to the tithe of herring and other fish, but the fishermen showed fight, and the clergymen renewed their complaint in the following year. It was enforced to the end of the century, when all mention disappears from the records (2). The bounties were repealed in 1771, and the next year the government gave permission to export herring caught *bona fide* off the Island to Great Britain, and a payment per barrel of 3s. 4d. for white herring, and of is 8d. per 1,000 red herring, was made. Herring could be exported to British colonies free, and salt loaded, provided it was only used for curing herring. In the same year, instead of the immemorial lord's maze, the payment was fixed at 10s. per boat, and the revenue arising from it handed over to the Harbour Commissioners to expend on the harbours.

It was about 1772 that "red herring houses for the cure of the Manx kippers were first erected at Peel and Douglas." The process is described in 1797 by Feltham, which I give for its interest:

The red herrings are first regularly piled up, he says, with a layer of salt between each row, and remain to purify some days; they are then washed, when dried sufficiently they are fixed by the mouth on small hazel rods, and hung up in large houses for the purpose, in length about 90 feet by 60 feet broad. Here the herring rods are hung as close as admissible, and reach from the roof till within 8 feet of the floor. Their regularity and lustre make a very beautiful appearance; fires are kept under them continually for four or five weeks, made of the dried roots of oak; when being sufficiently reddened, they are shipped for the Mediterranean ports.

There were five herring houses in Douglas in 1797, one of them costing £1,200, and a capital one in Peel.

In 1777 the Island boasted of 415 fishing boats, from 3–10 tons, employing 2,905 men and boys; in 1781 that number had sunk to 315 (3), which seems to point to a decline of the fishery; an act passed in 1785 prohibited the exportation of herring caught off the Isle of Man, unless actually caught there, while in 1786 the duties of 1772 were abolished and bounties granted of 1s. per barrel on white cured herring, and 2s. 8d. per barrel if exported direct, or via Great Britain to foreign parts. Red cured ones received a bounty of 1s. 9d. only when exported, the is bounty having been omitted by error (4).

1787 proved to be a disastrous year for Douglas; 84 yards of the lowest end of the old pier, with a light-house there, was destroyed by a violent gale, and great havoc was inflicted on the herring fleet, which was in full activity at Douglas; the *Mercury* writes 2nd October, 1787:

A few days since the most dreadful scene presented itself that ever was known at Douglas, 23 fishing boats out of the fleet were lost coming into this harbour, and many people perished, the wrecks are washed up from the rocks, and dead bodies taken up every hour; no less than four this afternoon, and 16 boats run on shore near Ramsey, but no lives lost.

The loss of life, *viz.*, some 161 people (23 boats with a crew of seven each) was appalling!

Feltham gives us the statistics of the exportation of red and white cured herring during 1787 to 1790, which I have grouped.

Red cured with a bounty of 1/9		
1787	2,636 for Italy	2,074 Gt. Britain
1788	5,468 for Italy & Dublin	4,435 Gt. Britain
1789	12,559 for Italy	3,015 Gt. Britain
1790	6,866 for Italy	2,747 Gt. Britain

White at 1/-		at 2/8 bounty
1787	1,935 for Italy	
1788	861 for Italy	
1789	2,616 for Italy	315 Cork, 10 Leghorn
1790	1,878 for Italy	125 Dublin

Or total exportation:

	1787	1788	1789	1790
Red	4,710	9,897	15,574	9,613
White	1,935	861	2,941	2,003
	†6,645‡	10,758	18,515	11,616

† This low return is, of course, principally due to the destruction of the fleet at the Douglas back fishing in 1787, and may also have affected the return for 1788, owing to the loss of so many boats.

The prices varying from 3s. to 1s. per 100; a barrel (600) costing the curer 12s., and selling in England 25s. for white herring. The quantity of red herring used for home consumption was also very large. 1789 was an exceptionally good year, and so was 1793. On September 22nd:

£5,000 worth of herring were brought into Douglas harbour alone, independent of what was carried to other markets. Following night the fishing quite as good, price twelve pence (Manks) per hundred (5).

Laughton's guide (6) also alludes to this remarkable catch:

The memory of persons still living recalls a season when the herring were so abundant that they were caught with the hand on the beach after being sold at 4d. a hundred, until purchasers could not be found they were carted off for manure.

At that period, writes Feltham:

Every village and parish is provided with public-houses, and the little huts thus privileged have mostly a small empty barrel outside the door to indicate their nature; if you venture in you will be gratified with excellent wine, plenty of rum, and improveable ale, and herrings and potatoes, of course.

The smuggling, in consequence of its lucrativeness, was still vigorously carried on, although followed under much greater risk, and gave the Government no little trouble. In 1791 large quantities of French brandy and Geneva were carried both into and out of the island; not one pound of tea nor a gallon of British spirits had paid duty for many years, though largely consumed. Tobacco was largely smuggled in, and so was salt for illicit re-exportation (6). The English gentility and half-pay officers and captains, who came in shoals to the Island, lived in clover, and one could get "drunk like a lord" for a mere trifle. Townley relates many stirring sea captures in his diary, during his stay in the Island:

15th February, 1790: Captain Cook has fallen in with the Laxey sloop and carried her to Kirkcudbright.

On the other hand:

1st February, 1790: The *Swift*, of Port Glasgow, a fine cutter-built brig, is come into the harbour on her return from Scotland to the French coast for another cargo of brandy, and other articles in the illicit trade. We were thought to expect a total suppression of the smuggling business, but I fear it is recovering much upon the coasts of Scotland and Ireland, as well as upon the east coast of England.

After 1798 smuggling still continued out of, not into, the Island; till about 1846, brandy, and tobacco between 1819 and 1826, were objects of smuggling (7).

In 1795 an additional bounty of 1s. for every barrel of herring landed in the Island was granted, and in 1799–1800 the same was taken out of the surplusage of the Manx customs (9).

In 1797, according to Feltham, 400 herring boats were employed in the fishery.

(1) See *Fargher's Isle of Man Annals*, 1771.
(2) See Moore's *History*, p. 660.
(3) See *Isle of Man Guide*, 1834, p. 84.
(4) See Moore, p. 957.
(5) See *Fargher's Annals*, pub. 1793.
(6) *Johnson's Isle of Man Guide*, by J.B. Laughton, Douglas, 1852, 6th edition.
(7) See Moore, pp. 598–99.
(8) See Moore, p. 601.
(9) See Moore, p. 957.

257. LETTER FROM J. W.

Sir,—The 21st of this month will be the anniversary of the loss of a large portion of the Manx herring fleet, 1787, in Douglas Bay. It is now about 115 years since those painful calamity took place. Many years after the event the fishermen would hesitate to go to sea on the 21st September. One hundred years ago the herring fishing boats were from 30 to 35 feet in the keel and had only a quarter deck, the other space being open to the rain and the waves. In the present day they were all decked all over, and the keel is about 40 feet long. The verses of poetry which I enclose herewith have hardly any history—the second verse is minus a few words. However, they are sent for your inspection, and publication, if you think proper.

J. W.
Castletown,
7th September, 1903.

DESTRUCTION OF THE HERRING FLEET IN DOUGLAS BAY, IN 1787
(Translated into English by Ny-Greie, Kirk Patrick.)

With pain we record in the year of our Lord
Seventeen hundred and eighty and seven,
When it so came to pass a good fishing there
Off Douglas, with a beautiful season.

But it was for a time——the weather too, kept fine.
Ere the week it had come ——ding;
The face of the sky ——ty
That a horrible s——ing.

On Matthew's eve, with the fleet on the wave,
It blew as with vengeance to hurry
Poor mariners there, from all that was dear,
Even life, by the element's fury.

Matthew's Day, how many could say
How sickening art thou to my feelings;
The fatherless there, their cries rent the air,
And widows how woeful their wailings!

Excitement and cries prevail'd through Kirk Christ,
Poor women who'd lost their defenders;
The fate of John Moore they lamented full sore,
And the unfortunate Kinleys.

Tom Grimshaw was too, with the rest of his crew,
In the cold arms of death they were sleeping;
There lived not a man of this twenty-one
Their friends they were bitterly weeping.

On a beautiful day these sailed away
From Douglas, along with their fellows;
On reaching the ground where the herrings were found,
Who'd think of the crashing that followed.

Alas 'twas too soon, the change it came on,
The easterly winds commenced roaring,
The sea running high, with its boisterous cry,
Whilst torrents of rain were downpouring.

Then up to the gale they quickly set sail,
Towards Douglas mov'd without ceasing;
But ere they got home, the sea out had flown,

'Midst storms with their fury increasing.

To hold in the bay, with the wind from the sea,
Alas for the boats which were riding;
Dark, dismal, and drear, without light on the pier,
Death there it seem'd quite unavoiding.

At anchor to ride—to wait for the tide—
It was frightful beyond comprehending,
Their cables gave way, boats sinking 'neath the spray,
And broke into pieces on landing.

Tempestuous and dark, who could see a spark,
The billows were over them breaking;
How dreadful it was to run for the coast
With every prospect so threat'ning.

The turbulent waves like mountains upheave,
The storm unabating in ardour;
The sea breaking white thro' the perilous night,
Completely obscuring the harbour.

An hour before day, Tom Grimshaw did say,
To run for the port he resolved;
There he and John Moore were lost in that hour—
Five crews in their fate were involved.

So Kinley was, too; he could not get through
With the task he so bravely attempted;
'Midst darkness most dread ran on for the pier,
His boat was immediately swamped.

258. SHORT RETROSPECT AT THE OUTGOING OF THE 19TH CENTURY
While I sat musing and picturing to myself the strange vicissitudes and events that had passed over Man during the last 900 years, noting the flotsam and jetsam of alternating invaders which the sea had incessantly cast up on its fair strands, methought I saw Mannanin Mac Leir rising before me in flesh and blood, his silver locks descending to his girdled loins, bent down with hoary age, and heaving a sigh for his unhappy children of Man, sorrowfully bewailing the fate that had befallen their inheritance. The torch and the sword, servitude and impoverishment had crippled their strength and nigh crushed them, agriculture stagnated, and famine and disease had mowed down their ranks; the herring, on whom their main hopes hinged, had proved a fickle, wayward friend, smiling and bountiful in fits and starts, and then mockingly forsaking them, and stealthily tripping away to leave them a

prey with sunken hearts. Its masters had been foreigners, their land passed merrily, a rolling coin, from hand to hand, by conquest, dower, or cast into a lord's lap by the favour of distant courts, the people merely so much chattel; when given to the Stanleys it was properly a question what could be got out of them in so much figure of revenue, an indifferent Governor presiding over as the ruling head, while the Keys were insignificant pawns to be pushed, who, weak and spiritless, did their lord's haughty bidding. Edward Christian, a real patriotic and level-headed Manxman, alone stands out, a bold and daring would-be reformer, towering head and shoulders above his puny compeers. The people did not progress or prosper under the Stanleys, and the influence of the succeeding Atholls was fraught with all sorts of evil. Their Government was corrupt and rotten, the system of wholesale smuggling licked away the moral and physical fibre of the race, and progress was, under the circumstances, a sheer impossibility. The Statute Book forms an eloquent monument and a faithful mirror of their legislation, and the administrative measures are blanks as far as the welfare and amelioration of the people were concerned. The British Government had to take over the unwelcome stock that was left behind as their share: poverty, corruption, and helplessness; neither the lord nor the church had been true to the people. Bishops Wilson (1698–1755) and Hildesley make honourable and bright amends amongst the list, both real and sincere fathers and helpers of the people. After Hildesley's death, the clergy rapidly deteriorated; there were repeated convictions against them for flagrant drunkenness and consequent removal from their office; and things went on in that fashion until the appearance of Bishop Murray (1819), who found matters "in a very scandalous state." No wonder, then, that Wesley (1777) was received with open arms. He lifted the people from the deep degradation into which they had sunk, due both to the vice and the greed of the Church. The British Government took over for practical reasons, Atholl's last Governor, John Wood, followed in 1777 by Edward Smith, and in 1793 by John Murray, fourth Duke of Athol. Legislation was naturally sterile during that period of utter confusion; the Governors, all perfect strangers, neither understood the real wants of the Island, nor did they take any active or beneficial initiative in improving the Insular conditions for the betterment of agriculture or the fisheries; they stood passively aloof and transacted their regular humdrum business in a hand-to-mouth fashion, satisfied with the being the paid and dignified figureheads of lovely little dominion.

259. PRICES IN ISLE OF MAN (1773)

A correspondent sent to the Manchester Mercury the prices of the following articles from Isle of Man, dated June 26th, 1773:

Beef, 3d. and 3½d. per lb.

Veal, 2½d. and 3d.—which is reckoned very dear.

Lamb 1s. 6d. to 2s. a side—about 2d. per lb.

Good Mutton, 3d. per lb.

Fowls, 6d. each.

Ducks, 6d. each.

Geese, with giblets, 15d.

Pigeons, 2d. each.

Rabbits, 2½d.

Salmon, 2d. per lb.

Lobsters, 3d. each.

Crabs, 6d. a dozen.

Oysters, 2s. a hundred.

Fine scalloped ditto, 6d, a hundred.

Fish of all kinds, 1d. per lb., and some cheaper (salmon excepted).

House of 10 rooms, from £6 to £8 per year.

He adds: "What an amazing difference between the above prices and those of this country."

It forms an interesting record, of ruling prices at that period in the Island, and deserves a corner in the Manx Notes and Queries.

260. CHAPTERS ON THE MANX HERRING FISHERY (1800–1897)

In 1801 the Manx fishermen and fish curers were put on the same terms as to bounties as allowed in Great Britain, and in 1808 this bounty was raised to £3 per barrel to all vessels employed in the white herring fishery on the coasts of Great Britain and Ireland (1). The number of fishing boats in 1810 amounted to 450, average 16 tons burden. There was much distress and discontent among the poorer farmers in 1816, and the ill-feeling rose considerably in consequence of Bishop Murray's attempt to revive the tithe on potatoes, turnips, &c., which had not been demanded for many years. The insular Exchequer Court decided in 1821 in favour of the Bishop; the farmers met it by appealing to the Privy Council, who in 1825 upheld the claim of the Bishop. The opponents, however, refused payment and combined together. On an attempt to enforce collection, a fierce riot broke out in Peel and in other places, and 5,000 armed men marched to Bishop's Court, compelling the Bishop by main force to desist from his attempt for that year. The barley and oats failed the next year, the Bishop therefore wisely gave way again, nor was the claim further pressed in 1827 (2). It will be recollected that the people rose *en masse* under the lead of Edward Christian in 1642–3 against the heavy extortions of the tithe, but the outburst in the 19th century, this time more successful, was even of a more serious nature, the long-suffering people were in dead earnest, and at last won the day (3). Not only were there bad crops in 1826, but the Island was visited in addition by a serious failure in 1827 of the herring. The distress was general, and great numbers of Manxmen were driven away between 1825–1840 to seek their fortunes in North America.

One would have expected that the Insular Government would have shown some practical concern about the fortures of the fisheries, that at least proper annual returns of the extent of the catches, the boats and men employed, or the capital sunk in boats and gear, the value realized by the sale, both for home consumption or export, the price obtained for the fish, should have been ordered, as a matter of course from the beginning of the 19th century upwards, but we look for them in vain, and this incredible indifference about the progress or condition of the deep sea fishery, a question at all times of vital insular importance, shows how little the House has been alive to its real interests. It is therefore not at all surprising that for any information we desire on these points we have to fall back on casual insular guide books, and some occasional reports of Royal or Official Commissions. Consequently we know next to nothing of the state of the fisheries between 1800 to 1839.

The number of herring boats in 1811 amounted to 331 (4).

In 1840 (5) the average price for the English market was 20s. per maze. The demand then for fresh fish in the English markets had greatly diminished the business in the Island of curing for home and exportation. Messrs Holmes were the only people in the Island engaged in this trade which they carried on at Douglas and Derbyhaven. They bad also a curing establishment at Wick. In cases of large takes they never offered less than 10s. or 12s. per cran. The following return of the fishing in 1840 presents a fair average of the annual value:

	MAZE	VALUE
Purchased and carried to Liverpool in Manx Boats	25,000	£35,000
Purchased in English and Irish boats	10,000	£12,000
Consumed in the Island, fresh and salt	15,000	£10,000
Cured in the Island for exportation in bulk and barrel	30,000	£15,000
	80,000	£72,000

1846	Value of all fish, £70,000	boats employed,	606
1850	£80,000	(————)	605
1852	28,845 barrels cured herrings (value not stated)		503
1859	34,357 (————)	(————)	574
1860	44,120 (————)	(————)	581
1861	48,112 (————)	(————)	591
1864	34,357 (————)	value of all fish £70,000	800
1876	Value of herring, £40,00	boats employed,	300
1883	£42,460	(————)	361
1886	£5,500	(————)	?
1887	£11,520	(————)	370
1892	£3,942	(————)	380
1896	£6,011	(————)	356
1897	£1,758	(————)	?

The period from 1840 to 1850 seems to indicate good seasons followed by low returns, more or less oscillating from year to year between 1852 to 1864. Statistics are missing for the interim between 1865–1875, and are erratic for the following years.

We notice a sharp fall in 1886; a temporary rise in 1887; a big collapse again in 1892; a flaring up during 1896; and a heavy decline in 1897.

Taking Peel by itself, the herring boats employed in 1881 were 309, and slowly decreased till we find them reduced to one-sixth in 1897, when the number of boats totals 55, and the fishermen were compelled during that time to sell or break them up.

It has been my object to bring out in bold relief the causes which have hampered and fettered the progress, both economic and administrative, of the Island in the past centuries, due partly to inherent natural conditions and partly to indifferent legislation, which prevented thrift and progress. The conditions have altered during our present times, and the old inane Man, void of life and aspiration and bestirring, has disappeared from the horizon, and shaken off the oppressive nightmare under which it has laboured so long. A more promising future has opened up, of larger scope, nationally and materially; and it appears even that the fisheries, on which it always so largely depended, show fresh signs of recovery, and a promise of renewed activity. It must be the great business and the duty of the Insular Government to further now this object by a proper re-consideration of its past legislation as to the fishery laws, and to undertake a careful marine survey and examination of the fishing ground, its conditions, extent, and to consider how best to foster and preserve the existing spawning beds and nurseries, both of herring, cod and flat-fish. Of the habitat of the Manx herring so little is actually known that we have everything to learn yet. The careless and inferior mode of packing and curing has been one of the points in the past which has largely interfered with gaining or attracting good markets for exportation, and it is late in the day that Mr Nicholls has to teach the fishermen and fish curers the art and mystery to make the herring acceptable and marketable abroad to the great profit of the Island.

(1) See Moore, pp. 957–58.

(2) See Moore, p. 661.

(3) The tithe was commuted in 1839.

(4) See *Isle of Man Guide*, Sam Haining, 1834, p. 84.

(5) See *Laughton's Guide to Isle of Man*, 1842, pp. 281–82.

261. MISCELLANEA IN CONNECTION WITH THE HERRING FISHERY

In making a start for the fishing, care is taken not to go out on Friday for the first time, or go out of the harbour third boat for the first fishing of the season. In the fishing fleet, Manx is a constant means of conversation among the older men; the compass is generally boxed in Manx by them. The only variation is that some box it from N. to E., others from N. to W. The men say they could box the compass in

Manx before they could box in English. A list is given at the end. Even when Anglo-Manx is spoken, distinct Manx names are used by *all* the crew for the various qualities of herrings. For instance, if down in the cabin at dinner and one man wanted a roe herring, or perhaps a milt herring, he would say, as the case might be, to the cook: "Ta mish laccal skeddan lesh *oghyr* aynjee," or "lesh *molg* ayn."

The following names are some, amongst others, which are in general use:

Herring= *skeddan;* masc. *molg;* fem. *oghyr.*

Young herring = *skeddan beg aeg,* or *skeddan beg,* or *skeddan aeg.*

Grown herring, *skeddan mie.*

Spent herring, *skeddan spendit* (an English loan word).

Fry, no particular name for herring fry, generalized as *fray.*

Skeddan fray are herring which chase and feed upon fray. *Skeddan fray* are big enough fish, but are of poor quality, as fray feeding makes herrings soft, and causes black gut.

Black gut is a little black round bag in the herring filled with small fray, which causes the herring to become bad almost directly after being caught. Some herrings will not touch this fray, or animalculæ, which floats in red patches on the water, but generally where it may be found, there too may the herring be found underneath, for some herrings always follow and feed greedily on this fray.

Sometimes they speak of the herring as the "lil bright fellas," but *skeddan* is the word generally used at sea or on land. The coral reef, banks, beds, or grounds, as the fishermen indiscriminately call the spawning grounds off Douglas, are of white and red colour. Many of the houses in Peel have a bit of this "coral" stuck on their mantlepiece for an ornament, taken out of the nets when at Douglas. When the boats "fish low" (close to land) or "drive over the banks," the nets invariably become studded with broken bits of "coral," which tangle the meshes and do injury both to hands and net in being got out. When a "let" (hindrance) is felt in the nets one hears: "*Ta'n snaa ta goaill grunt lane crossan*" ('The net is taking a groundful of coral'). When nets come on board full of coral the exclamation will be: "*Ogh! snaa lane crossan*" ('A net full of coral').

262. ENGLISH DIALECT WORDS

Herring pool = the English Channel (so called in Cornwall).

Herring dub = the Irish Sea (so called in Cumberland)

Herring dub = North Sea (so called in Aberdeen).

Herring drew = a drove of herring.

Herring bairn = sprat.

Herring gyte = herring spawn.

Herring siles = swarm of herring shoals.

Herring soam = the fat of a herring.

Herring tack = a shoal of herring.

Herring sile. East Yorkshire (white bait is nothing but herring sile.)

The name Herring occurs in:

Donegal (herren), Northumberland (harrin), Scotland (herren), Galloway, Aberdeen, Cumberland (Solway), Kent, East, West, and North Yorkshire, Lincolnshire, Devonshire, Norfolk, Cornwall, Dorsetshire.

263. THE COMPASS IN MANX

N	Twoaie
	Twoaie as lesh y shiar
NNE	Twoaie-shiar hwoaie
	Shiar-hwoaie as lesh y hwoaie
NE	Shiar-hwoaie
	Shiar-hwoaie as lesh y shiar
ENE	Shiar-shiar hwoaie
	Shiar as lesh y hwoaie
E	Shiar
	Shiar as lesh y jiass
ESE	Shiar-shiar ass
	Shiar-ass as lesh v shiar
SE	Shiar-ass
	Shiar-ass as lesh y jiass
SSE	Jiass shiar-ass
	Jiass as lesh y shiar
S	Jiass
	Jims as lesh y sheear
SSW	Jiass-sheear-ass
	Sheear-ass as lesh y jiass
SW	Sheear-ass
	Sheear-ass as lesh y sheear
WSW	Sheear-sheear ass
	Sheear as lesh y jiass
W	Sheear
	Sheear as lesh y hwoaie
WNW	Sheear sheear hwoaie
	Sheear hwoaie as lesh y sheear
NW	Sheear hwoaie
	Sheear hwoaie as lesh y hwoaie
NNW	Twoaie sheear hwoaie
	Twoaie as lesh y Sheear
N	Twoaie

264. A CORRECTION TO NOTE 254

In dealing with such a mass of information as Mr Roeder is now doing, it is not to be wondered at that he should occasionally be led into error by some of his authorities. In the note above mentioned, relating to the herring fishery of the Island, he states that Bishop Wilson had a petition inserted in the Litany, in 1705, to be read in the churches of the Isle of Man for the restoration of the blessings of the sea. This point he uses, and correctly so, in connection with the scarcity of herrings at the time. But later on in the same note, when dealing with the recurring failures of herrings, he makes use of the same point, and, I submit incorrectly. He says: "In the Book of Common Prayer in Manx, published in 1727, the Litany has the (same) petition inserted anew." And again: "The new edition of the Common Prayer (1738) renews the old petition."

For the sake of accuracy, I should wish to point out that the first printed edition of the Manx Prayer Book did not appear until 1765, so that the editions of 1727 and 1738, quoted by Mr Roeder, are (unfortunately for his argument) myths. When the first printed edition was prepared under the direction of Bishop Hildesley, the petition in question was incorporated, and so in the subsequent editions of 1777 and 1808; and even in the still later editions of almost our own time, 1840 and 1842.

The petition had evidently come to be considered an integral part of the Manx version, and had no specific reference to the failure of herrings at any particular date (as claimed by Mr Roeder) after that of 1705, when first inserted bv Bishop Wilson

G.W. WOOD, Streatham.

265. CORRECTION OF NOTE 254

In reply to Mr Wood's note, Fargher in his *Annals of the Isle of Man*, clearly speaks of an edition, published in 1727, with the insertion in question. It is strange he should mention such an edition, except he had seen it. But I do not rely simply for my argument of the scarcity of the herrings at the periods alluded to (1721–28, and 1735–37), nor do I insist particularly on this collateral reference of the Prayer Books, its failure for that purpose does not in any way affect the validity of my main point as to the herring famine in those years. The Lord's Revenues are quite conclusive, and enough for fully establishing that point, and my position remains the same.

266. THE JEWS IN THE ISLE OF MAN

There is some interesting information about them at an early time. Fargher states in his Annals: 1740. Bernard Frank, a Jew, presented for blasphemy against our blessed Saviour. In the *Manchester Chronicle and Anderton's Universal Advertizer*, we read *sub*. 5th October, 1762; in its Liverpool letter: On the 29th ulto., Joseph Levi a considerable Jew merchant (of Liverpool), renounced the errors of his religion, and was baptized by the name of Robert Joseph Levi, by the Rev. Philip Moore, Rector of St. Andrew's, and Vicar of Douglas, in the Isle of Man, and we are informed that many more Jews intend following his example.

267. LOSS OF A SMUGGLING SLOOP
In the same number it says: The *Betty*, sloop, Edward McCann, a smuggler from Isle of Man, lost on the Iron Wharf, and all hands on board perished, except one.

KARL ROEDER

THE HERRING

THE HERRING AND ITS HABITAT
(1903–04)

GASTRONOMICAL NOTES ON THE HERRING
(1903)

❀

KARL ROEDER

THE HERRING AND ITS HABITAT

(1)

Yn skeddan glass ayns shoalyn chin cloie
As cowrey lieen trooid ooilley y coamrey roie.

The pale-blue herring in thick "bushes" plays
And marks of netting on his robe displays.

My previous notes have been principally devoted to a cursory discussion of the origin and growth of the Manx herring fishery and its peculiar influence on the economical and sociological development of the Island. I intend now to speak of the herring itself, its habitat, and distribution in the Manx waters.

The herring, *clupea harengus,* is a gregarious fish, and divided into different local splits, or types, composed of distinctly differentiated hereditary types, of which each never leaves its more or less circumscribed area, or haunting ground. We have the pelagic, or high sea, and the littoral, or coast herring.

The female has two roes, containing between 20,000 to 50,000 eggs. The male has two milts of an oblong shape, and of whitish appearance, while the roe looks much darker.

After remaining on the coast for a certain number of weeks, the herring deposits its spawn on plants and hard rocky or gravelly ground, before leaving the bays or estuaries where it resorts. The shoals generally fix in one locality for deposition, and immediately after spawning proceed to sea.

The egg beds grasp firmly the stones, rocks, or seaweed, the young being thus protected from the effects of storms and currents, and, to a certain extent, from being devoured by fishes, and firmly fixed in a suitable feeding ground (1).

For fourteen days, or perhaps three weeks, the young are seen in great abundance near the shore, of a very small size; in six or seven weeks more they are observed to be about three inches in length, and move about in large shoals in winter and spring, in the various coasts, and in the rivers and bays generally resorted to by the herring shoals, and it is likely that they attain full size and maturity in about 18 months (2).

The full-grown herring visiting the British coasts, varies from eight to 12 inches in length.

Mitchell gives detailed measurements of the various sizes of the herring: (3)

From	West Coast of Britain	Ireland	East Coast of Britain
Total length	9¼	10	10½
Greatest height	2¼	2¼	2½

Young herring from five to six inches in length are called fry, or sill; here the milt and roe are exceedingly minute.

Maties are between six to 13 inches, and contain in them a large quantity of fat around the stomach and intestines; both roe and milt are of small size, and never fill the abdominal cavity, in herrings under ten inches these rarely exceed two or three inches in length.

While in the "matie" condition the herring feeds voraciously, and distend their stomach with crustacea and sand eels, in a more or less digested condition, and become so fat that they will not cure well.

Full herring have their milt and roe completely developed, so as to occupy the whole of the abdominal cavity; in this condition the fat about the abdominal canal has been absorbed.

Spent or shotten herring have lost all their milt or roe, and are in a very poor condition, having no fat about their intesines (4).

The spent herring, then, it is most probable, rapidly leave the coast and retire into deeper water, where they remain for a time and then return as maties to the shallows, and develop their reproductive organs, becoming full herring in the course of three or four months; the full herring appearing at first only scattered here and there among the shoals, but generally increasing in number, until they largely preponderate over the maties, or almost entirely constitute the shoal.

How many times a herring may run through the change from the condition of matie to full herring, and from full to spent, and from spent to matie, it is impossible to tell, but the Commissioners hold that the enemies of the fish are too numerous and too active to allow us to suppose the existence of any one individual to be prolonged beyond two or three reproductive epochs (5).

The herring advances through the water by means of the tail, which is moved in rapid elastic flexures. When it swims near the surface, if it is calm weather, the sound of their motion* is distinctly heard at a small distance (6).

In dark nights and in mild weather it swims nearest the surface, in moonlight and in cold weather it swims nearest the bottom. When the weather is clear and dry, in common seasons, the herring keeps at a distance from the nets, or at the bottom.†

Light and heat appear to have also very considerable influence upon the motion of the herring; for instance, when the spring or summer has been unusually clear and warm, it does not come so near our coasts as in ordinary seasons. In such weather they keep on the banks more distant from our shores and in deeper water than in ordinary seasons (7).

The effect of wind, likewise, seems to be very considerable on the visits of the herring, particularly in the winter. In that season the herring come nearer our shores, and in greater abundance when the wind blows for any length of time towards the coast (8)

The summer herring spawns from the end of September to beginning or middle of October, the winter herring in February and March.

The teeth of the herring are extremely minute and delicate. There are a few teeth in the upper jaw, there is a perfect tiny brush of teeth in four rows in the tongue, in the shape of transparent spikes, turned inwards slantingly, a few in the upper portion of the mouth and at the throat, and again four or five small teeth on each side of the lower jaw.

The aperture of the mouth for swallowing is comparatively large, and the distance between the upper and lower jaw, at the full opening out of the mouth, I have, on measuring, found to be ½ to ⅞ inch, wide enough, therefore, to gulp down fry, small fish, and sand-eels.

The plaice, when about ½ inch long, lives on plankton, when about 2½ to 3 inches it eats small crustacea; when about 6 inches and upwards it feeds chiefly on molluscs and annelids.

The herring, no doubt, subsists also on a large variation of diet, as it grows and advances; not only so, but to some extent varies or changes its feeding ground in the sea, accordingly with its gradual development to maturity.

The small herring fry or sill will be satisfied with plankton, that is, copepods, or water fleas: little free-swimming crustacea, which are exceedingly abundant in the sea. It has been shown that under each square metre of the surface of the Baltic there are one million copepods. These act as the scavengers of the sea, and live on the products of decomposition, or drainage matter.

In addition to copepods, the herring feeds on larval forms of the higher crustacea, such as the edible crab, larval worms, medusoids; besides, on its own ova, portions of spawned milt and roe, young fry, shrimps, and sand launces.

The quality and quantity of the distribution of plankton varies in the Irish sea, and is no less striking at Port Erin Bay (9). How far it affects the movements of the herring in its quest for its food dainties has yet to be ascertained: the herring, no doubt, goes nibbling from habitual ground to ground, for pastures new. It is now accepted that the herring inhabits the seas adjacent to the respective coasts, bays, or rivers, where they flock to for the purpose of spawning, after which they return to sea in the neighbourhood, where they continue and where they feed until the spawning season again draws near, while the fry, on being vivified, continues near the spawning ground until it is of sufficient size (10).

(1) See *The Herring, its natural history and natural importance*, by T.M. Michell. Edinburgh, 1864; pp. 29–30.

(2) See Mitchell, p. 30, *ibidem.*

(3) See Mitchell, p. 46.

(4) "The Herring and Herring Fisheries," *Westminster Review*, October, 1864, pp. 382–83.

(5) "The Herring and Herring Fisheries," *Westminster Review*, p. 383.

(6) Mitchell, p. 31.

(7) Do. p. 32.

(8) Do. p. 28.

(9) See 15th Report of the Liverpool Marine Biological Committee, 1901, pp. 22 and 64.

(10) Mitchell, p. 84.

* Through a shoal of herring. Quite recently the mail steamer *Nord*, of Calais, while crossing the channel, ploughed her way right through an immense shoal of herring swimming down channel, While the steamer's search-light was being used, the man on watch noticed a pecular agitation of the sea just ahead. The shoal was so thick that it affected the progress of the steamer, and thousands were churned up and killed with her great paddle-wheel (see *Daily Mail,* 30/11/1908).

† During the night the position of the herring in the water, or its distance from the surface, is much connected with the lightness or darkness of the night, and with the coldness and warmth of the atmosphere (Mitchell, p. 28).

(2)

HYDROGRAPHICAL AND PHYSICAL FEATURES

I have to notice the flow of the tides round Man, and will shortly allude to it. At Contrary Head, or Kione Roauyr, the stream of tides divides. It strikes off here in two opposite directions. One stream takes its course south, running round the Calf, passing thence along Langness, on to Douglas, and up Maughold Head. Near the Calf the spring tides, when strongest, run 6 miles an hour, near Langness Point 5 miles, near Douglas Head 4½ miles. Neap-tides near these heads run from two to one mile an hour. At Maughold Head these tides run off at a tangent out to sea. At Ramsey the stream runs nine hours northwards.

The other stream of tides flows up Peel northwards, and is here scarcely sensible; rounding Jurby Point it continues to Point of Ayre, running over Strunakile Bank, past Whitestone Bank and the Bahama Banks, off shore and out to sea south; it meets the stream running up at Maughold. At Point of Ayre the spring tides, when strongest, run about 4½ miles an hour; neaptides, 1½ mile.

On its whole western side, Man faces the North Channel; and longitudinally, between Ireland and the Isle, we have a long, deep, steep, narrow, and irregular trough, which, at a distance of about 11 miles from the Manx coast, quickly descends from 50 to a depth of 76 fathoms; while on the Irish side the plateau-like sea bottom, indicated by the 20–50 fathom contour-line, stretches out about double the distance before it drops sharply down into the trough.

The greater part of the coast-line is marked by a fringe of precipitous, rocky cliffs and headlands of schists; past Ballaugh, up Jurby, and from Kirk Bride to Ramsey, the Island exhibits a bold brow of boulderclay, while the Point of Ayre rolls out before you, a plain made up of sand and shingle beds. The middle part of the southern coastline is formed of carboniferous limestone strata, which are finally lost in the sea, and thickly grown over with sea weeds.

The larger bays sweep in extensive and graceful curves, a few sluggish and small, partly estuarine rivulets carry their offscour from the uplands, as mud, sand, gravel, and shingle, towards and into the sea. The marine basin, facing the Lancashire side, is very shallow, and of great range, not exceeding 16 fathoms in depth, with large wastes of sand banks and stretches of mud and silt, while the much narrower sea floor which separates Ireland and Man is comparatively extremely steep, sinking down at its lowest point in the centre to 76 fathoms, with a highly muddy and oozy bottom. For all these matters in detail I must refer the reader to Prof. Herdman's *Chart of the Irish Sea.*

In order to gain a clearer idea of the habitat of the various races, or individual shoals of herring which haunt the basin of the Irish sea, in which Man is almost centrally nestling, it will be instructive to take a general survey of the surrounding coasts, visited by the herring, in the enumeration of which I will follow T.M. Mitchell.

Firth of Clyde, Arran. Off the west end of this island, and in the adjacent Sound, there is generally a good fishing from July to end of November.

Loch Fyne, Loch Long. Frequently caught near the coast in June–July, and they appear sometimes in abundance in the Clyde; in Loch Fyne they may be caught all the year round.

Ayrshire Coast. Frequently caught near the coast in June–July, even in considerable quantities, off Irvine and Troon, as early as May.

The fishery upon the Ballantrae Bank (1) is of exceptional interest. The bank is about 12 or 14 fathoms deep, with a rough bottom; the herring taken here from the end of January up to March were partly maiden fish, and partly fish with roe: the only instance for full and spent herring, at that time of the year.

Solway Firth. Herring of small size, but good quality, appear here in considerable quantities, usual fishing time about September.

Liverpool Bay. During the reign of Queen Elizabeth (1558–1603) the herring fishery was rather extensively carried on, and strangers engaged in it were required to leave as soon as the fishing was over (2). Even within recent times herring has been caught in stake nets at the estuary of the Mersey, near Egremont.

Arklow. Onward to Arklow herring appear at different localities from August to December. At Arklow the fishing was formerly considerable from June to August, but now it begins about the the 1st October. The Arklow herring are similar in size to the Loch Fyne herring.

On the Wicklow coast there are sometimes considerable shoals from September to Christmas, and until within these few years there was a summer fishing in June and July (3).

Carlingford. At the Lough of Carlingford the herring was at one time fished abundantly, but the Irish Channel herring fishery is now considered the most advantageous, it lasts from June to November, and the fishing is pursued less or more by the fishermen at Newcastle, Dundrum Bay, *etc.**

Ardglass is a very considerable herring station, followed by the Penzance, Manx, and Irish boats.

Carrickfergus. The visits of the herring shoals are generally very regular at different parts of this coast, from Ardglass to Carrickfergus, from June to November, and herring in considerable shoals are said to enter Belfast Lough to spawn in September and October.

Larne and Fairhead. Herring of superior quality are caught from May to September between both places, but not in considerable quantities.

North Coast, Lough Foyle, *etc.* From Lough Foyle to Lough Swilley there are two herring seasons, *viz.*, in July–August, and from the middle of November to beginning of February.

The harvest herring are larger and finer than the winter herring—as is the case everywhere.

Haverford West (Cardiganshire). In 1752† herring seems to have abounded and gone down to Cardigan Bay. 18 busses then took in November, 9,000 barrels.

(1) See "Fish Cultivation," by John Fell, *Barrow Nat. Field Club*, vol. 3, 1878–79, p. 73.

(2) See *Rise and Progress of Liverpool* by Jas. M. Walthew, Liverpool, 1865, p. 15.

(3) Mitchell, p. 72, written 1864.

* There is a well-known spawning ground very close to Carlingford; the men know of no other place on the East coast of Ireland where spawn herring may be caught, but think it probable that there may be spots here and there in some of the Loughs.

† See "Chapters on the Manx Herring Fishery (1751–65)."

(3)

I have purposely entered more fully into the description of these topographical particulars as they may become useful for possibly tracing the routes and movements of some of the shoals of herring which are found in the Irish Sea, as well as to define the habitat of some of the apparently mixed races which visit the feeding areas between Ireland and the West of Man. After these preliminaries, I proceed to speak first of the Manx herring fishing in the Irish waters.

The shoal, which was followed, appears in May, off the South of Ireland; it works north, and seems to break into patches or bodies of herrings here and there, off the Irish and Manx coasts, many miles apart. Thirty years ago (1870) the Manx fishermen started from Cape Clear on May the 12th, or as near that date as possible;

they fished all along the Irish coast to the Tuscar, from that down to Rockabill, then between that and the Calf of Man, to St. John's Point, in Dundrum Bay, finishing up about the end of August.

When the Manx boats drew near to Arklow the fishermen of that port would enquire of them—"What sign is there?"; if told that herring had been caught lower down the coast the past night, the Arklow men—Tommy Artlars—would expect the herring to appear off their port the following night.

This shoal of herring, which enters the St. George's Channel from the South in the month of May, in which both the Cornishmen, Manx, and Irish participate, and joined in by the Arklow men, proceeds slowly to Ardglass.

It furnishes a second or winter fishery at Arklow in November. The Arklow fishermen state that the herring meshes with their heads always:

To the north in the summer fishery, and

to the south in the winter season.*

At the end of the Douglas "back" fishing, the Manx boats were rigged and fitted up again at the beginning of October, to go to the Howth fishing, which was continued off and about there to the end of November.

This Arklow shoal supplies the Howth fishing, once such an important one with the Manx boats. As far as they are concerned, it has dwindled almost away, but there are signs of its being revived once more, for last year several Manx boats which risked it again did fairly well, and more boats will probably go to the place this autumn (1903). Howth fishing, like that of Peel, is surface fishing.

North Channel.—The best part of the Peel fishing about 40 years ago was done "norrard" between Peel and the Mull of Galloway, and the herring caught came in from the North Channel. Purt Noo Moirrey (Port St. Mary) boats, too, at that time fished out "norrard"—which shows, at the same time, that herring were scarcer southward.

Jurby.—There is no remembrance of any fishing off Jurby. It is considered to have been most improbable, for the ground is said to be too rough and the tides too strong there to make it feasible.

Bradda Head Spawning Reef.—An odd reef of coral lies W.N.W. off Bradda Head, and it is said to be the nearest spawning ground to Peel, though there may be bits of reef here and there, elsewhere off the coast.

Port Erin.—The *Manks Advertiser* writes:

1802

July 3—A few herring caught off Port Erin.

July 10—Large take off Port Erin.

July 17—Very successful during the week, the largest draughts caught in shallow water, near the shore.

July 24—The largest take on Monday.

July 31—The herring fishery is a success, and continues.

August 7—Unusually plenty, and are caught on all coasts round the Island.

1803

July 2—Some few herring caught off Port Erin on Monday night.

July 16—The fleet is not successful.

The Shoulder or South Corner Fishing.—The Shoulder, Geaylin yn Choloo, is a corner of the Calf of Man. The well-known fishing ground, the Shoulder, is off this, say about 6 miles W.S.W.:

"Make out towards the Shoulder,

West at the Hen, out at the Clet."

(Moore's *Manx Ballads*, p. 177.)

In former times, when there were two lights on the Calf, the biggest shots would be made by getting these two lights in one, either opening out *geaylin twoaie* (= two lights in one to the north), or *geaylin jiass* (= two lights in one to the south).

The best of *all* herring caught by Manx boats is the shoulder herring, taken midway between the Shoulder and Carlingford. About forty years ago, no matter how plentiful and close to hand the Peel herring might be, the men would not catch them, but preferred going further south, for this South Corner herring. They knew that the Peel and the Wart small herring would lower the market once it was put on, so it paid them better to go the extra distance and catch the bigger herring south, and thus keep the price up as long as possible.

There is a great similarity between the Douglas, Big Bay, and the Shoulder or South Corner herring.

The *Manks Advertiser* informs us:

1805.

June 22—Some fresh fish caught off the Calf.

August 10—The herring fishery successful the last three weeks off Peel.

For the Peel fishing, the nets are sunk about 2½ fathoms.

Formerly herring that floated light—small stuff near the surface—was never thought of, and the nets would be given a long strap to escape it. The nets being about 8 fathoms deep, and with 4 fathoms or so of strap added, the whole sling of the net would be about 12 fathoms down in the water, and the surface fish would thus be missed. When deep fishing got scarcer, floating nets were made to catch this light fish.

* See also Report of the Committee of the Insular Legislature on the herring fishery on the coast, 1827. It is to be noticed that according to some very experienced Manx fishermen the fish are meshed in the nets according to the ebb and flow of the tides. Many a night two shots in the nets, herring are meshed first one side, and then another, but this remark would not apply here.

(4)

PEEL FISHING

Son y Feaill-Eoin
Bee mayd goll roin
Dy yeeaghyn son warpyn skeddan
Heear 'sy chione roauyr
Lesh yurnaa liauyr
—Goaill neose nyn shiaull fo'n Charrron
—As hie shin son y Gheaylin.

By St. John's feast day
We shall be away
To look for the warps of herring
West at Contrary Head
With a long journey
Furling our sails under Carron
And we made for the Shoulder.
  Manx Ballad

Formerly no boat went out to this fishing before June 18th; now, however, the nobbies make a start about May 18th, and it is continued till the Douglas back fishing is on.

The Peel fishing ground is a larger and more extensive one than that off Douglas, and extends right across the channel and down to the Calf.

As to the distance from Peel, and the depth at which they catch the herring, it is taken from 2 miles off the shore to right across the channel; the general fishing, however, is about 8 miles off, in about 20 to 30 fathoms water.

Herrings caught off Peel are of three qualities

(1) An average small-sized herring, known as Wart herring, hence the old couplet:
"Skeddan beg er y Wart.
  Best herring ever caught."

If an imaginary line was drawn between Peel and the Mull, it would pass over the Wart about two miles off Peel in a northerly direction. The fishing mark for the Wart was the top of Greeba mountain. The herring has disappeared off the Wart for some years past. The fishing on the Peel Wart is now confined to the nobbies, the nets of the luggers and nickeys being too deep to fish there. The Wart bank lies in about 9 fathoms of water and was noted for the abundance of small, sweet herring on it.

(2) The Peel herring of a greenish colour; not two of the same size.

(3) The Big Bay herring—the fishing should be spoken about in the past tense; it is that stretch of water which lies between the Niarbyl Point and Bradda Hill. For stock purposes, herring caught in the Big Bay were reckoned excellent.

A particular and characteristic feature of the Peel fishery is that the herring may be had all over this ground; it is what the Manx call a *reeayllagh* (= a scattering of the herring shoal), that is, scattered all over the area right across the channel and down to the Calf; while, on the other hand, in the Douglas ground there is not such a thing as a *reeayllagh*, for the herring comes there in *thick bushes* (= clustering, or closing) and if boats do not get in the thick of them, they are dead empty for that night.

Peel herring are considered of a finer flavour than those caught elsewhere.

The Big Bay (No. 3) herring are said to work in and out with the tides, and are supposed to come from the South Corner.

When coming round to Peel from Douglas back fishing, Peel herring has again been caught in the Big Bay, and off Peel. It is supposed, therefore, that the Peel shoal lies off Peel all the year round, coming in and out of the channel.

The Wart, near Spanish Head.—This is not much of a bank, and it lies low (close to land) and in about 7 to 8 fathom of water.

Strandhall (Castletown).—Mr W.J. Clague, of Ballabeg, informs me that about 35 years ago, when bathing at that place, an enormous shoal of young fry, about 1½ inches in length, was met with by him, and cartloads of them, which were thrown on the shore, could be noticed. This was either in August or September. The same fact has been noticed before.

(5)

DOUGLAS BACK FISHING

In former times Maughold Head was the first place where the fishermen looked for fish. The statutes define in 1613 that the boats "bring the Custome Heyrings and deliver them:

From and betwixt St. Maughold Head and Douglas, at Douglas.

Between Douglas and the Calf of Man, at Castletonne.

Such as fish on the North Parte of the Isle, at Peeletonne."

The first represents the "back fishing" the second the South fishing proper; and the third the Big bay and Peel fishing.

Maughold Head, therefore, appears to have taken the lead, and the fleet probably collected and proceeded from Ramsey Bay for the east fishing. It seems that the herring shoal, at that time, had their spawning ground spread out much further north than we find in our present times,

When they extend more between Laxey and Clay Head, a strip of coast line now particularly abundant in "coral banks." There is evidence that formerly Ramsey Bay* yielded good crops of herring. The *Manks Advertiser*, at the beginning of last century, informs us:

1802—August 7th: A great quantity of herring taken in Ramsey Bay.

1805—November 23rd: Considerable quantities of herring continue to be taken at Ramsey.

Mackenzie's Hydrographical Survey of 1775 marks a "coral" bank off Port Lewaigue, at Tableland Point, in 5½ and 6 fathoms water; and higher up, east off Kirk Bride, it delineates three "coral" banks in 3, 5, and 7 fathoms of water.

Douglas apparently was anciently but of secondary importance, and the Manx Ballad tells us

Yn chiagtoo laa jeh'n vee September
Hie shin er shiaulley ass baie Rumsaa
Kiarail dy gheddyn dys geaylin Vaughold
Dy akin caslys lane vie traa.

The seventh day of September month
We sailed out of Ramsey Bay
Intending to get to Maughold Shoulder
To see a sign there in good time.

Now, the fish seem only to work off there, on and off, during the Douglas back fishing, and I have no doubt that the constant shifting of the extensive sand banks at the Point of Ayre, as the Strunakile Bank, the Whitestone Bank, and the Big or Bahama Bank, and particularly the Great Bank, east off Maughold Head,† the former variously in 4¾ to 8 fathoms of water, and the latter in fully 8 to 10 fathoms, all of which have considerably moved, even since first surveyed by Mackenzie, rolling and spreading increasingly over a marine floor, at those points of an average depth of 12 fathoms of water, and thus probably dislodging and burying some old important feeding grounds, then habitually resorted to by the herring—I say I believe that these factors have doubtlessly contributed in a very great measure to shunt and drive off the fish from these, their former more chosen pasture grounds.

At the end of August, the fishermen following the Peel herring went around to Douglas, and worked that place till the end of September. This (1903) year the boats were engaged from August 27th to October 7th, and the fishing only ceased then because the weather broke. When it is time for Douglas "back" the boats put back to harbour to deepen their nets by more strap (longer thow), for Douglas herring lie lower down among the "coral beds," and the nets must be sunk down much deeper to catch them.

The Douglas back fishing is generally in about 20 fathoms of water, and the herring come within 3 to 4 miles off the land, and sometimes lower.

It travels in a tremendous body off Douglas, and with no scattering of the shoal as in Peel. Many a time the Douglas shoal moves about 2 to 3 miles square, many a time it may not be a mile square. If a boat misses the bush, or impact body of fish, by any very short distance, they are out of it, and will put back to port empty.

For the back fishing they fish as far out east as 12 miles off Douglas Head; if south-east they go about 8 miles, and if S.S.W. from 8 to 10 miles.

This is merely an average, as they are never confined to one spot, but fish off the coast from Maughold Head to Languess Point, sometimes going as far as Bahama Ship.

If it is east fishing in Douglas, as this September (1903), that is fishing from Maughold Head to Clay Head, and from thence to Douglas, the shoal going to Douglas for spawning is supposed to he that one which lies somewhat midway between Lancashire and Douglas during the summer. Men on the steamers can always tell the Manx fishermen the progress of this shoal to Douglas waters by the signs of the herring gulls, gannets, perkins, and the like. Sometimes they may report it to be 20 miles away; it was said to be 12 miles away a fortnight ago (27th June), and now (11th July) from 3 to 4 miles.

If it is south fishing the shoal is supposed to be South corner fish, which always went to east from the Calf.

The Inspector sent over to prove the herring for curing, said that the Douglas fish at the first of the season were second in quality and size only to Loch Fyne herring.

Mr Nicholls thinks with most fishermen that the Peel herring does not go round to Douglas. He affirms that Peel and Douglas herring are of two distinct qualities, and never come from the same feeding ground, as a Douglas herring would make two Peel herring, with both size, colouring, and shape alike differing.

He thinks, likewise, that the back fishing this season comes in from the south-west, viz., the Welsh and Lancashire Coasts, and that if the men fished higher out channel herring might be caught all the summer off Douglas.

He therefore advises the men:

"To start a month sooner next year, and go further out channel to meet the shoal coming in to spawn, and thinks that they ought to have been on the ground in the first week of August, for herring are then prime, and worth £2 a cran."

I hope the experiment will be made, for its result, let it be whatever it may be, either adverse or favourable to these speculations, will prove of the greatest possible importance in its practical and economical bearing. It is not good enough in our times to be satisfied merely to take out the boats as formerly, on the mere chance, and to discuss the eventful out-turn, or lament the decay of the fishery when expectations have been frustrated.

Let us recollect at this point the remarkable catches of:

1667—When an immense shoal visited the shores, such as had never been witnessed before.

1754—When at Douglas, within six weeks, more had been taken than in 6 years before, and upwards of 500 tons were salted and exported alone.

1765—The greatest take of herrings that has been known for many years past, so that upwards of 20,000 barrels were exported to foreign parts.

1789—18,515 barrels alone were exported to foreign parts, so that Townley could write on the 28th September: "The fishermen would not move to their employment, their pockets being still lined"; and on the 17th September "The number of boats, besides the smacks and other craft lying here for the purpose of purchasing fish! The whole number of people busily engaged this day in and about that business may be fairly computed at 5,000. It is computed that the abominable indolence of the fishermen for two nights past has been a loss to the public of more than £4,000."‡

1803—October 8th, the herring brought into Douglas Harbour on Wednesday are estimated at £9,000, and the two following nights even no less productive.—(*Manks Advertiser*).

1846—80,000 mazes, value £72,000, were taken.

1860—44,120 barrels were cured.

1876—The value of herring caught amounted to £40,000.

1883—It increased in this year to £42,460.

But in the past, how many fine seasons have been lost by the recklessness and indifference of the men after a rich herring harvest and money flowing in profusely, in addition to shortness of boats to follow on the success!

Speaking of the quality of the herring, Laughton writes (1842) in his guide, p. 63:

Their peculiar delicacy causes them to be greatly in demand among the manufacturers of anchovy sauce and pastes, by whom a single keg of Gorgona Anchovies is multiplied into 10 or 12; a very lucrative speculation, and contributing greatly to the commerce of the Island, if not to the reputation of the sauce-makers.

* About 100 years ago Ramsey and Laxey had their fishing fleets, as well as Peel and Port St. Mary. Ten years later or thereabouts the fishing declined to such a degree that the Ramsey and Laxey boats were sold to pay their debts, and only Peel and Port St. Mary kept boats going to sea.

† See also M. Mackenzie, Senior's Hydrographical Survey of Isle of Man, made 9th December, 1775; and Professor Herdman's *Chart of the Irish Sea*, prepared for the British Association, Liverpool Meeting, 1896.

‡ The herring was so abundant that they were caught with the hand on the beach; after being sold at 4d. a hundred, until purchasers could not be found, they were carted off for manure.

(6)

THE GREAT SPAWNING GROUND ON THE EAST SHORE OF THE ISLAND

From a very remote period, which is almost impossible to define, but certainly even historically traceable to some 400 to 500 years ago, an immense herring shoal, in densely closed rank and file, has ploughed its way, with occasional interruption and sometimes of greater or lesser magnitude, to the shallow waters which lave the east shore of the Island. They slowly make their way, in constantly increasing numbers, towards early autumn, to the well-known and intensely important spawning floor which at one time seems to have almost uninterruptedly extended from the

Whitestone Bark, south of the Point of Ayre, right down Ramsey Bay and Lewaigue to Laxey, and Clay Head to a little beyond that spot.

At present the northern grounds, which seem to have undergone a great change, destructive to the vitality of the spawning beds, are apparently but little visited, and the area favoured by the fish for the grand business of depositing their spawn is principally confined to the long strip of floor which stretches from about Dhoon and Laxey to Clay Head onwards.

Mackenzie's Old Chart of 1775 shows the old reefs and marks, eight of them in number. One east off Dhoon, in 15 fathoms; another a little N.E. off Laxey, in 15 fathoms; one in line with Ballabeg, in 7 fathoms; and another a bit further out in 15 fathoms; and 4 about Clay Head, 2 in 11 fathoms, one in 13, and another in 16 fathoms; extending from ⅜ to 1¾ miles from the shore, all of them of lesser or greater dimension. Some other beds lie about 5 miles S.E. off Douglas Head. The fishermen called these spawning grounds "coral" reefs, banks, or beds indiscriminately, and they are of white and red colour.

They are popularly called "coral" in consequence of their apparent similitude to them in their general appearance, but of course belong to the Red Sea weeds (Rhodophyceae) of the Corollina family, and refer more specially to the species of the Lithothamnion,* perhaps *L. varians, investiens, orbiculatum, tophiforme.*

The Lithothamnia generally grow gregarious, in great masses sometimes, most often only 1 or 2 species; sometimes, however, more club together. They form widely extended banks, even as far as about 2 miles in length, composed of millions of individuals. They are found fastened to one and the same substratum, covering each other, or one fastened to and growing over the other, on sandy and shingly bottoms. They are sublittoral, descending to 10 or more fathoms; preferring somewhat sheltered places. They are always attacked by animals, and the numerous passages made by worms, serpulae, &c., destroy and permeate the lower parts of the crust. Often they are covered with fustra. They harbour an immense lot of animalculæ. This so called coral is very hard and rough. When the boats fish low (close to land) or drive over the banks, the nets invariably become studded with it. It is a destruction of the nets, for it fastens into them like bons of ling, and can only be got rid of by stretching the net over a board and pounding and crushing the coral out with a heavy weight; it is apt, moreover, to tear the hands badly when the nets are being pulled on board.

When the fishermen fish low, they try to avoid the coral by giving less straps to the nets, so that they may thus be missed; but the tides often pack the nets and the whole bite will then drop down on the coral, and then is the mischief to play with them. (Nets are said to be packed when two corks drift together, and this causes the sling of the nets, the bite, between the corks to fall down into deep water).

Herring multiply by millions on these coral beds, millions of meases (if spawn were allowed to come to maturity) are destroyed by trawlers dragging their nets over these beds, breaking the coral and thus scattering the spawn; millions more are destroyed by the *bock* (a species of shark), and the *gobbag* (dog fish), for these fish hover closely around the beds, spawnfeeding, and if nets drift over the beds they are up like an army of soldiers to pick the herring out, and in doing this destroy the nets to a very great extent; in addition, they are preyed upon by the cod, ling, perkin, gannets, gulls, &c., to whom the ground is a paradise.

The herring delights at this season in these coral beds, as they afford harbourage for a great quantity of crustacea.

It is of paramount importance for the Island that these precious beds are jealously and properly protected from damage or decay, that the spawn is left undisturbed, and not suffered to be raked up from the ground while the incubation and hatching is in course of operation. I have been told that often enough it is brought up by the nets in vast masses; in that case it should be carefully replaced.

That trawling has occasionally done much harm, if it reaches these beds, or is carried across them, is fully acknowledged by all the fishermen. In fact, only recently I have been informed that the trawling has done vital injury in various spots.

TRAWLERS

The fishermen grumble that everywhere where trawlers go the herring and big fish disappear off that ground.

They think that trawling frightens the herring out higher channel, and near to the Welsh coast, and that the big fish and fry are both caught and destroyed.

Many places are instanced by the fishermen where big takes might be depended upon, and which were the order of the night before trawling came in vogue.

20 to 30 years ago, great quantities of hake and herring could be caught in a night, close in to land about the Calf, and it was no unusual thing for Peel men to come home from Purt le Muirrey 7 or 8 Saturday nights in the season.

Then the trawlers came and found that place so very suitable for trawling on account of its hard sea bed (Douglas Bay is not liked, the ground is too soft) that they made that bit of the coast line their favourite headquarters. So, seldom or never now can a fisherman catch a hake there, where once he caught a hundred, and the herring are far a-sea.

* See *The Norwegian Forms of Lithothamnion*, by M. Foslie, Trondhjem (1895), pp. 3, 85–86, 125, 132, 143.

(7)

MAXIMA AND MINIMA

GOOD YEARS	BAD YEARS
	1648—Of late years not half the herring.
1667—Enormous catch.	
	1693–4—The herring begins to fail, lasting up to 1711.
	1717–19—Bad.
	1721–28—Bad.
	1735–38—Bad.
1754—Splendid year, in 6 weeks more than in the 6 years before.	
1765—Another red-letter year.	
1789—Annus mirabilis.	
1803—A very successful year.	
	1827—Failure.
1840—Good.	
1860—Good.	
1876—Good.	
1883—Good.	
	1886—Bad.
	1892—Bad.
	1897—Lowest.
1903—Again improving.	

I have prepared a short table to show the years and periods of great plenty and scarcity of the herring "takes," as far as the Insular records go. These returns are extremely meagre, and anything but satisfactory for any definite conclusions. In future we require official and separate returns for the number of messes caught, both at Peel and at Douglas, and the same for cod, ling, &c.; men and number of boats employed, price of fish, and amount realized; and when the season begins there should be a regular daily record in the Peel, Douglas, and Ramsey papers to show the progress of the fishing from day to day, along with the daily takes, state of the weather and sky, temperature of the sea, &c., until the season closes. It would be also of great value to have a special column devoted to record any piscatorial observations obtained or obtainable from the fishermen, about items of special interest, such as the appearance of any shoals of fry or fish, and if mature, full or spent, and date and locality where seen; exact date of the first appearance of the fish at Peel, Big Bay, the Shoulder, Douglas, &c., and if mature, full, or spent; and particularly the occurrence at any place round the coast of the herring between November to June, and if fry, mature, or full and spent, that is, after the season is over; and all observations made by captains to and from the Island with regard to any shoals seen during the passage, date, and whereabouts.

Returning to the above returns: 1648 was apparently comparatively bad; 19 years later we notice an enormous catch; 27 years later the herring begins to fail, lasting for some 18 years; 17 years later is another bad crop; 6 years later there is a fresh bad period, lasting about 11 years; after 7 years we have again 3 bad years; after 16 years there is another splendid year; so again 11 years after, and again 14 years after that, and in 13 years again, a very successful year; 25 years after a great failure; a good season 13 years after this, in 1810; again 20 years after, 1860, and 16 years after, 1876; followed in 1886, 10 years after, 1892, 6 years between, by bad years, and the lowest, 5 years after, in 1897; with a revival in 1903, 6 years subsequently.

It has often been said that the herring disappears for years suddenly from large sea areas, known to be frequented by it for years consecutively and in vast shoals, by a freak, and apparently without rhyme or reason, and that it has been found suddenly forming up "in seas" abandoned by fishermen as hopelessly unproductive. (1)

Many instances are on record. We have the sudden reappearance at Gothenburg, of immense shoals of herring off the Swedish coast, after an absence of several years. The bulk of the eastern fishery centres about the Firth of Tay, the Moray Firth, and the Firth of Forth. Many years ago this fishing was found to be decreasing to some extent. It appeared as if the fish was leaving the coast entirely, it occurred however, to a carer at Montrose to recommend fishing some distance from land. This was done, and 20 or 30 miles from the shore they found the fish larger and in more abundance. (2)

We see from the Insular returns that on an average, during the last 250 years, there has been a failure every 13 years, while we notice there was a catastrophe lasting for some 18 years, and another for about 11 years. We also find that after an enormous sea-crop of herring, the following years have turned out rather tame, which looks almost as if it might be greatly due to over-fishing. Such a belief is reasonable.

But, of course, the greater and the more extensive and bulky the shoal turns out, the greater in proportion the havoc that is going on in its destruction. The inroads made by the cod and ling alone, and the gulls, gannets, and other sea birds, and dog fish, who accompany and chase the herring shoal, are simply enormous.

It has been stated that these enemies destroy 100th of 1,000th more than 96,000 fishermen could catch in a year, and that man does not destroy one herring for every 50 destroyed by other enemies. The late Lord Playfair expressed the opinion that migration was traceable possibly to the destruction of their natural food, small crustaceans, &c., or to the movements of their natural enemies, cod, ling, dog fish, &c.

We may well conceive that these facts can account to some degree for the disappearance, or lesser or even scarcer numbers of fish in the next few years subsequently. But when we have to deal with periods, persisting for, as in our case, 18 and 13 years, the causes must be of a different nature.

Not sufficient thought has been given to the mighty and silent changes which are going on from year to year, and sometimes quite suddenly, and more or less destructively, on the marine floor itself, often extending over vast areas, which vitally affect the habitat of the fish and marine life in general, both of plants and animals, due to sudden or slow depression or elevation of the coast line, and the marine bottom itself, brought about by complicated earth movements, earthquakes, &c.; not to reckon the filling and silting up of feeding and spawning grounds, caused by the deposition, and spreading out of estuaries and rivers into the sea basin, intensely charged with fine mud, sand, gravel, and other matter; and the consequent change of old channels and levels, which bring about, into the bargain, an inset of new conditions, such as, for instance, the formation of new currents and change of temperature of the various strata of water, &c.

And this powerful incessant work goes on day after day, year after year, and century after century.

It seems to me quite plain that these great factors affect to a large extent the sudden or slow shifting, for long periods, of the herring from their old habitual grounds to new areas, often far away from the original banks visited by them; as their food resources being cut off, and the spawning banks covered or destroyed, necessitate to look elsewhere for fresh pasturages. For the same reason they return sometimes, when things have assumed a favourable turn, to their old grounds which become again available and yield them fresh food.

To speak therefore of "freaks" of the fish is absurd, for it is of no use to visit any longer grounds which are "dead." We would do likewise. When the herring begins to show signs of deserting its old grounds something is physically wrong on the ground, and it is the business of the fishermen, as in Moray Firth, &c., to try and find and look out for any new areas likely the fish has gone to, in the search of which the biological marine zoologist may assist him.

It will be of interest and assist us also to re-state some conclusions arrived at by Cleghorn, of Wick, about the herring and its habitat:

(1) The herring is a native of the water in which it is found, and never (if not forced) migrates. It is more local than it is fancied.

(2) Distinct races of it exist at different places.

(3) There were fishing stations some years ago which are now exhausted, a steady increase having taken place in their produce up to a certain point, then followed by a violent fluctuation and final extinction,

(4) In districts where the tides are rapid, as among islands and in lochs where the fishing grounds are circumscribed, the fishings are precarious and brief, while on the other hand: Extensive sea-boards having slack tides with little accommodation for boats, are surer and of longer continuance as fishing stations.

(5) The extinction of districts attributable to over-fishing.

(6) He also recommends not to disturb the spawning grounds and their fry and spawn by the destructive trawling for flat fish, or by other means to drive away the shoal, such as fishing during the day.

(1) See *Toilers of the Sea*, vol 17, 1903, p. 35, Migration of the Herring.

(2) See "Fish Culture," by John Fell, *Barrow Natural Field Club*, vol. 3, 1878–79, pp. 73–74.

(8)

We come now to the more difficult and delicate question of tracing and fixing the particular areas of the Irish Sea to which the variety of herring to be found round the coasts of the Isle of Man are addicted to, in search of food, for purposes of spawning; and the grounds occupied by the young herring, or herring fry. This task which I approach now tentatively, becomes the more precarious because we have practically no official records or observations of any shape or kind to facilitate such an enquiry. The Manx fishermen have been content hitherto with hauling their catches during the season when the fish have made their appearance near the shores, indicated by the contemporaneous advent of the herring's great enemies, the gull, gannet, cormorant, and the divers, but what becomes of the spent herring, after the fishing is closed; how the fry thrives, and where it travels to after it is fully hatched, until it grows to maturity, are points upon which we are still in complete uncertainty, if not darkness.

It is, however, sufficiently clear that we have to deal with but a few perfectly distinct types of herring within the more proximate radius of the Isle of Man. I shall begin with the North Channel herring. This shoal used to visit the North-West side of Man, and Peel tradition still speaks of it. Even 40 years ago the best part of Peel fishing was done Norrard, that is, between Peel and the Mull of Galloway, and the herrings caught came from the North Channel. This herring was of a uniform size and colour, and, as stated before, so much alike are they, that out of a basketful no difference will be detected between any of the herrings in it—all being large in size and of a whitish colour.

It would seem that this herring moved in the deeper marine floor which extends north of Isle of Man, and then skirts the Mull of Galloway in a southerly direction, sweeping on to Solway Firth, thence descending south to King William's Banks, then creeping up, sharply projecting to the N.W. off Point of Ayr, and finally swinging round in a curved line down to Peel. This area lies in between 20 to 37 fathoms of water, more or less covered with mud. It seems to be a big feeding area. The Scotch fishermen assert that the herring caught by them in the Firth of Solway comes down from the North Channel.

It appears therefore that this Peel North Channel herring and the Solway visitor haunt the same basin together. Why it has deserted in more recent times the more southerly part (N.W. of Man) has not been ascertained.

The Peel herring proper.—Formerly no boat went out before June 18th. The fish was caught from 2 miles off the shore, but generally about 8 miles off in about 20–30 fathoms of water, and the nets were let down to 2½ fathoms deep.

Herring, exactly the same as the Peel herring, is caught in the spawning season between Ailsa and the land, and some of the Peel fishermen believe that the Peel herring go to spawn there. The fishermen stake their nets on this spawning ground.

Another fish peculiar to Peel is the Wart Bank herring, found about 2 miles off the town in a northerly direction in about 9 fathoms of water. It is a very sweet fish, and only found on that bank. Lately it also has become rather rare.

The two kinds are full fish, smaller and weaker than the Big Bay, Shoulder, and Douglas fish, and of a brighter green in colour. Professor Herdman marks down here a coral and gravel bed, it may, therefore, not unlikely turn out to have been once a much larger local (although now rather small) spawning and nursery spot. (1)

Before proceeding further it is important to point out at this stage a circumstance which may have or prove of a great bearing on the distribution of the various range of the particular types of herring found on the southern and northern side of the line of meeting of the tides extending across from Dundrum Bay, off St. John's Point, to Contrary Head (Kione Rouayr), a few miles south of Peel.

Any sort of fish, more especially herring, is thought better fed and of sweeter eating caught S.W. of Contrary Head, than N.E. of it. It also seems that the herring south of this demarcation does not invade or enter the Peel or northern side of this line, and thus may act as a barrier in their progress either north or southward of it.

The Big Bay herring, between Niarbyl Bay and Bradda Head, is not found north of the meeting of the tide, viz., at Peel. Like the Shoulder fish it is of big size, with big gills and black eyes, and of darker colour, and bigger and stronger every way. It is full, and before spending, next to Loch Fyne herring in quality. It is said to work in and out with the tides, and supposed to come from the South Corner.

At Fleshwick, about the end of August, for a few days only, just before the Spring tide, a bush may often be seen run into; when the spring tides come it shifts south. There is an odd reef or "coral" W.N.W. off Bradda Head, where in former times there was abundant spawning.

Tradition has it that in remoter times, on the west side, from Peel to Port Erin, the herring shoal used to come very close to land, and to enter the bays and shallows quite regularly. This fact has been also attested to me again by some very old men, within the last 20 years, and it is fully borne out by the *Manks Advertiser*, who speaks in 1802:

July 10th, of a large take off Port Erin.

July 17th—The largest draught caught in shallow water, near the shore.

It is my belief that in past centuries the spawning grounds, now either buried up or left in a few scattered patches, must have been pretty extensive on the west side of the Island within the narrow strip of the 5 to 10 fathom line which runs parallel with the shore from Peel to Port Erin, and that only in later times in consequence of their gradual decaying, the fish left these grounds for the extensive and more sheltered "coral" banks east of Douglas.

(1) See Prof. Herdman's *Chart of the Irish Sea.*

(9)

CONCLUSION

The Shoulder Herring.—The ground, as mentioned before, lies 6 miles W.S.W. of the Shoulder of the Calf of Man. According to the tides the fish works out and in on the ground from 2 to 3 miles up to 15 miles, and spring tides send them out further, that is, midway between the Calf and Carlingford. It is of excellent quality, and, when full, said to be equal to Loch Fyne fish. They range here in between 20 to 50 fathoms of water, and the sea abounds in mud and ooze.

The fish is caught here from June and July until the back fishing begins.

It is significant that fish has been caught off the Calf at unexpected times. One skipper took over 900 fine herring in February (they have been taken off Carlingford in March) and according to the *Manks Advertiser*, on November 13th, 1802:

Great quantities of herring were caught within the last fortnight off Port St. Mary, and so successful that several boats were refitted for sea—after the "back" fishing had terminated.

The conclusion would be that the herring is always on the ground, and never goes far away from its habitual haunts, and that if weather permitted and if in season, herring might be caught all the year round off Man.

It appears when the great period of spawning draws near, the shoals from Big Bay and the Shoulder, which up to then freely range over the great south-western feeding ground of Man, draw more closely together in serried and ever-increasing numbers to form the enormous and closely united general shoal which picks up the straggling battalions on its way during their gradual and slow march to the breeding banks, off Douglas Bay, keeping on their course thither, within the 20 fathom line south-east of the Island. How long it takes them to reach their destination we don't know.

Before that great process they roam, broken up, in smaller swarms over the great south-western feeding ground, as a *reeayllagh* of herring, scattered and spread, but when the time of spawning is up, they unite then into the bush (= closing in), on their customary track or route to the spawning ground, which, as we have seen, is east of

Douglas. After the spawning is over they disband and go back to their old quarters. Their movements off Douglas seem to extend to a radius of 20–25 miles, from south to north, for feeding purposes, up to Bahama Banks in the deeper ground, circumscribed by the 20 fathoms line, where they probably rove and linger on for some time to recoup their strength.

The fry which is left behind does probably not go far away from the "coral beds" before it has reached a certain size. Their subsequent local movements have not been ascertained, and we want careful observations on this point to settle this matter.

I am also inclined to think that the Carlingford or Arklow herring adhere in their movements to the Irish side of the channel, without invading the western coast line of Man, or intermixing with the Peel, Big Bay, or Shoulder herring; and the same holds good with the Manx herring, both, no doubt, move within their own habitual zones roughly defined by the deep longitudinal trough, midway between Ireland and Man.

The Douglas herring is so much alike the Shoulder and Big Bay herring that apparently they are identical. The Douglas side being the shallow part of the sea basin, and of a more sheltered nature, forms an excellent and extensive breeding ground and nursery, while the deeper floor, characteristic of the southern and western part of Man, is *par excellence*, and remains the great feeding ground of the Manx herring.

The herring, which was abundant in the 16th century in Liverpool Bay, has since almost entirely disappeared, due no doubt to the encroachment of the estuarine deposits of the Mersey and the Ribble; probably it migrated to Manx waters.

As far as the herring from St George's Channel, up Cardigan Bay, is concerned, I don't think it ever reached the spur of the Calf, at least we have no records, and it is not very likely.

In addition, I may remark that specimens of all the various types of herring found round the Manx water and in the Irish Sea at large, should be kept and preserved as standards for comparison, with full description of colour, weight, dimension, and any particular features, time of capture, and locality where taken, and contents of the stomach, so that gradually we may be able to learn more about its habits, movements, and life history. And many may help in this and thus assist any future labours of the Biological Station at Port Erin.

DIALECT WORDS

"Two eyed steak" or "Purt ny Inshy beefsteak" was a slang used for the Peel herring, also "Peel duck."

"Clean herring" was applied in contradistinction to the fray herring or skeddan fray.

Ymmyr corraa (= the butt of spawn herring) = the bush of spawn.

Creeping—After being shot an hour or two the nets were proved to see, as the fishermen say, if they are "creeping."

Bumming yawls—Buyers' boats.

The earnest—A shilling or a bottle of rum passed between fish buyer and seller to clench the bargain.

Tailley—An account, particularly of fish which is kept by notching a stick. Every fifth notch crossed the other four; This cross denoted a mease.

Scoltey—A boat's supper. This was formerly held either on Old St. Stephen's, or Old New Year's nights.

God's money—When crews settled balance accounts, at the end of the season, any odd shillings or pence was put aside for the poor. In old times Manx folk thought that the right time to cure herring for winter stock was between the two Lammas Days—the old and new.

Mr Holmes, who died in 1852, cured herring for the Royal Navy.

KARL ROEDER

GASTRONOMICAL NOTES ON THE HERRING

(1)

THE SHAD, OR SCEADD, HERRING, SKEDDAN AND SILD

After having said so much about the herring and its history, folklore, and habitat, it will not he out of place to dedicate a few remarks to its philological side.

It is now accepted and sufficiently proved that the Romans were practically unacquainted with the herring as an article of food; and even granted they should have employed a few boats occasionally on the east coast of England, from the Wash down to the Thames, it was not likely that they would fit up a regular annual fleet of smacks for following the herring fishery on the coast of Norfolk on an economic basis. Their boats were otherwise employed for purposes of commerce and naval requirements, and it is not to be supposed that the British coast tribes dared, or had the means of getting together an efficient fishing fleet; and we must not forget the great peril and insecurity, even in Roman times, of the eastern and southern shore attached in any such attempt, due to the frequent piratical attacks and incursions which required the constant watch of the Count of the Saxon shore to stem the inroads of the streams of continental marauders.

It is only when the Anglo-Saxons had got a firm foothold on British soil that the herring fishery began slowly to develop, and Swinden* thinks that it must have been soon after the landing of Cedric in 495. Great Yarmouth is said to have been the resort of fishermen during the herring season, as early as the 6th century, carried on by no other methods than drift nets.† In early times the fishery was principally confined to the great rivers and estuaries, such, for instance, as the Thames and the Severn, and probably it was then the shad the natives fished. The shads differ from other members of the herring family in their habit of ascending in big shoals some of our rivers in the Spring in order to deposit their spawn in fresh water. They are similar in appearance to the common herring, and from their larger size are called by fishermen "The mother of herrings," "The king or queen of herrings." Before the erection of weirs at Worcester and other places, shad used to ascend the river about middle of April.

The Anglo-Saxon name *sceadd* is probably derived in the first instance from the Britons, and from the Irish *scaoth, scaoith,* = a swarm, multitude; Gaelic *sgaoth* = a, shoal. When the Britons became seafishers they encountered a smaller form, similar in appearance to their shad, which they called *sgathan, ysqgaden,* Welsh; *sgadan,* Irish and Gaelic; *skeddan,* Manx, or the *little* shad.

The Celtic fishermen have clung to the name skeddan, while the Angles, Saxons and Frisians, who had been great sea-fishers long before the Britons ventured on high sea fishing, brought their native name with them, calling it *haering*, ahd. = *hâring* = herring, pointing to *heri* = an army (in consequence of their appearance in great shoals or swarms).[‡]

The herring does not descend beyond Normandy, and the French, Portuguese, Spanish, and Italians, adopted therefore the current Anglo-Saxon name.

Another name for the herring is *sild*, used specifically by the Norwegians, Swedes, Danes, and the Icelanders. They were the people who were supreme in the North Sea, the Skager Rack, the Cattegat, and the Sound; the Slavic nations who, in ancient times, held the whole coast line of the Baltic Sea, and who also pursued the herring fishery of the litoral fringe for their sustenance, borrowed their name from the Norsemen; the Russian word for it is *seld, sioldka;* Polish, *sledz;* and each of the leading seafaring nations kept a jealous guard on their respective fishing grounds. The Slavs would not infringe on Norse fishing grounds, nor would the latter, even in early medieaval times, permit an encroachment of either English, Scotch, Dutch, &c., within their zones for the purpose of fishing herring or cod, and the very name of sgadan, herring, and sild, expresses the privileged areas over which the respective nations held command, and challenged interference.

We thus see what an interesting light is thrown on the history and development of ancient fishing and fishery right, even by a philological examination of the various names for the herring.

* See *History and Antiquities of Great Yarmouth.*—Swinden.

† The oldest document relating to herring fishery dates from 709, and is found in the Chronicles of the Monastery of Evesham.

‡ See *Etymological Dictionary of the German language.*—Friedr. Kluge Jena, 1859.

(2)

...... Fresh herring on the dish
Would leave no Roman epicure a wish,
When drest with all our garnishes of art.

White and red herring has for centuries formed a staple mess of the masses. The general demand of Catholic Europe for it, during Lent and fasting days, laid the foundation of the Dutch Republic, whose wealth and development was built on the herring. They were the great curers and purveyors. But the exquisiteness of fresh herring was naturally known to the favoured few who happened to live about the great fishing ports. There is all the difference in the world between the taste of cured and fresh herring. The one, candidly, you may eat out of doctrinal duty to satisfy the Church, or constrained by poverty and necessity; the other, on the contrary, is a feast to allure a born epicure. Ask, I pray, a Manninagh, what he thinks of Manx freshly-caught skeddan. Brillat-Savarin missed much not to have tasted it at Peel, where, you know, you get the "lil silvern fellas," as in no other spot in the wide world, for deliciousness and delicacy of flavour. Hill,* a fine English connoisseur, describes a method of dressing the fresh fish, which I offer to the housewives of Mona for trial:

With a sharp penknife make three or four incisions across the fish on each side, cut an onion in thin slices, place both on the gridiron, and turn them occasionally till done. Have melted butter ready, in which two tablespoonfuls of mushroom catchup has been poured, and a little fresh mustard; eat your herrings hot, with the prescribed sauce, and you will ask yourself why people have made such a fuss about John Dories.

For those who are curious about ancient cookery, and the fancies of the English gentry in the times of the merry monarch, I have copied a recipe "to make minced herring pies":†

Take salt herrings, being watered, crush them between your hands and you shall loose the fish from the skin, take off the skin whole and lay them in a dish; then have a pound of almond paste ready, mince the herrings and stamp them with the almond paste, two of the melts or roes, five or six dates, some grated manchet, sugar, sack, rose water and saffron; make the composition somewhat stiff, and fill the skins, put butter in the bottom of your pye, lay on the herring, and on them dates, gooseberries, currants, barbaries, and butter; close it up and bake it; being baked, liquor it with butter, verjuyce, and sugar.

OTHER WAYS

"Bone them and mince them, being finely cleansed, with two or three pleasant pears, raisins of the sun, some currants, dates, sugar, cinnamon, ginger, nutmeg, pepper, and butter; mingle all together, fill your pies, and being baked, liquor them with verjuyce, claret, or white wine."

It may tempt some fair reader to prepare it afresh and report.

The Herring Pie made 1734,‡ in the Georgian period, has rather degenerated from its high ancestral lineage:

Take about eight middle-sized herrings (the soft roes are the best), slit them down the backs, and, taking out the bones, rub them over with pepper and salt, mince onions, leeks, and apples, and scrape in lemon peel; strew over them some nutmeg, finely grated, half-a-pound of currants, and mix a pound of butter with a little flour; and place it above-and beneath in thin slices.

Here is a more homely way from 1788, for making a herring pie:§

Scale, gut, and wash them very clean, cut off the heads, fins, and tail. Make a crust, cover your dish, then season your herrings with beaten mace, pepper, and salt; put a little butter in the bottom of your dish, then a row of herrings, pare some apples and put them in thin slices all over, take the peel off some onions and cut them in slices all over thick, lay a little butter on the top, put in a little water, lay on the lid; bake it well.

Herring pies are forgotten now, but old tastes may revive.

Stewing of Herring seems to have come in early in the eighteenth century. I have a preparation from 1714,¶ evidently intended for the rich:

First broil them very brown, then have ready some white wine made hot with an anchovy, a blade of mace, and a bit of onion, with a little whole pepper all stewed in the wine; then cut off the heads of the fish and bruise them in the wine and spice, and take them out again before you put in your herrings; let them stew over coals, in a dish that they may lie at length in; let them stew on both sides, till they are enough at the bone; take them out and shake up the sauce with butter and flour.

Pottage of Red Herring is mentioned in 1730:‖

First make a stock of meager soup with herbs, roots, and bread, and season it with the same seasoning, but not too much salt; take six red herrings, and broil them and beat them in a mortar; put to them some of your stock and strain and force them through your strainer; make a ragoust of old onions, strain them into the rest; take a little celery and endive, a little spinach, sorrel, and parsley; mince them and pass them in brown butter thickened till very tender; put all together and stove it up; put in fry'd French manchet, dish it up, and broil some more red herrings and lay them round your dish; and garnish with sliced lemon and scalded spinach.

Vincente La Chapelle, "Chief Cook to the Right Honourable the Earl of Chesterfield," published in 1744, *The Modern Cook*. It is a treasure-house of noble recipes brought together from every corner of Europe, but amongst the many kinds of fish mentioned in it, the herring alone has no place. It was no doubt too vulgar a thing for the palate of Chesterfield to be patronised.

We get an early recipe to bake herrings:**

Take 30 herrings, scale them, cut off their heads and pull out their roes, and wash them very clean, and lap them to drain four or five hours, and roll them in a dry cloth. Season them with pepper and salt, and lay them in a long venison pot at full length. When you have laid one row, shred a large onion very small and mix with a little cloves, mace, and ginger cut small, strew it all over the herrings; and then another row of herrings and seasoning, and so do till all is in the pot. Let it stand seasoning an hour before it is put in the oven, then put in a quart of claret and tie it over with paper, and bake with household bread.

Here is also a recipe from 1749:††

Season them with a little mace and cloves beat, a very little beaten pepper and salt; lay them in a deep pan, lay two or three bay leaves between each lay; then put in half vinegar and half water, or rap vinegar. Cover it close with a brown paper and send it to the oven to bake; let it stand till cold, and then pour off that pickle and put fresh vinegar and water, and send them to the oven again to bake.

* *The Epicure's Almanac*, by Benson E. Hill, London, 1841.

† *The Accomplisht Cook, or the Art and Mystery of Cookery, approved by the fifty-five years' experience and industry of Robert May, in his attendance on several Persons of Great Honour*, London, 1678.

‡ *The Family Dictionary, or Household Companion,* by the late Wm. Salmon, M.D.; London, 1734.

§ *The Art of Cookery made plain and easy,* by Mrs Glasse; London, 1788.

¶ *A Collection of Receipts in Cookery, Physick and Surgery,* by several hands; London, 1714.

‖ *A Complete Practical Cook—A New System of the Whole Art and Mystery of Cooking,* by Charles Carter; London, 1730.

** *The Compleat Housewife, or Accomplish'd Gentlewoman's Companion,* by E. Smith; London, 1744.

†† *The London and Country Cook,* by Charles Carter, Cook to his Grace the Duke of Argyle; London, 1749.

(3)

Among the great number of schemes for establishing companies in London in 1720, that for the British fishery was not the least considerable. The Society of the Free British Fishery was renewed in 1723, and subsequently an Act of Parliament was obtained, in 23 Geo. ii, for the "encouragement of the British white herring fishery"; the charter of incorporation passed the great seal on 12th April, 1750, Frederic, Prince of Wales, being nominated its first governor. The Society had apartments in the Royal Exchange.

The herring, says Rolt,* is become so much in vogue, since the establishment of the new fishery, that it is allowed at the politest society, in imitation of the signal honour done it at the table of his Majesty. The great popularity of the herring, either boiled, baked, broiled, fried, pickled potted, or made into pies, or as stuffing, thus properly dates from the moment King George II began to patronize it, to encourage the British white herring fishery; it was honourably received into all good English households, and Penelope Bradshaw hastens, in her *Family Jewel,*† to give us, in 1754, "receipts or various ways of dressing Pickled Herrings, as British pickled Herrings are now brought to the best of Tables." One way is, "to cut it into slices (after skinning and dividing it), and to eat between bread and butter, or minced and mixed with a salad of any kind, or else made into a Salomongundy, with chicken, rabbit, or veal, they eat very well with green peas, Windsor beans, kidney beans, or Potatoes, if, after these are drained off when boiled, a pickled herring or more be thrown into the same water and then taken out, after the water has bubbled up a minute. Herring-pickle may be used for that of anchovy; and a little of this pickle thrown into the butter, made as sauce for eels, takes off from their lusciousness."

Then follows a receipt for making Pickled Herring Soup, which I will pass over.

"To Stuff a Fillet of Veal, or Calf's Heart with Pickled Herrings:

Take 2 herrings, skin, bone, and wash them in several waters, chop them very small, with a quarter of a pound of suet, add a handful of bread grated fine and the like quantity of parsley, cut very small, throw in a little thyme, nutmeg, and pepper to your taste, and mix all together with 2 eggs."

"Stuffing of Pickled Herrings for a Roast Turkey:

Wash in several waters 2 pickled herrings, which afterwards skin and take the bone out carefully; take half a pound of suet and two large handfuls of bread grated, chop the herrings, suet and bread (separately) very small, beat all these together in a marble mortar, with the white of an egg, after throwing in a little nutmeg and white pepper."

"Pickled Herring Pudding for a Hare:

Take ½lb of the lean of fine veal, which clear of the skin and strings, 2 pickled herrings, which wash in 2 or 3 waters, then skin, and clear them of the bones; a ¼lb. of suet, two handfuls of bread grated fine, and a handful of parsley; chop all the above separately, then mix them, throwing in half a nutmeg grated, a little thyme, sweet-majoram, and one egg, beat the whole together in a marble mortar."

The later recipes, down to Elizabeth Raffald (see her *Experienced English House Keeper*), *viz.*, to the end of the 18th century, are more or less repetitions of the previous ways; many in time dropped out, and we hear principally but of methods to boil, fry, bake, and pot them.

The French‡ have their:

Harengs frais à la sauce à la moutarde,

Harengs frais en matelote, an fenouil,

Harengs sees on hors-d'oeuvre,

and very good things they are.

I have troubled to delve a little into the cookery-quarries of the past to show my fair readers how the herring was culinarily handled by their forebears. Perhaps they may resuscitate same of the old recipes. Cooks are not negligible quantities in one's life. All honour and praise to them. They are the sweet-mouthed bees, ever mindful of our comforts; the "Lares" of our domestic hearth, who preside over our palate and bodily welfare, pouring out cheerful sun-glints into our homes, and no little happiness on poor, plagued mankind in general—from the King down to the humble thrall. The herring is and continues, ever since first meshed in the salt sea, one of our sweetest favourite morsels—a little fish, to boot, which, in centuries past, has had a great share both in making and unmaking nations.

A Manx song runs:

"*Cha nel veg gull-rish praaseyn as skeddan*"

(There is nothing like potatoes and herring)

The primitive and chosen way of the old Manx to take it was: To put mashed potatoes in a long wooden tray, a cup of butter placed besides, into which all dipped, and in that manner the boiled herring and all were eaten with the fingers.

I have now come to the end of my pleasant journey, and so good-bye, and: *Semper floreat et crescat Harengus Monensis—applaudite!*

* *A New Dictionary of Trade and Commerce,* by Mr Rolt; folio, 2nd edition. London, 1761.

† *The Family Jewel and Compleat Housewife's Companion, by Mrs Penelope Bradshaw, Housekeeper forty years to a Noble Family of Great Table, but proper Oeconomy;* 3rd edition. London, 1754.

‡ See: Baron Brisse, *La Cuisine à l'usage des menages bourgeois, etc.*; Paris.

FINIS

❀

KARL ROEDER

FRANCOIS THUROT (1727 AND 1760)
AND HIS NAVAL ENGAGEMENT
OFF THE ISLE OF MAN
(1902)

❀

KARL ROEDER

FRANCOIS THUROT (1727 AND 1760) AND HIS NAVAL ENGAGEMENT OFF THE ISLE OF MAN

(1)

The career of Francois Thurot offers many features of great interest, and particularly so for Manxmen, and a revival of his memory, and the circumstances which drove him into Manx waters cannot but add fresh zest to an episode in Manx history which, at the time formed the great topic of the day, not only in the Island, but in the whole country. Indeed, his defeat was looked upon as an event of almost national importance, for the sharp blow the destruction and capture of Thurot's squadron inflicted on French naval renown.

In 1756 England declared war against France, and an interesting notice of the act is preserved in the Manchester paper, dated June 8th, 1756. We read:

Manchester, June 7th.—On Saturday War was proclaimed in this town and in Salford. The Under Sheriff was attended by the Justice of Peace, the Borrough Reeve, Constables, and a considerable number of gentlemen, a body of Halbertmen, and also by the Towns musick, which played *Britons strike home*, before and after the reading the Declaration of War. There was a great concourse of people, who expressed their satisfaction by three loud huzzas. Soon after many hundred of the Declarations of War were given away to country people, the better to enable them to judge of the justice of his Majesty's proceedings and the perfidiousness of the French.

The rupture between the two great powers naturally called into activity a numerous bellicose host of cruisers and privateers, and heavy blows were exchanged, and the coast and the high seas bristled with ships of all descriptions hotly chasing and engaging each other. Reprisals and captures were the order of the day. It was during this intense period of clashing of arms that Thurot eminently steps to the front, a man whose daring, popularity, and ability eventually procured him from his Government the proud position of commodore of a squadron wherewith to harrass and damage the enemy's shipping.

He was born at Nuits (Côte d'or), France, on July the 21st, 1727, and at an early period took to smuggling as a profession, running goods between the Isle of Man and Ireland, until be rose to become the acknowledged "King of Smugglers," and it is stated that during his reign he did not export and import less than £20,000 worth of contraband a year.

The King of France, afterwards, when the war had already been carried on for a few years, gave him the command of the *Marshal de Belleisle*, fitted out for a privateer, and from that period he became an antagonist who made himself quickly known for prowess and activity to English merchant vessels on the English, Scotch, and Irish coasts and the Baltic. He appeared in the North Channel in September, 1758, and had taken in this cruise alone 36 prizes, and he hoped as he said, "to increase that number." He cruised along the coast of North Britain, the Shetlands, and kept himself in watchful evidence for captures on the north coast of Ireland, and was greatly feared at Belfast, Carrickfergus, and the Isle of Man. In the beginning of the summer of 1759, in consequence of his great success, the King of France advanced him to take charge of a whole squadron of five ships, with the retention of the *Marshal de Belleisle*, consisting together of 168 mounted guns, 700 sailors, and 1,270 soldiers, all veterans.

The completion of this expedition took some time. It began under very unfavourable and bad auspices, and was followed by misfortunes throughout its whole course. Thurot's plan was to descend upon North Britain, Scotland, and then fall on Ireland through St George's Channel, and perhaps touch upon Whitehaven, the Lancashire coast and Liverpool, and finally to return round the Bristol Channel and the English Channel to Dunkirk, with a view to capture and destroy as many English vessels as he possibly could during his progress in English waters. Pitt became soon aware of the French intentions, and initial steps for land and coast defence were in full preparation. It was thought that Thurot's aim tended in particular to attack and plunder the rich port of Liverpool. We learn that:

On the news of Thurot's sailing from Dunkirk the magistrates of Liverpool assembled and entered into an association for the defence of that opulent town. It was proposed to raise 20 companies of 100 men each, to be armed and paid by the inhabitants, and to erect batteries, to mount 50 pieces of cannon.

His fleet actually embarked on the 5th September, 1759, but being blocked up by 26 English ships under Commodore Boys, set sail only on the 15th of October, and anchored off Ostend, arriving in Gothenburg on the 26th, and on the 17th November in Bergen, during which passage they lost the *Begon* in a violent storm.

Extract of a letter from Alex. Wallace, Esq., his Majesty's Consul at Bergen, Dec. 6th, 1759:

Capt. Thurot with four ships of his squadron has been lying in harbour, three leagues from this place, these 18 days. The ship that is missing is the *Begon* of 40 guns. He begins to be in doubt of her safety, but seems resolved not to stir till he has some account of her. I am much surprized that in all this time none of his Britannic Majesty's ships of war have appeared here. Last evening Thurot put to sea with the four ships under his command, wind N.E. (*Manchester Mercury*, 29th January, 1760).

In these two places they had to stay a considerable time to repair their ships, which had been much damaged in the foul weather. They left after nineteen days, provisions growing short, and soon arrived off the Islands of the North of Scotland, beating about and collecting what they possibly could.

On the 24th of January, 1760, they made for Derry, but such a tremendous storm began to blow that they were almost lost, and the *Marante*, with 24 guns and 140 men, was lost sight of for good off Barrahead; the *Le Blond* had to throw four guns overboard, and the commanders begged Thurot to return to France, lest they should perish with famine; which the commodore refused. On the 13th February they entered the Sound of Islay in Clagin Bay, where he landed his men. The poor wretches the moment they got out of the boat began to dig up everything green they saw upon the ground. They levied 48 steers and 24 hags of oatmeal, for which Thurot made handsome payment, and on the 19th weighed anchor, sailing for Carrickfergus, where they landed their forcess on the 21st, which were reduced now from 1,270 to 600, and marched on the town. A French officer, who was taken prisoner, tells us in his journal: "All the wine on board the ships was given to the men to animate their courage that day." The siege of Carrickfergus, which led to its capitulation, is too well known to dwell upon. The French suffered considerably, and had at least 100 men killed, besides the wounded. Upon the reduction of the garrison a French officer, we read, arrived at Belfast with a flag of truce, demanding 50 hogsheads of claret, 30 pipes of brandy, 25 tons of bread, two tons of onions; and the inhabitants agreed, and furnished most of the material as fast as they could be collected.

Whilst they were in the bay the French took the brig *Clyde*, Captain Taylor, from Glasgow to Carrickfergus, laden with sugar and tobacco, valued at £2,000, and having taken out the lading burnt the vessel; they also took a brig with coals, and a sloop with herrings, the latter vessel they burnt after taking out her cargo; before they arrived in the bay they likewise took the *Boyne*, of Drogheda, for New York with flax seed, and a letter of marque ship, of 14 carriage guns, bound from Lisbon to Glasgow, both of which they sent to Bergen, the latter supposed to be the *Ingram*, of Glasgow.

(2)

The *Manchester Advertiser*, from news received and reproduced from Carrickfergus, writes:

Feb. 26th.—Last night the French troops began to re-embark, which they did from the quay, and completed it at four o'clock in the morning, leaving behind them a French General Fobert, who is so ill of his wounds that it was not thought proper to take him on board, but they took with them Willoughby Chaplain, Esq., Deputy-Mayor of Carrickfergus, and George Spaight, Esq., as hostages for the payment of a contribution of £1,000, which they had demanded of the town and county of Carrickfergus, although by this capitulation they were not to plunder the town. They embarked in such a hurry as to leave 80 casks filled with water behind them; they have carried off one brass cannon, a 12 pounder, and spiked up the iron guns in the castle, and have thrown into the sea upwards of 300 barrels of gunpowder which was in the magazine, supposed to be unfit for service.

Although they had embarked, says a report, a little later, the French ships lie very quiet at anchor in their former situation, it being impossible for them to sail to the northward, as the wind blows now.

Things became now very stirring, for this night it was reported that three English ships of war were seen to-day off *Killough*, steering to the northward. The hawk is already pouncing on his quarry, for the Lord Lieutenant of Ireland had meanwhile hastily dispatched circular letters addressed to all Irish naval stations for succour. It happened then that the *Æolus* was stationed at Kinsale by accident of the weather, having got separated from the *Intrepid*, of 64 guns, under orders of Sir Edward Hawke, who had sailed from Quiberon Bay on a cruise, and provisions running short the *Æolus*, Capt. Elliot, put into Kinsale, on the 21st January, 1760, where it was still on the 24th February, and so were the two other 32 gun frigates, the *Pallas* and the *Brilliant*, who had taken shelter a few days before.

We have now lost complete sight of the two squadrons, which have disappeared on the grey horizon. The English are in desperate pursuit, in the wake of Thurot's ships, and shortly the two young commanders, Elliot and Thurot, are engaged measuring each other it fierce combat. The guns are bellowing forth their thunder, and the action all the while is keenly and coolly watched by John Kelly, the Irish pilot of Elliot's fleet, who follows the fight on board the *Æolus*. We have his graphic description:

> *An account given by John Kelly from the 26th of February, when he boarded the Æolus, of the Bay of Dublin, and undertook the pilotage of her to the Lough of Belfast, in quest of three French ships of war.*

The 26th.—Stood to the northward and made the Copeland Isles before dark, then came to blow so very hard from N.N.W. that it put them under their two courses; in which situation they continued that night and next day, between the Copeland Isles and the Mull of Galloway, and with great difficulty kept that station, which they effected by taking advantage of the tide, being obliged to wear ship every time they tacked.

27th.—About two o'clock in the morning they tacked and stood for the Scotch shore, the weather being more moderate; about four that morning, John Kelly, the pilot, and others, perceived the enemy standing S.E., intending for the Isle of Man: but when they made the English man of war distinctly, they changed their course by hauling close on the wind to the Scotch shore, being then somewhat less than a league to windward. The English men of war hauled their wind, and crowded sail after them; and about sunrise came up with the *Belleisle*, and after Captain Elliot gave her a broadside she returned it, and then put him aweather, in order to board the *Æolus*, but her bow sprit coming between the main and fore shrouds it was carried away, then her stern scraped the *Æolus* and fell astern of her. It was during this time that great execution was done among the French by the constant firing of the great and small shot; she then dropping astern, the *Æolus* bore down on her, and gave her a starboard broadside; the *Æolus* falling then astern, the other two English frigates came up and gave the *Belleisle* a broadside each, one of which carried away her main yard, and passed ahead of her to make room for the *Æolus*, who was coming up again, and went so close before he fired that his bowsprit went in between his main and mizen shrouds; and in that situation continued firing at each other till the *Belleisle* struck; a little while before which the *Æolus* carried away the *Belleisle's* mizen mast with her bowsprit.

The other two French frigates made but a poor fight, one of them struck to the commodore, with the *Belleisle*.

The *Terpsichore* endeavoured to escape, but was pursued by the *Pallas*, who soon came up with and took her.

The prizes were taken to Ramsey Bay, and the *Belleisle* was in such a shattered condition that it had five feet of water in the hold when she struck. A sailor who came with the express from Elliot's fleet in Ramsey Bay, affirms that Thurot fought and was killed, dressed like a sailor in a blue jacket in order—it is supposed—the better to disguise himself. People, meanwhile, had hurried and flocked from all parts of the Island to witness the scene presented in Ramsey Bay, and an eye witness writes:

On receipt of the news of Thurot being brought into Ramsey Bay on Thursday, last night, I went there to see the ships, *etc.*, at daylight. I got on board the *Belleisle*, and was struck with astonishment; turn which way I would nothing but scattered limbs of dead and dying men presented themselves to my view, the decks and ship's sides could be compared to nothing but a slaughter-house; the English not having time to clear the vessel the night before, near 200 men being killed on board her, besides what the other two French ships lost.

Thurot's body was thrown, by mistake, overboard amongst the rest.

The French must have plundered all before them at Carrickfergus, for I saw one of them stript who had eight women's shifts on him. They had plenty of women and children's shirts, caps, ruffles, shoes, petticoats, stays, bed curtains, sheets, buttons, thimbles, pins, bleached and grey yarn.

Mr Richard Wright, painter, formerly of Liverpool, was on board. and is now drawing a sketch of the whole (Extract of a letter from Douglas, Isle of Man, dated March 4th, 1760, from Whitworth's *Manchester Advertiser*.)

Liverpool, 2nd March.—Yesterday evening, late, one Watts, master of a codsmack, met with the Isle of Man packet, who came with an express from the Island, giving an account that Thurot's squadron was taken. As it was quite calm, he left the vessel off Formby Point and rowed up to town. About eleven o'clock a pilot boat, come from Ramsey, brought a young gentleman whose name was Mungo Smith, passenger, and some letters from people of the Island. This account is, that on Thursday morning, very early, several guns were heard, which were conjectured to be signal guns. This occasioned many persons to go to a place called Jurby, or Jurby Point, from which place they saw the engagement between three frigates, Captain Elliot, commodore, and Thurot's three frigates, which lasted two hours and a half. He says that about 50 of the English were wounded, of which number 29 dangerously, and 6 killed; that orders were sent to Douglas to provide quarters for them. This vessel which brings this express is not arrived, but is expected to be in this tide. I write you only what I heard from the gentleman giving the account to the Mayor and officers. I took the account in writing and gave it to the Town Clerk, who from it, and what more might be said, wrote a letter, which was by an express sent to Mr Pitt. He left the town about one o'clock this morning. I believe what I write may be depended upon, as the private letters which I have heard of are to the same purpose (A letter from Liverpool to Manchester.)

Extract of a letter from a gentleman in Liverpool to a gentleman in Manchester, March 3rd, 1760 (Manchester Mercury).

At the first setting out of Mons, Thurot was not free from apprehensions, and on that account contributed my mite towards a defence; but now I really look upon his all at Belfast as out of mere necessity, to satisfy the cravings of nature. Be that as it may, three of our frigates, some accounts say two, and a sloop, were dispatched by the Lord Lieutenant of Ireland, from Kinsale, in quest of him.

On Tuesday they passed on the west side of the Isle of Man, and next day I suppose ferreted him out of Carrickfergus Lough, and so they had a fair race for it till they came up to the north side of the Isle of Man. Off Jurby Head, which is on the north side of the point, he caught up with him, and about 5-30 on Thursday morning began of engaging.

Thurot was killed the second broadside, but they continued fighting very close, near two hours and a half, when his squadron struck, and in the afternoon he brought them into Ramsey Bay. The *Belleisle* is terribly mauled, having early in the engagement lost her mizen mast and bolt sprit.

The *Æolus*, commodore Elliot, a youth of mettle, about 25 years of age, engaged him and lost his fore top gallant mast. They have about 20 wounded, which he was sending ashore, the killed not then mentioned. I believe all Thurot's land forces were on board, and if so there's great slaughter. We shall have all particulars next tide.

P.S.—Most or all of the folks in the Island saw the action, which they say was terribly hot. They have made very liberal contributions for the men, and boat-loads of wine, brandy, etc was sending to the fleet.

There were found on Thurot's three ships upwards of 100 bales of linen, which they had taken from the two ships in Belfast Lough for Scotland.

Although Elliot had given orders to bring Thurot's body on shore, it was thrown in the bustle, by mistake, into the sea with the rest of the dead men, but it was found afterwards cast ashore near the Mull of Galloway, Mochrum, and subsequently interred in the graveyard of Kirkmaiden. According to one of Elliot's officers, Thurot received his death wound by a ball which entered his throat close to the windpipe, and when the *Belleisle* struck he was found among a great number of dead bodies on the quarter-deck. Thus perished Thurot at the age of nearly thirty-three. His young and handsome wife, Henrietta, daughter of a rich apothecary in Paddington, named Smith, with whom he eloped, and whom married about 1750, was, it is stated, a sorrowful witness of his last moments. She had accompanied him, ever since, in all his enterprises by sea and land, and was with him his last expedition to Carrickfergus.

The bowsprit of the *Belleisle*, two yards circumference, came ashore near Bishops Court, and in commemoration of the action and as trophy of the victory, Bishop Hildesley caused it to be erected on a tumulus which he named Mount Æolus, a little above the garden of the episcopal residence, where, as he said, "being painted, it makes a handsome appearance at a distance."

By a letter from on board the *Pallas*, in Ramsey Bay, dated 29th February, we are informed that Thurot intended to have landed on the Isle of Man, and raised contributions there, and also to have attempted taking the shipping at Liverpool and Whitehaven, before returning to France. The destruction of his ships, writes another correspondent, relieves the trade of this kingdom, particularly the Baltic, from a troublesome flying squadron, and France has not only sustained a fresh loss by this event in her little navy, but more so in the death of an active and experienced naval partisan.

His expedition was indeed doomed; if he would have escaped Elliot's clutches he could not have evaded the *Bienfaisant*, man of war, and several frigates, which had sailed from Plymouth for Ireland on the news becoming known. From Portsmouth, the same time, the *Dorsetshire*, Captain Campbell, with others, in quest for him was hastily despatched; while, if he had advanced on Belfast with his reduced land army, melted down to almost 500 men in number, 3,000 militiamen (of the Irish Northern Militia), aided by some troops of standing army, would have utterly annihilated him. Thurot's undertaking has, from the very beginning, says a Dublin report, appeared a most desperate one, and should he persevere in the enterprise and risk an engagement, we have little reason to doubt of success.

(3)

Not only were his movements carefully watched and prepared for in Ireland, but Liverpool had already taken energetic measures for his coming, should he make an attempt on the port.

The Manchester paper announces on the 26th February, 1760:

Last night at eight o'clock an express arrived from the Mayor of Liverpool to the commanding officer of the Lincolnshire militia, quartered here, with certain intelligence that Mr Thurot is landed at Carrickfergus, and immediately the drums beat to arms, and the militia marched off to Liverpool about ten o'clock in high spirits amidst the acclamation of the populace.

Liverpool, Feb. 29.—On Monday morning an express arrived here from the Lord Lieutenant of Ireland, addressed to the commander of any of his Majesty's ships in the port, which was immediately forwarded to the tender lying at the rock at noon. The commanding-officer sent a message up to the magistrates acquainting them that his Grace the Duke of Bedford had informed him that Thurot with three frigates put into Carrickfergus Lough on Thursday, the 21st inst. Upon which expresses were sent to Warrington and Manchester, agreeable to former instructions from the War Office, requesting all the military in those parts to march immediately for the town, as it was not known whether Thurot intended to visit us or not, and also about nine o'clock on Tuesday morning, four companies of the southern battalion of the Lincolnshire militia, under the command of Col. Sir John Cust, Lieut.-Col. Welby, Capt. Nevile, Capt. Thourel, came into town, having begun their march from Warrington at two o'clock in the morning, and at eight o'clock at night the two northern battalions of the Lincolnshire militia came in from Manchester, consisting of ten companies under the command of the Earl of Scarborough, Lieut-Col. Vinor, Major Dashwood, Capt. Mathew Lister, Captains Blackinborough, Wood, Dymoke, Lister, Coldercote, Pilkington, Amcotts. On Wednesday morning came in the remainder of the southern battalion, consisting of six companies, under the command of Major Glover, Capt. Scrope, from Stockport; Capt. Silthorpe, and Capt. Welby, of Knutsford ; Capt. Buckworth and Capt. Boulton, from Macclesfield. To the honour of the British militia we can assure the public that immediately in receipt of the express from the magistrate their officers ordered the drums to beat to arms, and they marched off to this town in a few hours, each company consisting of sixty privates, two drums, and three sergeants, with their officers.

Of the prisoners taken on Thurots ships:

220 were brought to Carlisle,

500 to Carrickfergus, *

90 to Cove,

84 to Dublin,

894 [in total]

and part of the seamen and officers were left on board the *Æolus*, etc., while the captured prizes were brought by Elliot to Kinsale.

When the victory became known, there were great rejoicings and celebrations throughout the country, and in an appendix I have given some of the accounts preserved in the old country newspapers. At Liverpool particularly great doings marked the occasion, and the troops stationed there, disappointed in meeting with Thurot in person, took the opportunity of having a great manoeuvre, and deploying their ranks along the shore lines, to the immense delight of 10,000 eager spectators. The *Gentleman's Magazine* wrote a long epitaph on the death of Thurot,† beginning:

Here lies the pirate, brave Thurot,

To merchants' wealth a dreadful foe,

Who, weary of a robber's name,

Aspired to gain a hero's fame.

and the poet took the occasion to enlarge a lot on the glorious achievements of the British arms, and bespattering Thurot's memory.

The longest poem in Manx ever wrote was inspired by this memorable sea fight off the Point of Ayre, and it stirred the bosoms of the Islanders to the highest pitch of patriotism.

It also gave rise in the Island to a bit of Folklore, for it is said that "on the day of Elliot's engagement with Thurot, at Ramsey some man near Dalby met an old woman standing by a stream of water, and she asked the man to lift her over the water, for the fight between the ships would continue until, she got to them."

The Rev. John Francis Durand published it 1760 a little pamphlet, which gives us a picture of Thurot, from which it appears that he must have been a very remarkable person. He had many romantic adventures in his younger days, and came often to London, and particularly to Paddington, where Durand made his personal acquaintance. Thurot was also instructed here in mathematics by "one M Donelly, an Irish gentleman famous for his knowledge and abilities in that branch." It was also here that Thurot made the acquaintance of his future wife. He spoke, we are told, English to a degree that he was taken by everyone for a native, and there has been a popular belief that he was descended from the race of the O'Farells which, however, has been proved to be erroneous, and also energetically denied by Thurot himself. There is an oil painting of his preserved in France,‡ in the dress of a French commodore, and it shows him to have been a very fine looking, gentlemanly person, with a large featured face, brilliant eyes, and well formed nose and mouth. He was of a generous disposition and honourable in all his dealings, and his men, we are told, loved him as a parent. There cannot be any doubt that he was a attractive figure, who quickly secured the esteem and respect of everyone who came into personal contact with him, both enemy and friend. We have a description left to us, while he was staying in Bergen and Chritiansand to repair his ships, which is very interesting:

Commodore Thurot is a well-built, genteel man, very humane and affable, and understands several languages very well. I was one day in company with him at dinner with a great many other gentlemen, one of whom asked him whether or not he was a native of France upon which Thurot smilingly replied: "I hear that it is reported and believed by a great many people that I am a native of North Britain, and that the name I go by at present is not real, but a feigned one; I assure. you, gentlemen, this is a mere fiction, and chiefly founded on my knowledge of the English language. I was born and educated in France; I still retain the name of my forefathers, and I never will, on any account, deny my name or country." (A letter from a gentleman of Gothenburg; see Whitworth's *Manchester Advertiser*, January 15th, 1760, p. 2, column 3.)

From a gentleman who dined frequently on Thurot's own ship, when he put into Christiansand to repair his fleet, we learn that he was scarce 33, a well-looking man, fresh coloured, extremely well bred, and of the greatest good nature, surprisingly active, being almost instantly in every part of his ship, to see whether his men, who valued him as a parent, were at their respective posts. Any gentleman was welcome to his table, but he would permit none to speak to any of his people. His mistress was a young woman, excessively handsome. (From same paper, March 18th, No. 3,413.)

Thus, yet in the prime of his life, ended the career of a man whom we cannot refuse our tribute of admiration and pity. He fought for the glory of his country, and when misfortune and disaster crowded round him, beset with starvation, and drifted by storm and weather, conscious of the approach of disease and destruction, he declined to forsake his charge, although be fully realised his position. The victory gained over him was no great feat the odds were dead against him, and although the victory of Elliot was blazed about as a most brilliant achievement, from the facts described we cannot join in that great glorification. To defeat this wretched, starved-out crew, with leaky and drifting vessels, and its overcrowded decks and short ammunition, was an affair that could be settled without much difficulty, as Simson wrote from Islay, by "one of our 50 gun ships, which could take Thurot's three vessels, for they are crowded with men so much that they are scarce able to fight her guns." The expedition was ill-planned, and little short of madness, considering the trivial number of his ships set to eventually encounter the full brunt of the British naval forces, sure to oppose him in his cruise.

The writer of the article on Elliot in the *English National Biographical Dictionary*, takes a similar view; he says:

The action, creditable enough in itself, was almost absurdly magnified by popular report, to such an extent, indeed, that even 44, years after, Nelson, writing to Lord Minto, speaking of Elliot, said: "This action with Thurot will stand the test of any of our modern victories. In point of fact, the French force, though nominally superior, was disintegrated by dissatisfaction, mutiny, and sickness. The ships, too, had been severely strained by the long persisting bad weather to which they had been exposed, and many of their guns had been struck below."

The English sources of Thurot's exploits are extremely meagre and incomplete, and consequently scarcely give the reader a true idea of the career of this gallant officer, who was the bugbear of the English mercantile fleet. I have therefore copied the account given in Larousse, which will give a better view of the man:

Thurot engaged himself as surgeon on the Dunkirk corsair, fell into the hands, a little after, of the English, who carried him to Dover. He learned English during his captivity, and succeeded to escape one fine day, crossing the channel in a bark.

Far from being disgusted with the marine by the perils which he had run, Thurot enrolled himself as a sailor, and became in a very short time captain, and distinguished himself by his bravery in various engagements with the English. The peace of 1748 compelled him to navigate for the trade; but at the beginning of the seven years war (1756–63) the privateers asked him to recommence his cruises, and confided him the command of various ships, with which he ruined the English trade in the northern seas. These brilliant expeditions procured him an entrance into the Royal Navy. Having been appointed to the command of the corvette La Friponne, he cruised the channel, fought numerous sea battles with the enemy, and took about 60 merchant vessels.

Marshal Belle Isle, who had long appreciated his merits, entrusted him in 1757 the command of a division, at the head of which he covered himself with glory, made a great number of prizes in the channel and on the coast of Norway, and swept the whole of the North Sea. In 1758 he beat four English ships, then routed a fleet of 17 armed pirogues, escaped the pursuit of 30 English vessels, and came back to Dunkirk after, having inflicted enormous damage on the enemy and covered himself with fresh glory. Having gone to Versailles, where he received the most honourable reception, he proposed to make a descent on the coasts of Great Britain. He succeeded in his project, and was called to the command of five frigates, *etc.* (See notice on Thurot in the *Grand Dictionnaire Universelle*, by Pierre Larousse, Paris, 1865.)

* The occasion of bringing the prisoners to Carrickfergus was to ease the ships, to prevent an infection from the number of wounded. (*Universal Magazine.*)

† There is also an epitaph on him in French and English in the *Universal Magazine*, vol. 26, 1760, p. 154.

‡ Given by his daughter, Henriette Thurot, 1823, to the Town Hall of Nuits, his native place, to which my attention has been drawn by Mr L. Fournier, of Beaune, France, who is at present engaged in a compendious "life" of Thurot, and who sent me an engraving of it. Thurot's daughter died in 1830.

APPENDIX

DISPOSAL OF PRISONERS AND CAPTURED SHIPS *

Carlisle, Thursday, 6th March, 1760.—220 of the prisoners belonging to Thurot's fleet came in hither from Whitehaven, as also the officers on whom the command devolved on Thurot's fall. These are the best looking and most genteel Frenchmen we have seen (having 400 here before), and have been all picked from different corps. Everybody speaks well of Thurot, and had he been taken alive, would certainly have been treated more like a petty prince than a prisoner. The prisoners of war consisted of 207 soldiers and 13 officers, the seamen and officers were left on board His Majesty's ships *Æolus, etc.*

Liverpool, Tuesday, 7th.—By a vessel arrived from Belfast we have an account of 500 French prisoners from Thurot's fleet being landed at Carrickfergus, prisoners of war, on Saturday last, the 4th, by the *Pallas* frigate, who were full as kindly received as they were ten days before.

Cork, 10th March.—This eve the *Nightingale*, man of war, Capt. Campbell, arrived at Cove from Ramsay Bay, with 90 prisoners taken on board M. Thurot's fleet.

Dublin, 12th March.—The *Weezle*, sloop of war, Capt. Bowles, commander, having on board 84 of the French officers and soldiers, taken in the last engagement with M. Thurot, arrvied in our bay from the Isle of Man.

Kinsale.—In the evening on the 10th, arrived at Kinsale His Majesty's ship *Æolus*, Capt. Elliott; *Pallas*, Capt. Clements; *Brilliant*, Capt. Loggie; and brought in with them the *Marshal Belleisle, Le Blond, Terpsichore.*

They finally arrived at Spithead on the 25th of March.

LIST OF PRISONERS SENT TO CARRICKFERGUS

March 25, 1760. Belfast, March 7th.—The following is a list of the French prisoners of war, landed out of His Majesty's ship *Pallas* at Carrickfergus on the 1st inst., and now here, viz, French Guards: Mr de Cavena, Lieut.-Colonel; le Comte de Kersallo, commandant of the detachment; Chevalier de Brugelonque, Major; le Marquis de Parogee Gentic, Capt.-Lieut.; le Marquis de Panise, Capt.-Lieut.; Chevalier de Miramont, Capt Lieut.; and 98 sergeants, corporals, and private men. Swiss Guards: Castellas, commander of the detachment; Carrer, Capt.-Lieut.; 27 sergeants, corporals, and private men: and 5 gunners and miners. Burgundy, De Russily, commandant; Dortoman, Adjutant and Captain; Delwailly, Captain; Beaumale, Captain Chamborant, Lieutenant; Duple, Lieutenant Mailleleau, Lieutenant; Garson, Lieutenant of Grenadiers; Parisol, Lieutenant; and 108 sergeants, corporals, and private men. Cambise, Frechancourt, Capt. Commandant; Barantin, Lieutenant; De Joye, Lieutenant; and 43 sergeants, corporals, and private men. Hussars: Le Conite de Shordeck, Lieut.-Colonel; and 72 private men. Voluntaires etrangers: 17 sergeants, corporals, and private men. Sea officers: Laine, Second Captain; Malet Laine, Lieutenant; Malet Cadit, Lieutenant; Antoine Delatre, officer; and 27 seamen and officers' servants. Total, 25 officers and 416 sergeants, corporals, and private men. (*Manchester Mercury.*)

HONOURS

March 25th, 1760 (from *Universal Magazine*).—The Mayor, Sheriffs, and Common Counc of the pity of Cork have unanimously ordered the freedom of the said city to be presented the Captains Elliott, Clements,† and Logic, for their gallant conduct in defeating the French squadron commanded by Mr Thurot.

Dublin, March 4th.—Yesterday the thanks of the House of Commons were unanimously voted to Captains Elliott, Clements, and Logic, for their gallant behaviour in attacking and taking the French fleet commanded by M. Thurot (*ditto*).

London,—Several gentlemen took ship, last Saturday se'nnight (March 1st), in the evening from Whitehaven to wait on Captain Elliott, with the thanks of the town, and a handsome present is intended to be made him for his gallant behaviour in taking Thurot's squadron. Captain Elliott, of the *Æolus*, is brother to Gilbert Elliott, of Minto, Esq., one of the Lords of Admiralty. Elliot was also presented to the King and very graciously received by him.

London, March 18th.—We hear that Captain Elliot, for his gallant behaviour in taking the *Marshal Belleisle*, is to be promoted to the command of a 60 gun ship.

REJOICINGS

Bristol, March 8th.—Wednesday last upon receiving the great and joyful news of the defeat of Thurot's squadron, the bells of the several churches were rang, and in the evening the gentlemen of the Corporation met at the Council House, where his Majesty's and the Royal Family's healths were drank, a company of soldiers answering to the several toasts by repeated vollies of fire arms.

Carlisle, March 6th.—We have had the most extraordinary rejoicings on account of the victory over Thurot, that have been known here. Sir James Lowther, Brigadier-General, and Colonel of the Westmoreland Militia, now quartered here, ordered a double round of the great guns, bonfires, illuminations, and music bells; invited all the gentlemen to a tavern, where many loyal healths were cheerfully drank, and in the evening an elegant ball was given to the ladies, which was both a full and brilliant one. The Westmoreland Militia did honour to the day by three excellent vollies of their fire arms, and went through their exercise with great dexterity. They being all stout, clever fellows, and dressed in their uniform, made a most delightful appearance.

Liverpool, Thursday night, 45 minutes past 10, Feb. 28th.—"This letter will come too late to bring the first intelligence of Capt. Elliot's good fortune in taking Thurot's three ships with a much less force. All the letters agree that the brave Thurot was killed the second broadside. There were several valuable Liverpool ships at the Island, so that he might have done very great damage there. Our battalion has just given us a *feu de joie* on the occasion." (From a gentleman in Liverpool to his friend in Manchester.)

MOCKFIGHT AT LIVERPOOL

Liverpool, March 7th, 1760.—On Friday last (1st March) the North and South Battalion of the Lincolnshire Militia, and the company of Invalids quartered here, accompanied by two of the independent companies of the town, marched from hence along the sea shore with the town's train of artillery, opposite the Rock Point, which forms the west side of the mouth of the harbour, with their colours flying, French horns sounding, fifes playing and drums beating. As soon as they came to the ground which was presumed would be the landing place of any enemy who might attempt this town, several of the detached parties took possession of the hills and heights, whilst others formed a body reserve. A supposed attack of the enemy was made; sallies from the camp to oppose their landing; regular retreats, and lining the hills with the different evolutions; flying parties were dispatched; bush fighting and pursuing an enemy two miles in the country over hedges and ditches, executed in order to skew the whole corps the nature of service in case of any attempt from the enemy.

It was supposed there were upwards of 10,000 spectators, and the serenity of the weather added to the regularity of the whole.

THUROT AT ISLAY

Extract of a letter from Mr David Simson, dated at Islay, in Scotland, Feb. 13th, 1760, to a merchant in Liverpool.

Saturday last Commodore Thurot with three French ships, *viz.*, one of 54 guns, one of 32, and one of 20, came in here from the westward, and betwixt this Island and Cantyre they were hovering for five or six hours; at length they came close to this land and hoisted an English ensign, which made us believe they wanted a pilot. Your friends Archibald and Hugh McDonald went out with a boat and five men, and brought them to an anchor at the entry of the Sound of Islay, in Clagin Bay. I was there on Sunday last, where they landed about 600 men in order to plunder the country, and surrounded a parcel of cattle belonging to a gentleman of that place, which they carried off, and they said would be paid for by a bill on the French ambassador at the Hague. Our sloop lay in a harbour close by them loaded with kelp, bound to Liverpool, and had 21 bags of flour on board, which Thurot likewise took away; but did no other prejudice to the vessel. They have about 1,500 land forces on board, with a great number of officers, mostly genteel men, with whom I was in company. They are almost starved for want of provisions, being at allowance of 4oz. of bread per day. The land officers and Thurot have disagreed on account of his coming into these channels, and they want him to proceed immediately to France. Thurot's vessel, the *Belleisle*, is very leaky. I send you now by the bearer one of the swords they left on board my sloop on the sword is struck the words, *Volontaire e Belleisle.* Five days before the French put in here they parted with one of their comrades of Barrhead (the *Marante*), which they imagine is foundered at sea, or driven into some of the Highland Islands. (It got, however, finally safe back to St. Maloe.) The *Belleisle* broke her rudder, which he told me forced him into these channels. I have been these two days past ranging the coast, in hopes of meeting the codsmack before, in order to dispatch her express to England, and having now met with her, immediately send her. One of our 50 gun ships would take Thurot's five vessels, for they are crowded with men so much, that they are scarce able to fight her guns; but Mr Thurot says that if he once gets half gun-shot from the best ship in England, he could clear himself by his fast sailing. The season here is very rough; but Thurot will go either through St. George's Channel, or round Ireland, as best suits him, being determined to execute his original scheme; there are a number of English and Irish amongst his crew. We have sent an express to Edinburgh, however, hope the codsmack will bring the first intelligence to you. We are deprived of the use of arms here, or should have been able to have defended our country from being plundered. The ships lay close in shore between M. Arthur's Head and Ardmore Point, and you may depend on this relation, as I was eye witness to the facts here.

It plainly appears by the accounts we have of Mons. Thurot's expedition, received by the codsmack, that he was creeping home through St. George's Channel, and the late southerly winds preventing him, necessity, with the season of the year, forced him into Carrickfergus Lough, where he remained on Sunday evening.

Glasgow, Feb. 29th, 1760.—By a gentleman who arrived here last night from Islay, we learn that while Thurot remained in that Island he behaved more like a friend than an enemy. All the provisions he got there he paid for, even beyond their value; he allowed 30s. for every cow, 23s. 6d. for every goose, 1s. for every hen, and in proportion for flour and other things. He kept the best discipline, suffering none of his crew to pillage. One of his officers having gone to a gentleman's house, and robbed it of £60—in cash—a complaint was made to Thurot, who immediately went out, in a long boat, and searched all his ships in person for the fellow who was charged with the robbery. The delinquent at first denied that he had taken anything, but being ordered ashore and threatened to be shot, he at last confessed that he had taken £51 only, which he was obliged immediately to restore.

SOME OF THUROT'S EARLIER MOVEMENTS

Liverpool, 15th Sept., 1758.—Capt. Hutchinson, of the Liverpool privateer, of 22 guns, upon hearing of the *Belleisle*, privateer, being in the North Channel, bravely offered himself, upon the owners fitting her out with 200 seamen, to go in quest of the *Belleisle*, and in two or three days near that number were engaged for one month, but the wind proving contrary this scheme was dropped, as the *Belleisle* could not be supposed to remain upon that station for so long a time. (Sept. 19th, 1758, Manchester paper.)

Britannia, Butler, bound for New York, had been taken ten days before by the *Marshal Belleisle*, privateer, but was retaken by the *Lockhart*, privateer, going into Brest. The *Belleisle* took this vessel off Belfast, and was proceeding to France with his prizes. (Manchester, 26th September, 1758.)

Liverpool, September 29th, 1758.—Last night arrived here Capt. Hassey, late of the Charles Town, of this port, who was taken the 2nd inst. by the *Marshal Belleisle*, privateer, and by her carried into Bergen, in Norway. He left her there last Thursday refitting, and imagines she will be ready for sea again in a few days. He gives a very favourable account of the good usage the prisoners received from Mr Thurot; that he had taken 36 prizes this cruise, and hoped shortly to increase that number. Off Shetland he was seen by two English men of war, the *Experiment* and *Sapphire*, at less than a league distant, and was so apprehensive of being taken by them, that all the officers and men went down to dress themselves, and not a man was ordered to his quarters or the least preparation for resistance. Why the the English men of war did not pursue her is unaccountable. By the captures she had made she was apprised of our Jamaica fleet being expected, but could not wait on the station for them, all her powder having received damage.

Liverpool, October 13th, 1758.—From a letter of a gentleman at Killough, Scotland. "There is a vessel arrived here which was chased into Loughendall by a large French privateer that was cruising in the channel; she is thought to be the *Belleisle*, privateer."

* Amongst the French prisoners detained as wounded, in the Island itself, was a Mr LaMothe, who having fallen in love with a Manx girl, when exchanged, returned to the Isle, where he married her. A daughter of his, Jane, born in 1767, died at the age of 17, and is buried in Kirk Malew Church. He is the ancestor of the present Manx LaMothes

† Clements took *La Terpsichore* and Logic the *Le Blond.* (See Feltham's *Tour in Isle of Man*).

‡ They were not plundered, but paid for every thing, as we see from the Glasgow letter.

A JOURNAL OF THE LATE EXPEDITION UNDER M. THUROT

From a French Officer of the said Expedition, and now a Prisoner in Dublin

LIST OF THE SHIPS ON THEIR FIRST SETTING OUT

	GUNS		SAILORS	SOLDIERS
	DESIGNED FOR	MOUNTED		
Marshal Belleisle	54	48	200	400
Le Begon *	36	36	200	400
Le Blond †	36	36	200	200
Le Terpsichore	36	24	60	170
Le Marante *	24	24	60	100
	186	168	700	1,270

* Lost company. † 4 thrown overboard.

There embarked on board the above vessels 1,270 men, on the 5th September, 1759, and they set sail on the 15th of October, being blocked up for 40 days by 26 English ships, during which time they put on shore upwards of 200 sick, and under favour of a hazy night, they arrived and anchored off Ostend. Next morning a storm, arising, the *Begon* broke her cable and drove to sea, which obliged us to cut ours and follow her. In 10 days we arrived at Gottenburgh, stayed there 15 days, set sail and arrived at Bergen in Norway, during which passage we lost company of the *Begon* in a violent storm. After staying there 19 days, we were obliged to set sail again, provisions growing short, we soon arrived off the Islands on the North of Scotland, where we beat about, collecting from the Islands what we possibly could; at length the wind springing up from the north, we made sail for Ireland, which was the 24th of January, 1760. In a few days we discovered the land, all preparations were made for landing the next day. In the night a most violent storm arose, which prevented our landing, and we made sail then for Derry, which we should have reached that day, but M. Thurot not being willing to land the troops in the evening, ordered us to be ready to land the next morning, but as we were doubling the point of the harbour of Derry, the wind changed, and we were blown to sea. Such a storm arose that we were all like to be lost. The *Le Blond* was obliged to throw four guns overboard to save herself. We lost sight of the *Marante* this night for good, and as we had been bearing about for so long a time at short allowance, the next day each ship made towards M. Thurot, and the commanders desired him to return to France, lest they should perish with famine. Thurot positively answered that he would not return to France without doing something, and to refresh us would put us on shore on the Island of Islay. We arrived there the same day and all the troops landed. We found there some few cattle, and a brig laden with oatnteal, suffcient to subsist its 12 days at 6oz. per day each man. After three days' stay on that Island, we sailed for Carrickfergus, and the next day we arrived in the bay. All the wine on board the ships was given to the men to animate their courage that day. The 21st of February we came to anchor at twelve o'clock, and landed at three in the afternoon, amounting in all, by sickness and death:

But	600 men
Lost in the *Beyon*	400 men
In the *Marante*	100 men
Died and sick on the voyage	170 men
	1,270

ADDITIONAL ALLUSIONS TO THUROT

Naval Biography of illustrious British Heroes, London, 1806, 9th, pp. 293–94:

John Elliott: ... On the 28th of February they descried the enemy and gave chase, in sight of the Isle of Man: and about six in the morning, Capt. Elliott in his own ship engaged the *Belleisle*. In a few minutes his consorts were also engaged with the other two ships of the enemy. After a warm action, maintained with great spirit on all sides for an hour and a half, Captain Elliott's lieutenant (Forbes) boarded the *Belleisle*, and striking her colours with his own hands, the commander submitted. His example was immediately followed by the other French captains. Though the *Belleisle* was very leaky, and had lost her bowsprit, mizen mast, and main yard, the victory would have remained longer in suspense, if the gallant Thurot had not fallen during the action. The victor had not even the consolation to perform the last offices to his brave enemy, for his body was thrown into the sea by his own people in the hurry of the engagement. The enemy had about 300 men killed and wounded. The service performed on this occasion was deemed so essential to the peace and commerce of Ireland, that the thanks of the House of Commons in that kingdom were voted to the conquerors of Thurot, and the freedom of the city of Cork was presented in silver boxes to the Captains Elliott, Clements, and Logie. Having refitted the prizes, Capt. Elliott got into Kinsale with them, and in his squadron, and from thence proceeded to Spithead, where he arrived on the 26th March soon after which he was introduced to his Majesty and most graciously received.

Smollett in his *History of England*, London, 1760, vol. iii, gives a very succinct account of the progress of Thurot's expedition (pages 390–95): He says, amongst other things:

His instructions were to make occasional descents upon the coast of Ireland. and by dividing the troops, and distracting the attention of the Government in that kingdom, to facilitate the enterprise of M. De Conflans. While this spirited adventurer struggled with these wants and difficulties, his arrival in those seas filled the whole kingdom with alarm. Bodies of regular troops and militia were posted along the coasts of Ireland and Scotland; and besides the squadron of Commodore Boys, who sailed to the northward on purpose to pursue the enemy, other ships of war were ordered to scour the Bristol Channel and cruise between Scotland and Ireland. The name of Thurot has become terrible to all the trading seaports of Britain and Ireland, and therefore the defeat and capture of his squadron were celebrated with as hearty rejoicings as the most important victory could have produced.

The *Annual Register*, 1760, pp. 55–57, speaking of Thurot's expedition, has some generous words to say on his behalf:

Thurot did all that could be expected from the intrepidity of his character. The public, indeed, lamented the death of the brave Thurot, who, even whilst he commanded a privateer, fought less for plunder than honour; whose behaviour was on all occasions full of humanity and generosity, and whose undaunted courage raised him to rank and merited distinction. His death seemed the glory he always sought, he did not live to be brought a prisoner into England, or to hear in France those malignant criticisms which so often attend unfortunate bravery.

Thurot's expedition was the fate of the last remaining branch of that great armament (De Conflans, whose other fleet intended to make the principal descent in some of the southern parts of Great Britain, having been defeated) which had so long been the hope of France, the alarm of England, and the object of general attention to all Europe.

And finally, let me allude to Thackeray, who, in his *Irish Sketch-Book*,* has immortalized Thurot's memory in a few brilliant and genial strokes. Speaking of Carrickfergus he writes:

Carrickfergus rejoices in a real romantic-looking castle, jutting bravely into the sea, and famous as a background for a picture. It is of use for little else now, luckily, nor has it been put to any such war-like purposes since the day when honest Thurot stormed, took, and evacuated it. Let any romancer who is in want of a hero, peruse the second volume, or it may be third, of the *Annual Register*, where the adventures of that gallant fellow are related. He was a gentleman, a genius, and, to crown all, a smuggler. He lived for some time in Ireland, and in England in disguise; he had love passages and romantic adventures; he landed a body of his countrymen on these shores, and died in the third volume, after a battle gallantly fought on both sides, but in which the victory rested with the British arms. What can a novelist want more?

* By Mr M.A. Titmarsh, London, 1843, vol. ii, p. 236.

MANX NOTES AND QUERIES

LATER CONTRIBUTIONS BY
KARL ROEDER AND G.W. WOOD
(1905–06)

❈

MANX NOTES AND QUERIES

LATER CONTRIBUTIONS BY
KARL ROEDER AND G.W. WOOD
1905–06

(1)

A SONG, COMPOSED 1900

Ta'n arragh er jeet lesh feayraght as rio,
Ta'n aer jeeaghyn quaagh dy mie;
My hig eh er sniaghtey ny kirree vees fo,
Eisht gow shiu dy gheddyn ad thie.

Ta'n gheay feayr nish sheidey er voish yn niar hwoaie,
As bodjalyn dorraghey gaase;
Nagh faag shiu ny kirree as colbeeyn mooie
As gow shiu kiarail jeih yn maase.

Son shimmiey cretoor boght ta'n sniaghtey er stroie,
'Syn imbagh ta shaghey er gholl—
T'ad mennick ve riojit ny lhie rish ny cleigh,
Ny rouail ersooyl veih nyn oayll.

Eisht jean shiu goaill tastey as kiarail ayns traa,
Dy haglym ny shellooyn stiagh;
As nish trog shiu erriu ayns soilshey yn laa,
Dy hauail yn maase veih yn çhagh.

Ny eayin as yn keyrragh gys fastee yn chlea,
Nish eiyrt shiu ad sheese veih yn clieau;
As nyn moiraghyn neesht dy vod ad goaill fea,
Shen cliaghtey t'er ve er dy rieau.

FREE TRANSLATION

The springtide is come with cold and with frost,
The sky looks so dismal and drear;
If it comes on to snow the sheep will be lost,
So now of the flocks take good care.

The cold north-east wind is howling about,
And dark clouds overshadow the hill;

Then leave not the sheep and the heifers all out,
But drive them all home with good will.

For many poor creatures the snow has destroyed
In seasons that long since have flown—
They've frozen been oft on the steep mountain side,
Or wandered away and quite gone.

So now, boys, be careful, and hasten away
And gather the sheep to the fold;
Be careful and haste in the light of the day,
And shelter them all from the cold.

The lambs from the hill to the sheltering roof—
Go, drive them all down from the steep;
The cows and the heifers with every hoof,
Beside the young lambs and the sheep.

    F.

(2)

MANX NOTES AND QUERIES

There is an unwritten chapter of Manx history to be gleaned from the columns of the *Manchester Mercury*, which throws some very interesting sidelight on the various steps and proposals that were either intended, or actually carried out, in connection with the annexation of the Island to the Crown of Great Britain.

ORIGINAL SUGGESTED CREATION INTO A DUKEDOM
1765
March 5th.—"It is confidently said that should the Government take the Isle of Man into their hand, the present title of King in Man will be converted into a Dukedom and recognised in one of the branches of the Royal Family."—If, therefore, such a measure would have been carried, the Island would have had its Royal Duke of Man.
May 14th.—"'Tis said that the Isle of Man will be invested with a right of sending a certain number of members to the British Parliament."—The Island is still excluded from that privilege or right of Imperial representation.

THE DUKE OF ATHOL'S CLAIM AND THE LAND PROPRIETORS
March 12th.—-"It is said that £70,000 is the sum agreed to be given to the Duke of Athol for giving up his charter for the Isle of Man, and that the proprietors of land are to enjoy their rights and privileges as lords of manors."

AN ASSEMBLY TO BE FORMED

May 14th.—"We hear as Assembly, composed of the principal inhabitants, is going to be introduced on the new form of Government of the Isle of Man."—There was, therefore, an idea of first doing away with the House of Keys and the Tynwald, unfortunately, we may say, left unaccomplished.

DISPOSAL OF GOODS SUBJECT TO DUTY

March 12th.—"The people of the Isle of Man have six months allowed to dispose of their stock in hand, and all after that to be subject to the customary duty as in all parts of England, and under the same regulations and restrictions, for which purpose an Excise Officer and Custom House will be immediately established."

March 19th.—"We hear that three Manks Keys are come to London in order to to present a petition to be allowed a farther time for the conveying their effects from that place."

RAMPANT SMUGGLING

May 14th.—"Though there have been several of his Majesty's cutters stationed in different ports of the Isle of Man to prevent the illicit trade of smuggling, they are said to have imported into the Island from the month of December to the month of April above 3,000 chests of tea from Holland, Denmark, and Sweden, principally at a creek called Port le Murray, from whence they export it in large quantities to England, Ireland, and Wales, to the great detriment of the revenue."

July 9th.—"It is remarked that among the goods obliged to he entered to pay duty in the Isle of Man have been several hundred bales of wool, which, it is said, were intended to have heen shipped occasionally for France and Holland."

FURTHER EXTENSION OF TIME ALLOWED FOR DISPOSAL OF GOODS

July 30th.—"It is said that in consequence of some vigorous dispositions now taking place for the benefit of his Majesty's Revenue in Jersey and Guernsey, the inhabitants of these Islands will have a limited time granted them to dispose of their mercantile effects, subject to the duties of the Customs and Excise, after which such as shall not be properly entered will be liable to confiscation the same as the Isle of Man."

THE POOR CHILDREN TO BE SENT TO THE IRISH CHARTER SCHOOLS

May 7th.—"It is said that a considerable number of poor children in the Isle of Man will be sent over to the Irish Charter Schools for the benefit of their education, from whence, after the expiration of a stated period, they will be ordered home and put apprentices to the various artificers of their own country."

MILITARY ARRANGEMENTS

June 4th.—"We hear there will soon be a review of the out-pensioners and invalids of Chelsea Hospital, in order to make draughts for garrison duty in the Isle of Man."

July 2nd.—"We hear that a large train of artillery is now getting ready for the Isle of Man, where some regular fortifications will soon be erected."

July 16th.—"A quantity of gun carriages are ordered to be shipped from the Tower for the Isle of Man."

August 6th.—"Castle Rushen is ordered to be filled up with barracks for the accommodation of his Majesty's garrison in the Isle of Man."

APPOINTMENT OF GOVERNMENT OFFICERS

July 23rd.—"The following gentlemen are appointed to office in the Isle of Man by the Lords of Trade and Plantations —Charles Lutwich, Esq., Receiver-General of the Island; Mr Curling, searcher; Messrs Broomfield, Jackson, and Hamilton, Comptrollers; and Messrs Fry, Rentham, and Grant, Collectors."

ENGLISH PETTIFOGGERS SWAMPING THE ISLAND

Sept. 10th.—"Letters from Douglas in the Isle of Man advise that the sober-minded inhabitants there begin to have apprehensions of an evil hitherto unknown, namely, that of frequent litigation, as a number of pettifoggers in the law are arrived there from different parts of England since the accession of that Island to the Crown of Great Britain."

THE MINES TO BE MORE DILIGENTLY WORKED

Sept. 10th.—"We hear that some experienced miners will soon be sent on the Government's account to the Isle of Man, where some valuable mineral ores are said to abound, but hitherto neglected by reason of the poverty of the country and the people's great application to a clandestine trade."

ANNEXATION

June 1st.—"The English colours were hoisted on the Castle in the Isle of Man, the sovereignity of that Island being now annexed to the Crown of Great, Britain, and the inhabitants in every respect subjected to the laws, customs, and privileges of their fellow subjects."— (*Gentleman's Magazine*).

(3)

A HYMN TRANSLATED INTO MANX
BY THE REV. JOHN CLAGUE

The following hymn is taken from, a Catechism by the Rev H. Grossman, Rector of Little Bromley, Essex, published early in the eighteenith century. This Catechism was translated into Manx by the Rev. John Clague, Vicar of Rushen, under the title "Aght giare dy heet gys tushtey as toiggal jeh'n chredjue Creestee ayns daa ayrn," and published by Beatson and Copeland at their offices on the Custom House Quay, Douglas, in 1814. It is thought that the hymn, in its Manx dress, may be of special interest just now, when the Metrical Version of some of the Psalms in Manx by the same hand is about to be published in book form. I am sure I shall only echo the sentiments of many others of your readers if I express the hope that some at least of the Rev. John Clague's Manx semons may follow his version of the Psalms in the pages of the *Examiner*.

G.W. Wood
Streatham.

> "A verse may find him who a sermon flies,
> And turn delight into a sacrifice."
> Herbert

ON PRAYER

When morning comes, the birds arise
And tune their voices to the skies,
With warbling notes and hallow'd lays,
To sing their great Creator's praise.

Shall I, then, from my chamber go,
Or any work presume to do,
Before I've sought the God of Heaven,
And my first morning tribute given?

Lest every bird's harmonious song
Reproach me, as I walk along
Thoughtless of Him whose guardian power
Upholds, and saves me every hour.

Come, then, my soul, awake and pray,
And praise thy Maker day by day:
Bless Him for raiment, health, and food,
And for each peaceful night's abode.

Heathens, who never knew the Lord,
Nor saw the brightness of His Word,
Religions honours duly paid
To deities themselves had made.

The Turk, to various errors bred,
Yet learns the living God to dread:
Five times a day, at Mah'met's shrine,
He prays, and offers things divine.

These shall in judgment rise and shame
Many who bear the Christian name;
The Judge in wrath shall cast them out,
Who in their day their God forgot.

The beasts and fowls, craving to eat,
Beg, as it were, their daily meat:
The hand which feedeth them they know,
And to it grateful homage shew.

Shall Christians, then, the hand above
Refuse to know, whose boundless love
Pours blessings out, like kindly show'rs,
To fill with goodness us and ours?

Let man and wife, each little one,
Incessant hearts and voices join,
In ev'ry household, rich and poor,
One God and Father to adore
From this time forth for evermore.

MANX VERSION

Foddee eer Sharnaaae ve jeh beggan bree,
Choad's nee Arrane moyllee roshtyn y Cree.

MYCHIONE PADJER
'Sy vadran hene, ta eeanlee'n aer,
Dy gennal geeck da'n Chiarn e chair,
Lesh coraa bingys as lesh cree,
T'adsyn dy kinjagh moylley Jee.

Jeanyms my lhiabbee eisht agaill,
As noon as noal, gyn tort rauaill,
Fegooisch my Yee y voylley neesh',

Liorish 'sy voghrey cur da booise?

Nagh jean yn eean beg veih yn chrow,
Goltooaney, gra, oh! cre'n aght t'ou
(Coamrit, lesh tushtey mooar as keayll),
Jarrood dty Yee? Nagh treih yn skeayll.

Tar, eisht, my aunym, dooisht as guee,
Lesh padjer imlee gys dty Yee:
Son cur dhyt cadley feagh as fea,
Son cooid as gerjagh, slaynt as bea.

T'adsyn gyn toiggal ta jeh Jee,
T'er ve ayns Dellid anchreestee
Goaill padjer jeean daa cheayrt 'sy laa
Gys jallooyn gyn feeu imraa.

Yn Turk, 'sy chredjue shaghrynagh,
Ny yeih t'eh hene, 'sy hie dy bragh,
Shirveish nyn Yee, queig cheayrt 'sy laa,
Goll gys e hie myr pointat da.

Irree ad shoh ayns briwnys seose,
Naaragh dagh Creestee t'ayns meerioose,
Mychione e churrym, gys e Yee,
Ta stowal er dy chooilley nhee.

Ta maase as eeanlee gagyrts bee,
Son shoh, myr veagh eh, tar ad guee;
Yn phooar ta stowal eh shione daue,
As dy chur booise, cha vel nyn daaue.

Jean Creestee, eisht jarrood e Yee,
Ta coyrt da bioys marish dagh nhee;
Bannaghtyn erskyn, earroo mooar,
T'eh deayrtey neose er dagh cretoor?

Lhig aeg as shenn, yn slane lught-thie,
Gloyr chur da Jee va rieau cha mie,
Lhig ooilleyn seeihll lesh un choraa
Berchagh as boght nyn mooise choyrt da
Veih'n traa shoh magh er son dy bragh.

(4)

LEGEND OF FINN MACCOOIL

With the recent death of John Kennish ("Pete," or Jacky Ballure, as familiarly known amongst his neighbours and close friends) another link of the old-world Manx types has gone. He was born 66 years ago at Ballure Farm, a genial, sunny old fellow with a large human heart and a receptive mind, with a face that tinkled with merry humour and good nature. His popularity did not spoil him, he was a simple hearted growth and one of nature's happy children. His knowledge of Manx ways, and folk-tales, customs, and fairy lore and superstitions, was apparently inexhaustible, and it is only a pity that no Ramsey or Northern Manxman—it is the centre of the Manx Natural History and Antiquarian Society—has ever besought himself to take the trouble or the interest of collecting and preserving his rich store of folklore, a loss which is by no means light to those who fully appreciate the importance of the subject; for we specially are very poor in material from the northern parts of the Island, which on the whole has shown great indifference of a systematical study or survey of the folklore extant among the peasantry and fishermen. The *Ramsey Courier*, in its issue of September 21st, has given a very readable account of John Kennish and also, fortunately, recounts in a chatty way one of his stories.

It treats about the old Manx Giants. The writer of the article says: He used to tell how a giant from the West of the Island had a feud with another in the North, so he came over to settle accounts. Arriving at the home of the latter, so his story goes, he was met by the giant's wife, who told him the giant sought after was not at home, but his son was. The Western giant requested to see the son, and observing his son fled with the reflection: 'If the son is such a giant, what must the father be?'"

I have no need to say that we have here the garbled, contracted, and confused version of one of those few true Celtic Manx traditional legends so precious to the Island, viz., of Finn MacCooil of the Sound, who was challenged by the giant of South Barrule, which is fully given *sub note* 216 in my *Manx Notes and Queries, 1904.** The second version, then, of Kennish, from the Ballure district, is a confirmation of the genuineness of the Southern legend which travelled North. The only pity is that he had no folklorist at hand who could fully draw from him, and preserve the whole substance of the story.

It emphasises again the need of collecting—especially from the old people—the decreasing lore of the Island. He was, and perhaps is even now, only one of the many old people who have still many recollections illustrating the past; what is required is more serious workers like Miss S. Morrison, of Peel, who is enriching us with a succession of lovely, golden, bi-lingual folk-tales in the *Isle of Man Examiner* that in every respect quite equal in beauty, freshness, and value Grimm's *German Fairy*

---

* As Note 231 here.

Tales. They are a delight to read, and make the heart of the young Manx joyous and eager for more. We wish Miss Morrison every success in her ardent and laudable endeavours of still adding to the number of these Insular gems of folk-literature.

(5)

THE HERRING IN LANCASHIRE WATERS

Having previously treated so amply upon the Manx Herring Fishery, an additional note on its habitat in Lancashire waters will be interesting in connection with the subject.

The information is contained in the *Victoria History of Lancashire*, vol. i, 1906, where it says, subject "Fishes," written by James Johnstone, B.Sc (London): "There is no real fishing now for herring in Lancashire waters, though they are caught off the Isle of Man and in Welsh waters. They used to be abundant in Morecambe Bay, but have deserted this district for many years on account of the increased steam traffic in the bay, some fishermen say. They were, however rather abundant in the Mersey, between Rock Ferry and Eastham a few years ago, and some boats from Morecambe followed the fishing there with much success. They occur very frequently, however, though not in sufficient numbers to make a remunerative fishery, and are constantly met with in the trawl nets."

�֎

BIBLIOGRAPHY

MANX NOTES AND QUERIES
THE ISLE OF MAN EXAMINER COLUMN

(1)
THE NUMBERED SERIES *

1901

Karl Roeder, "Manx Notes and Queries, Nos 1–2," *Isle of Man Examiner* 21 September 1901, 3c; 2–5, 28 September 1901, 3a; 6–12, 5 October 1901, 7d; 13–17 19 October 1901, 3g; 18, 26 October 1901, 6a; 19–21, 2 November 1901, 7b; 22–24, 9 November 1901, 8e; 25–28, 16 November 1901, 5e; 29, 23 November 1901, 7b; 30–32, 30 November 1901, 6a; 33–37, 7 December 1901, 6a; 37–40, 21 December 1901, 6a; 41, 28 December 1901, 6a.

1902

Karl Roeder, "Manx Notes and Queries, Nos 39–40," *Isle of Man Examiner* 4 January 1902, 6a; 41–50, 11 January 1902, 7d; 51–55, 18 January 1902, 7f; 55–60, 25 January 1902, 7a; 61, 1 February 1902, 6a–b; 62, 8 February 1902, 6a; 63, 15 February 1902, 6a; 64, 22 February 1902, 6a; 65, 1 March 1902, 6a; 66, 8 March 1902, 6a; 67, 15 March 1902, 6a; 73–78, 22 March 1902, 6a; 79, 29 March 1902, 6a; 80–83, 5 April 1902, 6a; 84, 12 April 1902, 6a–b; 85–86, 19 April 1902, 6a; 87–90, 26 April 1902, 6a; 91–96, 3 May 1902, 6a; 97, 10 May 1902, 6a; 98, 17 May 1902, 6a; 99, 24 May 1902, 6a; 100–101, 14 June 1902, 6b; 102–109, 28 June 1902, 6b; 110–115, 5 July 1902, 6a; 116–124, 12 July 1902, 6a; 125–131, 19 July 1902, 6a; 132–140, 26 July 1902, 6a; 141–148, 2 August 1902, 6a; 149–154, 9 August 1902, 6a; 155, 16 August 1902, 6a–b; [155], 23 August 1902, 6a; 156–164, 6 September 1902, 6a; 165–73, 13 September 1902, 6a; 174–82, 20 September 1902, 6a; 183–87, 4 October 1902, 6a–b; 188–91, 11 October 1902, 6a; 192–93, 1 November 1902, 6b; 194, 8 November 1902, 6b; 195–96, 15 November 1902, 6a; 197, 22 November 1902, 6a; 198–201, 29 November 1902, 8b; 202, 6 December 1902, 8c; 203–04, 20 December 1902, 8b; 205, 27 December 1902, 8a.

1903

Karl Roeder, "Manx Notes and Queries, No. 206," *Isle of Man Examiner* 3 January 1903, 8b; [206], 17 January 1903, 8c; [206], 24 January 1903, 8b; [207], 31 January 1903, 8b; 208–12, 14 February 1903, 8a–b; 213, 21 February 1903, 8c; 213, 28

---

* NB—The numbering of the column is inconsistent.

February 1903, 8b; **214–15**, 7 March 1903, 8b; **216–17**, 21 March 1903, 8f; **218**, 28 March 1903, 8d; **210**, 4 April 1903, 8e; **220**, 11 April 1903, 8d; **221**, 18 April 1903, 8d; **222**, 25 April 1903, 8d; **233**, 5 May 1903, 8f; **234**, 23 May 1903, 8f; **235**, 6 June 1903, 8a; **236**, 13 June 1903, 8e; **237**, 20 June 1903, 8a; **238**, 27 June 1903, 3a–b; **239**, 4 July 1903, 3a–b; **240**, 11 July 1903, 8a; [**241**], 25 July 1903, 7e–f; **242**, 1 August 1903, 8a; **243**, 15 August 1903, 8e; **244**, 22 August 1903, 8a; [**245**], 29 August 1903, 8a; **256**, 5 September 1903, 8a; [–], 12 September 1903, 8a; **257–58**, 19 September 1903, 8a; **259**, 3 October 1903, 8a; **260**, 10 October 1903, 8a; **261**, 24 October 1903, 8b.

(2)

THE HERRING AND ITS HABITAT (1903–04)

Karl Roeder, "The Herring and Its Habitat (1)," *Isle of Man Examiner*, 26 December 1903, 8a–b; (2) 9 January 1904, 8a; (3) 16 January 1904, 8a; (4) 23 January 1904, 8b; (5) 30 January 1904, 8a–b; (6) 6 February 1904, 8a; (7) 13 February 1904, 8a–b; (8) 20 February 1904, 8a; (9) 27 February 1904, 8a;* (10) 14 May 1904, 8a.

* Contains at end, "Dialect Words," as No. 245 and reproduced as such in *Manx Notes & Queries* (1904) where it is the last numbered note in the text reflecting the re-numbering of the notes needed for consistentcy ("The Herring and Its Habitat," Parts 1–9 together become No. 244 in the 1904 edtion).

(3)

GASTRONOMINAL NOTES ON THE HERRING (1904)

Karl Roeder, "Gastronominal Notes on the Herring (1)," *Isle of Man Examiner*, 28 May 1904, 8a–b; —— (2), 6 June 1904, 8a.

*

MANX NOTES & QUERIES
(1904)

MANX NOTES | AND | QUERIES | WITH AN ACCOUNT OF | FRANÇOIS THUROT | AND HIS | NAVAL ENGAGEMENT OFF THE ISLE OF MAN | [short rule] | Reprinted from the Isle of Man Examiner | [short rule] | EDITED BY C. ROEDER | [short rule] | Douglas: | S. K. Broadbent & Co. Ltd. "Isle of Man Examiner" Office. | 1904

[i] + 155 pp + i–xvi. With Introduction (unpaged) by Karl Roeder. Cost 2/-, post free. First advertised in the *Isle of Man Examiner* on 17 September 1904: "To be Ready in a few Days." A review of the book appeared on 1 October 1904, mentioning that "[t]his volume has just made its appearance." A second advert is from 13 May 1905. Sale notices appear in issues for 24 & 31 December 1904; 7, 21, 28 January 1905; 4 February 1905; 15 & 29 April 1905; 27 May 1905; 3, 10, 24 June 1905; 1 & 8 July 1905 (nothing further after this date).

CONTENTS

1. THE ISLE OF MAN EXAMINER COLUMNS

Manx Notes & Queries brings together (1) the ninety columns published under the heading of "Manx Notes and Queries" from the *Isle of Man Examiner,* together with (2.1) nine of the ten (unnumbered) contributions published as "The Herring and Its Habitat." These are numbered from 1 to 245 and are a re-numbering of the series due to the inconsistencies in the original columns. (3) The final column from (2) together with (2.2) the two further additional (again, unnumbered) contributions, "Gastronominal Notes on the Herring," are reproduced following, unnumbered, and under the heading of "Herring Recipes." Omitted from the 1904 edition is the column (unnumbered) for 12 September 1903.

2. G.W. WOOD'S CONTRIBUTIONS

Three pieces by Wood appear: (1) "The Isle of Man in 1671," (2) "A Sketch of the Early Printers of the Isle of Man," (3) "An Old Manx Bard." (1) never appeared in the original column; (2) was advertised to appear in the *Isle of Man Examiner* but never did (see adverts in issues for 21 & 28 February 1903, and 14 March 1903); (3) appeared (unnumbered) in the column for 2 May 1903.

3. FRANCOIS THUROT (1727 AND 1760) AND HIS NAVAL ENGAGEMENT OFF
THE ISLE OF MAN (1902)

Karl Roeder, "Francois Thurot (1727 and 1760) and his Naval Engagement off the
Isle of Man (1)," *Isle of Man Examiner* (31 May 1902), 6a; (2), 7 June 1902, 6a–b; (3),
14 June 1902, 6a–b;* (4), 21 June 1902, 6a–b; (5), 28 June 1902, 6a. These pieces were
never part of the column and close the volume (paginated in roman numerals).

* Pseud [signed as "Manninagh Dooie"], "[Letter to the Editor] The Longest Manx Poem:
Alleged Inaccuracy," *Isle of Man Examiner,* 21 June 1902, 6b. This letter a comment on
(3). Passage corrected when reproduced in *Manx Notes & Queries* (1904).

(3)

MANX NOTES AND QUERIES

LATER, OCCASSIONAL CONTRIBUTIONS

KARL ROEDER

Karl Roeder, "A Song, composed 1900," *Isle of Man Examiner,* 18 March 1905, 8d.
——, "Manx Notes and Queries: [Untitled]," *Isle of Man Examiner,* 8 April 1905,
8b–c.
——, "Manx Notes and Queries: Legend of Finn MacCooil," *Isle of Man Examiner,*
3 November 1906, 8d.
——, "Manx Notes and Queries: The Herring in Lancashire Waters," *Isle of Man
Examiner,* 3 November 1906, 8e.

G.W. WOOD

G.W. Wood, "Manx Notes and Queries: A Hymn translated into Manx by the Rev.
John Clague," *Isle of Man Examiner,* 22 April 1905, 8a.

❀

BIBLIOGRAPHY

MANX NOTES AND QUERIES
THE ISLE OF MAN EXAMINER COLUMN

(1)

THE NUMBERED SERIES *

1901

Karl Roeder, "Manx Notes and Queries, Nos 1–2," *Isle of Man Examiner* 21 September 1901, 3c; **2–5**, 28 September 1901, 3a; **6–12**, 5 October 1901, 7d; **13–17** 19 October 1901, 3g; **18**, 26 October 1901, 6a; **19–21**, 2 November 1901, 7b; **22–24**, 9 November 1901, 8e; **25–28**, 16 November 1901, 5e; **29**, 23 November 1901, 7b; **30–32**, 30 November 1901, 6a; **33–37**, 7 December 1901, 6a; **37–40**, 21 December 1901, 6a; **41**, 28 December 1901, 6a.

1902

Karl Roeder, "Manx Notes and Queries, Nos **39–40**," *Isle of Man Examiner* 4 January 1902, 6a; **41–50**, 11 January 1902, 7d; **51–55**, 18 January 1902, 7f; **55–60**, 25 January 1902, 7a; **61**, 1 February 1902, 6a–b; **62**, 8 February 1902, 6a; **63**, 15 February 1902, 6a; **64**, 22 February 1902, 6a; **65**, 1 March 1902, 6a; **66**, 8 March 1902, 6a; **67**, 15 March 1902, 6a; **73–78**, 22 March 1902, 6a; **79**, 29 March 1902, 6a; **80–83**, 5 April 1902, 6a; **84**, 12 April 1902, 6a–b; **85–86**, 19 April 1902, 6a; **87–90**, 26 April 1902, 6a; **91–96**, 3 May 1902, 6a; **97**, 10 May 1902, 6a; **98**, 17 May 1902, 6a; **99**, 24 May 1902, 6a; **100–101**, 14 June 1902, 6b; **102–109**, 28 June 1902, 6b; **110–115**, 5 July 1902, 6a; **116–124**, 12 July 1902, 6a; **125–131**, 19 July 1902, 6a; **132–140**, 26 July 1902, 6a; **141–148**, 2 August 1902, 6a; **149–154**, 9 August 1902, 6a; **155**, 16 August 1902, 6a–b; **[155]**, 23 August 1902, 6a; **156–164**, 6 September 1902, 6a; **165–73**, 13 September 1902, 6a; **174–82**, 20 September 1902, 6a; **183–87**, 4 October 1902, 6a–b; **188–91**, 11 October 1902, 6a; **192–93**, 1 November 1902, 6b; **194**, 8 November 1902, 6b; **195–96**, 15 November 1902, 6a; **197**, 22 November 1902, 6a; **198–201**, 29 November 1902, 8b; **202**, 6 December 1902, 8c; **203–04**, 20 December 1902, 8b; **205**, 27 December 1902, 8a.

1903

Karl Roeder, "Manx Notes and Queries, No. **206**," *Isle of Man Examiner* 3 January 1903, 8b; **[206]**, 17 January 1903, 8c; **[206]**, 24 January 1903, 8b; **[207]**, 31 January 1903, 8b; **208–12**, 14 February 1903, 8a–b; **213**, 21 February 1903, 8c; **213**, 28

---

* NB—The numbering of the column is inconsistent.

February 1903, 8b; **214–15**, 7 March 1903, 8b; **216–17**, 21 March 1903, 8f; **218**, 28 March 1903, 8d; **210**, 4 April 1903, 8e; **220**, 11 April 1903, 8d; **221**, 18 April 1903, 8d; **222**, 25 April 1903, 8d; **233**, 5 May 1903, 8f; **234**, 23 May 1903, 8f; **235**, 6 June 1903, 8a; **236**, 13 June 1903, 8e; **237**, 20 June 1903, 8a; **238**, 27 June 1903, 3a–b; **239**, 4 July 1903, 3a–b; **240**, 11 July 1903, 8a; [**241**], 25 July 1903, 7e–f; **242**, 1 August 1903, 8a; **243**, 15 August 1903, 8e; **244**, 22 August 1903, 8a; [**245**], 29 August 1903, 8a; **256**, 5 September 1903, 8a; [–], 12 September 1903, 8a; **257–58**, 19 September 1903, 8a; **259**, 3 October 1903, 8a; **260**, 10 October 1903, 8a; **261**, 24 October 1903, 8b.

(2)

THE HERRING AND ITS HABITAT (1903–04)

Karl Roeder, "The Herring and Its Habitat (1)," *Isle of Man Examiner,* 26 December 1903, 8a–b; (2) 9 January 1904, 8a; (3) 16 January 1904, 8a; (4) 23 January 1904, 8b; (5) 30 January 1904, 8a–b; (6) 6 February 1904, 8a; (7) 13 February 1904, 8a–b; (8) 20 February 1904, 8a; (9) 27 February 1904, 8a;* (10) 14 May 1904, 8a.

* Contains at end, "Dialect Words," as No. 245 and reproduced as such in *Manx Notes & Queries* (1904) where it is the last numbered note in the text reflecting the re-numbering of the notes needed for consistentcy ("The Herring and Its Habitat," Parts 1–9 together become No. 244 in the 1904 edtion).

(3)

GASTRONOMINAL NOTES ON THE HERRING (1904)

Karl Roeder, "Gastronominal Notes on the Herring (1)," *Isle of Man Examiner,* 28 May 1904, 8a–b; —— (2), 6 June 1904, 8a.

*